FOUNDATIONS OF CANADIAN POLITICAL BEHAVIOUR

Stability and Change in the Twenty-First Century

Edited by Amanda Bittner, J. Scott Matthews, and Stuart Soroka

Foundations of Canadian Political Behaviour aims to place contemporary Canadian electoral politics in comparative perspective, particularly with respect to its peers among the established democracies of western Europe and North America. The book pays tribute to political scientist Richard Johnston and his diverse contributions to the study of Canadian politics and electoral politics in general.

Presenting original empirical research by leading Canadian and international scholars, the volume is organized around the three themes that animate Johnston's nearly five decades of scholarship: the impact of electoral and party systems on political conflict, change and persistence in the social foundations of party competition, and the role of election campaigns in voting behaviour. Chapters utilize diverse approaches, including quantitative analysis of survey data and electoral statistics, experimentation, systematic analysis of media content, historical narrative, and critical conceptual analyses. The book is anchored in general theoretical concerns; half of the chapters centre on Canadian cases, while half highlight key comparators including the United States, Germany, and the United Kingdom.

AMANDA BITTNER is a professor in the Department of Political Science at Memorial University of Newfoundland and Labrador.

J. SCOTT MATTHEWS is a professor in the Department of Political Science at Memorial University of Newfoundland and Labrador.

STUART SOROKA is a professor in the Departments of Communication and Political Science at the University of California, Los Angeles.

Foundations of Canadian Political Behaviour

Stability and Change in the Twenty-First Century

EDITED BY AMANDA BITTNER, J. SCOTT MATTHEWS, AND STUART SOROKA

UNIVERSITY OF TORONTO PRESS
Toronto Buffalo London

ISBN 978-1-4875-0742-8 (cloth)   ISBN 978-1-4875-3622-0 (EPUB)
ISBN 978-1-4875-2511-8 (paper)   ISBN 978-1-4875-3621-3 (PDF)

Library and Archives Canada Cataloguing in Publication

Title: Foundations of political behaviour : stability and change in the 21st century /
    edited by Amanda Bittner, J. Scott Matthews, and Stuart Soroka.
Names: Bittner, Amanda, editor. | Matthews, J. Scott, editor. | Soroka, Stuart Neil,
    1970- editor.
Description: Includes bibliographical references and index.
Identifiers: Canadiana (print) 2024037021X | Canadiana (ebook) 20240370228 |
    ISBN 9781487507428 (cloth) | ISBN 9781487525118 (paper) |
    ISBN 9781487536213 (PDF) | ISBN 9781487536220 (EPUB)
Subjects: LCSH: Political sociology—Canada. | LCSH: Political parties—Canada. |
LCSH: Political campaigns—Canada. | LCSH: Voting—Canada. |
    LCSH: Canada—Politics and government.
Classification: LCC JA76 .F65 2024 | DDC 306.20971—dc23

Cover design: Liz Harasymczuk
Cover image: Anna Davidovskaya/Shutterstock.com

We wish to acknowledge the land on which the University of Toronto Press
operates. This land is the traditional territory of the Wendat, the Anishnaabeg, the
Haudenosaunee, the Métis, and the Mississaugas of the Credit First Nation.

This book has been published with the help of a grant from the Federation for the
Humanities and Social Sciences, through the Awards to Scholarly Publications Program,
using funds provided by the Social Sciences and Humanities Research Council of Canada.

University of Toronto Press acknowledges the financial support of the Government of
Canada, the Canada Council for the Arts, and the Ontario Arts Council, an agency of
the Government of Ontario, for its publishing activities.

Canada Council Conseil des Arts
for the Arts du Canada

ONTARIO ARTS COUNCIL
CONSEIL DES ARTS DE L'ONTARIO
an Ontario government agency
un organisme du gouvernement de l'Ontario

Funded by the Financé par le
Government gouvernement
of Canada du Canada

Canadä

Contents

PART THREE: Campaigns and Persuasion

FOUNDATIONS OF CANADIAN POLITICAL BEHAVIOUR

FOUNDATIONS OF CANADIAN POLITICAL BEHAVIOUR

Introduction

AMANDA BITTNER, J. SCOTT MATTHEWS, AND STUART SOROKA

This book approaches the study of Canadian politics from a cross-national context. Consider first the context in which these papers began. In 2016, fuelled in large part by a rising wave of right-wing populism, political change was evident across Western democracies. In June 2016, British voters' decision in a national referendum to exit the European Union ("Brexit") shocked political leaders across Europe and around the world. Mainstream politicians in France nervously observed far-right candidate Marine Le Pen's ascent to the final round of voting in that country's presidential elections in 2017; and, only months later, German voters sent a far-right populist party, Alternative für Deutschland ("Alternative for Germany" [AfD]), to the national Parliament for the first time in the country's post-war history. And late in the year, voters in the United States delivered an even bigger surprise when they selected Donald J. Trump for president, a bombastic reality-TV star and political novice, over Hillary Clinton, arguably the most well-credentialed candidate ever to seek the US presidency.

Six years later the situation is no less striking, with both generation-defining transformation and, perhaps, hopefully, also signs of a return to normalcy. We are now nearly two years into the COVID-19 pandemic, which is changing fundamentally the politics and economics of countries around the world. Arguments and counter-arguments rage about the use of masks (and vaccines) and about personal freedoms and government over-reach. A functioning agreement over Brexit has been approved. The latest polls in France suggest the 2022 presidential election may be a replay of 2017, with incumbent Emmanuel Macron likely to face Le Pen for a second time in the final round of voting. In Germany, support for the party of long-serving Chancellor Angela Merkel, the Christian Democrats, surged during the pandemic, though she was ultimately succeeded by the Social Democrats' standard bearer, Olaf Scholz, after an election in which both the far left and far right lost support. In the US, finally, the populist Donald Trump has been replaced by the consummate politician, Joseph R. Biden, but the outgoing president continues to wage a years-long disinformation campaign alleging widespread electoral fraud.

Where does Canada fit into all this international turmoil? At the time of writing, a quick answer is pretty clear: Prime Minister Justin Trudeau's popularity is at an all-time low, and after three weeks of occupation of downtown Ottawa by a convoy of truckers protesting continuing COVID-related restrictions, the government passed the Emergency Measures Act in order to restore order. This book is focused on a somewhat broader time period, however. Our aims are twofold. The first is to situate Canada's democratic history and prospects among the trends evident in many of its peer democracies. Post-industrial economic dislocation, challenges to "majority" culture, and potentially long-lasting shifts in the nature of party systems, political competition, and partisan debate are as salient in Canada as in other established democracies.

There are some ways in which Canada seemed, until very recently, relatively unique. For some time, Canada largely avoided the right-wing populist trend that has been prominent in other established democracies. The 2019 federal election saw the emergence of a credibly far-right People's Party, for instance, although the party captured no seats and only a tiny sliver (1.6 per cent) of the popular vote. While the governing Liberals lost seats, votes, and majority status in 2019, like many of their peers in other democracies, the party's support grew in the early months of the pandemic, and the party maintained a consistent lead over its opponents for nearly a year. Less than three years (and a global pandemic) later, Erin O'Toole has been ousted as the leader of the Conservative Party of Canada – most would argue for being too moderate; and demonstrations not just in Ottawa but across Canada and at border crossings have put on display small groups of right-wing activists that were until very recently only visible outside the country.

It is perhaps a difficult time to argue that Canadian politics is entirely unique. But Canadian democracy has long been seen as a "deviant case" (Lijphart, 1971) among its comparators: a "deeply divided" society that is nonetheless politically stable (Noel, 1971); a Westminster parliamentary democracy in the British mould that, paradoxically, supports three (and sometimes five) significant political parties (Cairns, 1968); a system that exhibits profound electoral volatility – today's partisan "hero" becomes tomorrow's "zero" with remarkable frequency – yet has been governed by one or the other of just two parties for 150 years (Bakvis, 1988; Clarke et al., 1996). These peculiarities of the Canadian case are a key theme in Richard Johnston's recent monograph, *The Canadian Party System: An Analytic History* (2017). The book – the culmination of decades of work by one of the country's leading political scientists and a critical source of inspiration for our collection – presents a comprehensive statement on Canadian democracy's foundations and tensions that is already reshaping scholarly understanding. For all that, Johnston's analysis is historical: his "analytic history" tells us where we are and how we got here but is mostly silent on where we're going. This book aims, therefore, to pick up where *The Canadian Party System* leaves off, placing special emphasis on understanding Canada's electoral future by drawing from the experiences and contemporary patterns of other countries. Johnston could not possibly have anticipated the consequences, political and otherwise, of a global pandemic. But the analytic history that Johnston provides, in combination with the breadth and legacy of his work, may offer some valuable clues about what to expect in post-pandemic Canadian politics.

This brings us to the second aim of the current volume: to celebrate the fundamental contributions that Richard Johnston has made to the study of politics in Canada, the United States, and elsewhere. The chapters that follow first came together at a conference held in Vancouver, BC, as a celebration of Johnston's work. It is testament to his role in the discipline that we were able to attract such an impressive group of scholars; and testament to the impact of his work that so many were readily able to highlight the ways in which his research has informed their own.

Where both that conference and the current volume are concerned, what is perhaps most motivating about Johnston's work (especially although not exclusively *The Canadian Party System*) is that it identifies features of Canadian politics that we might expect to condition the kind of right-wing populism that is recently evident in Canadian politics, including the historic electoral dominance of a party of the ideological centre (the Liberal Party); the pivotal role of a single region (Quebec) in making and breaking parliamentary majorities; the relatively weak influence of class identity on voting behaviour; the volatile interaction of multiparty competition, first-past-the-post (FPTP) electoral rules and public opinion polling; and, not least, the still-evolving symbolism of the "nation" in a deeply diverse – and still diversifying – society. While some of these factors may inoculate the country from populist insurgency, others point to the system's vulnerabilities.

It is with these considerations in mind that the current volume features scholarship on the mixture of social and institutional factors highlighted by Johnston's analysis, along with research focused on contemporary political dynamics across nations, in order to frame conclusions about the likely course of politics in the Canadian context. Three themes will orient the research contributions and structure the book: (1) the electoral system and the party system; (2) social foundations, in particular traditional questions in the contemporary context; and (3) campaigns and persuasion, focusing in particular on media and polling. We consider each of these themes in more detail below.

The Electoral System and the Party System

Electoral systems and party systems have been central in the study of Canadian politics, at least since Alan Cairns's foundational piece, "The Electoral System and the Party System in Canada, 1921–1965" (1968). Since then, Canadian scholars have made influential contributions, not only pertaining to the study of Canada, but also to the voluminous cross-national literature (Bakvis and Macpherson, 1995; Blais and Carty, 1991; Gaines, 1999; Cross et al., 2016). In Johnston's (2017) analysis, electoral systems and party systems can only be reckoned in relation to one another. In Canada, he argues, the historic challenges of the electoral system have typically involved failures of voters to coordinate on viable alternatives – birds of a feather not flocking together – seemingly in spite of efforts to do so (187–213).

Another theme is the differential electoral opportunities presented to parties across levels, that is, across the federal and provincial arenas, and the manner in which success (or failure) in one arena can bleed into the other (214–38). We note, in particular, that challenges of coordination bedevil incipient right-wing populist (RWP) parties everywhere, but may be especially poignant in Canada, with its patchwork of parties varying by province, both within and across levels. At the same time, these very same dynamics suggest opportunities for RWP movements: Could an electoral toehold in one or two provinces be levered for entry into national politics? While there is so far no evidence of this in Canada, it has happened before: Germany's AfD rose to national prominence only after electoral success in other arenas.

Chapters by Carty, Shafer, and Shugart and Struthers serve to ground the Canadian case squarely in a comparative tradition, assessing the institutional features that structure Canadian electoral politics. In "The Politics of Party System Transition in Canada," Carty argues that current models of the Canadian party system(s) provide an oversimplified understanding of its development. Building on the observations of Johnston that periods of recognizable organizational equilibrium have been interrupted by considerable periods of change, it explores these "transition" periods in terms of the extent and patterns of competition, the consequences for governments and parliamentary life of MPs, and the internal life of the parties themselves. The bigger question to be asked is whether these differences simply constitute regularities in transition mechanics or whether they constitute an alternate model of Canadian electoral competition.

In "Modern American Politics: The Analytic History," Shafer imports the "analytic history" approach in Johnston's *The Canadian Party System* to the United States. On Shafer's interpretation, analytic history consists in identifying the interaction of a small set of pivotal, structural drivers that fuse to generate, at specific historical moments, fundamental change in the operating logics of politics. Shafer renders American politics since 1938 into three periods, each typified by a characteristic pattern of electoral outcomes and style of policymaking, which reflect the combination of three central factors: the prevailing partisan balance, the level of ideological polarization between the dominant parties, and the nature of the substantive conflicts on which politics centres. For students of the current moment in American politics, one critical insight resulting from the approach is the revelation of important continuities uniting the Trump and Biden presidencies with their predecessors stretching back to the Clinton era.

In "Generalizing the Engine of Fragmentation," Shugart and Struthers upend the notion that Canada's persistent multipartism makes it a deviant case in comparative terms. This is a feature of the country's electoral history that Johnston emphasizes in *The Canadian Party System*, particularly the degree to which the case combines national *and* local multipartism. The syndrome is deeply peculiar given the conventional wisdom that first-past-the-post electoral systems tend towards two-party politics, especially at the local level. Shugart and Struthers, by contrast, situate Canada within an alternative framework – the Seat Product Model – that finds the country's politics perfectly ordinary, at least with respect to average numbers of parties competing nationally and locally.

Social Foundations: Understanding Traditional Questions through the Lens of Contemporary Contexts

A large literature, crossing both political science and sociology, has investigated the imprint of Canada's demography and economic development on the pattern of political identities that have – and have not – been influential in the country's politics, particularly in relation to parties and elections (Alford, 1963; Laponce, 1972; Myles, 1979; Schwartz, 1974; Johnston et al., 1992; Blais, 2005; Bittner, 2007). For Johnston, the electorally pivotal identities ultimately embody contending visions of the nation itself, involving, especially, conflict over the country's ethno-religious and linguistic character (2017, 101–32). His analysis also emphasizes the historic weakness of class politics in the Canadian context, a syndrome he links (as he does to many features of the country's politics) to the political dominance of the centrist Liberals (163–86).

Both of these conclusions – about the politics of the nation and of social class – suggest questions concerning interactions with right-wing populism. Does the historic fragmentation of national identity limit the plausibility of chauvinistic appeals to "make Canada great again"? Does the traditional anaemia of class politics create fertile ground for the distinctive material claims of contemporary populists? Six chapters address these questions either indirectly or directly, considering questions of voter behaviour through the lens of contemporary politics.

The first is by Richard Johnston himself. In "Families and the Fate of Party Systems," Johnston returns to a topic he famously explored in relation to Canada's religious cleavage (Johnston, 1985): the heritability of party loyalty. One contribution of the chapter is to clarify that variation in rates of (apparent) within-family partisan inheritance largely reflect the size of the party in question: as Johnston writes, "the larger the party, the higher the inheritance rate." This regularity – which emerges powerfully in the cross-national data he analyzes – underlines the fundamental importance of the partisan environment *outside the home* in reinforcing, or undermining, whatever intra-family partisan socialization as may occur. Johnston's second key claim follows from the first: to the extent that cross-national variation in average inheritance rates is simply a reflection of party-system arithmetic (i.e., parties' relative sizes), then this variation cannot – *contra* conventional arguments traceable to Converse (1969) – be expected to systematically shape patterns of partisan alignment and dealignment. And, as it turns out, Johnston shows that the relationship between inheritance rates and electoral volatility is nugatory.

In "Gods and Votes," Bibeau, Bodet, and Dufresne explore the historical relationship between Catholics and the Liberal Party of Canada. In *The Canadian Party System* Johnston showed with great effect how, despite the ideological incongruities between the Liberal Party of Canada and Catholics, the two have been able to build a relationship that has allowed for a long succession of Liberal governments during the twentieth century. Bibeau and colleagues note that much less has been done to understand how parties in Canada were able (or not) to build systematic bases of support among other religious denominations, however. That is the focus of their analysis, using novel data from a combination of Canadian Election Studies and Vox Pop Labs' Vote Compass.

Fournier and Blais's "Is Quebec's Distinctiveness an Artefact?" begins by noting that respondents from Quebec often hold political opinions that differ from those of respondents from the Rest of Canada (ROC). Since most interviews in Quebec and the ROC are conducted in different languages, however, translation of survey questions could be partly responsible for the gaps in opinions. That possibility is explored in this chapter, focusing on thermometer ratings of groups. Since 1997, the English endpoints of the scale have been, 0 means "really like," and 100 means "really dislike"; the French endpoints have in contrast been, 0 means "really do not like/love at all," and 100 means really like/love a lot." Fournier and Blais suggest that the French labels are more extreme and may consequently be more difficult to agree with – and this may produce lower evaluations of minority groups in Quebec. The authors test whether this thermometer wording matters, using a question wording experiment in the 2015 Canadian Election Study. Differences do not appear to hinge on question wording, however. Quebec's distinctiveness (on these issues) is thus not a methodological artefact.

In "Identities, Intersectionality, and Engagement: Examining Women's Political Participation," Brenda O'Neill is motivated by two claims in the literature: first, that incorporating intersectionality into the study of gender and political behaviour is critical, in spite of the difficulties involved (Harell, 2017); and second, that larger gaps in participation across women than between men and women suggest that a richer understanding of women's participatory decision-making is likely to be gained by concentrating on the various forces working to restrict and encourage women's political engagement (Gidengil, 2007). O'Neill's chapter focuses on women's political participation, incorporating an intersectional lens. Using original survey data of Canadian women, the chapter examines how differently situated women engage in various political activities and how intersectional analyses help to explain these differences. More specifically, it asks two questions: How does political participation vary across differently situated women? And second, to what extent are differences in participation explained by differences in access to resources? The chapter adds to our theoretical understanding of women's political participation by, first, showing that not all participatory acts require similar resource requirements; certain groups of women are able to overcome resource deficits under certain conditions. Second, it underscores the limitations of the resource model – one focused on available time, money, and civic skills – across activities for explaining these gaps across differently situated women.

Matthew Wright's "Multiculturalism Policy in the Vernacular: Public Opinion in Canada and the US" begins by highlighting two rather different positions on multiculturalism: a "cultural pluralist" approach which supports a redefinition of society in a more diverse, multicultural way, and a "cultural monist" approach which emphasizes immigrants' integration into the existing national culture. To what degree do citizens in the United States and Canada support one position or the other? As Wright notes, existing evidence suggests support for the "monist" position – but there is little work that directly examines these attitudes in relation to modern multiculturalism policy. Drawing on recent survey data, then, Wright explores the structure of, and levels of support for, a range of multiculturalism policies. He finds some coherence in support (or not) for various multicultural policies, but little evidence of the multidimensionality we might expect from citizens carefully weighing pluralist- and monist-oriented policies. The nature and sources of policy support (both attitudinal and political, attitudinal) are in Wright's view an important theme for future work.

In "Immigration Attitudes and Partisanship in Canada, 1980–2017," Banting and Soroka suggest that Canada has in some regards been seen as an exception to the major currents in contemporary democratic politics. Backlash to globalization and migration produced significant political shifts in some countries (including the election of Donald Trump and Brexit), but the same dynamic has been less evident in the Canadian case. This chapter challenges this perception, at least in part, by tracing the evolution of public attitudes towards immigration and analyzing the factors that have shaped their trajectory for over three decades. Their particular focus is on the increasing connection between partisanship and immigration preferences. Commercial survey data from the early 1980s to the present makes clear that immigration preferences were not systematically linked to partisanship until the mid-2000s; since that time, however, immigration has become an increasingly partisan issue.

Campaigns and Persuasion

Political scientists have long been skeptical about the influence of election campaigns on the behaviour and attitudes of voters (Berelson, Lazarsfeld, and McPhee, 1954; Lenz, 2012), reasoning that strong partisan attitudes and fitful attention to politics render the "average person" largely immune to political persuasion. Canadian scholars, however, have been central in challenging this conventional wisdom (Johnston et al., 1992; Mendelsohn, 1996; Nadeau et al., 2008), and evidence that campaigns can have sizable effects on voter attitudes and electoral outcomes continues to accumulate (Hart, 2013; Matthews, 2019). Johnston (2017) presents, as noted, a treatment of Canadian politics that is first and foremost a historical one: he foregrounds relatively stable institutional configurations (e.g., the electoral system) and long-term processes of social and political change (e.g., the slow eclipse of the "British" definition of Canada), rather than the short-run dynamics of election campaigns.

Even so, Johnston's analysis of the historic fragmentation of party support in Canada ironically turns on a short-run effect of the information presented to voters during elections. He suggests that campaign events (like a party leader's strong debate performance) and surveys of vote intention, or "horserace polls," also have an influence on voters' beliefs about the electoral viability of the alternatives (190–202), and it is these highly malleable beliefs that open up (and foreclose upon) possibilities for like-minded voters to coordinate on a common electoral choice. For a right-wing populist party seeking to enter the Canadian system, these campaign effects will be critical determinants of success. Does the party catch an existing player in a vulnerable moment, as the (arguably proto-RWP) Reform Party did to the Progressive Conservatives in the 1993 general election? Or will the party merely encroach on, but fail to capture, another party's turf, and simply allow a third party (probably the Liberals) to more easily conquer its divided opposition? The third section of our book looks at these questions directly, focusing on campaign dynamics, media, and polling.

In "Do Election Campaigns Tighten the Margin of Victory? A Cross-Country Comparison of the Dynamics of Vote Margins," Julia Partheymüller notes that a well-known phenomenon in US presidential election campaigns is that the electoral margin tightens over the course of the campaign. Can this pattern be found elsewhere, outside the United States? Relying on a comparable conceptualization of competitiveness, Partheymüller evaluates the dynamics of vote margins in comparative perspective using the "Dataset on Polls and the Timeline of Elections" (Jennings and Wlezien, 2018). Results suggest that vote margins tend to narrow across a wide range of different institutional settings. Yet, the analyses also uncover some heterogeneity in the trends across countries as well as deviant cases. Overall, her results contribute to the ongoing debates about the functions of election campaigns in modern democracies.

In "Media Bias, Voters, and Rolling Cross-Sections," Schmitt-Beck and Staudt examine the persuasive effects of the statement bias of TV news coverage of parties and lead candidates – the positive or negative tone in which these political actors are addressed in news reports – on German voters' electoral preferences. The expectation, they argue, is that voters' views of the parties and their lead candidates are more favourable (unfavourable), the more positive (negative) the tone of this coverage. This is an idea with a very long history but a shaky empirical record. Drawing on data that were collected at four German federal elections (2005, 2009, 2013, and 2017), the chapter explores the persuasive effects of "statement bias" of German TV news. The analyses draw on merged data from rolling cross-section voter surveys conducted during the four election campaigns and parallel content analyses of the major TV primetime news shows broadcast by the major public and commercial broadcasters. As dependent variables, the paper looks at thermometer scales indicating voters' evaluations of the major parties and their lead candidates and as a safeguard against the possibility of selection bias, the analyses utilize an approach suggested by Brandenburg and van Egmond (2012) in an analysis of persuasive effects of the British daily press. Findings suggest that party and candidate evaluations are indeed sensitive to persuasive media effects.

In "Media Image and Voter Perception of Candidates in the 2015 Canadian Election," Bittner and Peterson reconsider the ongoing debate about the importance of candidates' personalities during election campaigns. There is a growing body of evidence to suggest that personality has an influence on election outcomes, they argue; but a number of scholars have suggested that part of the reason the issue is still up for debate is based on measurement (e.g., Bittner, 2011; Peterson, 2014). Simply put, candidates' traits are measured differently over time and across space through election surveys, and most academic studies do not directly measure one of the key issues to understanding the role of personality in elections: the movement of candidate's image over the campaign. Recent analysis in the American context (Peterson, 2014) indicates that images of the candidates' personalities in the 2004 presidential election shaped voters' perceptions of candidates' traits as well as candidates' overall standing among the electorate. Recent work in the Canadian context (Peterson and Bittner, 2015) suggests that media image has some impact on voter perception of candidates. In this chapter, the authors differentiate between the measurement of candidates' image and voters' perceptions using data collected during the 2015 Canadian election to evaluate the extent that personality has an impact on both (a) voters' assessments of candidates; and (b) their subsequent decisions on election day.

Finally, Cutler, Matthews, and Pickup's "Cognitive Preconditions for Direct Poll Effects on Voters" considers the impact that polls may have on voting. As polls of vote intentions have become central to media coverage of elections, some analysts have worried about polls' potentially deleterious effects on voter deci-sion making. Cutler and colleagues assess the plausibility of such direct effects of polls on voters by investigating the cognitive preconditions for the mechanisms of poll influence theorized in the literature. They argue that direct (as opposed to mediated) influence from poll information requires attention to polls and (some) retention of poll information; and that "rational" mechanisms of influence, such as cue-taking and strategic voting, also require a belief in the applicability of poll results to the vote decision. They evaluate the presence of these preconditions during elections in Canada and the United Kingdom, and conclude that a poten-tially sizable minority of voters is susceptible to direct poll influence, although only a subset of these exhibits the preconditions for "rational" poll effects.

Looking Forward

This is a disparate body of work, to be sure. It reflects not just diversity in the study of political behaviour and institutions, but diversity in the scope and impact of Richard Johnston's scholarship. While disparate, we see an important cumulative story to the chapters that follow.

Understanding the nature and impact of electoral and party systems, of "social foundations" as drivers of political behaviour, and of political campaigns – and the many intersections between these three guiding themes – requires an eye for detail. We can each recall as doctoral students instances of looking at a simple cross-tabulation (likely in a coffee shop) and marvelling at Professor Johnston's ability to see the hint of something that was for each of us entirely undetectable. This was not just a valuable lesson in the importance of listening to our dissertation adviser – it was a lesson in the inevitable complexity of po-litical behaviour. All the chapters in this volume reflect that complexity, in the heterogeneity of campaign and polling effects across individuals, in the chang-ing structure of political institutions and attitudes over time, in the changing structure of party systems, and in the importance of careful measurement of institutions and attitudes in order to identify these complexities – to name just a few examples!

This volume brings together researchers working on the above three themes in order to shed light on our core question of the likely course of contemporary Canadian politics. It has taken some time to pull together this body of research, to be sure. But it is striking to us that roughly six years after we and our col-leagues started down this path the basic motivations of our investigation still apply. Even as the pandemic has highlighted some of the similarities between Canada and other established democracies, Canada remains in some ways a peculiar case. The basic premise of this book is that the case's eccentricity is understandable only in light of the more fundamental and enduring peculiarities of Canadian politics so well captured in Johnston's decades of research.

References

Alford, Robert R. 1963. *Party and Society: The Anglo-American Democracies.* Rand McNally.

Bakvis, Herman. 1988. "The Canadian Paradox: Party System Stability in the Face of a Weakly Aligned Electorate." In *Parties and Party Systems in Liberal Democracies,* edited by Steven B. Wolinetz. Routledge.

Bakvis, Herman, and Laura G. Macpherson. 1995. "Quebec Block Voting and the Canadian Electoral System." *Canadian Journal of Political Science* 28(4): 659–92.

Berelson, B.R., P.F. Lazarsfeld, and W.N. McPhee. 1954. *Voting: A Study of Opinion Formation in a Presidential Election.* University of Chicago Press.

Bittner, Amanda. 2011. *Platform or Personality? The Role of Party Leaders in Elections.* Oxford University Press.

Bittner, Amanda. 2007. "The Effects of Information and Social Cleavages: Explaining Issue Attitudes and Vote Choice in Canada." *Canadian Journal of Political Science* 40(4): 935–68.

Blais, André. 2005. "Accounting for the Electoral Success of the Liberal Party in Canada." *Canadian Journal of Political Science.* 38(4): 821–40.

Blais, André, and R.K. Carty. 1991. "The Psychological Impact of Electoral Laws: Measuring Duverger's Elusive Factor." *British Journal of Political Science* 21(1): 79–93.

Brandenburg, Heinz, and Marcel Van Egmond. 2012. "Pressed into Party Support? Media Influence on Partisan Attitudes during the 2005 UK General Election Campaign." *British Journal of Political Science* 42(2): 441–63.

Cairns, Alan C. 1968. "The Electoral System and the Party System in Canada, 1921–1965." *Canadian Journal of Political Science/Revue canadienne de science politique* 1(1): 55–80.

Clarke, Harold, Jane Jenson, Lawrence LeDuc, and Jon H. Pammett. 1996. *Absent Mandate: Canadian Electoral Politics in an Era of Restructuring.* Gage.

Cross, William P., Ofer Kenig, Scott Pruysers, and Gideon Rahat. 2016. *Promise and Challenge of Party Primary Elections: A Comparative Perspective.* McGill-Queen's Press – MQUP.

Gaines, Brian. 1999. "Duverger's Law and the Meaning of Canadian Exceptionalism." *Comparative Political Studies* 32(7): 835–61.

Gidengil, Elisabeth. 2007. "Beyond the Gender Gap: Presidential Address to the Canadian Political Science Association, Saskatoon, 2007." *Canadian Journal of Political Science/ Revue canadienne de science politique* 40(4): 815–31.

Harell, Allison. 2017. "Intersectionality and Gendered Political Behaviour in a Multicultural Canada." *Canadian Journal of Political Science/Revue canadienne de science politique* 50(2): 495–514.

Hart, A., 2013. "Can Candidates Activate or Deactivate the Economic Vote? Evidence from Two Mexican Elections." *The Journal of Politics* 75(4): 1051–1063.

Jennings, Will, and Christopher Wlezien. 2018. "Election Polling Errors across Time and Space." *Nature Human Behaviour* 2(4): 276–83.

Johnston, Richard. 2017. *The Canadian Party System: An Analytic History*. UBC Press.

Johnston, Richard. 1986. *Public Opinion and Public Policy in Canada: Questions of Confidence*. University of Toronto Press.

Johnston, Richard, André Blais, Henry E. Brady, and Jean Crête. 1992. *Letting the People Decide: Dynamics of a Canadian Election*. McGill-Queen's University Press.

Laponce, Jean A. 1972. "Post-Dicting Electoral Cleavages in Canadian Federal Elections, 1949–68: Material for a Footnote." *Canadian Journal of Political Science* 5(2): 270–86.

Lenz, G.S. 2013. *Follow the Leader?: How Voters Respond to Politicians' Policies and Performance*. University of Chicago Press.

Lijphart, A. 1971. "Comparative Politics and the Comparative Method." *American Political Science Review* 65(3): 682–93.

Matthews, J. Scott. 2019. "Issue Priming Revisited: Susceptible Voters and Detectable Effects." *British Journal of Political Science* 49(2): 513–31.

Mendelsohn, M. 1996. "The Media and Interpersonal Communications: The Priming of Issues, Leaders, and Party Identification." *The Journal of Politics* 58(1): 112–125.

Myles, John F. 1979. "Differences in the Canadian and American Class Vote: Fact or Pseudofact?" *American Journal of Sociology* 84(5): 1232–37.

Nadeau, R., N. Nevitte, E. Gidengil, and A. Blais. 2008. "Election Campaigns as Information Campaigns: Who Learns What and Does It Matter?" *Political Communication* 25(3): 229–48.

Noel, S.J.R. 1971. "Consociational Democracy and Canadian Federalism." *Canadian Journal of Political Science* 4(1): 15–18.

Peterson, D.A. 2014. "The Social Construction of Candidate Image." *Atlantic Provinces Political Science Association*, 2014.

Peterson, D.A., and A. Bittner. 2015. "Candidate Image and Voter Perception: Unpacking the Impact of Personality." *Biennial Meeting of the Association for Canadian Studies in the United States*, Las Vegas, Nevada, October 14–17, 2015.

Schwartz, Mildred. 1974. *Politics and Territory: The Sociology of Regional Persistence in Canada*. McGill-Queen's University Press.

PART ONE

Parties and Party Systems – Canada in Comparative Context

1 The Two Faces of Canadian Party Politics

R. KENNETH CARTY

For three decades analyses of Canadian party politics have been commonly framed in terms of a developmental model that tracked the evolution of partisan organization and activity over the century from Confederation. In its initial formulation that model of the national party system described a sequence of three distinctive eras in which the set of continuing individual political parties' social roots, organizational features, and basic activity patterns emerged in response to a continually changing society, and to the unique governance challenges of each period (Smith, 1985; Carty, 1988). Building on that interpretation, subsequent accounts have sought to identify the arrival of successive party systems but, with little agreement on their emergence or character, they have not been able to identify them as distinctive phenomena. In this chapter I suggest this reflects insufficient attention being paid to the political dynamics that marked the transitions from one party system to the next. A more focused examination of those processes reveals a second peculiarly volatile face of Canadian party competition, regularly alternating with the more settled pattern portrayed in traditional accounts.

While classic accounts of established European party systems typically focused on the number and dynamic interactions among the parties (Sartori, 1976, ch. 5 and 6), the developmental model of the Canadian party system was more broadly cast. It argued that, in each of three successive periods, the parties differed in terms of their dominant governance challenges, geographic focus, organizational dynamic, and leadership, as well as their principal financial and communication modalities. And in each distinctive era the relationship between party and state was reordered. Thus, in the first system, parties overwhelmed the formal institutions of government, adopting patronage politics in aid of state-building; in the second, the state co-opted the governing party as an instrument for regional brokerage to foster nation-building; and in the third, the party-state relationship produced a politics of pan-Canadian partisan agendas to support national policy goals. Thriving in the political environments of their time, these systems persisted only as long as they served the (latent) governing functions for which they had been established. As a structural-functional analysis, that interpretation identified the key social and institutional changes that usurped the parties established political tasks, so opening them up to a redefinition of their structure and activity.

Given the multi-dimensional cast of the political parties, and the continually evolving character of their environments, providing precise dates for this set of sequential systems was always somewhat arbitrary. As major elections provide obvious political turning points, they serve as convenient identifiers, and the three great Conservative party election sweeps in the second, sixth, and ninth decades of the century stand as obvious markers of significant partisan change. While the years before and after those contests give evidence of an old foundation crumbing, those elections dramatically revealed the erosion of established political and electoral balances that underlay decades of party system equilibrium. As a consequence the Borden, Diefenbaker and Mulroney Conservative governments have generally been recognized as heralding a transition from one party system to the next.

Political parties are complex and cumbersome organizations that don't change easily or smoothly. While the "three party system" model of Canadian party development points to the larger overarching features of the parties in their mature and fully developed form, it gives little attention to how, or how long, it took the parties to make the shift from one type and pattern of activity to another. Simply observing that the transitional years were periods of considerable uncertainty seems to fudge the issue and may confuse important aspects of a transition process with a new system's dynamics. In their book on the contemporary *Rebuilding* of the country's party politics Carty, Cross, and Young (2000) suggested that the system was then in transition, and speculated on several features of a new system struggling to emerge – new parties, increased fragmentation, regionalization, and internal democratization. However, without a clear understanding of the difference between the politics of transition and those of settled party competition it is difficult to be sure that they were not simply describing the dynamics of a long transition following the collapse of the third system.

The challenge is to turn our attention from a preoccupation with the essence of the successive distinctive party systems to consider more carefully the nature of the processes that mark the shift from one to another. To do so begins with moving beyond the assumption that these party systems simply followed one another in a seemingly seamless fashion. It requires recognition of the temporal dimensions of transition politics. Few accounts of Canadian party politics do this – the notable exception is Johnston and colleagues (1992, ch. 2) in their important book on the 1988 general election. In a careful analysis that tracks electoral realignments reflecting redefined political interests and party strength,

Johnston demonstrates both the geography of these changes and identifies the time it took for them to work through into the basis for a new party system.[1] Using general elections as the markers, the transition from the first to the second party system is recognized as having occurred during the decade from 1921 to 1930, although he suggests it was probably not fully completed until 1935. Johnston suggests the second transition may have been shorter, perhaps from 1957 until 1962, but however they might be dated, it is clear that both these first two transitions took place over several elections as the constellation of interests and the geography of the competing parties was reorganized and a new equilibrium slowly developed.

A striking fact about these processes is that they were, in considerable part, launched by a massive crash of the standing system that was driven by massive Conservative victories over the governing Liberals. But then, in both cases, the Liberals managed to rebuild a base that quickly allowed them to reclaim their position as the country's dominant national party. Writing in the early 1990s, Johnston raised the possibility that the Conservative sweep of 1984 might have been the precursor to a third transition although, given the subsequent record of the Mulroney government and its then still uncertain prospects in the face of the parties' reordered policy orientations, he remained agnostic on the prospects for another cycle marked by Liberal recovery and reassertion (1992, 76–7). In retrospect it now seems clear that another significant transition, which would destabilize the country's national party system, was about to begin. And, as before, the Conservatives would pay the biggest (short-term) price and the Liberals would again find a way to return to office.

If we recognize that these party system transitions played out in extended multi-year processes, rather than as a single point distinguishing two distinctive political eras, then we are driven to ask about the character of party competition in these periods. Is it simply a rather piecemeal evolutionary mixture of the periods being separated (and joined), or is some different, characteristic pattern regularly being played out during these several periods? And if so, what are the common dimensions of transition politics? To answer these critical questions, we need to start by considering the periods to be examined. Election dates, with their results that signal the state and shape of party support, provide an obvious indication of the competitive balances defining the party system. However, for individual parties, and the working of the wider political system itself, other important events and corresponding organizational adjustments can also indicate the changing state of play in the system. They also need to be recognized as defining the transition periods with their consequent impact on the country's party politics.

While the 1917 wartime election, fought under its unique conditions and institutional arrangements, undoubtedly broke the first party system, it wasn't until after the war ended, and the political dust began to settle, that the first transition to a new system really got under way. Two significant events signalled its beginning: first, the reunification of the Liberal party broken over conscription and the war effort; and second, that party's adoption in 1919 of a radical new method of choosing its leader, a process that challenged the autonomy of the "party in public office" and would quickly come to define the distinctive organization and internal politics of Canada's parties. Indeed, it was the Conservative's subsequent decision to adopt the same convention-centred procedures in 1927 that indicated that the country's two principal parties were now different organizational creatures than they had been in the previous party era. By 1930 an apparently familiar choice between the Liberal and Conservative parties was restored as the central competitive electoral dynamic governing the selection of national governments. Thus it seems reasonable to define the first transition as running for the decade from 1919 to about 1929. During this period there were three general elections (1921, 1925, and 1926).

In 1958 the Conservatives won the largest general election vote share of any national party in Canadian history.[2] This "Diefenbaker Revolution" restructured national voter alignments and eroded the regional brokerage party politics of the second party system. But by 1968 the Conservatives were bitterly divided in opposition while the Liberals had come back from their worst result in the century (to date) and, led by dynamic new leadership, were back in office. During these years the internal politics of both parties were again reshaped by the adoption of a new leadership politics that drove competition down into the "party on the ground" (Carty, 2007). This second transition period, which saw this organizational transformation, was squeezed into the decade between 1958 and 1968, a period in which the parties fought another three general elections (1962, 1963 and 1965).

As Johnston speculated, the oversized electoral victory won by the Conservatives in 1984 unleashed a set of political events that eventually culminated in the collapse of the third party system in the 1993 election with the arrival of the Reform party and the Bloc Québécois as the two largest opposition caucuses in Parliament. It would be over a decade before a new national party system would even begin to crystalize. This longer transition, which really started with the victory of federalist forces in the 1995 Quebec sovereignty referendum, ran through until near the end of the first decade of the new century when the Bloc finally ceased to be a significant player in the country's parliamentary life. These transition years, from about 1996 until 2009, saw the parties compete in five national general elections (1997, 2000, 2004, 2006, and 2008). While the subsequent shape of party competition is still unclear, it might represent an embryonic fourth system.

This mapping of the temporal dimensions of Canadian electoral history suggests we can identify three quite distinctive sets of electoral events. There are the periods of stable institutionalized party competition, between the big battalions of the Liberal and Conservative parties, in recognizably distinct party systems; there are periods of transition between each of these party systems; and there are the individual elections that saw an old system crash and opened the way to the transition years' rebuilding of a new one. These different periods of party competition can be summarized (in terms of their general elections) as follows:

Periods	Election years	Number GEs
Party System 1	1896–1911	5
System crash	1917	1
1st Transition	1921–1926	3
Party System 2	1930–1953	6
System crash	1957–1958	2
2nd Transition	1962–1965	3
Party System 3	1968–1988	7
System crash	1993	1
3rd Transition	1997–2008	5
Party System 4?	2011–	3

Since 1896, when the Liberals came to power and established themselves as the country's "natural governing party," and the end of the first decade of the twenty-first century when a new stable fourth system may have been emerging, there were 33 national general elections.[3] By this account only 18 took place during well-defined, stable party systems in which the Liberals and Conservatives vied for office. More than half as many (11 – a third of all the contests) occurred during multi-year periods of transition when the character of the individual parties and the structure of the competitive system were in flux. Each of three breaks followed a party system crash characterized by an oversized Conservative victory and successively new low points for the Liberals.[4] Yet in the aftermath of each restructuring of party politics that stretched over several elections a much changed Liberal party (Carty, 2015, ch. 3) once again came out on top of a new, but superficially familiar, pattern of party competition that could lay claim to being the oldest continuously running party system in any of the established parliamentary democracies.

The Electoral Dynamics of Party System Transition

Each of the transitions was preceded by years of social, geo-demographic, and economic change. When the then existing patterns of partisan alignments no longer reflected the country's underlying political pressures, the result was voter rebellion, the growth of new parties and movements, and an electoral explosion. Figure 1.1 demonstrates this, charting the average effective number of

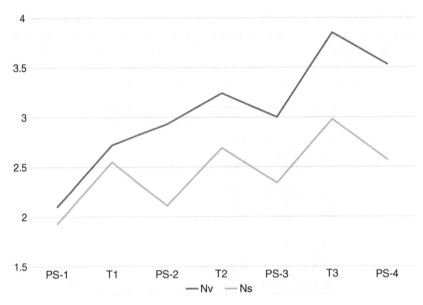

Figure 1.1. Effective number of parties: 1896–2019

parties (measured in terms of both votes and seats) across the distinctive party systems and years of the transition period elections. The distinctive character of the transition periods is clear. Despite a gradual increase over the century, the number of parties (at both levels) in each transition was always greater than in the party system that preceded it, and larger than in the party system that came after – the single exception to this pattern being the permanent increase in the number of parties winning votes after the first transition. The greater competitiveness of electoral politics in the transitions reflected the electoral uncertainties generated by ongoing realignments, but it also generated incentives for working politicians to reconstruct their party organizations.

The basis for the growth in the number of parties during these transition periods was never particularly even. It reflected the continually changing demography of the country and the consequent recurring pattern of attack on the country's existing partisan equations.[5] The story of these party eruptions is a familiar one. In the decade after the First World War, Conservative strength in Quebec sharply declined as the province's voters saw the Liberals as their natural defenders, while in Ontario and the Prairie West the successful rise of farmers movements disrupted both the old parties. In the aftermath of Diefenbaker's Conservative sweep of the west, and the Ralliement Créditiste's split from its western Social Credit (nominal) co-partisans in the wake of the Quiet Revolution in Quebec, the parties' standing electoral coalitions were again threatened.

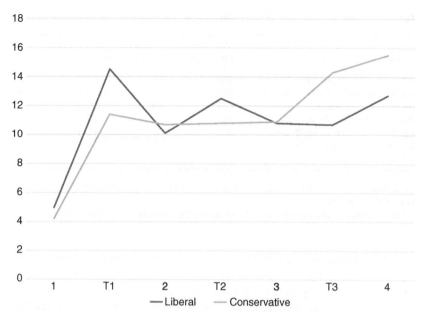

Figure 1.2. Geographic concentration of the parties' vote: 1896–2015

And then in the early 1990s the emergence of the Reform party and the Bloc Québécois once again shattered the regular contest for office between the Conservatives and the Liberals. The common thread running through these stories is a persistent regionalization of competitive impulses and organizations, centred in both the prairies and Quebec. That form of electoral protest was a seemingly inherent characteristic of Canada's transition politics.

In an important paper Johnston (1980) explored the shifting character of federal and provincial voting for the parties over the century. To measure the extent of regional divergence of a party's national support he calculated the standard deviation of its vote across the (changing number of) provinces for each election. Figure 1.2 reports the average of these scores for each of the party systems and subsequent transition periods.[6] A high score indicates greater provincial variation in a party's vote shares; a lower score suggests a more nationally homogeneous support base.

Four observations leap out from this picture. First, as Johnston (1980, 145) noted the "tightly contested, geographically homogeneous system ended with a bang in 1917." Canadian electoral politics really was very different after the war.[7] Second, both the major parties have been more regionally heterogeneous (i.e., with less of a balanced national support base) during transition elections than in the election years of the settled party systems. Third, the Liberals, while going into the

Table 1.1. Stable party system vs transition politics: 1896–2019*

Period	Years	No. of elections	Maj / min Governments	% Majority Governments	Lib + Con avg vote share
PS 1	1896–1911	5	5/0	100	94.5
1st Transition	1921–26	3	0/3	0	81.7
PS 2	1930-53	6	6/0	100	80.0
2nd Transition	1962–65	3	0/3	0	73.7
PS 3	1968–1988	7	5/2	72	75.4
3rd Transition	1997–2008	5	2/3	40	58.5**
PS 4?	2011–	3	2/1	66	65.8

* Excludes the four "crash" elections: three (1917, 1958, 1993) produced big majorities, one (1957) a minority
** Conservative share includes both Progressive Conservative and Reform parties.

transitions as the normal party of government, typically suffered the most from the regional challenges and so were left with a more geographically varied base than their Conservative opponents in those transition year elections.[8] And fourth, the reverse was true once the transition politics had worked themselves out. The Liberals reestablished their place as the most nationally inclusive of the major parties, and the Conservatives were again pushed into trying to organize a national opposition while burdened with a more regionally imbalanced electoral base.

With election contests being more frequent and competitive, vote and seat shares more fragmented, and the impact of regional forces dividing the contestants both internally and from each other, one might expect that the outcomes in the transition period elections to differ systematically from those in the more settled eras. Table 1.1 which summarizes the election results in terms of their production of majority or minority governments, indicates that this was the case. Of the 18 general elections held in the three settled party systems, 16 led to a majority government, a "success" rate of almost 90 per cent: by contrast, in the 11 elections fought in transition years, there were just two majority outcomes, a rate five times lower. The First-Past-the-Post's vaunted ability to produce stable majority governments apparently worked during the institutionalized periods of normal party competition, for only twice (in 1940 and 1984) in the post-World War I era did a majority government actually rest on a majority of the vote.

In transition year elections the much-altered dynamics of competition regularly led to parliamentary minorities despite the same inherent biases of the electoral system. Indeed, the only times majority governments emerged from a transition election were in 1997 and 2000 when the hyper-regionalism generated by quite different insurgent parties in the west and Quebec, and a divided Conservative vote, allowed the Liberals to sweep the large, seat-rich province of Ontario. Two of three (2011 and 2015) general elections in the post-transition period returned majority governments – evidence, perhaps, that a fourth party system was struggling to emerge.

Responding to Changing Electoral Dynamics

With a number of new parties effectively competing for votes in a realigning electorate, and with the established parties rethinking their appeal and rede-fining themselves, transitions inevitably generated considerable political un-certainty on the ground. For many parliamentarians it created a new political world; for some it forced them to relocate themselves in the altered political space, whether for electoral imperatives or ideological reasons. While party switching by members of Parliament is hardly a regular or normal event, nei-ther is it as exceptional as excited journalistic reports of floor-crossing might suggest. A careful study of year-by-year changes in declared party affiliations of sitting members of the House of Commons notes that there were 229 switches from 1921 to 2005. In more years than not (six in 10) at least one MP changed sides; on average there were 2.7 moves per year (Morton, 2006).[9]

Given the slow and modest rate at which changes occurred, years in which a disproportionate number take place demand attention. Over the eight-and-a-half decades there were only seven years in which 10 or more MPs changed their parti-san affiliation. Five of the seven were in the midst of the transitions: 1926 in the first, 1963 in the second, and 2000, 2002, and 2004 in the third. These, and the few years around them, accounted for over half of all the switches over the entire period. The turbulent third transition itself generated 54 changes of alignment in the House from 2000 to 2005 as the party system wrestled a new political formula, with its reshaped Conservative party, into existence. Of the only two non-transition years in which large numbers of switches occurred, the first (in 1935) reflected a final, somewhat delayed, mopping-up of prairie voters into the second party system; the second (in 1990) was a prelude to the looming departure of Quebec from contem-porary national electoral politics that was to soon help ignite the third transition.

Given the powerful regional impulses that drove the transitions, it is not sur-prising that the great majority (73 per cent) of MPs switching their party came from either Quebec or the prairies. Quebec alone accounted for almost half of all the party switchers over the years, some admittedly moving out of and then back into the Liberal party. That partisan ambivalence of Quebec politicians, apparent even during the otherwise stable 1940s when 17 of the province's MPs switched sides, was an important aspect of both the breakups and reorganiza-tions of national party competition in Canada.

In the face of new electoral imperatives, and the need to cope with altered parliamentary realities, the parties were driven to examine and reform some of their basic internal organizational relationships. As Siegfried (1966) had ar-gued as early as 1906, the most important of these in Canadian parties was the position of the party leader. Over the course of the twentieth century party leadership was transformed from being in the gift of (and responsible to) the parliamentary caucus to a democratically held mandate conferred by the ordinary grassroots membership (Carty, 2007). This process took place in three stages as the parties struggled to find a new way to organize and to compete: each of them occurring during one of the system transitions, each led by a different party.

As part of their process of reuniting a party split during the First World War, the Liberals took the right to choose the party leader from their (geographically) unrepresentative caucus and established a convention selection process that, while nominally fed from their local associations, was largely managed from the top. The immediate result was the choice of a new leader from outside the sitting caucus – a revolution in parliamentary terms but one quickly sanctified by electoral success. Towards the end of this first transition period the Conservatives reluctantly followed suit. Their 1930 electoral win quickly solidified a delegate convention process as the norm for choosing leaders to lead the parties' organization and national election campaigns. This development clearly differentiated Canadian parties, and their leadership politics, from those in other Westminster-style parliamentary systems.

The bitter disputes that divided the Conservative government in the early 1960s as the second transition was underway led to a ferocious intraparty battle over Diefenbaker's leadership of the party. In a publicly fought series of party meetings the extra-parliamentary organizations successfully asserted the right to dismiss the national leader in what was euphemistically referred to as a "leadership review." In the process the grassroots were mobilized in a fashion that then transformed the selection process, making it more open and competitive. The example of the Conservatives was not lost on the Liberals, who soon follow suit. This vigorous activation of ordinary local party members spilled over into constituency nomination processes leaving parties in the third system as complex stratarchical networks of mobilizable citizens (Carty and Cross, 2010, 196–7), vulnerable to personalized intraparty conflict.

The 1980s saw a number of provincial parties experiment with one member – one vote leadership selection mechanisms that engaged all their supporters. During the third transition the Reform/Alliance party's enthusiasm for reshaping the country's democratic practices led them to utilize broad membership votes for key internal party decision-making, including leadership selection. Their example spurred on the other national parties to adopt various forms of that principle. In doing so the old issue of leadership accountability and removal reasserted itself. With no easy solution at hand, unhappy Alliance party MPs resorted to splitting the parliamentary party (one source of the large number of party switches in the third transition) – a crude reassertion of caucus power and testimony to the organizational as well as electoral volatility generated by the dynamics of transition politics.

The Two Faces of Canadian Party Competition

The sequential party systems model provided a portrait of the distinctive patterns of party organization and activity that were institutionalized to serve the changing demands of linking society and polity in distinctive periods over a century of national development. The attraction of the model was its comprehensive multi-dimensional portrait of the parties as structural responses to the functional demands of governing in the respective periods. Each of the several consecutive stable party systems provided its own unique pattern of party life and political competition. While it is possible to read that interpretation as suggesting successive systems passed readily from one form to another at a moment when critical governing modalities, such as civil service reform or the establishment of federal-provincial diplomacy, suddenly made established patterns obsolete, Johnston's careful rendering of the temporal dimension of the electoral alignments underpinning the parties points to a more nuanced reality. He demonstrates that realignments were not the business of a moment, or just one electoral eruption, but took place over a more extended period, of up to about a decade, in each of three cases in the twentieth century.

This detailed focus on these periods reveals that electoral party politics during those transition years differed considerably from those during the periods dominated by a stable, institutionalized party system, and secondly, that there was a regularly recurring common pattern in their dynamics. Taken together this describes the regular existence of two distinctive faces of Canadian party competition.

Two Alternating Faces of Party Competition

Settled	Volatile
Limited party fragmentation	Increased party numbers
Parties regionally heterogeneous	Regionalized parties
Stable parliamentarianism	Volatile parliamentary loyalties
Organizational stability	Organizational turbulence and restructuring
Majority governments	Minority governments

The striking reality is that these two patterns of party competition regularly alternated over the century. The years in which stable party competition prevailed lasted longer, but it still only accounted for just over half of the elections held between 1896 and 2008. A third were characterized by the volatile dynamics generated by the increased regional tensions driving representational interests and generating less conclusive outcomes. And separating these two different competitive constellations were earthquake elections that produced the greatest turnovers in the country's electoral history, and indeed that of any

Western democracy during the century. The cyclical character of this alternation slowly eroded the two-party character of electoral competition as the combined Liberal and Conservative vote share regularly declined with every transitional turn as it generated a new party system equilibrium.

The very use of the term "transition" might imply that the periods of settled party organization and competition are 'normal' while the years and elections between are mere interregnums. But is that how they ought to be understood? The regularity with which the party system has been broken, and the consistency in the shape and character of competitive politics in these successive interregnums, raises the issue of whether they may just represent an alternative face of Canadian party politics.

Over the century the emergence of each new party system depended upon the Liberal party reconstructing itself as a viable organization able to dominate national electoral competition. It continually managed this rebirth but "each time the party did so it emerged a different organization, one smaller in reach and narrower in range than the one that had preceded it" (Carty, 2015, 34). It was this succession of four different Liberal parties that provided the appearance of continuity and stability to the country's political competition. But a smaller and less representative Liberal party only insured that another system collapse would come, each in its turn increasing party system fragmentation, shrinking the Liberal's base, and complicating a subsequent inevitably limited recovery. The last, prolonged multi-election transition at century's end, a consequence of Quebec's flirtation with the Bloc in those years, appears to have undermined the Liberal's capacity to count on Quebec, long the basis for its easy preeminence and majority governments. That consequences of that dynamic have yet to fully unfold and is likely to shape a fourth party system. Given the Liberal party's role as the anchor for the previous stable party systems (Johnston, 2017, ch. 3), it may be that the traditional norms of Canadian electoral politics will give way and a politics thought to be merely transitional could become a new normal face of the future.

NOTES

An early draft of this paper was presented at the October 2018 workshop on "Canada's Electoral Future in Comparative Perspective." I am much indebted to Matt Shugart and Bill Cross for perceptive comments.

1 Although the book is a collective effort, there is little doubt that the historical analysis is by Johnston. It reflects his long interest in the development of Canadian electoral alignments that culminated in his *The Canadian Party System: An Analytic History*, UBC Press, 2017.

2 The Borden-led government won a larger vote share in the 1917 general election but it was a coalition of Conservatives and Liberals.

3 Johnston et al. (1992, 44) argue that 1896 defines the start of a distinctive second half of the original, first party system and the beginning of Liberal party dominance. For the purpose of this analysis, I assume a fourth party system can be dated from the 2011 election although it remains to be seen whether, or in what form, it may be institutionalized.

4 The system crash in the 1950s took place over two elections held only nine months apart. In the first (June 1957) the Conservatives won the most seats – but not votes – but then in the second (March 1958) they scored the largest vote share in Canadian history.

5 On the changing demography and geography see Carty (2015, 4–9).

6 Johnston (1980) provides the data through the 1974 general election, scores for subsequent elections by the author.

7 It should be noted that 1921 was the first national general election in which there was (nearly) universal adult suffrage.

8 In the third transition the Conservatives split along regional lines, making none of the resulting pieces regionally heterogeneous.

9 Comparing absolute numbers of party switchers over time can be hazardous as the size of the House grew considerably during the period. In 1921 it had 235 members; by 2004, the last year in Morton's database, it had 308.

References

Carty, R.K. 1988. "Three Canadian Party Systems: An Interpretation of the Development of National Politics." In *Party Democracy in Canada*, edited by G.C. Perlin. Prentice-Hall.

– 2007. "Leadership Politics and the Transformation of Canadian Parties." In *Political Leadership and Representation in Canada: Essays in Honour of John Courtney*, edited by H. Michelmann et al. University of Toronto Press.

– 2015. *Big Tent Politics: The Liberal Party's Long Mastery of Canada's Public Life*. UBC Press.

Carty, R.K., W. Cross, and L. Young. 2000. *Rebuilding Canadian Party Politics*. UBC Press.

Carty, R.K., and W. Cross 2010. "Political Parties and the Practice of Brokerage Politics." In *The Oxford Handbook of Canadian Politics*, edited by J.C. Courtney and D.E. Smith. Oxford University Press.

Johnston, R. 1980. "Federal Provincial Voting: Contemporary Patterns and Historical Evolution." In *Small Worlds: Provinces and Parties in Canadian Political Life*, edited by D. Elkins and R. Simeon. Methuen.

– 2017. *The Canadian Party System: An Analytic History*, UBC Press.

Johnston, R., A. Blais, H. Brady, and J. Crête. 1992. *Letting the People Decide: The Dynamics of a Canadian Election.* McGill-Queen's University Press.

Morton, D. 2006. "A Note on Party Switchers." *Canadian Parliamentary Review* 29 (2).

Sartori, G. 1976. *Parties and Party Systems: A Framework for Analysis.* Cambridge University Press.

Siegfried, A. 1966: 1907. *The Race Question in Canada.* McClelland & Stewart.

Smith, D. 1985. Party Government, Representation and National Integration in Canada." In *Party Government and Regional Representation in Canada*, edited by P. Aucoin. Canada: Royal Commission on the Economic Union and Developmental Prospects for Canada.

2 Modern American Politics: The Analytic History

BYRON E. SHAFER

In *The Canadian Party System,* Richard Johnston has used the framework for what he calls "an analytic history" to unpack major puzzles in Canadian politics (Johnston, 2017). These begin with the dynamic inescapably central to that politics, involving the role and behaviour of a true centrist party, the theoretically anomalous Liberals. We come to know how they came to be, what they do in this role, and how they came to play it. But we also know, and much more than just in passing, how this central dynamic is tied to the governmental forms and electoral system above, to a set of major social cleavages below, and to an evolutionary path, one that morphs into a partially autonomous influence all its own. Along the way, we learn to treat such things as a dissident electoral region, namely Quebec, and a changing mix of social groups, from settlers at the start to immigrants and Inuits at the end, less as idiosyncrasies and more as ongoing structural facts.

Yet the same exercise, so richly focused on Canada as its case, has also gifted us with an *analytic approach,* capable of being carried elsewhere. So if this exercise gives Canadian politics a powerful synthesizing treatment on its own terms, it simultaneously makes the result available for – but really, it injects its approach forcefully into – comparative work on the same grand level. In this, the notion of an analytic history imposes a small set of explanatory demands on the writing of both political science and political history. Seen this way, the notion of an analytic history asserts that an acceptable explanation must occur within an explicit hierarchy of causal engines and at specified (historical) points in time. Causally ordered but beautifully focused, the Canadian case thus opens the door to a specific kind of further comparison. So perhaps the best tribute to its analytic framework and the resulting specifics is to take that framework elsewhere – and see what fresh propositions emerge.

Here, the focus is American politics across the years since the Second World War. Three simple concepts provide a way to organize the journey: *partisan balance,* that is, the competitive equilibrium or imbalance of party loyalists in society;

ideological polarization, that is, the nature and degree of preference differences within and between two dominant parties; and *substantive conflict*, that is, the actual focus of major disputes over public policy. Together, these contribute a *policy-making process*, and it is this process that ultimately distinguishes political periods, those where politics has a recognizable and continuing character. Though its elements do contribute simultaneously to the patterning of electoral outcomes, these outcomes are more useful in driving a search for the changing interaction among its contributory elements than as causal agents in their own right.

To that end, this chapter tackles American politics since the end of the Second World War with an eye to isolating a small set of structural influences, ongoing shapers that themselves evolve across time but that interact differently at different periods. The overall product is by definition a second analytic history, progressing in this case through an old world of incremental policy-making, to a transitional world of grand coalitions, into a modern world of stasis, spikes, and omnibus legislation. What this particular analytic history suggests most pointedly about the modern world is that the years from 1992 to the present – and thus the presidencies of Bill Clinton, George Bush, Barack Obama, and Donald Trump – constitute a more or less integrated whole. One final contribution of the general approach and its specific application thus lies in separating what is consequentially different in current American politics from what is just an idiosyncratic twist on an established order.

The Late New Deal Era, 1938–1968

There have been three great break points in the evolution of American politics since its beginning. The first was the Revolutionary War, 1775–83. The second was the Civil War, 1860–65. And the third was the Great Depression, 1929–36. Each functioned as a kind of giant political reset for American politics, while each also possessed an intense and tightly focused politics specific to the crisis. For an analytic history, these three serve additionally as a means of isolating a point in time that was sufficiently self-contained to allow the search for causal ordering and temporal evolution to proceed. For a focus on modern American politics, it is the third of these that becomes the starting point.

The lone structural characteristic among our four key elements that continued from the short High New Deal rupture, 1932–8, was a lasting shift in partisan loyalties. From 1896 to 1932, there had been only one Democratic presidency, that of Woodrow Wilson, and even this required a Republican implosion with *two* Republican candidates in 1912 to produce a minority-party victory. From 1932 to 1968, by contrast, there was to be only one Republican presidency, that of Dwight Eisenhower in 1952, whom some Democrats had considered to replace the majority-party *Democrat*, Harry Truman, in 1948. What was additionally different this time was that there would be continuing and systematic data to confirm the partisan balance in the general public beneath these results, with the launch of what would become the American National Election Study (ANES) in 1952. Figure 2.1 shows the result for the years 1952–64 in two canonical ways, first as a simple two-party division of Democrats versus Republicans, then as a seven-part tally of strong, weak, and independent identifiers plus pure independents.

Either way, the point for an analytic history is straightforward. There was a solid Democratic majority in the country as a whole, such that the default result for any presidential election should have been a Democratic president, while the default result for a congressional election should have been a Democratic Congress. As indeed they were. The Republicans succeeded in capturing the presidency exactly once between the election in 1938 that blew up the fantasy of an extended High New Deal and the one in 1968 that signalled the end of its extended successor. Just as these Republicans succeeded in capturing control of Congress exactly twice during this entire period, and then only for a single term in 1947–8 and again in 1953–4.

Inside this emergent (and then lasting) Democratic majority, the short High New Deal had simultaneously featured an unprecedented *unipolarity* to American politics in ideological terms. It was during these years, 1935–6 and 1937–8, that Northern Democrats achieved their only majorities – still, as this is written – in all of American history. Party politics was thus effectively unipolar (Shafer, 2017, 7–8, figures 1.1 and 1.2). Northern Democrats had no need of any extra-party support from the Republicans nor even of any intra-party support from the Southern Democrats in order to legislate. The real ideological conflict that remained was instead between a presidency committed to what would be the new Democratic orthodoxy and a Supreme Court still committed to what was the old Republican counterpart (Leuchtenberg, 1995).

Yet what had momentarily appeared to be a new and uniform ideological majority had already reverted by 1938 to a new version of the classic *factional* story of American politics, in which enduring regional factions inside the two major parties provided the real building blocks for policy conflict and policy-making (Truman, 1959; DiSalvo, 2012). Now, each party featured a major factional divide. The more famous Democratic version involved a deep divide between Northern Democrats and Southern Democrats with major ideological implications. Yet the Republican version was noteworthy too, featuring Northeastern Republicans versus the Regular Republicans elsewhere (Rae, 1994; Rae, 1989).

For social welfare, continuing as the lead policy focus of the new era, the implications were straightforward. Democrats could legislate on welfare policy when Northern Democrats either retained a substantial share of Southern Democrats or attracted a serious share of Northeastern Republicans. Republicans could legislate instead when Regular Republicans either retained a substantial share of Northeastern Republicans or attracted a serious share of Southern

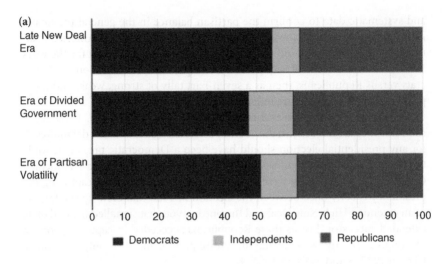

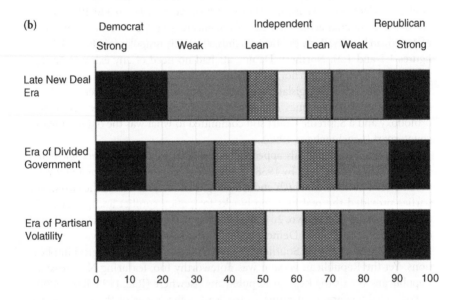

Figure 2.1. Party identification in the nation as a whole: Underpinnings for postwar political eras
Source: American National Election Studies, University of Michigan and Stanford University, "ANES Time Series Cumulative Data File (1948–2016), Ann Arbor, MI.

Democrats. That was already a much more complex strategic environment for legislative conflict than that of the High New Deal era.

Yet this still understates the changed factional situation. For in the High New Deal, a fleeting Northern Democratic majority had been able to focus nearly all of its legislative activity on social welfare, the single dominant policy domain of the time. But after 1938, social welfare was insistently joined by issues of foreign affairs, driven by the Second World War and then institutionalized by the long Cold War to follow (Hamby, 2004; Hamby, 1976; Gaddis, 2007). After 1948, both major domains would likewise be joined by civil rights, driven from the bottom up rather than from the outside in but more and more insistent as time passed (Valelly, 2004; Graham, 1990). So policy-making would almost surely have become more complex merely through the arrival of a tripartite rather than a unipartite substantive focus. Yet even this continues to understate the changed strategic situation.

For in fact, each of these three domains for major policy conflict aligned the four partisan factions in a different ideological order, a further structural story that is presented schematically in table 2.1. Social welfare remained as it was, with Northern Democrats on the left, Regular Republicans on the right, and Southern Democrats plus Northeastern Republicans as the swing factions. But on foreign affairs, Southern Democrats were the internationalists, Regular Republicans the isolationists, and Northern Democrats plus Northeastern Republicans the swing factions. And on civil rights, factions (and their ideologies) lined up differently yet again. Here, Northern Democrats were the integrationists, Southern Democrats were the segregationists, and Northeastern Republicans plus Regular Republicans were the pivotal blocs.

The policy-making process that followed from this complex array was perhaps the most distinctive of all between the short High New Deal and this long aftermath, now best seen as the Late New Deal. In the former, policy-making was executive-dominated in a way that has never been true at any time since. The bulk of legislation came from the White House. Its timing was largely determined by the White House. And serious congressional initiatives were ordinarily coopted by that White House. Possibly no other policy-making process was so executive-centred in all of American history, not even excluding the Civil War.

After 1938, there were instead four major factions rather than just one; there were three major policy domains rather than just one; and those four factions lined up differently on these three policy domains. So what resulted was a multi-level complexity for policy initiatives. Policy details had to be squared with a majority that could be extracted from the interaction of the main factions, of course. But every initiative of any size had to be considered simultaneously for what it would do to possible policy majorities in the *other two* major domains, the ones that were not explicitly part of the initiative in question but that were inherent in legislation of any size, given the new and ongoing structure of American politics.

Table 2.1. Factional alignments in the late New Deal era

"Progressives"	"Pivots"	"Conservatives"
A. Social Welfare		
Northern Democrats	Southern Democrats Northeastern Republicans	Regular Republicans
B. Foreign Affairs		
Southern Democrats	Northern Democrats Northeastern Republicans	Regular Republicans
C. Civil Rights		
Northern Democrats	Regular Republicans Northeastern Republicans	Southern Democrats

The arrival of this complex policy world, as it happened, coincided with the rise of a self-consciously empirical political science to study it. "Incrementalism" was the term that practitioners produced to capture this world in summary form (on political science at the time, see Hotson, 2017; on incrementalism as concept and as process, see: Wildavsky, 1964). Some found this incrementalism to be the "genius" of American politics. Others found it to be the curse (for the celebratory, see Boorstin, 1958; for the critical, see Burns, 1963). Yet a sense of its general outlines was widely shared. Moreover, and this was the crucial buttressing fact for an institutionalized process of policy-making, the major players all came to understand its inherent logic: four factions, three major issues, differential alignments by faction and by issue, all interacting in any serious policy move (Fenno Jr., 1966). As a result, there were also generalized norms of behaviour along with regularized strategies for approaching legislation, both adopted by the major players in order to make policy in an institutionalized world like this one.

A Generation of Divided Government, 1968–1988

This world, like all worlds demarcated by a distinctive process of policy-making, was being undermined piecemeal as time passed. So, it was not some single eruption, or even some single development, that brought it to a close after 1964. A shift in electoral outcomes did suggest an actual change of political eras. Yet this shift was initially treated as an anomaly, more or less, by all sides. Richard Nixon, Republican candidate for president, secured election, while solid Democratic majorities returned to control both houses of Congress. It would take a while for all sides to recognize that this was a template, not an exception: a generation-plus of "divided government" – split partisan control of the elective institutions of national government – had arrived. A collateral result was that social scientists had to return to looking for those gradually emerging elements of change that came together in 1968, to live on together for a further generation (Jacobson, 1990; Cox and Kernell, 1991; Thurber, 1991).

Nothing about the balance of party identifiers would have foreshadowed such a change. ANES tallies of party identification in the mass public for the next twenty-plus years showed a modest decline in the share of Democrats but almost no increase in the share of Republicans (for a comprehensive consideration of party identification as a concept, addressing strengths and weaknesses, applications and misapplications, see Johnston, 2006) (figure 2.1). This made survey-based party balance a bad indicator for a sharply changed pattern of electoral outcomes that was afterward quite stable. Indeed, if the one-term Carter "accidency" was chalked up to the Watergate crisis and the Nixon resignation, then total domination of presidential elections by the Republicans was coupled with near-total domination of congressional elections – truly total for the House – by the Democrats.

As a result, change had to come from some mix of ideological (re)balance and substantive (re)focus, as indeed it did. For an extended era of divided government, what had been a unipolar ideological alignment in the High New Deal and a multipolar alignment in the Late New Deal became what has to be called a split-level alignment in this successor period. On the elite level, party activists – and hence the active parties – were increasingly polarized in ideological terms. On the mass level, the general public remained obstinately and consistently depolarized. And in between, elected public officials sought to accommodate their activists while remaining more concerned, when push came to shove, with their mass electorates.

The engine for this split-level alignment was a long-running secular trend in the structure of American political parties, a trend which reached the breaking point around 1968. There had in fact been a long war over party structure, built upon opposite approaches to party politics and democratic representation (Shafer and Wagner, 2019). The Jacksonians, from the 1820s onward, pioneered the organized model of this politics, where a hierarchy of long-serving party officials used the concrete rewards of government to build an army-type structure of operatives who could contest elections and manage the governments that followed. The Progressives, from the 1880s onward, offered the opposite model, a volunteer approach in which self-starting participants mobilized by issues of the day undertook to free politics from those organized parties and turn it over to an enlightened citizenry.

The dominant lore about the course of this conflict was that it featured a long, slow, but ineluctable one-way flow from organized parties to volunteer counterparts. Serious enquiry by political scientists in the 1960s then produced two correctives, with opposite implications (Ware, 1985, and Mayhew, 1986). In the first, the inevitability of this structural drift proved to have been greatly exaggerated. Organized parties were alive, well, and well represented in the United States as the 1960s arrived. But in the second, the hypothesized pivot point did finally arrive around 1970, changing the party structure underpinning American politics in a major way.

For this, a politics involving social networks of issue activists was closely tied to volunteer party structure, and these volunteer parties were on the rise not just courtesy of a long-running secular trend. They were also the beneficiaries of participatory reforms that swept through the United States in the 1960s and 1970s. The most widely recognized part of this was root and branch changes in the institutions of presidential selection, and presidential nominating politics became the opening home ground for newly advantaged issue activists. But the same movement went on to colonize political parties much more broadly, while restructuring the institutional processes of government itself – in Congress, in the federal bureaucracy, and in state counterparts across the country.

So the social identity and policy preferences of a rising body of issue activists came to matter, arguably more than it ever had (for a theoretical framework involving organizational structures and social characteristics, see Clark and Wilson, 1961; for its application to American political parties, see Wilson, 1973). Their rise was easiest to recognize in its early days among national convention delegates, who were the most direct product of sweeping participatory reform (table 2.2.). In the Late New Deal era (as here in the data for 1956), partisan publics had been moderate; active Democrats had been modestly off to the left of their partisans, and active Republicans, driven principally by ideology once the Great Depression deprived them of governmental largesse, had been strongly off to their right of theirs. With the coming of an era of divided government (as here in the data for 1972), this picture was temporarily inverted to yield two moderate publics, Republican activists only slightly more extreme than their rank and file, but Democratic activists far off to the left of theirs.

Yet even before the modern era appeared, these activists had begun to polarize more symmetrically (as registered here in 1976 and 1980), a division that was to be institutionalized in the modern world. Moreover, there was a set of issues, generally gathered as "social" or "cultural," that were rising with these activists and stimulating their active participation while simultaneously benefiting from it. The liberal side of these issues among Democrats, but soon the conservative side among Republicans as well, were particularly attractive – motivating – to party activists. Yet they ran head on into the split-level polarization characterizing the era.

For what was attractive at the elite level was not necessarily motivating (or even attractive) among the rank and file. Put simply, there were many rank-and-file Democrats who were long-time supporters of the welfare state but were deeply conservative in cultural terms. Just as there were many rank-and-file Republicans who were long-time non-supporters of the welfare state but were liberal on cultural issues. Figure 2.2 offers one snapshot of the situation,

Table 2.2. Ideological representation at National Party conventions

Years	Rep Delegates	Rep Identifiers	All Voters	Dem Identifiers	Dem Delegates
2008	+62	+48	0	−20	−50
2004	+48	+39	0	−29	−52
1980	+49	+15	0	−11	−54
1976	+49	+14	0	−8	−42
1972	+24	+12	0	−9	−55
1956	+45	+6	0	−6	−9

* Positive scores are conservative and negative scores are liberal; the national median becomes the zero point; cell entries are then the balance of conservative over liberal or vice versa as a distance from that national median. For the specifics of creating these measures across time, see Shafer 1988, 100–107. Source: Shafer (2010, 270).

with the two mass parties clearly aligned on economic issues, Democrats liberal and Republicans conservative, but both neatly cross-cut by culture.

In a unitary political system, this would have created a democratic problem: vote for one party and get one mix of things that you did not want; vote for the other party and get a different unwanted mix. In the United States, however, the solution was simple: register one majority in one elective institution – in this case, cultural values in the presidency – and the other majority in the other main elective institution, hence economic values in Congress. In that sense, an extended period with a Republican presidency and a Democratic Congress was not just a perfectly reasonable outcome, but in fact a democratic triumph – though Democrats and Republicans did experience this "triumph" differently.

Possessing most of the remaining organized parties, the Democrats began with a major institutionalized resistance to participatory politics, making the dramatic implosion in their presidential nominating campaign of 1968 more traumatic when it arrived to fuel the surge of participatory reforms. By contrast, the Republicans had moved earlier to being a party of issue activists, more or less by compulsion. Having been blamed for the disaster of the Great Depression, they had been forced to shift to the volunteer model. Yet they had staved off the resulting split-level tensions by retaining sufficient power in a skeletal party structure to continue nominating moderates – Dewey, Eisenhower, Nixon – who might succeed in breaking the hold of a Democratic voting majority on the big industrial states.

All of that was stressed past the breaking point in the era of divided government, with clear-cut impacts on the creation of a national policy-making process distinctive to the era. Republicans would always win the presidency, so they always had to be dealt into any successful policy-making. No Republican support, no legislation. But Democrats would always control Congress, so they too had to be dealt into any successful policy-making. No Democratic support,

(a)

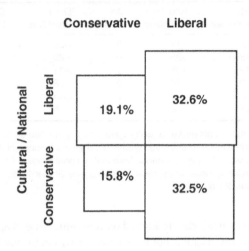

(b)   **Economic / Welfare**

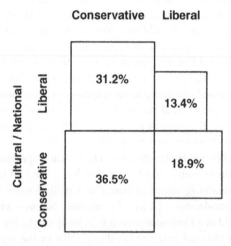

Figure 2.2. Economic and cultural preferences: (a) Democrats in an era of divided government; (b) Republicans in an era of divided government
Notes: (a) $N = 3,994$; (b) $N = 3,294$.
Source: Shafer and Claggett (1995).

Table 2.3. Era of divided government: policy-making as cross-party coalitions

House Votes
Opening Legislation of the Period
Coal Mine Safety, 334–12
Social Security Increase, 399–0
Draft Lottery System, 383–12
Comprehensive Tax Reform, 391–2
National Environmental Policy Act, 372–15
Deregulation
Airline Deregulation, 363–8
Banking Deregulation, 380–13
Trucking Deregulation, 367–13
Staggers Rail Act, 337–20
Environment
Surface Mining Control Act of 1977, 325–68
Clean Water Act of 1977, 346–2
Clean Air Act Amendments of 1977, 326–49
Toxic Wastes Superfund of 1980, at 274–94

Source: Mayhew (1991) with coverage extended through the author's personal website

no legislation. The public had some major and consensual matters on which it wanted action, the fate of the environment and a response to stagflation being the leading examples. Yet elected officials knew that the next election would produce no relief, no matter what they did: the president would again be Republican, Congress would again be Democratic.

The result, unintentional but probably inevitable, was a politics of grand coalitions, coalitions capable of reaching across political parties *and* across governmental institutions. Nothing else can explain the distinctive policy-making process of the period. Much major legislation was in fact produced, passed by large cross-party majorities in Congress and signed by a president who could shape but not dictate their content yet was unwilling to be an obvious roadblock to them. Said more pungently, nothing else can explain how President Richard Nixon could become the great environmental legislator or how President Jimmy Carter could become the great governmental deregulator.

The Modern World, 1992–2020 – and Counting?

Hindsight would allow analytic historians to see the election of 1992 as the first to register the structural contours of a successor era, effectively the modern world of American politics. Hindsight would also confirm that 1992 shared two

further characteristics with 1968, as superficially different as these two election years otherwise were. First, the collective partisan outcome had clearly
changed. Reliably divided government, that is, split partisan control, was replaced by unified partisan control – but for how long? – with the presidency
and both houses of Congress in the same hands. And second, while no one
failed to notice that particular change, almost everyone again treated it as an
anomaly, awaiting correction to a now-departed status quo.

Analysts should rarely be criticized for failing to foretell the future. Yet an application of the same analytic tools from previous periods – party balance, ideological
polarization, substantive conflict, and an associated process of policy-making –
can make the modern break clear and its structural underpinnings apparent, at
least in retrospect. Survey-based party identification had been relegated to a structural sideshow during the era of divided government, so that following its minimal
changes in the modern era was inherently unpromising Yet if actual voting behaviour is substituted as the real standard of party balance, then it becomes possible to
elicit an underlying counterpart structure for the contemporary political period, in
the same way that it was possible to elicit the nature of change around 1968.

Seen this way, the two political parties had become as closely balanced in the
modern world as they had been since the late nineteenth century, and perhaps
ever. The simplest way to see this is just to sum the vote for the two major parties
in presidential *plus* congressional elections from the 1860s onward (figure 2.3).
Despite the length of that historical span, the modern era veritably jumps out
of the comparison. Yet there was even more to an emergently narrow balance.
Four presidential elections went on to provide unprecedented testimony to an
overall balance by generating an alternating succession of two-term presidencies, each in turn captained by the out-party: Democrats in 1992–2000, Reubli-
cans in 2000–08, Democrats in 2008–16.

This had quite literally never been seen in American political history. Yet the
underpinnings for a new outcome that was patterned but different had to come
from some new mix of ideological polarization and substantive conflict, as of
course they did. For its part, ideological polarization reached a level never-be-
fore seen in the era of survey research, and last seen at several points in the
nineteenth century. The result was so extreme as to bring a comprehensive bipolarity to American politics overall, a bipolarity between two parties that was
sufficient to reshape the nature of substantive conflict over public policy, pulling all the previous major domains of potential policy conflict into one single
left-right ideological dimension (for a wide-ranging introduction to the period,
see Nivola and Brady, 2008 as well as Hopkins and Sides).

An analyst with mysterious foresight might have recognized this gallop-
ing polarization even in its earliest days by looking at the policy preferences
of delegates to national party conventions, polarizing relentlessly, as they
were, from the 1970s onward. Yet the era of divided government had featured

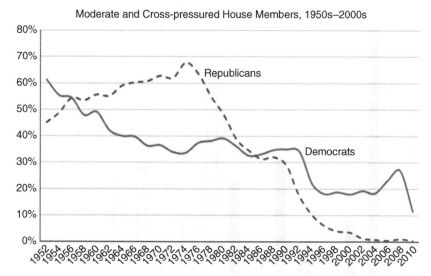

Figure 2.3. Partisan polarization among public officials: moderate and cross-pressured
House members, 1950s–2000s
Source: Lee (2015, 77).

countervailing forces to constrain the reach of national convention activists
while insulating many public offices, most especially Congress. A generation
later, this divide was increasingly breached, such that the same forces – and
now, for that matter, the same people – were shaping the identities of those who
held public office as well.

The canonical register of this too was the composition of Congress (see
figure 2.3). Once upon a time – not very long ago and for a very long stretch –
there were numerous members whose individual preferences were closer to
the median preferences of the other party, along with even more members
who were at least closer to the mid-point of Congress than to that of their
own party. Democratic members of Congress with these characteristics had
been in long-run decline across the postwar years, a decline that accelerated
after 1992. The counterpart Republican fall began later but plunged even more
sharply in the 1990s, to the point where, as the modern world aged, there was
no Democratic member to the right of any Republican, no Republican member to the left of any Democrat.

Where had this expanding (and substantively dominating) polarization come
from? Two big structural changes – one regional, one national, and both interacting – appear to be the best answer. One was the coming of two-party politics to the American South, that is, the demise of an established and extensive

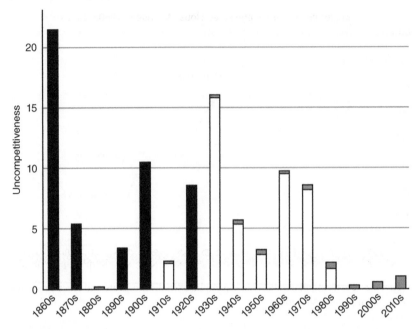

Figure 2.4. Party balance as reflected in voting behaviour: the presidency, the Senate, and the House combined
Source: Adapted from Fleisher and Bond, 2004 (as graciously extended by the authors). See also Theriault, 2008.

one-party system. One-party systems depolarize a political system by drawing all policy views into the same party. When such a system constitutes 30 per cent of a nation and then splits into two competing parties, it is not just the region but the entire nation that receives a major polarizing jolt. And the second great force, driving crucially in the same direction, involved the triumph of the participatory approach to politics, the participatory institutional structures associated with it, and the participatory elites who were the most obvious products of their interaction, namely the party activists who made volunteer parties work and whose influence was at the same time was magnified by them.

The shifting politics of a changing American South – a counterpart to Quebec in the Canadian story, in that both had to be understood in regional terms before being placed back inside national politics – was widely recognized (trumpeted, even) by analysts at the time. These analysts did go on to argue about whether its roots lay in racial desegregation, in economic development, or in some mix thereof (one pole of this debate can be represented by Shafer and Johnston, 2006; the other by Black and Black, 2002). But here, the point is legal desegregation did occur and, indeed, the battle over it had provided one of the substantive fulcrums in the structure of the Late New Deal era – just as economic development likewise occurred, at long last and to an eye-opening degree, for a region that was more or less the third world when the postwar period began. Yet almost none of this debate was focused on the associated, major, and ongoing contribution to partisan polarization in the nation as a whole that was intrinsic to the change.

At the same time, the participatory thrust associated with the triumph of volunteer parties and the institutional reforms that accompanied this triumph reached an apogee of its own (for the dynamics of this rise, see Carsey and Layman, 2006 and Layman et. al., 2010). The balance of party structures in the United States was altered. The nature of the incentives to participate in politics was altered. The social identity of the newly active partisans was altered. And in the modern world, the latter finally broke through into major public office, again most especially in Congress, though there was a major irony in this. In the old world, theorists of volunteer parties had attacked the long-serving individuals who managed their organized-party opponents for usurping power over nominations to public office and disproportionately shaping the public policy that resulted.

Yet in the new world, the activists managing these volunteer parties found equally effective ways to close off nominations from outside their own ranks and demand adherence to the public policies that they favoured. One succinct summary captures this process as well as anything in a burgeoning literature:

> Nominations are made in primaries that typically have low turnout, little advertising, no rival party labels among which to choose, and virtually no media attention until they are over. For these reasons, nominations are often easily controlled by political insiders, including legislative leaders, interest groups, activists, and others. I call this collection of actors the *informal party organization*, or IPO, and I argue that these IPOs are the heart, soul, and backbone of contemporary political parties. Since activists are a prominent and energetic component of these organizations, IPOs tend to seek the most ideologically extreme candidate they feel they can get elected in a general election. And, since most general elections are not seriously contested today, winning at that stage is often not much of a constraint.
>
> My claim, then, is that the parties control the public behaviour of their office-holders by acting as gatekeepers to public office. Just as it is nearly impossible to win office without the nomination of a major political party, so it is nearly impossible to win the nomination of a major political party without the backing of a local IPO. (Masket, 2014, 9)

Ramifications for the substantive conflict at the heart of modern politics were immediate. In the Late New Deal Era, there had been three major issues to help explain why four principal factions interacted in a complex fashion to create the incrementalism that distinguished the period. In the era of divided government, the key policy division was boiled to two major axes, economic and cultural, but these remained ideologically orthogonal and socially cross-cutting, such that the two parties could still be split into four political pieces. But in the modern world, the partisan polarization dominating national politics not only shrank four major factions to two homogeneous parties, but also reduced all five previously autonomous realms of policy conflict – social welfare, foreign affairs, and civil rights in the Late New Deal; economic welfare and cultural values under divided government – into one encompassing dimension.

This closely competitive but sharply polarized world did offer one clear benefit to the voting public, though it came at the cost of an inextricably associated punishment. The benefit was strategic. It was easier than ever to choose between polarized candidates: policy preferences were clear, and if the vast majority of voters inevitably fell between them, these voters could still readily judge which one was closer to them. Yet there was a major sting in the tail: for a voting public that reliably fell in between the two active parties would find the modern world to be reliably and recurrently disappointing. Which is to say: when the losing candidate was gone and the public now had to evaluate only the incumbent, a public that was always right of the Democratic candidate and always left of the Republican candidate was reliably displeased by whatever that incumbent turned out to be.

Fortunately, at the end of this causal change, the general public did possess a simple salvation. If close party balance, distant ideological positioning, and simplified choice ordinarily resulted in buyers' remorse, remorseful voters could more easily than ever express their displeasure by denying the winning party its initial unified partisan control of government. Indeed, this was a resolution that further connected the years since 1992 into a coherent modern whole. At bottom, a new era of partisan volatility could simply re-divide control of the presidency and Congress. Consider:

- Bill Clinton secured unified partisan control in Democratic hands in 1992.
- A disappointed public restored divided control in 1994.
- George W. Bush secured unified control in Republican hands in 2000.
- Public disappointment was delayed by 9–11, but could not be stalled in 2006.
- Barack Obama secured unified control, back in Democratic hands, in 2008.
- A disappointed public restored divided partisan control in 2010.
- Donald Trump secured unified control, back in Republican hands, in 2016.
- And a disappointed pubic, as ever, restored split control in 2018.

Trump would fail to secure the usual second term that belonged to his predecessors. But by then, the point had long since been established that it was the component parts of an extended political period – its party balance, ideological, polarization, substantive conflict, and associated policy-making process, and not its election outcomes – that drove both these election results and the subsequent policy outcomes, rather than vice versa. So the question for the Trump administration (and prospectively for a Biden counterpart) was whether the policy-making process that was the critical result of this underlying structure had continued on. And here, the key interpretive tool remains the final element in this comprehensive structure, which is the process of policy-making that came to characterize the period – and that appears to pull all five presidencies into one coherent whole.

Without showing any comprehension of where it came from or how it actually operated, critics summarily disparaged this modern policy-making process as "gridlock and stasis." Admittedly, policy does get made differently – that much is true – through a recurrent process of policy-making unlike those characterizing the immediate postwar years or the successor period of divided government. Moreover, the signature product of this modern policy-making process was actually isolated early in the modern period. Dubbed "omnibus legislation," this is a process whereby extended gridlock is unpredictably but unfailingly interrupted by major spikes of policy-making, driven by the build-up of pressures for governmental action (the term itself belongs to Sinclair, 1997). The fact that this modern form of legislative production tends to be both large and compressed discourages analysts from thinking about it as an integral part of an overall process, but so it is.

For this, there are three recurrent drivers (pursued in considerably greater detail in chapter four of Shafer, 2016). Sometimes these spikes are the result of a consensual crisis, as with 9–11 for George W. Bush or the Great Recession for Barack Obama. Other times spikes can instead be the result of an unavoidable reauthorization, as with raising the debt ceiling or producing a new budget to fund an inevitably changing government. Still other times, spikes can be the simple product of a collective build-up of policy wishes, one so intense as to precipitate what is politely described as omnibus legislation – really a giant logroll pulling all these pent-up demands into one legislative spasm. Though note that the appearance of any one of these inescapable stimuli ordinarily provides what is known among the major players as a legislative "Christmas tree," the opportunity to link other ongoing policy demands to the underlying deadline.

In less than the full run of a single Congress, Donald Trump was actually to generate a major example of each generic form of the policy spikes that respond to the ongoing background of the modern era, though two of these were actual successes while the third was a dramatic failure. The first major win came on tax reform (all three Trumpian examples are pursued in greater detail in Shafer and Wagner, 2019). The House passed legislation in the stereotypically polarized form by a vote of 224–201, which covered a Republican split of 224–12 and a Democratic split of 0–189. The Senate did the same, just as narrowly, 51–48, while covering a perfect Republican split of 51-0 and a perfect Democratic counterpart of 0-48.

The Trumpian example of the second generic policy spike came with a new, two-year operating budget for the federal government, a project recurrently left for dead by pundits and commentators. Yet Republicans overwhelmingly wanted to escape the spending strictures that they themselves had extracted from then-President Obama in 2011, so as to do a major increase in military spending. While Democrats, never enthusiastic about those fiscal constraints, were even more desirous of escaping their strictures in the name of a major increase in domestic spending. The resulting $1.3 trillion spending bill was excoriated from both ends of the ideological spectrum. Yet the bill passed the House comfortably, 256–167, losing the most liberal Democrats on the left and the most conservative Republicans on the right while securing majorities of both parties. The Senate was then anticlimactic, threatened only by the question of whether one or another senator would exercise their personal prerogative to delay it for a few further days.

Modern presidents often try consciously to manipulate this recurrent pattern of legislative production in one further way, by capitalizing on the (often sudden and surprising) appearance of unified partisan control at the very beginning of their administration. Polarized partisan divisions always remain, but for a brief stretch it appears that a new partisan majority might be harvested in a common opening policy thrust. For President Trump, this perceived need to strike while the iron was hot became the driving force behind his opening healthcare initiative, though this time, the result was to be a failure.

When push came to shove, the necessary generalized pressure for change was simply not there. Too much of the congressional Republican Party was committed to the complete repeal of the Affordable Care Act (ACA). Too much of the congressional Democratic Party saw no need to adjust anything. The handful of Republicans who coalesced around reform, headquartered in the Senate, found few allies in their own party. And what was probably a larger smattering of Democrats from both houses of Congress who saw particular things in the ACA that they would like to fix proved unready to coalesce as a group and be dragged back into an ideologized policy morass.

Modern American Politics as Analytic History

The world of modern American politics began for our purposes on 29 October 1929 with the stock market crash, followed by the Great Depression, followed by the New Deal. Collectively, those events constituted one of three critical crisis-and-response moments in all of American history. The notion of an analytic history, borrowed from Richard Johnston's *The Canadian Party System* and imported to the United States, contributes a rich theoretical framework for pursuing periods of stasis and change in national politics since that time, through its insistence on a hierarchy of causal influences and on locating this hierarchy at specified points.

In the case of the United States, after a short High New Deal – the immediate crisis plus only 1932–8 – this politics would evolve through three distinctive and extended successor eras. There was to be a long Late New Deal, 1939–68. There was to be a period of divided government, from 1968–92. And there is our current world, 1992–2020, and counting. For these periods, three continuing structural elements – party balance, ideological polarization, and substantive content – can be used to tease out a collective process of policy-making. The latter is what truly distinguishes the periods, though a sharp break in the pattern of electoral outcomes can provide an initial sign that it is time to search for change in the policy-making process.

In the first of these extended eras, the Late New Deal period, survey-based party identification confirmed the consolidation of a predominant Democratic majority for the nation as a whole. Yet ideological polarization within this balance went on to distinguish it sharply from the High New Deal. What had been an effectively unipolar legislative and electoral politics in this High New Deal became a strikingly depolarized politics in its Late New Deal successor. From one side, this was courtesy of the resurrection of geographic factions as crucial building blocks for policy coalitions. From the other side, it was the result of a shift in the substantive focus of politics, away from a concentration on social welfare and towards a tripartite focus on social welfare, foreign affairs, and civil rights, where the factions lined up in a different ideological order in each policy domain. The need to make policy across factions and across domains then contributed a generalized incrementalism, in which this policy was made and unmade while coalitions were built and un-built, over and over for thirty years.

This arrangement gave way around 1968 to an initially anomalous but ultimately stable successor. A changed electoral pattern, namely split partisan control of American national government, was what first brought this shift to the attention of many analysts. Their attempt to unpack the new era was handicapped by the fact that party identification, touchstone of many political scientists in the Late New Deal Era, stopped working. Yet with voting behaviour as the measure of party balance instead, the patterning within this change became clear: Republicans won the presidency while Democrats won Congress, over and over. So the explanation had to lie with ideological polarization and substantive content, as in fact it did.

Split-level polarization now characterized the major parties, aligning party activists against their own putative rank and file, while a cross-cutting substantive focus, economic welfare versus cultural values, was both product and goad to this polarization. A participatory revolution in party politics became central to both effects, but the policy-making process that resulted was curious and ironic. Since elected public officials still wanted to make public policy and were indeed under pressure from the general public to deliver it in several major areas, but since the main players quickly came to see that Democrats were unlikely to control the presidency and Republicans unlikely to control Congress, grand coalitions – across parties and across institutions – sprang up continually in major policy domains.

In its time, that world was already being undermined by two great and implicit but additionally polarizing influences. The first was the demise of a distinctive one-party politics in the American South, which was rejoining a national two-party system. The second was the further spread of participatory politics, such that the previous tension between self-starting activists and elected officials declined – as the former ultimately morphed into the latter, becoming more not less ideologically extreme as they did so. So an old world again broke up and a new one arrived around 1992, with a fresh combination of diagnostic influences. Party balance, now as indexed by actual voting, was as close as it had been in a very long time. Yet two closely balanced parties were simultaneously as far away from each other programmatically as they had been in that same period. And the resulting polarization was sufficient to collapse all previously autonomous substantive domains into a single left-right continuum.

A general public that reliably sat between those two parties responded accordingly, creating a pattern of alternating partisan presidencies but then saddling their presidents – Messrs. Clinton, Bush, Obama, and Trump – with split partisan control of American national government at its first practical opportunity. Yet back behind all this was a regularized policy-making process to go with this changed political structure, even if critics wanted to dismiss it as gridlock and statis. There were indeed long periods of policy inaction, but in each of these presidencies, those periods were punctuated by sharp spikes of policy-making, always on a major scale and often rolling multiple policy domains into the same spike. Policy was made *differently* from both predecessor periods, but there was reason to believe that policy output was not otherwise much reduced in either its scope or its bulk (Mayhew, 1991 as reconfigured in Shafer and Wagner, 2019, Table 1).

So in the end and circling back, *The Canadian Party System* remains a marvel of national interpretation, giving Canadian politics a powerful synthesizing treatment on its own terms. Yet this treatment arrives wrapped in the notion of an analytic history, an approach that, in principle, has no national limits. In practice, what results here is an effort to follow its injunctions in a different society, through a tour of 80 years of the changing structure of American politics. One may hope that what also results is an implicit comparative exposition of Canadian and American politics, yet one that escapes the obvious temptation to take details central to the politics of one nation and go searching for counterpart details in another. Finally, and likewise in the process, the result is a kind of second-order tribute to the intellectual power of the initial effort and its initial product, in that analytic history of the Canadian party system.

References

American National Election Studies (ANES). *ANES Time Series Cumulative Data File (1948–2016)*. University of Michigan and Stanford University, Ann Arbor, MI.

Black, E., and M. Black 2002. *The Rise of Southern Republicans*. Harvard University Press.

Boorstin, D.J. 1958. *The Genius of American Politics*. University of Chicago Press.

Burns, J.M. 1963. *The Deadlock of Democracy: Four-Party Politics in America*. Prentice-Hall.

Carsey, T.M., and G. Layman. 2006. "Changing Sides or Changing Minds? Party Identification and Policy Preferences in the American Electorate." *American Journal of Political Science*, no. 50: 464–77. https://doi.org/10.1111/j.1540-5907.2006.00196.x

Clark, B., and J.Q. Wilson, 1961. "Incentive Systems: A Theory of Organizations." *Administrative Science Quarterly*, no. 6: 129–66. https://doi.org/10.2307/2390752

Cox, G., and S. Kernell, eds. 1991. *Divided Government*. Westview.

DiSalvo, D. 2012. *Agents of Change: Party Factions in American Politics, 1868–2012*. Oxford University Press.

Fenno, Jr., R.F. 1966. *The Power of the Purse: Appropriations Politics in Congress*. Little, Brown

Fleisher, R. and J.R. Bond. 2004. "The Shrinking Middle in the US Congress." *British Journal of Political Science*, no. 34: 429–51. https://doi.org/10.1017/S0007123404000122

Gaddis, J.L. 2007. *The Cold War*. Penguin.

Graham, H.D. 1990. *The Civil Rights Era: Origins and Development of National Policy, 1960–1972*. Oxford University Press.

Hamby, A.L. 1976. *The Imperial Years: The United States since 1939*. Weybright and Talley.

– 2004. *For the Survival of Democracy: Franklin Roosevelt and the World Crisis of the 1930s*. Free Press.

Hotson, L.A. 2017. "Scholarly Solutions: The Development of American Political Science from the Gilded Age to the Great Society." D.Phil. Thesis, Oxford University.

Jacobson, G.C. 1990. *The Electoral Origins of Divided Government: Competition in House Elections, 1946–1988*. Westview.

Johnston, R. 2006. "Party Identification: Unmoved Mover or Sum of Preferences?" *Annual Review of Political Science*, no. 9: 329–51. https://doi.org/10.1146/annurev.polisci.9.062404.170523

– 2017. *The Canadian Party System: An Analytic History*. UBC Press.

Layman, G.C., T.M. Carsey, J.C. Green, R. Herrara, and R. Cooperman. 2010. "Activists and Conflict Extension in American Party Politics." *American Political Science Review*, no. 104: 324–46. https://doi.org/10.1017/S000305541000016X

Lee, F. 2015. "American Politics Is More Competitive Than Ever, and That Is Making Partisanship Worse." In *Political Polarization in American Politics*, edited by D.J. Hopkins, and J. Sides. Bloomsbury.

Leuchtenberg, W.E. 1995. *The Supreme Court Reborn: The Constitutional Revolution in the Age of Roosevelt*. Oxford University Press.

Masket, S.E. 2014. *No Middle Ground: How Informal Party Organizations Control Nominations and Polarize Legislatures*. University of Michigan Press.

Mayhew, D.R. 1986. *Placing Parties in American Politics: Organization, Electoral Settings, and Government Activity in the Twentieth Century*. Princeton University Press.

– 1991. *Divided We Govern: Party Control, Lawmaking, and Investigations, 1946–1990*. Yale University Press.

Nivola, P.S., and D.W. Brady, eds. 2008. *Red and Blue Nation?* (Vols. 1 and 2). Brookings.

Rae, N.C. 1989. *The Decline and Fall of the Liberal Republicans: 1952 to the Present*. Oxford University Press.

– 1994. *Southern Democrats*. Oxford University Press.

Shafer, B.E. 2010. "The Pure Partisan Institution: National Party Conventions as Research Sites." In *Oxford Handbook of Political Parties and Interest Groups*, edited by Sandy Maisel. Oxford University Press.

– 2016. *The American Political Pattern: Stability and Change, 1932–2016*. University Press of Kansas.

Shafer, B.E., and R. Johnston 2006. *The End of Southern Exceptionalism: Class, Race, and Partisan Change in the Postwar South*. Harvard University Press.

Shafer, B.E., and R.L. Wagner. 2019. *The Long War over Party Structure: Policy Responsiveness and Democratic Representation in American Politics, 1952–2008*. Cambridge University Press.

– 2019. "The Trump Presidency and the Structure of Modern American Politics." *Perspectives on Politics* 17, 340–57. https://doi.org/10.1017/S1537592718003353

Shafer, B.E., and W.J.M. Claggett. 1995. *The Two Majorities: The Issue Context of Modern American Politics*. Johns Hopkins University Press.

Sinclair, B. 1997. *Unorthodox Lawmaking: New Legislative Processes in the U.S. Congress*. CQ Press.

Theriault, S.M. 2008. *Party Polarization in Congress*. Cambridge University Press.

Thurber, J. 1991. *Divided Democracy: Cooperation and Conflict between the President and Congress*. CQ Press.

Truman, D.B. 1959. *The Congressional Party: A Case Study*. John Wiley.

Valelly, R.M. 2004. *The Two Reconstructions: The Struggle for Black Enfranchisement*. University of Chicago Press.

Ware, A. 1985. *The Breakdown of Democratic Party Organization, 1940–1980*. Oxford University Press.

Wildavsky, A.B. 1964. *The Politics of the Budgetary Process*. Little, Brown.

Wilson, J.Q. 1973. *Political Organizations*. Basic Books.

3 Generalizing the Engine of Fragmentation: Quantitatively Modelling the Observed Contra-Duvergerian Patterns

MATTHEW S. SHUGART AND CORY L. STRUTHERS

Canada is one of the largest democracies employing a first-past-the-post (FPTP) electoral system to elect a national parliamentary body. It is often perceived as an anomalous case of FPTP because of its persistent multiparty system. Over several decades, it has tended to result in minority governments, and this tendency appears to be on the increase with such governments resulting from five of the seven national elections held over the two decades before and including the 2021 election.

A defining feature of any FPTP system is that all seats are assigned via contests in districts (ridings) that elect only one member of Parliament. Thus, in a sense, if there are 338 seats, as in the Canadian House of Commons in recent elections, then there are 338 distinct contests, with the winner being the candidate with the highest vote total – not necessarily a majority of votes. The established wisdom on FPTP systems has been that the electoral system's disproportionality at the district level – and corresponding lack of realistic seat-winning prospects for locally trailing parties – leads to votes being concentrated among two viable parties. Moreover, the common assumption is that this local two-partism somehow projects up to the national level. Therefore, according to this thinking, the national result is likely to be something like a two-party system. This wisdom is essentially that expressed by "Duverger's law" and was given its most detailed and elegant formulation by Cox (1997), who developed models of district-level "coordination," inspired by a game-theoretic approach, and of "linkage" of districts into a nationwide party system.

As well established as this approach is, it contains a critical flaw. This flaw is most clearly represented by the previously noted fact that Canada has national multipartism and frequent minority governments. In fact, in both 2019 and 2021, the largest party won barely a third of the votes. Even in the United Kingdom, where minority (or coalition) governments have been less common, the party system is nonetheless far from being two-party, given significant presence of other parties in Parliament and especially in the votes distribution. Most analysts promoting the standard view about coordination and linkage allow the relaxation of their strict assumptions under certain conditions. These conditions typically include regional cleavages, which might sustain local or regional two-party systems that involve different pairings of parties in different clusters of districts, or they might hold that ethnic diversity or other social factors inflate the number of parties. However, an alternative possibility is rarely considered: it may be that party systems develop with more than two viable parties due to *national* political factors, and then this national party system is reflected at the district level. In other words, we should entertain the opposite of the common wisdom: party systems might be national phenomena that play out in arenas we call districts, rather than district-level coordination games that get projected into a national system.

The idea of primacy to the aggregate, national dynamics that drive party-system development is central to Johnston's (2017) magisterial study of the Canadian party system. As Johnston puts it, "the standing claim in the study of electoral coordination is that the crucial arena is the local district." In contrast to this standing claim, he says, "I argue that actors respond to information about the whole electorate" (p. 8). Supporting and building on Johnston's alternative view, this chapter builds quantitative predictions from *the whole electoral system* in which each district is "embedded." Moreover, the argument about the impact of the whole electoral system is generalizable to the universe of FPTP electoral systems, including not only the allegedly "anomalous" case of Canada (Johnston, 4) but also the otherwise theoretically challenging case of India.

To advance the central arguments of this chapter, we situate FPTP systems in the Seat Product Model. This model of how key features of national electoral systems shape party systems was introduced by Rein Taagepera (2007) and was the principal contribution cited in his winning the Skytte Prize (https://www.skytteprize.com/), the most prestigious international prize in political science. We will not recapitulate the entire logic of the SPM in this chapter, although we will summarize its most relevant points in order to situate the extension we develop in this chapter in its theoretical context.

The basic conclusion of this chapter is that we can model with great accuracy the average *district-level vote* fragmentation as a product of the *nationwide seat* fragmentation. We are able to establish that the direction of the effect runs from the national to the district setting, and not the reverse, by virtue of the fact that the Seat Product Model is both logically grounded and known to be empirically accurate to cross-national variation in electoral institutional variables (Shugart and Taagepera 2017, 2018). Moreover, it is accurate for Canada specifically. By contrast, there is no district-level institutional variation under FPTP, by definition, and thus a district-level institutional model always predicts the "Duverger's law" outcome – towards local bipartism (Duverger 1951, 1954).[1] Thus, our findings offer strong support for Johnston's claims and contrary to the leading alternative, which Johnston (2017, 28–31) aptly refers to as the Neo-Duvergerian Synthesis (most represented by Cox 1997).

The remainder of this chapter is structured as follows. First, using the now-standard index of fragmentation, the *effective number of parties*, we show how district-level voting outcomes are systematically related to nationwide seat outcomes. This systematic relationship, which is shown for the first time in this chapter, can be generalized from the Seat Product Model and verified with Canadian and other FPTP-system data. Then we offer a new extension of the Seat Product Model for FPTP systems, which can encompass India, another case often seen as anomalous. The connection to India is important both theoretically and empirically, as it shows the broad applicability of the model to a setting where the posited direction of effect – national to local – can't plausibly run in the opposite direction. In India, national politics is structured around a few *national* multiparty alliances each containing various *state* parties. It would be thus impossible for voters or other actors at the district level to be the engine of fragmentation (or coordination) in India. Rather, the engine driving the district-level effective number of parties must be grounded in the processes that shape national political forces. We show that the logic we apply successfully to Canada also applies to Indian national alliances. This is an important contribution, given that both India and Canada are regularly branded as exceptions to Duverger's law or as atypical for FPTP. We show, by contrast, that neither country is exceptional when we start with the national level and explain, via the Seat Product Model, how the district level reflects patterns of national party politics.

How the District Level Connects to the National

In this chapter, we draw on the set of "quantitatively predictive logical models" developed by Taagepera (2007) and Shugart and Taagepera (2017): the *Seat Product Model* (SPM). An important point about the SPM is that the models are based on deductive logic – how two or more quantities can be expected to be related, in the absence of any other information and, critically, prior to conducting statistical regression tests (see Taagepera, 2008, for a general introduction to the methodology). The process of deductive logic leads to mathematical formulas, expressing a relationship between the quantities. These formulas can then be tested on data via both visualization (graphing) and regression analysis. The "absence of any other information" criterion means that the models do not incorporate "political" factors, like the coalitions of social groups underlying a political party's voting bloc, or the popularity of governmental or opposition leaders. Incorporating such political factors should be the next step – explaining any deviations we observe from SPM baseline predictions that emerge from considerations of how the electoral rules constrain the party system.

The "Seat Product" and Baseline Expectations for Party Systems under FPTP

The absence of political factors in the SPM is a feature, not a bug – it allows the analyst to have a baseline expectation against which actual election outcomes can be compared. It thus allows the analyst to ask: Is this election, or series of elections in some country, anomalous? Or is it about what we should expect, *given the electoral institutions* in place? The electoral-system components most important for shaping party systems are, according to the SPM, the mean district magnitude (the number of seats elected from a district, abbreviated M) and the assembly size (the total number of elected house seats, S). The insight that powers the SPM is that, for a given number of seats available, the number of parties that can win seats is bounded. Thus, the number that can win at least one of the M seats in a district must not be less than one, nor can it be more than M. The same applies to an entire assembly: the number of parties winning seats can range from one to S, the total number of seats available. If M or S is larger, neither extreme is likely, so where might the central tendency lie? The best guess (Shugart and Taagepera, 2017, 11–13), in the absence of other information, is that the number in a district should tend to be around the square root of M, and the number in the national assembly should be around the square root of S. For instance, if $M = 9$, we expect about three parties; if $S = 100$, about ten.[2] The Seat Product Model puts these two insights together, suggesting that we can estimate the likely number of parties from the *product* of M and S in a given electoral system. Moreover, it states – and empirical analysis confirms – that the logic applies both to single-tier proportional systems (where average $M > 1$) and to FPTP ($M = 1$). An important point of the SPM is that one should start with the seats and then estimate likely votes distributions from that. The reason is that seats are more directly constrained (by M and S), whereas votes are only constrained by the tolerance of elites and voters for disproportionality.[3]

The raw number of parties winning at least one seat is not especially interesting in its own right. For instance, saying that there were six parties that won at least one seat in the Canadian election of 1993 is a true statement,[4] but not a very interesting one, given that one of them won three-fifths of the seats and the party of the incumbent government at that time won only two. Thus, a more interesting party-system output to measure and model electoral systems, commonly used in the literature, is the *effective number of parties*, abbreviated N_S.[5] Given a previously established connection (Taagepera, 2007, 59–60) between the actual number (winning any number of seats) and the effective number, the logic behind the SPM leads to the following central prediction:

$$N_S = (MS)^{1/6} \tag{1}.$$

Equation 1 tells us that we can expect, on average, that the effective number of seat-winning parties (N_S) tends to be the seat product (mean magnitude times assembly size), raised to the power, 1/6. This deductively derived model[6] is tested on hundreds of election outcomes in Shugart and Taagepera (2017) and shown to account for around 60 per cent of the variance. This is an impressive performance for a deductive model containing only two purely institutional inputs. However, the 40 per cent of unexplained variance tells us there is still plenty of explanatory power in political factors like social cleavages, the process by which elites construct political parties, the issues that dominate a given campaign, and how voters evaluate politicians' performance.

Because this chapter is focused on FPTP systems, in which each district elects only a single member of Parliament, meaning $M = 1$, Equation 1 reduces, *for this class of electoral system only*, to

$$N_S = S^{1/6} \tag{2}.$$

In words, the average expectation for the effective number of seat-winning parties in a system of first-past-the-post is the number of seats in Parliament, raised to the power, 1/6. Given our primary focus on Canada, we should ask how well Equation 2 fits the Canadian context. The dataset for this chapter (see appendix) includes 23 Canadian elections from 1949 to 2021. Over that timeframe, the mean number of seats in the House of Commons is 282. Based on Equation 2, we would expect that $N_S = 2.561$, on average. In fact, the average of this period of time is $N_S = 2.509$. In other words, Equation 2 closely describes Canada's long-term average. Individual elections are expected to vary around the average, due to election-specific political factors, and indeed they do. Over the 20 elections covered, N_S ranges from a low of 1.54 in 1958 to a high of 3.22 in 2006. The interquartile range is 2.33 to 2.84. As for the recent period, S averaged 308 between 1997 and 2021, and the mean N_S for this period was 2.82. We would expect about $N_S = 2.60$ based on Equation 2. That is, the actual party system has been 1.09 times the expectation over past quarter century. While fragmentation has run a little higher than predicted in recent elections, the bigger picture result is that the SPM predicts the average Canadian national effective number of seat-winning parties very well. Moreover, it is noteworthy that the 2019 and 2021 elections, both of which resulted in minority governments that the common (Duvergerian) wisdom sees as anomalous for FPTP, saw N_S around 2.8, very close to expectation, given a seat product, *MS*, of 338.

Now we turn our attention to the district level. The Neo-Duvergerian Synthesis claims that "coordination" around a limited number of parties – about two – takes place at the district level, and then links upward to a national party system. However, our approach, following Shugart and Taagepera (2017), stands this notion on its head. It claims that the national party system can be predicted based on the national electoral system – described simply by assembly size when all districts have $M = 1$. Our approach is consistent with Johnston's (2017) interpretation that voters respond to information about the whole electorate, rather than primarily about the likely outcome of their local district.

Extensions of the SPM predict the average level of electoral fragmentation at the level of the individual district. These extensions are based on the premise that any given district is "embedded" in the wider electoral system. Because each district represents some fraction of the entire assembly, a key insight of Shugart and Taagepera's (2017, chapter 10) district level model is that the more seats there are in play *outside the district* the more fragmented the voting will be *inside the district* (all else equal). This means that we can predict the average trend in the effective number of vote-earning parties at the district level (which we will denote as N'_V, with the prime mark indicating a district rather than nationwide quantity) based on the national-level seat product. For FPTP, the only needed variable is thus assembly size, given $M = 1$. The formula derived and empirically confirmed by Shugart and Taagepera (2017, 170) for district level fragmentation in FPTP is:

$$N'_V = 1.59 S^{1/12} \tag{3}.$$

It must be expected that data points will scatter around the average trend implied by Equation 3, because even if national politics strongly conditions the trend, there still is room for local politics (including each district's own set of candidates) to shift a given contest above or below the trend. Yet the ability to account for the trend by using *only assembly size* as a right-hand-side variable tells us something important about the dynamics of district-level competition in FPTP systems: A key engine of fragmentation at the district level in FPTP systems is simply *how many seats there are outside the district*, that is, the size of the assembly in which each district is embedded.

In this chapter, we extend the logic of this national impact on district fragmentation by showing a relationship that has been previously overlooked, between the *election-specific* aggregate parliamentary outcome – the effective number of seat-winning parties (N_S) and average district voting fragmentation (N'_V). We do so by a simple algebraic substitution of Equation 2 into Equation 3. In doing so, we need to replace S in Equation 3 with N_S; given we have $N_S = S^{1/6}$ (Equation 2) it must be that $S = N_S^6$, allowing us to combine the equations as follows:

$$N'_V = 1.59 (N_S^6)^{1/12} = 1.59 N_S^{0.5} \tag{4}.$$

This equation[7] (which can also be expressed as $N'_V = 1.59\sqrt{N_S}$) states that, on average, *the effective number of vote-earning parties in districts of a FPTP system is the square root of the effective number of seat-winning parties in the national parliament, times 1.59.* Can that possibly be so? We can look at data to find out.

In figure 3.1, we plot 81 elections in Canada, the UK, New Zealand (prior to 1996), and numerous other parliamentary systems using FPTP, including both small and large assemblies.[8] The x-axis is the effective number of seat-winning parties in the national assembly (N_S). The y-axis is the district-level effective number of vote-earning parties (N'_V).

The small data points in figure 3.1 are the individual districts – all 15,590 of them – whereas election averages are shown with the larger symbols. To our knowledge, the dataset we employ here is the largest ever used for the study of district-level fragmentation in single-seat districts. All Canadian election district averages are depicted with a square, while election averages in other countries are shown as diamonds. For the individual districts, the darker marks are the Canadian districts. Selected Canadian elections are labelled with the final two digits of the election year.

Before discussing specific elections, let us explain the logic and statistics underlying the systematic relationship between the two quantities plotted in figure 3.1. The diagonal line is the logical model (Eq. 4), *not* a regression best fit. The arrangement of data points in figure 3.1, especially those of the election means, suggests that the logically derived Equation 4 is on the right track, at the very least. Moreover, regression analysis (see table A1 in the appendix) strongly supports the logically modelled relationship.

It must be noted that, contrary to the claims of the Neo-Duvergerian Synthesis, our logical model leads us not to see as "anomalous" a FPTP system in which the effective number of vote-earning parties at the district level (N'_V) is well above 2.0. In fact, unless the national parliamentary party system is quite lopsided (e.g., around $N_S = 1.5$), the district-level mean N'_V is *not expected to be near 2.0*. If the nationwide parliamentary $N_S = 2.25$ (consistent with two major parties having most of the seats but some other small parties also having some seats), Equation 4 predicts that the mean district will have $N'_V = 2.39$. This expected value is thus deviant from the Neo-Duvergerian claim that the voters should systematically abandon third parties and thereby concentrate district outcomes near $N'_V = 2.0$. When we have $N_S = 3$, we should expect, according to Equation 4, that N'_V would tend to be around 2.75, which is hardly a co-ordinated, "Duvergerian" outcome. As we see in Figure 3.1, several Canadian elections (including 1962, 1997, and 2008) are in this region, and tend to agree quite closely, in their district averages, with Equation 4. It might be further noted that Canadian elections since 2011 are only slightly on the higher side of the model expectation, even as overall nationwide N_S in these elections has varied from 2.40 to 2.78 in this period. The district mean N'_V in these elections has tracked these changes in N_S well, and the average district is more fragmented than expected from Equation 4 to only a very small degree.[9]

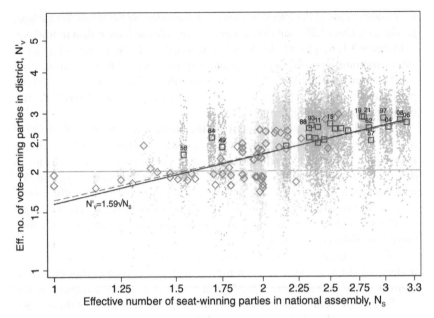

Figure 3.1. How the effective number of vote-earning parties at the district level (N'_V) is systematically related to the effective number of seat-winning parties nationwide (N_S) in FPTP systems

What We Can Learn from Equation 4

The logical foundation of Equation 4 could only be discovered by taking a starting point like that of Johnston (2017), in contrast to the more common starting point of district-level "coordination" and "linkage" up to the national level. That is, the logic assumes that voters, even though voting in local district contests in which the candidate of only one party can win, *tend to cast their votes with the national outcome in mind*. The national outcome is itself, of course, a product of a national electoral system made up of these many districts (among other factors[10]). The point is that the two phenomena – how voters behave in districts and the shape of the party system in Parliament – are interlinked in a way that can be defined by a formula, specifically Equation 4.

Equation 4 captures the relationship between the two levels as follows: If an additional party wins representation in the national Parliament, thus increasing nationwide N_S to some degree, then this new party has some probabilistic chance of inflating the district-level voting outcome as well. It may not inflate district-level voting fragmentation everywhere (so the exponent on N_S is not 1), but it will inflate it in more than just the few districts it wins. If it did so only in those districts the exponent would be near zero for the average district in the whole country. A party with no seats obviously contributes nothing to N_S, but as a party wins more seats, it contributes more.[11] According to Equation 4, as a party emerges as capable of winning more seats, it tends also to obtain more votes in the average district.[12]

As Johnston and Cutler (2009, 94) put it, voters' "judgments of a party's viability may hinge on its ability to win seats." Our logical model quantitively captures precisely this notion of "viability" of parties as players on the national scene through its square root of N_S component. Most of the time, viability requires winning seats. For a new party, this might mean the expectation that it will win seats in the current election. Thus our idea is that the more voters see a given party as viable (likely to win representation somewhere), the more they are likely to vote for it.[13] This increased tendency to vote for viable national parties is predicated on voters being more tuned in to the national contest than they are concerned over the outcome in their own district, which might even be a "sideshow" (Johnston and Cutler 2009, 94). Thus, the approach starts with the national party system, and projects downward, rather than the conventional approach of starting with district-level coordination and projecting upward.

So far the explanation has centred on the second term in Equation 4, the square root of N_S. What about the other term, the constant, 1.59? Where does this come from? It certainly does not look very logical! However, it is. Whereas N_S is, by definition, a national factor, the constant expresses something fundamental about competition in single-seat districts that even the most die-hard Duvergerian can accept: there tend to be two "pertinent" parties in a single-seat district. A party can be said to be "pertinent" when it either wins, or comes up just short. When there is one seat – the district magnitude is one ($M = 1$) – there is obviously one winner; this party and the first loser can be thought of as "pertinent" to the competition in the district. However, the formula's left-hand side is the effective number, not the real (or pertinent) number of vote-earning parties. From established work on the relationship between actual and effective numbers (Taagepera 2007), we know that the average relationship between the two quantities can be expressed as the effective number being approximately the actual number, to the power, 2/3. If we have an actual (here, "pertinent"[14]) number of 2, then we should tend to have an effective number of $2^{2/3} = 1.5874$.

Thus the two terms of the right-hand side of Equation 4 express a district component (two locally pertinent parties) and a nationwide one (how many seat-winning parties are there *effectively* in the Parliament being elected?) Note, again, that only the latter component can vary (with the size of the assembly, per Equation 2, or with a given election's national politics), while the district component is always the same because there is always just one seat to be fought over. Consider some hypothetical cases as illustration. Suppose there are exactly two evenly balanced parties in parliament ($N_S = 2.00$), these contribute $1.41 = \sqrt{2}$ to a district's N'_V, while the district's essential tendency towards two pertinent parties contributes $1.59 = 2^{2/3}$. Multiply the two together and get $1.59*1.41 = 2.25$. That extra ".25" thus implies some voting for either local politicians (perhaps independents) not affiliated with the two national seat-winning parties or for national parties that are expected to win few or no seats.[15] On the other hand, suppose the nationwide N_S is close to three, such as the 3.03 observed in Canada in 2004. The formula suggests the national seat-winning outcome contributes $\sqrt{3.03} = 1.74$ at the district level; multiply this by our usual 1.59, for a predicted value of $N'_V = 2.77$. As we see from figure 3.1, this is almost precisely what the actual *average* value of N'_V was in 2004.[16]

Of course, actual individual districts will vary widely around the average, as the smear of small markers in figure 3.1 shows is the case for every election. No formula can predict the outcome of each individual district. What Equation 4 accomplishes is to establish a *baseline* that allows one to ask: Given the nationwide balance of parties winning seats in the election, was this district more or less fragmented than expected? Without a systematic way to ask what is "expected," we are unable to answer the question. This is the value of a logical model.

Individual Elections and Provincial Variation

While having a baseline is useful, we also need to have a sense of how much real variation there is from the trend, election by election. Moreover, given the importance of federalism in Canada, we should also explore patterns at the provincial level in national elections. A glance at figure 3.1 shows that those Canadian elections that have the *highest* national seat fragmentation see this fragmentation reflected at the district level, in a predicted way. In other words, the high national level of parties does not result principally from different regional patterns (i.e., different "two-party systems" in different places) as the Neo-Duvergerian Synthesis would expect.

Nonetheless, some elections obviously diverge from the pattern; the political context of a given election campaign still matters. It is precisely in such deviations that we may learn something especially interesting about the limits of a logical model. Moreover, deviating elections allow us to ask, what was it about this election that is "surprising," a question we obviously can ask only if we have the baseline provided by a logical model. To compare actual to predicted results, we can simply take the ratio,

$$(\text{observed mean } N'_V)/(N'_V \text{ predicted from Equation 4}).$$

Among all elections depicted in figure 3.1, one Canadian election ranks as the third greatest outlier on the high side – that is, with average district-level N'_V that is substantially greater than predicted, given nationwide N_S. This is the 1984 election, which has a ratio of 1.22.[17] That election is, of course, well known to students of Canadian politics for the magnificent scope of the win by the Progressive Conservatives (PC) under leadership of Brian Mulroney. The PCs more than doubled their seat total from the preceding election (1980). Not only did they earn over half the votes nationwide (itself a rare occurrence), but they won nearly three-fourths of the seats (the second highest between 1949 and 2021). So, what was it about this election – or more narrowly, about the way the national and district levels connected – that causes it to deviate rather greatly from the model? It is not principally that districts were markedly different from the national party balance; that is, it is not a tale of differential coordination in districts where the PCs faced different opponents in different districts or regions. This is clear from a consideration of the nationwide effective number of vote-earning parties (N_V): at 2.75, this does not differ by much from the district average (N'_V) of 2.52. It is simply that the nationwide seat outcome, in which $N_S = 1.69$, was so much less fragmented than that in votes. In other words, it was simply an unusually *nationalized* election in terms of which party tended to receive the local pluralities. Yet it is evident that a high degree of multiparty competition persisted in the typical district – even more than our national-focused model predicts. (It would have expected $N'_V = 2.07$, which would actually have been quite a good deal more "coordinated" and "Duvergerian" than the actual result!).

No other Canadian election is higher than the sample's 90th percentile in its ratio of observed mean N'_V to the formula's prediction. The next highest ratio is from 1958, which was a similar large sweep by the Conservatives (under John Diefenbaker). One of the key themes of Johnston (2017) is that occasional Conservative victories have occurred from the party's "soaking up the sectional tensions of the preceding years" (p. 31); it is thus not unexpected that the greatest deviations from Equation 4 would occur in precisely those elections in which there is a temporary recombination of political alignments. These tend not to be sustained, and subsequent elections revert to closer approximations of the national–local relationship predicted by Equation 4.[18]

To visualize the Canadian context in a more granular way, figure 3.2 shows a separate plot for each of the eight largest provinces. Here, instead of using the nationwide average for N'_V, we will consider each province's mean N'_V. Within each plot, we compare the province's mean district voting outcome to the predicted value from Equation 4 (which is necessarily the same for all provinces). The diagonal line in each plot would indicate perfect correspondence of the provincial average to the prediction of our model.

From figure 3.2, we see that Ontario conforms most closely to the model, with few elections deviating by much. Perhaps this is not surprising; after all, Ontario is the province with the greatest number of districts and thereby contributes the most to the national mean that we already know (from figure 3.1) generally fits well. When we look to Quebec, the province with the second greatest number of districts, there are more elections that deviate from the expectation, including

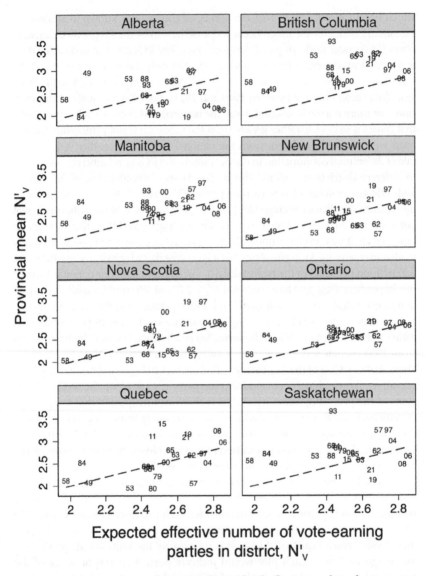

Figure 3.2. Correspondence of the mean district-level effective number of vote-earning parties to Equation 4, by Canadian province

2011, when the NDP emerged as the second largest party nationally with a surge in Quebec. In fact, each election from 2011 through 2021 is on the high side of the equality line. The more telling pattern about Quebec, however, is that only a few elections fit the established neo-Duvergerian wisdom about the province's regional distinctiveness, which would lead one to expect two-party competition within the province (and its districts), even as the national system was multiparty. From the Quebec plot, the neo-Duvergerian explanation appears reasonable for 1953, 1957, and 1980 (and perhaps 1979), but for few other elections, given that most tend to be either on the equality line or above it. If any province has a district-level party system strongly at variance with the model presented in this chapter, it is British Columbia – every election except for 2006 and 2008 is above the equality line. Of course, with such fragmentation at the district level, BC certainly fails to fit any better with the neo-Duvergerians' standard explanation!

We have seen that the Seat Product Model, including extensions derived in this chapter, accurately captures the tendency of district-level vote fragmentation to follow the national parliamentary outcome. It does so notwithstanding variation in individual elections and the tendencies of some provinces to fragment to a greater or lesser degree than the national scene. We now offer a further extension to an especially hard case for the model: the notoriously fragmented party system of India.

Indian Alliances as a Hard Test of the Model

The Indian case is a hard test for our model because its unusually high degree of fragmentation has marked it as an outlier, at least according to conventional approaches, among FPTP systems. India has long puzzled comparative electoral-systems scholars. It has always seemed to defy the Duvergerian expectation, in the first decades of independence because it had a single dominant party, and then later due to extensive fragmentation of the party system. The fact that India is the world's largest example of the FPTP electoral system – or any democratic electoral system – means it is hardly desirable if it stands as an exception to the subfield's theories and empirical generalizations. In his use of "Duverger's law" as a case study in the history of political science, Riker (1982) explained the Indian exception as being due to a dominant party (the Congress) standing in the centre. This large centrist party was, Riker claimed, a Condorcet winner, which other parties could not normally combine to defeat (see also Nikolenyi, 2009). Johnston (2017, 210, quoting Johnston and Cutler, 2009) comments on this point by suggesting that Riker's claim for India "also" applies to Canada.

The logical models of this paper are silent as to the placement of a country's political parties in issue space. We agree with one of Johnston's fundamental points in his book, which is that the presence of a centrist party (the Liberals) is a "pivotal" factor for understanding the Canadian party system, and also one that sets it apart from the left-vs.-right positioning of the two major parties in the British system (or that of the US, Australia,[19] or pre-reform New Zealand). Moreover, we will not address whether Riker's (1982) point was accurate for India in the time that he made it. Rather, the conclusion here is that, once we take account of how political competition in India has been structured in recent years around national alliances, we see that India's current party alignment – like that of Canada – may not be exceptional after all.

Why consider alliances instead of their component parties in the Indian case? Because most of the parties do not contest nationally, but only in one or a few states. It is the alliances that provide the competition over control of the national government. They thus represent national elites' efforts to coordinate a fractious political scene. Yet in the districts, voters see candidates running under banners of various parties, with each alliance presenting no more than one component party-affiliated candidate per district.[20] India is thus a hard case for the model presented in this chapter, in that it may be unexpected that district patterns would mirror national ones, given the different actors (parties and alliances) at each level – unless, that is, Equation 4 captures something essential about how local competition is shaped by the balance of national political forces.

India's National Democratic Alliance (NDA) consists of the Bharatiya Janata Party (BJP) and numerous state-based regional parties (Sridharan 2005). In response to the electoral success of the NDA (which won an absolute majority of seats in 1999), the previously dominant Congress Party formed a similar alliance with other regional parties, branded the United Progressive Alliance (UPA). Various other alliances have also competed, such as the Left Front and Fourth Front. Governments have alternated between the NDA and UPA in several recent elections, making the alliances equivalent to national parties in terms of calculating N_S for purposes of Equation 4 in that they are the collective actors competing to control the assembly and form government.

To test whether Equation 4 can be extended to include the Indian case, we will calculate the nationwide effective number of seat-winning "parties" on the alliances as well as on the component parties.[21] At the district level, we calculate N'_V exactly as always – it is simply derived from the vote shares of the various candidates running in a given district. We then plot the national and district quantities, and also run regressions including Indian data.

Figure 3.3 is a data plot similar to figure 3.1, except that it includes India. Moreover, it includes India plotted both ways. To include the component parties in the nationwide N_S requires a considerable lengthening of the x-axis, because N_S>4 in all but one of elections for which the alliances are in effect.[22] Each of these Indian elections is thus plotted twice. One plot accords to the effective number of seat-winning *alliances*. Elections represented via this calculation are shown with the black squares. The other plot accords to the component *parties*, and thus appears as a diamond just like the others (including, in this plot, Canada). The calculation of the value is not affected on the y-axis, because the district N'_V (individual district and the means) is the same either way; it is a strictly district-level measure, and an alliance will be represented by just one party having nominated a candidate in any district.

If Equation 4 captures the dynamic between national seat-winning alliances and district voting in India approximately as well as it connects the

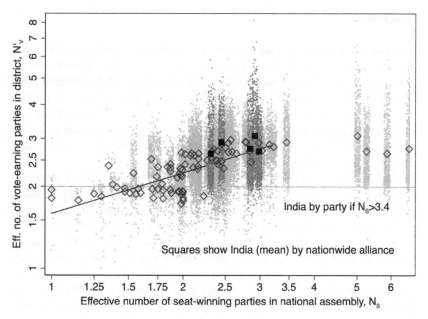

Figure 3.3. How the effective number of vote-earning parties at the district level (N'_V) is systematically related to the effective number of seat-winning parties/alliances nationwide (N_S) in FPTP systems, including India

national–district party dynamic in other countries, the black squares should be located near the diagonal line that defines Equation 4. That is precisely what we see. The relationship between the effective number of seat-winning alliances in the Lok Sabha and the district-level mean effective number of vote-earning parties is fundamentally the same in India as it is in the broader set of FPTP systems. India, at least in this recent period of alliance politics, is not in any sense anomalous, just as Canada is not.

The pattern seen in figure 3.3 shows that the degree of district-level voting fragmentation closely follows the balance of competition for control of Parliament in India as well as in other FPTP parliamentary systems. The only difference is that the control of Parliament in India is carried out by alliances, in lieu of nation-spanning parties. The local–national connection looks fundamentally the same. The ability to include the Indian case in the generalization of the local–national connection in FPTP systems is a significant advance. It implies that the process producing the patterns captured by Equation 4 reflects some essential feature of how national politics plays out within the districts of a FPTP system.

Conclusion

It has been common for some time now for scholars to understand the party-system dynamics of FPTP parliamentary systems as being set by the district magnitude – a single seat per district – and to conceive of the national party system as an aggregation of district-level outcomes. This is, in broad outline, the approach that Johnston (2017) calls the "Neo-Duvergerian Synthesis." It expects the typical outcome of competition for each district's one seat to be "coordination" and sees cases of vote fragmentation at the district level as possibly indicating "coordination failure."

This chapter takes an alternative view of how district and national party systems are related. It is compatible with the "whole electorate" approach Johnston (2017) takes in his "analytic history" of the Canadian party system. In Johnston's explanation, voters respond to information from the whole electorate rather than information about which candidates are most likely to win in their district. The result is not only a nationwide party system that typically has more than two significant parties – a result that is not, in itself, contrary to the neo-Duvergerian expectation – but also a district-level competition that likewise often features some considerable degree of vote fragmentation. The approach of this chapter is at once narrower and broader than Johnston's. It is narrower in that it makes no reference to public opinion, ideological positions, or social coalitions underlying the party system. It is a "whole electoral system" approach, focused solely on institutions, following the Seat Product Model (Shugart and Taagepera 2017, 2018). For a system of all one-seat districts, the seat product is simply the size of the assembly – in other words, how many districts are there? At the same time, the approach is broader in that it applies the Seat Product Model's predictions to a wide range of FPTP parliamentary systems, and brings the Indian pattern of alliance politics (since 1998) into its purview.[23]

The advantage of the approach taken here is that its narrowness and sparseness of factors allows it to make predictions that play out successfully *on average*. It offers baseline expectations that are more specific than the neo-Duvergerians' "the districts should tend to feature two-party competition"; in some cases, they should not. If the Parliament is large (as in Canada, India, and the UK) the expectation should be that often no party would win a parliamentary majority, corresponding to an effective number of seat-winning parties (or national alliances) closer to three than to two. The disadvantage of the approach is that it obviously is unable to account for factors that push a given election out of expectation, because such factors are not included in the model. A further agenda is to take this disadvantage and run with it: analysis of election outcomes, both national and district, might start with the premise that, given the national electoral system, we have a given expected value for the effective number of parties. However, in this given election, or this district, the outcome was not the expected one; why?

As Johnston (2017, 200–1) observes, if Canadian voters are actually making strategic choices, they are using a "blinkered" strategy, because they are not looking at their district (as expected under neo-Duvergerian assumptions) but at extra-district information. On the contrary, perhaps their strategy is the "correct" one for participating in the *national* election. In a given election in Canada, under its current seat product (338), the expected N_S is 2.64. Based on other results shown by Shugart and Taagepera (2017) such a value of N_S would tend to be associated with a largest party having around 48 per cent of the seats. In other words, a minority situation, such as that of 2021 when the Liberals won 46.4 per cent of seats. While voters' votes for a third party in their district are often said to be "wasted" because they can't help that party win a seat, such "blinkered" voters are looking beyond the local outcome and may even be doing so strategically. They perhaps want to register support for a party that may have seats in a House that lacks a majority party, allowing the party potentially to bargain with the government over policy.[24] To uncover whether voters think this way, we need surveys that ask about scenarios (landslide for this or that party, close call, likely minority, etc.). Do these scenarios, which would roughly capture what voters think nationwide N_S would be, shape voter decisions? By having a baseline for expected district-level fragmentation, on average – derived from the whole electoral system and not just district magnitude – we may be able to develop answers to questions like these and gain a deeper insight into how district-level party-system dynamics operate. Perhaps voters' "blinkers" are directing their attention where it should be, after all, as suggested by logically predictive models. Voters are participating in a nationwide election of a relatively large Parliament that holds confidence authority over the government, and thus might be expected to vote in a way that is generally consistent with the logical models of this chapter on how the national shapes the local. It can be hoped that further research on voter behaviour in FPTP (and other) electoral systems can benefit from quantitatively predictive logical models such as we have presented here.

Appendix

In this appendix, we present the regression tables, corresponding to tests of models derived in the body of the paper regarding district-level party-system outcomes.

To run a regression test of Equation 4, we need to transform it into its logarithmic equivalent[25]:

$$\log N'_V = 0.201 + 0.500\log N_S.$$

Table 3.1 shows the regression output for which the dependent variable is the district-level effective number of vote-earning parties (N'_V), and the

Table 3.1. Regression output

Random effects GLS regression	
	Log(N'_V)
Log N_S (national)	.469
	(.0425)
	.385 – .552
Constant	.213
	(.0132)
	.187 – .239
Observations (districts)	15,590
Number of groups (elections)	81
R^2 (between)	.5275

Note: Standard errors in parentheses, clustered by country; 95% confidence intervals shown.

Table 3.2. Countries and years included in regression analysis

Country	No. of elections	Range of years
Bahamas	1	2002
Bangladesh	1	2001
Barbados	8	1971–2008
Belize	1	2003
Bermuda	1	2003
Canada	23	1949–2021
Grenada	1	1999
Jamaica	3	1993–2002
New Zealand	15	1946–1987
St. Lucia	1	2001
St. Kitts and Nevis	1	2000
St. Vincent and the Grenadines	8	1979–2010
Trinidad and Tobago	7	1991–2010
United Kingdom	10	1983–2019

independent variable is the nationwide effective number of seat-winning parties (N_S). The sample is 15,590 districts within 81 elections, all of which are parliamentary with FPTP elections, consistent with the theory articulated in the chapter. The five Indian elections shown in figure 3.2 are not included in the regression shown, although including them (using alliance-level N_S) results in almost precisely the same estimated parameters. The regression is random effects generalized least squares (GLS) where the grouping variable is a country's election. Unlike fully pooled ordinary least squares (OLS), GLS is a multilevel model that accounts for the nesting of the districts in a given election.[26] The table shows that the regression result is

$$\log N'_V = 0.213 + 0.469\, N_S.$$

These outputs translate into an equation of $N'_V = 1.63 N_S^{0.47}$, which is obviously a minor difference from the logically derived $N'_V = 1.59 N_S^{0.50}$. As reported in the table, the expected logged values are within the 95 per cent confidence intervals of the regression estimates.

The data used in this chapter are mostly from Struthers, et al. (2018), and have been augmented with data from elections in several smaller-assembly cases used in Singer (2013), generously shared by Matt Singer, and by data collected by the authors on more recent elections in Canada and the UK, sourced from the Constituency Level Electoral Archive[27] and from Elections Canada. We thank Adam Ziegfeld for assistance with the Indian data. The complete list of countries and years included in the regression analysis is shown in table 3.2.

NOTES

1   On skepticism that there is, in a scientifically meaningful sense, a "law" of Duverger, see Shugart and Taagepera (2017, 117–20).

2   This is the geometric mean; for why it, and not the arithmetic mean, should be used in this type of analysis, see Taagepera (2007, 119).

3   Shugart and Taagepera (2017) show that one can derive predictions for the indicators of votes distribution among parties, and that these are empirically as successful as the those for seat-winning parties. We will not review these models in this chapter.

4   Counting the one elected independent as a de facto single-person party.

5   The "effective" number is by now the standard index of party-system fragmentation (originally introduced by Laakso and Taagepera, 1979). It is simply a size-weighted count. It can be calculated on either the votes for individual parties in a given election, or on the seats the parties win. The formula is to take each seat share (s_i, or vote share, v_i) and square it – thus weighting it by itself – then sum the squares, and take the reciprocal: $N_S = 1/\Sigma(s_i)^2$.

6   A very brief overview of the steps is as follows. If the number of parties winning at least one seat, N_{S0} (with the subscript zero indicating it is the unweighted count rather than the effective number) is $N_{S0} = M^{1/2}$ and also $N_{S0} = S^{1/2}$, as noted above, then it must be that $N_{S0} = (MS)^{1/4}$. Taagepera (2007) further found that, logically and empirically, $N_S = N_{S0}^{2/3}$. Thus, by basic algebra it must be that $N_S = [(MS)^{1/4}]^{2/3} = (MS)^{1/6}$. Readers desiring a more detailed overview, along with graphs and regression results showing the models' accuracy, are referred to Shugart and Taagepera (2017, 2018).

7 Recall that when one exponent is raised to another, as in the first expression to the right of the first equal sign in Equation 4, we multiply their values, hence 6 x (1/12) = .5.

8 The cases included in the data analysis are listed in the appendix. The figure excludes India, for reasons that will be clear later. In a subsequent section, we bring in the Indian case to generalize the result.

9 In comparison, a few recent British elections have been somewhat more fragmented at the district level than expected. The three diamonds just above the point for Canada 2015 represent, from left to right, the elections of 2005, 2015, and 2010. On the other hand, the elections of 2017 and 2019 are much closer to the predictions of Equation 4 despite little change in N_S across these elections. It might be further noted that the most aberrant elections in figure 3.1 on the lower side of the predictive line are from Trinidad and Tobago, signalling that this small island nation actually has more regionally distinct outcomes at the district level than Canada, as its mean district N'_V is lower than expected for its actual N_S. See Shugart and Taagepera (2017, 78–84) for a discussion of this case.

10 Perhaps one of those other factors may be federalism, which is obviously a critical factor in the Canadian party scene. Nonetheless, one must acknowledge that adding some variable to take account of federalism would not improve a model fit to the case that is already extremely good. We will explore provincial-level patterns further later in this chapter.

11 Because the formula for the effective number squares each party's seat share, larger parties contribute more to the final calculation.

12 Obviously, a party like the Bloc Québécois, which does not contest seats outside its home province, is not able to inflate N'_V other than in Quebec. Nonetheless, our simplification based on how voters respond to parties' national seat viability works in practice and thus a further adjustment to Equation 4 to account for non-national parties seems like an unnecessary complication. Perhaps it still works because voters outside Quebec are aware of the BQ's likely contribution to the national parliamentary fragmentation (and likelihood of a minority government). Disentangling the importance of regional parties that do not participate in national alliances (see also the Scottish National Party in the UK) would be a worthwhile extension but will not detain us further here.

13 Likely the key effect is earlier in the sequence of events in which voters decide the party is viable. For instance, parties themselves decide they want to be "national" and so they recruit candidates, raise funds, have leaders visit, etc., even for districts where they may not win. Breaking out these steps is beyond the scope of this paper but would be essential for a more detailed understanding of the process captured by our logic.

14 Because the actual number of vote-earning parties (or independent candidates) is a useless quantity, inasmuch as it may include tiny vanity parties that are of no political consequence.

15 A party having one or two seats in a large Parliament makes little difference to N_S. However, having even one seat may make some voters perceive the party a somehow "viable" in the national policy debate – for instance the Green parties of Canada and the UK in some elections.

16 The actual average was 2.71.

17 The only higher ratios are found in two Caribbean elections, Grenada 1999 and St. Vincent and the Grenadines 1979.

18 The election immediately following 1958, in 1962, can be found near the far right of the graph, perfectly straddling the line representing Equation 4; it resulted in a Conservative seat plurality. The election following that of 1984 was that of 1988; it resulted in a second Conservative majority and is much less far above the predictive line than 1984.

19 Australia, of course, does not use FPTP. However, it is included as one of the "Anglosphere" reference cases by Johnston. It also has a nationwide party system that conforms closely to the SPM, as if it were FPTP (Shugart and Taagepera 2017, 286–9).

20 We draw on Ziegfeld (2018), Heath, et al. (2008), and Carroll and Shugart (2008).

21 For instance, suppose there are four parties, each with 25 per cent of the seats. In turn, each of these parties contested the election in alliance with one of the other parties, and the two alliances each have 50 per cent of the seats. Then $N_S = 4$ if calculated on the component parties, but $N_S = 2$ if calculated on the alliances.

22 The elections included are 1998 through 2014; one of these has a lower N_S (3.45 in 2014, when the BJP itself won a majority of seats, although it contested at the head of the NDA; N_S on alliances was 2.45 in this election).

23 The application of the SPM actually leaves the UK system looking like the more anomalous example of the major FPTP systems. However, this is so only for the relation between the seat product and the national party system. The connection between the observed effective number of seat-winning parties and the district-level vote fragmentation in the UK is consistent with our expectations.

24 In other words, voters may believe that by voting for such a party, they put some wind in its sails in terms of the national debate, even if it is only voters in *other districts* who are able to contribute to its winning any seats. Johnston (2017, 212) gives some specific examples of policy influence by the New Democratic Party, even in situations of Liberal Party majority governments. Is it a stretch to think voters have some awareness of such potential influence on the national scene, and vote accordingly? We think not, but it remains to be demonstrated systematically in the way we are proposing here.

25 The reason for taking logs (and the associated exponential format of Equation 1) is that both variables can be only nonzero and positive (Taagepera, 2008). Moreover, they have somewhat skewed distributions. Additionally, the difference between $N'_V = 1.7$ and $N'_V = 2.7$ is theoretically more important than that between $N'_V = 4.5$ and $N'_V = 5.5$, and assemblies of 500 and 550 should have effects more similar to

one another than assemblies of 25 and 75 even though the pairs in these examples differ by the same amount.

26 We check for the presence of random effects using the Breusch-Pagan Lagrange multiplier (LM) test, the results of which (p-value < .00001) indicate random effects are preferred to pooled OLS. Note that although districts are also nested in a country, N_S (the input variable) is, as predicted by the Seat Product Model, strongly conditioned on assembly size (S), which rarely changes (and when it does, the differences are minimal). Correlation among district values in the same election is therefore captured through N_S. Note that there is no "within" variation captured in the regression (because we are not estimating correlates of individual district deviation from the election mean), only "between" (election level). By clustering standard errors by country, we account for the likely non-independence of election averages by country, across time. (If we do not cluster in this manner, standard errors are slightly larger, but not consequentially so.)

27 https://electiondataarchive.org

References

Carroll, Royce, and Matthew S. Shugart. 2008. "Parties, Alliances, and Duverger's Law in India." Paper prepared for presentation at the Annual Meeting of the Western Political Science Association, March 18–20.

Cox, G.W. 1997. *Making Votes Count: Strategic Coordination in the World's Electoral Systems*. Cambridge University Press.

Duverger, M. 1951. *Les partis politiques*. Paris: Armand Colin.

– 1954. *Political Parties: Their Organization and Activity in the Modern State*. John Wiley and Sons.

Heath, A., S. Glouharova, and O. Heath. 2008. "India: Two-Party Contests within a Multiparty System." In *The Politics of Electoral Systems*, edited by M. Gallagher and P. Mitchell, Oxford University Press.

Johnston, R. 2017. *The Canadian Party System: An Analytic History*. University of British Columbia Press.

Johnston. R., and F. Cutler. 2009. "Canada: The Puzzle of Local Three-Party Competition." In *Duverger's Law of Plurality Voting: The Logic of Party Competition in Canada, India, the United Kingdom, and the United States*, edited by B. Grofman, A. Blais, and S. Bowler. Springer.

Laakso, M., and R. Taagepera. 1979. "The 'Effective' Number of Parties: A Measure with Application to West Europe." *Comparative Political Studies* 12 (1): 3–27. https:// doi.org/10.1177/001041407901200101

Nikolenyi, C. 2009. "Party Inflation in India: Why Has a Multiparty Format Prevailed in the National Party System?" In *Duverger's Law of Plurality Voting: The Logic of Party Competition in Canada, India, the United Kingdom, and the United States*, edited by B. Grofman, A. Blais, and S. Bowler. Springer.

Riker, W.H. 1982. "The Two-Party System and Duverger's Law: An Essay on the History of Political Science." *American Political Science Review* 76: 753–66. https://doi.org/10.2307/1962968

Shugart, M.S., and R. Taagepera. 2017. *Votes from Seats: Logical Models of Electoral Systems*. Cambridge University Press.

– 2018. "Electoral System Effects on Party Systems." In *The Oxford Handbook of Electoral Systems*, edited by Erik Herron, Robert Pekkanen, and Matthew S. Shugart, Oxford University Press.

Singer, M.M. 2013. "Was Duverger Correct? Single-Member District Election Outcomes in Fifty-Three Countries." *British Journal of Political Science* 43 (1): 201–20. https://doi.org/10.1017/S0007123412000233

Sridharan, E. 2005. Coalition Strategies and the BJP's Expansion, 1989–2004. *Commonwealth and Comparative Politics* 43 (2): 194-221. https://doi.org/10.1080/14662040500151093

Struthers, Cory, Yuhui Li, and M. Shugart. 2018. "Introducing New Multilevel Datasets: Party Systems at the District and National Levels." *Research and Politics*. https://doi.org/10.1177/2053168018813508

Taagepera, R. 2007. *Predicting Party Sizes: The Logic of Simple Electoral Systems*. Oxford University Press.

– 2008. *Making Social Sciences More Scientific: The Need for Predictive Models*. Oxford University Press.

Ziegfeld, Adam. 2018. "Electoral Systems in Context: India." In *The Oxford Handbook of Electoral Systems*, edited by Erik Herron, Robert Pekkanen and Matthew S. Shugart. Oxford University Press.

PART TWO

Social Foundations: Understanding Traditional Questions through the Lens of Contemporary Contexts

4 Families and the Fate of Party Systems

RICHARD JOHNSTON

... parental traditions are shared collectively rather than individually ...

Berelson et al. (1954, 136, Chart LXVII)

The heritability of partisanship is commonly presented as a critical component of the multi-generational anchoring of individuals to parties. The first systematic statement of this claim is Converse (1969). Just as individuals' identification with a party, when aggregated across large numbers of individuals, is critical to the stability of a party system, so too is the anchoring of individuals to their parents. As partisan inheritance is the initial push in a life-cycle process of partisan reinforcement, the higher the rate of consistency between parents and children in a given system, the more stable that system should be in the aggregate.

I contest this claim by showing that variation in intergenerational consistency within families is itself the product of the probability of extra-familial reinforcement, which in turn is the product of the fractionalization of the party system. There are very few party systems where a majority in the current generation could possibly have inherited their loyalty. Further, the probability of such inheritance is essentially unrelated to the volatility in the systems. And properly measured, there is little variation across parties or systems in heritability. This is not to deny that individuals' partisan dispositions are potentially heritable, with follow-on implications for motivation and cognition. The claim, rather, is that these within-family rates of inheritance are epiphenomenal. The argument and the findings cast serious doubt on accounts of partisan alignment and dealignment that rely solely on individual-level indicators. They also have implications for the proper measurement of turnover. At the most general level, the chapter is a call for rethinking the foundations of electoral aggregation. In essence, aggregate patterns require aggregate explanations.

I stake these claims with data from 37 parties in 10 countries and a combination of aggregate analyses and hierarchically modelled estimations with survey data. The survey data are rather old and are far from representative of the totality of the world's party systems. But as the systems in this study range across constitutional forms, electoral fractionalization, and historical starting points, they embody the variance required to test my argument. Even if it is not comprehensive, the analysis stands as a proof of concept.

The Stakes

"Of Time and Partisan Stability," by Philip Converse (1969), is a landmark in the comparative study of party systems. It links socialization within families and self-reinforcement over the life course to the macro-stability of party systems:

> … we conceive such aggregate levels of loyalty to existing parties in a democratic system as an important ingredient of democratic stability, and perhaps, for the mass level, *the* most important ingredient …. (142)

The paper is a logical extension to the comparative realm of the work by Campbell et al. (1960) on the United States. Notwithstanding the variability in the twentieth-century experience of representative democracy, the United States was not alone as an example of continuity. In many countries, electoral patterns still visible in the 1960s date back at least to the 1920s and commonly include elements stemming from the Protestant Reformation and from early state-building sequences (Lipset and Rokkan 1967). It was exhilarating to think that insights of survey research could unlock the secrets of such continuity.[1]

But the twentieth century was also a site for democratic breakdown or, for some countries, chronic volatility. Here too, Converse (1969), building on earlier work by Converse and Dupeux (1962), suggests that survey evidence can explain variation – failure as well as success – in system consolidation. The critical exhibit is a US/France comparison of partisan heritability. Among children of partisans, the probabilities of success or failure in acquiring a partisan identity are 80:20. Among children of non-partisans, the rates are 50:50. The American and French turnover patterns are essentially identical. The difference between the systems lay in the partisanship of parents: few French respondents could remember such partisanship. In a simple Markov framework, however, the near identity of the French and US turnover patterns implies that the aggregate patterns would eventually converge. But the convergence would be gradual, requiring two to three generations to be fully accomplished.

Converse (1969, 167) concludes on this note:

> We assume that the state of a democratic system in this regard—the degree to which it is frozen or remains fluid with respect to mass loyalties—is a significant datum. We see these loyalties as having something of the same conservative or

preservative influence on democratic system stability as does socialization into the rules of the democratic game at an elite level. This is not to imply that the possibility of radical change in party structure, or even in the nature of the regime, disappears as a system approaches this type of "maturity." But it is to argue that the probabilities decline in a significant degree or, if one wishes, that the severity of shock necessary to induce such system change must be progressively greater the more completely the system has jelled in these terms.

This picture seems to have maintained its grip on our imagination. Its citation count continues to grow, and its role is only rarely that of a straw man.[2]

Converse's model has two parts. The US–France comparison is about partisan inheritance. On the arithmetic of cross-national comparison, this is the more important part.[3] For this reason, most of the rest of my chapter is taken up with it. Much of the actual content in Converse, however, is devoted to the growth of partisan intensity over the life course, for which inheritance is a major boost. And most of the literature in the grip of Converse focuses on the life course.

It may help that one central proposition seemed to derive theoretical warrant from an earlier generation of research. This is the work on "political immunization," notably by McPhee and Ferguson (1962). It may also help that the immunization argument was deployed with dramatic effect in Butler and Stokes (1969) and by Converse (1976) himself. For individual-level mechanisms, fieldwork by the Columbia School (of which McPhee and Ferguson was the last hurrah) supplied the earliest evidence of motivated cognition: Berelson et al. (1954) documented self-directed bias in perception (Chart LII, 221) and retention (Chart CIII, 222), whose impact was amplified by an individual's psychological commitment to a side (Chart CIV, 224). Once a party preference is initiated, motivated cognition will reinforce it. And at least one formal model, a Bayesian one proposed in Achen (1992), predicts damping of response to new political stimuli over the life course. Achen's model does not claim that the weight attached to new information diminishes as citizens grow older, only that the accumulation of information that comes with age makes it harder for new information to displace the older information.[4] Achen's model requires no boost from motivated cognition, only that – Bayes-style – priors count for something.

Empirically, however, the life course component of the model has not fared well. Indeed, it stumbled right out of the gate. Early disconfirmation came from France, the very electorate that Converse and Dupeux saw as the foil to the United States. Inglehart and Hochstein (1972, 344–5) show that by the late 1960s, not only was party identification as ubiquitous in France as in the US but there were no discernible life-course gains in its intensity. They also pointed out that Lipset and Rokkan (1967) attributed the "freezing" of patterns to the locking-in of the group and issue basis of competition. In turn, this was the result of choices by elites; little agency was attributed to mass electorates.[5] In the French case, the transition from the 4th to the 5th Republic brought a rapid stabilization of the bases of choice and with this, a correspondingly swift locking-in of the electorate. Life-cycle predictions similarly failed in Switzerland, the US South, and Mexico (Niemi et al., 1985), Germany (Norpoth, 1984), and Britain (Abramson, 1992). Abramson (1976) was an early skeptic for the United States, non-South as well as South.

Converse's (1969) argument might have been tempered in the first place – and its subsequent staying power rendered less impressive – had more attention been paid to the full import of McPhee and Ferguson. After walking through a model predicated on the implantation of resistors to new information, these authors conclude:

> ... there *is* an immunization effect ..., a "damping" of the oscillatory swings in response to the same stimuli in successive decades ... but ... the degree of such damping of response is *small* in any one decade's time (or slow if we consider many decades). The latter results had not been expected of the intuitive theory and are contrary to the impression given by voting research, namely, that party loyalties rapidly "rigidify" with maturity. If they do not rigidify quickly, however, and the effect of previous experience in damping out new responsiveness is no more than that ... in the real American circumstances today, then the immunization effect would be of only academic interest, and insufficient for any real protection. (159–60)

The chapter concludes (pp. 171–9) with a section wanly entitled "Lack of Effective Immunity."[6]

The other part of the Converse (1969) story – the intergenerational component – has been largely neglected. Yet, the Inglehart-Hochstein finding implies that this intergenerational component was an especially portentous prediction failure: in a mere decade, French respondents achieved a frequency of party loyalty that they should not have approached until the turn of the millennium. For all that, it remains an article of faith that partisanship is heritable, and that this heritability reflects prepolitical social influence[7] *within the family*. Although evidence of such influence is hard to find, given the privacy of intergenerational bonds, a recent report from the largest single study of parent-child pairs (Jennings et al. 2009) reaffirms patterns of continuity across generations within families, and shows that continuity is conditioned on certain features of the parent-child bond.[8]

But this is evidence from the United States, a system that is highly stable and, no less important, very simple in its persistent two-party-ness. Even for the US, the emphasis on family socialization is curiously blinkered, considering the origins of electoral studies in the extraordinarily detailed and sophisticated work by the Columbia School, especially Berelson et al. (1954). That book's chapter 7 is a rich discussion of personal influence. To be sure, much of this influence stabilizes individuals' behaviour – makes them consistent with themselves. But the volume of exchange between sides is not trivial. The dominant motif combines the vulnerability of individuals within minorities to social pressure from the larger community with an equilibration logic that limits the aggregate susceptibility of the minority groups. In the short run, a lot of movement is "homing" – the return of individuals to their original position – but the forces that produce this are commonly external to the individual. By implication, the maintenance of patterns is less the result of intra-individual factors than of stable vectors of external pressure:

> … religious and socio-economic status (SES) groups remain more or less constant from one generation to the next, and equilibrium states within them link the vote of the two generations for the whole community, even if there is no exact parent-child association *within* any specific social stratum. (136)
>
> After the parents' starting point, the distribution of offspring's preferences tends to parallel the distribution of influences to which they are exposed. But since these "influences" are each other's preferences, the distribution of them more or less parallels the parental traditions of years and years before! A political tradition is a class and religious (i.e., a social) heritage as well as a purely family inheritance. (137)
>
> … the question of persistences and survivals probably turns in many cases less on the identity of individual opinions from one time to the next than on the sluggishness of change in the collective distributions of preferences …. (137–8)

Few scholars have taken up the challenge of extending the logic in these passages. The principal exceptions seem to be Butler and Stokes (1969) and Johnston (1985).

An argument closely akin to this has surfaced in the recent literature. Achen (2002) extends his 1992 Bayesian work to links between parents and children. He argues that the similarity of their social circumstances is the key. More often than not, these circumstances, although rarely identical, are generally similar, such that *the appearance of inheritance within families relies on the extent of reinforcement from the outside.* Contrariwise, as circumstances diverge, including as offspring proceed on their adult life course, so does the parent-child correspondence diminish.

Achen's argument turns on objective circumstances. The Columbia argument turns on the flow of social influence. For both, the key causal force lies outside the family. This intuition has implications for comparison between parties within systems and for comparisons between systems. First, we need to define an inheritance rate, I_j^s, as p_{jj}^s, where p^s_{jj} is the proportion among those whose parents identify with the jth party in system s who also identify with party j themselves.

Think of this as a diagonal entry in a transition matrix where the entries sum to one across rows. The size of the jth party could be represented as either $p^s_{.j}$, the jth party's share on the *row* margin – that is, its share in the *parents'* generation – or as $p^s_{.j}$, the jth party's share on the *column* margin – its share in the *current* generation. In equilibrium these shares are the same, and for convenience call this quantity p^s_j.

1 Within a system, the larger the party, the higher its apparent inheritance rate. That is,

$$I^s_j = f\left(p^s_j\right).$$

Critically, the two quantities are not required to be identical, just that the relationship be monotonically positive. If p^s_j is the probability of selecting a supporter of party j at random from system s, then I^s_j is that probability conditional on his or her parents also supporting party j. Other things equal, that conditional probability should increase with the size of the party, just as the unconditional one does. That is, variation in the size of I^s_j should be diagnostic of the size of the parties in question. It is, of course, almost certain that $I^s_j > p^s_j$. Everything we know about the empirics of party support tells us that the difference is positive and is so whatever the mechanism. To identify factors specific to parties or systems, the key diagnostic is the difference between I^s_j and p^s_j, the gain that knowledge of parental partisanship gives over a merely random draw.

This logic extends to comparisons across systems. Define the inheritance rate for a country as $I^s_u = \left(\sum_j I^s_j\right)/N^s_i$ where parties are unweighted or as $I^s_w = \left(\sum_j p^s_j I^s_j\right)/\left(\sum_j p^s_j\right)$ where parties are weighted for their electoral share. N^s_i is the arithmetic number of parties in the system[9] and $\sum_j p^s_j$ is the sum of each party's share in system s.[10]

2 By either indicator, $I^s = f\left(\bar{p}^s_j\right)$. The average inheritance rate in a country will be a function of the average size of a party in each country. The less fractionalized the system, the higher the average rate, and vice versa.

None of this is terribly complicated and is mostly just arithmetic. Within a country, the ratios among the rates along the major diagonal of the transition matrix – the inheritance rates – and the off-diagonal rates in each row – the rates of exchange among parties--must jointly reflect the sizes of the parties on the row and column margins.

The impact of variation in I_j^s for the stability of a party system is unclear. On one hand, it does follow that the smaller I_j^s is, the more gross volatility there must be in a system. Just as the smaller entities in a system are subject to more turnover (gains as well as losses) relative to their base size, so do systems with many small units exhibit more gross turnover than do systems with a small number of large units. And where there is more gross movement, so might there be more net movement. But if the Columbia School intuition is right, the key to stability overall is stability in the vector of external influences. Where there are many parties, each with its own influence system or each representing a sharply distinct interest, the sum of those influences might be highly stable, more stable even than in a system with large entities but porous boundaries. No observable implication leaps off the table, but the matter bears empirical investigation.

Data and Method

I explore these propositions with data drawn mainly from the Political Action survey, an eight-country study conducted in the 1970s. The data have the virtue of constant wording for the party identification measure across the cases, along with questions about parental partisanship. I extend the dataset to include roughly contemporaneous survey data from Canada and Australia. The Political Action surveys are oriented to elections between 1970 and 1975. The Canadian data are for the 1974 election and the Australian data are for 1966. The period is also fortuitous, as respondents' political lifespans ranged from before the First World War to the unsettled years of the early 1970s. In some countries, the party system had been fully consolidated for the lifetimes of all respondents. Other countries experienced authoritarian rule or military occupation, such that fully functioning democracy was only two decades old and older respondents came late to a competitive party system. For each system I also incorporate data based on official returns for the elections in question and for four temporally adjacent ones.

Survey Items

The core survey variables purport to capture party identification for the respondents and their parents. The item wordings for the Political Action surveys are not the standard ones for the English-speaking world, however. For most countries, the question is as follows:

Which political party do you usually feel closest to?

For Germany and Austria, the question is the standard one for election surveys in those countries:

Many people in Germany/Austria lean towards a particular party for a long time, although they may occasionally vote for a different party. How about you: Do you in general lean towards a particular party? [If so, which one?]

For Canada and Australia, the questions are closer to the form that predominates in US election studies. For Australia:

Generally speaking, do you usually think of yourself as Liberal, Labor, Country Party or DLP?

A follow-up asks if the respondent understands the question to be about the federal or state arena or both. Almost all say both arenas and only a miniscule fraction mean the state level only. For Canada, the wording is conditional on arena:

Thinking of federal politics, do you usually think of yourself as a Liberal, Conservative, NDP, Social Credit, or what?

In some countries a follow-up was asked, with a wording such as "closer than any other" and referring to the moment. The time referent is inappropriate and, as often as not, the follow-up was not asked. Party identification in this chapter, then, means the party named in response to the first query or no identification at all.

The percentage identifying with a party ranged from 65 (Switzerland) to 87 (Australia). It makes intuitive sense – and is consistent with Converse (1969) – that three of the four lowest percentages (Germany, Italy, Austria in ascending order) are for countries that exited authoritarian rule only after 1945. But Switzerland does not fit this description. And among countries with 80 per cent or more identifiers, the Netherlands and Finland had interrupted experiences. Note also (table 4.1, below) that the percentage of US respondents naming a party is higher than normally observed after the first query in the standard ANES battery.[11]

The question about the respondents' fathers[12] is the following:

Which political party did your father favour during your youth?

Aggregate Indicators

The basic representation of electoral volatility is the Pedersen (1979) index of net electoral turnover across consecutive elections. For each country the elections in question are the one referred to in the survey question and the election immediately before it. Each of these election pairs is then bracketed by the two immediately preceding pairs and two succeeding pairs and the results across the five pairs are averaged. The temporal spans range from one to two decades. This reduces the scope for idiosyncrasy, and the resulting values capture differences in chronic instability.

Calibration

Before proceeding to the heart of the argument, I relate my data first to those used by Converse and then to some facts on the ground. One point is to show that my data exhibit patterns for individual-level partisan inheritance and life-cycle gains consistent with the propositions in Converse. This rules out the possibility that my difference in interpretation is the product of divergence in the underlying data set. The second point is to show that the aggregate frequency of partisan inheritance is low. In very few countries could a majority of respondents be said to inherit their partisanship. This is true not just for systems whose democratic pedigree was short but even for some systems that are truly venerable.

The joint effect of age and inheritance on partisanship appears in figure 4.1. For all terms, the coding is essentially identical to that in Converse: whether or not partisanship is imputed to the respondent's father and whether or not the respondent her/himself gives a partisan response to the first query. The underlying estimation is by probit with a fully-dummy-interactive setup, including a quadratic representation of age. The fine print in Converse about resistance to new information and forgetting of old information is not reproduced here. Note also that, at this point, nothing is said about the direction of partisanship, just its mere presence.[13]

As Converse (1969) argued, having a partisan father makes a big difference in the respondent's own politics, an average gain in partisan likelihood of about 20 points. Children of non-partisans do make life-course gains – slightly more, in fact, than children of partisans – but the gap ceases to close after middle age. Averaged across the 10 countries, the pattern conforms remarkably to the standard expectation. Children of partisans and (especially) non-partisans are more likely to claim partisanship themselves than implied in the original Converse-Dupeux finding. But the qualitative similarity is unmistakeable. Even more impressive is the negative acceleration in partisan gains in both groups, but especially among children of non-partisans. This conforms to both the standard expectation and the theoretically predicted one in Achen (1992).

The pattern varies from country to country, but not in a way that is consistent with the fine print in Converse. In every country the partisan line lies above the non-partisan one: the first derivative of the slope on age is always positive, and the second derivative is almost always negative. What is not visible in variation across countries is impact from forgetting or resistance, Converse-style.[14]

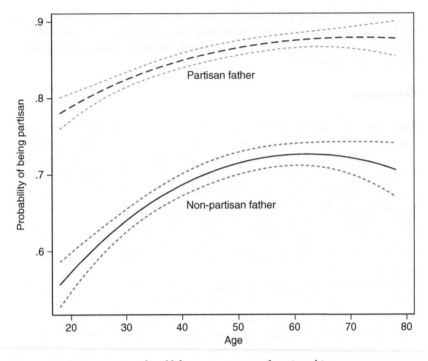

Figure 4.1. Intergenerational and life-course sources of partisanship
Note: Entries are modelled values and 95 per cent confidence intervals from a fully specified underlying probit estimation.

Figure 4.1 masks an awkward fact, however. Table 4.1 (leftmost column) shows that only in four countries could a one-sided majority of respondents impute partisanship to their fathers and the cross-national variation in this incidence is unrelated to the age of the party system. In Canada and Switzerland, only a bare majority could do so. That Germany, Austria, and Italy are extreme cases should come as no surprise. They exemplify the autocratic interruptions that figure prominently in Converse's model. But Finland, Switzerland, and Canada are all examples of uninterrupted electoral history. The contrast between Canada and Australia, otherwise so similar, is also striking.

No less striking is the variation in inheritance rates. In every country, this rate is calculated for respondents who claim to have partisan fathers and is the average share who support the same party as their father. For the unweighted rate (middle column), only in the United States, Australia, and Finland is the rate above .50. Where the rate is weighted by party size (rightmost column), the cross-national variance is smaller. Even so, three countries still have rates

Table 4.1. Aspects of partisan inheritance by country

Country	Proportion no father's party	Inheritance rate – raw	Inheritance rate – weighted
Canada	.44	.43	.53
Britain	.28	.49	.58
West Germany	.53	.45	.53
Netherlands	.31	.43	.43
Austria	.57	.46	.66
United States	.24	.67	.69
Italy	.57	.33	.44
Switzerland	.48	.47	.45
Finland	.52	.56	.56
Australia	.28	.64	.64

Note: For calculation of rates, see text.

below .50, and in the systems where weighting has lifted the average rate above .50 the resulting odds still seem like a coin toss. In only three countries does a majority of respondents both impute a loyalty – any loyalty – to their fathers and claim to have the same one themselves. These are Britain (barely), the United States, and Australia.

Consider some examples for how these numbers cash out in the scope of paternal influence, in table 4.2. In each subtable, cell entries are diagonal percentages, the number in the cell as a share of the whole table. This enables us to identify the weight of each pathway. Note that the bottom-right cell divides its total into two parts: above the diagonal appears the fraction who claim a loyalty for both their fathers and themselves, but *different* ones; below the diagonal is the fraction with the *same* loyalty in both generations.

The United States is a boundary case with a high level of intergenerational transmission. About three respondents in four could, in principle, inherit their party loyalty. One in 10 imputes a loyalty to their father but claim none for themselves and 15 per cent report a change across generations. This leaves 52 per cent who have the same loyalty as their fathers.

Elsewhere the scope for inheritance is typically smaller. Consider the subtly different cases of Canada and the Netherlands. In the Netherlands, 70 per cent of respondents could conceivably inherit their partisanship, a share only slightly smaller than in the United States. The partisan share among the children of partisans is also like that in the US. But among partisan children of partisan fathers, only half report the same loyalty as their father. The share of the whole sample that could be said to inherit their partisanship is only 30 per cent. Canadians arrive at the same percentage by a different route. Canadians are much less able than the Dutch to claim a loyalty for their father. This is

Table 4.2. The scale of partisan i-nheritance

	Respondent partisan?				
Father partisan?	No	Yes		No	Yes
	Netherlands			Canada	
No	10	20		10	34
Yes	10	30/30		9	17/30
	US			All	
No	9	15		13	30
Yes	10	15/52		8	17/32

Notes: Cell entries are diagonal percentages, summing to 100 in each subtable. Entries in bottom-right cells are for partisan respondents who impute a different (above the diagonal) or the same (below the diagonal) partisanship to their father as to themselves.

plausibly the result of Canada's high rate of postwar immigration from diverse sources.[15] Among those who can identify a paternal party, however, the rate claiming the same party for themselves is the same in Canada as in the Netherlands. But many fewer Canadians arrive at a present party by abandoning their father's; the bulk of new recruits comes from families without a partisan father. In the Netherlands, a partisan is as likely to be a defector from the father's party as to be an inheritor.

The Canadian pattern typifies the 10 countries, as seen in the bottom right subtable. As point estimates, numbers for the 10-country sample should obviously be taken with a grain of salt. The choice of countries is arbitrary, and the countries are weighted only by the relative sample sizes. But a basic point stands: partisanship is heritable but not always inherited. In most countries, only a minority are partisan inheritors. Inheritors are outnumbered by contemporaneous non-partisans, children of non-partisans, and intergenerational defectors. Even among current partisans, the number with a non-partisan father rivals that with a father of the same partisan stripe.

Table 4.3. Party size and partisan inheritance

Categories	Dependent variable			
	Same party as father[1]		Inheritance rate[2]	
	(1)	(2)	(3)	(4)
Party share, 20-year average	2.03	2.31	2.30	2.53
	(.55)	(.48)	(.31)	(.34)
Britain		.27		−.04
		(.26)		(.14)
Germany		.00		−.06
		(.27)		(.14)
Netherlands		.90		.21
		(.24)		(.17)
Austria		−.05		−.12
		(.28)		(.22)
United States		.41		−.00
		(.32)		(.17)
Italy		−.08		−.05
		(.25)		(.21)
Switzerland		.74		.27
		(.24)		(.13)
Finland		−.08		.43
		(.27)		(.15)
Australia		.49		.40
		(.27)		(.24)
Constant	−.89	−1.23	−.64	−.82
	(.23)	(.22)	(.11)	(.13)
Variance (constant)	.25	.11		
	(.07)	(.03)		
Observations	11,267	11,267	38	38
Number of groups	38	38		

Notes:
[1] Multi-level probit estimations with country-party combinations at level 2. Reference country is Canada.
[2] Fractional polynomial regressions with probit link. Reference country is Canada.

Aggregate Sources of Inheritance

This leads to the empirical heart of my argument: the apparent heritability of partisanship is a function of the probability that the parental push is reinforced by forces *outside* the family. That probability is a quite smooth function of the simple size of the party, exactly as argued by the Columbia scholars years ago. Heritability is, in a word, epiphenomenal.

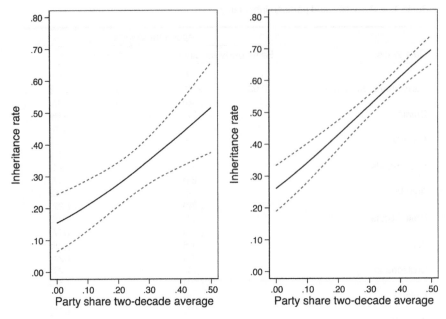

Figure 4.2. Party size and partisan inheritance (multi-level estimation and aggregate estimation)
Note: Based estimation models (1) and (3) in table 3.2.

The key evidence is in table 4.3 and figure 4.2. I present two different esti-mation strategies and two different models. One strategy uses the 10-country merged file of individual survey response. Estimation is multilevel, with level 2 being 38 country-party combinations. The dependent variable is a dummy, indi-cating whether or not the respondent's and the father's party are the same. Only children of partisans appear in the dataset. This is, in effect, a weighted estimate of the inheritance rate, where the weights are the relative shares of each party among current identifiers in each sample. The other strategy is aggregate, with 38 observations. The dependent variable is the inheritance rate for each party. As the rate is scaled from zero to one, estimation is by fractional polynomial regres-sion with a probit link. In this estimation all parties, large or small, are weighted equally. In both setups, the key independent variable is "party share," the par-ty's average share as reported in official returns over roughly the two decades preceding the survey fieldwork.[16] Each estimation is run twice, first as bivariate with the party's election share only and then repeated with country dummies, to see if and in what direction the average rate in a country differs from what would be predicted from party size alone. Canada is the reference country.

The basic patterns are similar between estimation strategies and with and without country dummies. As the coefficients do not speak for themselves, the bivariate relationships are reproduced as marginal effects estimations in figure 4.2. In the cross-level estimation, the plausible range of election shares induces a shift in inheritance rates of about .3 points. For a small party – with, say, a share below 10% – the estimated inheritance rate is about .20. Such a party loses many more supporters than it retains, but the rate itself represents a huge gain over the tiny baseline of a random draw. The gain diminishes as the baseline grows – as the party share itself grows – and the modelled rate approaches .50.

The aggregate estimate produces a more dramatic relationship, roughly one-to-one. A vanishingly small party is predicted to have an inheritance rate of about .25. A party with a 50% share is estimated to have an inheritance rate close to .70. The gain over a random draw is .20 to .25 across the board. The confidence intervals are tighter in the aggregate case because all the individual-level "error" is burned off by aggregation. The aggregate estimate is, however, true to what meets the eye in party-by-party comparisons. For parties like the two US or Australian major parties or the British Conservatives and Canadian Liberals, the inheritance rate is greater than .60. The basic point in both estimations is that the rate is not so much a freestanding social fact as a by-product of other forces.

The country dummies in estimations (2) and (4) pick up whether the country's transmission process reflect factors outside simple variation in party sizes. Depending on the estimation, two to four countries merit comment. Australia stands out in both estimations as having a peculiarly strong father-child link. The same is true for Switzerland in both estimations, for the Netherlands in the cross-level estimation, and for Finland in the aggregate estimation. No obvious explanation covers all cases. Three of the countries – the Netherlands, Switzerland, and Finland – are very fractionalized systems. One might think that there is some heritability floor for hyper fractionalized electorates. But Italy is also highly fragmented yet has inheritance rates that lie right on the prediction line. In any case, if the floor were higher for small parties, this should have shown up in the base estimates. And the Australian system, far from being fragmented, rivals the United States for consolidation. The Netherlands and Switzerland exemplify "pillarized" or "consociational" systems (Lijphart, 1977). Social relations in these societies are – or were – compartmentalized by religion, region, or class-based civil society. So perhaps citizens in such places have higher probabilities of encountering self-reinforcing social influence (Berelson et al., 1954). Or social locations may be more heritable in such societies (Achen, 2002). But Finland has never been considered a pillarized society. Aside from the dwindling Swedish minority, it is a relatively homogenous and tightly connected society. And Austria – a classic case of consociationalism

(Lijphart, 1977) – does not stand out as distinct. In sum, the deviant cases remain to be accounted for.

Their presence should not distract us from the main story. Most of the variation in inheritance rates across countries (like variation across parties within each country) is the product of the relative fractionalization of each country's electorate. Big parties beget high inheritance rates. Small parties beget low inheritance rates. The differences are not the result of within-family factors. Rather, the differences in rates reflect the likelihood that forces within families are reinforced by forces outside the family. Nor is it the case that a party is big because it has a high inheritance rate. Rather, it has a high inheritance rate because it is big.

Aggregate Impact

As epiphenomena, inheritance rates might be irrelevant to the stability or instability of party shares. This section provides the empirics to test this proposition. The primary demonstrations are 10-country regressions of an indicator of electoral volatility on country-level inheritance rates.

The inheritance rate in the setup is the unweighted ("raw") one from table 1. The indicator of electoral volatility is based on the Pederson (1979) index, the minimum proportion of the electorate that would have to shift between parties to transform the distribution in one election into the distribution in the next election. To avoid potentially idiosyncratic election pairs, I calculate index numbers for five consecutive election pairs centred on the last election before the country's survey fieldwork and take the average value.

But we immediately confront an issue with the United States. The US stands apart from the other systems in being a system of fully separated powers. The others, with the partial exception of Finland, are parliamentary systems with either a constitutional monarch or a ceremonial president. Until recently, US presidential elections were quite volatile. A common sequence featured re-election landslides for incumbents from opposite parties bracketing highly competitive open races. Elections for the US House, in contrast, were (and are) among the most stable in the world. As neither arena by itself represents the totality of US elections, the United States will appear twice, one estimation for each electoral arena. I also present an estimation that simply excludes the United States.[17]

The results appear in figure 4.3. Each panel in the figure presents the regression line, its coefficient values, and the scatterplot. For all non-US entries, the scatterplot does not change from estimation to estimation. With US House elections, the relationship between partisan inheritance and system stability is negative. For a theory predicated on individual voter psychology, this would be good news. The problem is that the result is reversed when House elections are supplanted by presidential ones: now the relationship is positive. This reflects

(a)

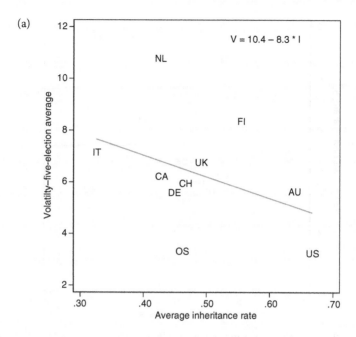

(b)

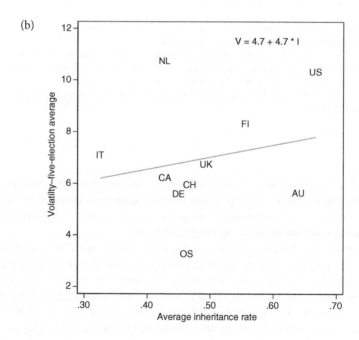

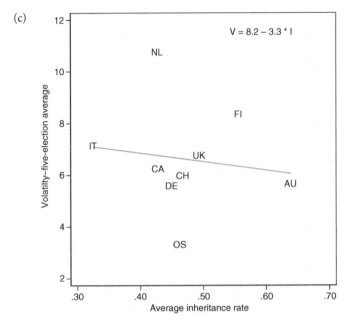

(c)

$V = 8.2 - 3.3 * I$

Figure 4.3. Partisan inheritance and system stability: (a) 10 systems, US House; (b) 10 systems, US Presidential; (c) 9 systems, no US

Notes:
1. Dependent variable (V, vertical axis) is five-year average inter-election volatility (Pederson index) with survey election year as the median election.
2. Independent variable (I, horizontal axis) is a country's average inheritance rate (percentage claiming to identify with a given party conditional on respondent imputing support for that party to his or her father, unweighted average across the parties in the system).
3. Estimations by OLS. All absolute values for slopes are either smaller or slightly larger than their standard errors.

the fact that the United States flips from being an extreme case on the bottom to being an extreme case on the top. When the United States is removed entirely, the relationship slips back to slightly negative. In none of these estimations is the apparent relationship anything more than noise.

The same is true for any variations in the setup. Focus on volatility over the specific election pair predating the survey also yields null relationships. Perhaps the operative factor is the gain or loss in within-family transmission relative to party sizes. But replacing the observed inheritance rate with residuals for each country – basically the unweighted average departure of the observed inheritance rates in a country from the rates predicted by party size (roughly as in table 3) – also yields nothing.

Of course, the analysis is of only 10 countries over a decade of elections more than four decades ago. A different mix of countries and periods might yield different patterns. But it is unclear on what principled basis we should replace or augment this set of countries. And the countries in this paper range from long-standing consolidated democracies to ones that experienced autocratic rule within the lifetimes of many in the electorate. The life spans of the respondents range as far back as the late nineteenth century. Certainly, the countries were not chosen to prove my argument or – more to the point – to disprove the argument in Converse (1969).

Most telling, perhaps, is the very presence in the data set of the United States. It is ironic that US survey data served as the basis for the development of an argument about electoral stability. And yet the United States exhibits extremes of stability and volatility, depending on the arena. To be sure, the presidential arena has not seen the bases of competition between the two leading parties disrupted by an invader since the 1850s. But the scale of presidential tides is striking, and the presidency is the arena in which insurgents make the greatest inroads.

Conclusion

As we have known for years, party identification is heritable, in the minimal sense that there is a father-child correspondence in party support. But the actual incidence of partisan inheritance is typically low. In very few countries can a majority of survey respondents be said to inherit their loyalty. Often, the percentage who cannot impute any party label to their fathers is large. Even where a large fraction can impute a loyalty to their fathers, the incidence of defection from the parental brand is often high. The most powerful effect on the incidence of inheritance is the average size of the party in the system: the larger the party, the higher the inheritance rate, and vice versa. The basic parameter of this relationship holds across many systems. System-level departures from this simple expectation are rare and modest. Whatever their source, variance in inheritance rates is unrelated to variance in systems' inter-election volatility.

One implication is clear: the driver of variation in heritability is the extent to which influence within the family is reinforced by factors existing *outside* the family. The pattern observed by Bernard Berelson and his colleagues (1954) for elections in the 1940s remains as pertinent as ever.

What is more, it covers not just variation among parties within a system but also variation across an array of systems. The parameters of relationship that hold for a given system could be said to follow from logical necessity. For a system's structure to persist, the relationship between party sizes, on one hand, and the rates of exchange among parties, on the other hand, must hold. If rates converge, the system's energy will run down, leaving all parties the same size overall and with no variation across the politically relevant elements of the social structure. But the requirement that a system's parties differ among themselves and across contexts in rates of exchange does not also imply that inheritance rates – understood as the *difference* between diagonal and off-diagonal rates – be identical across countries. And there is variation in such differences across countries, although we have no ready explanation for it. The variance is modest, however, and the bigger point is that country-specific idiosyncrasy is modest relative to the predictive power of simple aggregation. The fact that children of partisans in the United States seem to inherit their fathers' loyalties at higher rates than their Canadian counterparts do, for instance, indicates not that partisanship is intrinsically more heritable in the United States than in Canada, only that US parties are smaller in number and bigger in size than the Canadian ones.

In the account of impact from inheritance on volatility – or lack thereof – what leaps to the eye is the United States. Its place in the volatility league tables is contingent on which electoral arena supplies the data. The House is a global benchmark for stability; the presidency was a leader in volatility. This arena difference extends to other facets of electoral choice, including the very foundations of the vote (Shafer and Johnston 2006). The divergence captured in this paper probably reflects the geography of messaging. This in turn affects how individual shifts translate into aggregate ones. In the presidential arena, gross individual turnover is quite efficiently converted into net shifts between parties. Major-party presidential candidates send nationwide signals. Indeed, these signals are probably more consistent across locales than the appeals made by parties in Westminster systems. In the latter, some of the party signal is distorted as it passes through local candidates. In US House elections, this local distortion is carried even further, as much of the signalling is purely local and often at cross purposes with the rest of the party. By implication, this increases the surplus of gross turnover relative to countrywide net shifts. It bears repeating that the US electorates exhibiting these contrasting patterns comprise the same people. The temporal gap between the behaviours in question is often no more than a few seconds.

One might object that this divergence no longer holds. Successive presidential elections now resemble each other closely, much as House elections traditionally did. House elections, for their part, have come to resemble parliamentary ones, as ideologically cohesive teams now fight for all the marbles, and control of the chamber changes hands every few years. The two US arenas have, in short, converged. But this objection proves the point. It is hard to believe that US voters have undergone a fundamental change in their individual psychologies, certainly not in the cognitive part. And yet the system has changed profoundly.

Both US observations – divergence in earlier decades and convergence in recent ones – go to the same point. We cannot account for aggregate patterns, much less for differences in such patterns, simply by summing up individual propensities. These propensities may co-vary with aggregate patterns, but this is as likely to be effect as cause. As Achen (2002, 166) puts it:

> ... the great majority of the evidence cited in this article refers to studies of population or subpopulation averages. Often these averages are the only socially relevant outcomes. But then, as long as the average voter responds correctly, the data will look as though everyone did. The fact that the model is rather poor at the individual level may make almost no difference for the purposes of social explanation. A large group covers a multitude of individual sins.

Or as Berelson et al. (1954, 297) put it, paraphrasing Durkheim (1938), "the essence of sociological method is its concern with *rates*." Aggregate outcomes require aggregate explanations.

Appendix: Sources of Survey Data

Each survey used in this chapter embodies a multi-stage sample and face-to-face interviews. Questions about electoral behaviour are all retrospective. Influence from the American National Election Studies is substantial in all the surveys.

Political Action I

This is the common core of an eight-nation project, where individual national surveys had additional country-specific content. Fieldwork took place from 1973 to 1976. Co-principal investigators are Klaus R. Allerbeck, Max Kaase, Hans-Dieter Klingemann, Leopold Rosenmayer, Anselm Eder, Inga Findl, Elfriede Urbas, Philip C. Stouthard, Felix Heunks, Cees J. De Graaf, Mark Abrams, Alan Marsh, Samuel H. Barnes, Ronald Inglehart, M. Kent Jennings, Barbara G. Farah, Pertti Pesonen, David K. Matheson, Risto Sänkiaho, Giovanni Sartori, Alberto Marradi, Giacomo Sani, Henry H. Kerr, David Handley, Charles Roig, and Dusan Sidjanski.

Accessible from GESIS Data Archive as ZA0765. Further details can be found at https://doi.org/10.4232/1.0765. Additional cross-sections and panels were conducted in some of the participating countries.

The principal publication from this project is Samuel H. Barnes and Max Kaase, *Political action: Mass Participation in Five Western Democracies.* Beverly Hills: Sage, 1979.

Canadian National Election Study, 1974

This study was conducted by Harold D. Clarke, Jane Jenson, Lawrence LeDuc, and Jon Pammett. Accessible from the Inter-university Consortium for Political and Social Research at https://doi.org/10.3886/ICPSR07379.v1

Australian National Political Attitudes Study, 1967

This study was conducted by Donald Aitkin, Michael Kahan, and Donald E. Stokes as part of a projected two-wave study. The second wave never materialized. Details on the survey and downloads are available at https://www .icpsr.umich.edu/web/ICPSR/studies/7282. No subsequent Australian study used this study's sampling strategy and mode.

NOTES

1   Although see below for a different reading of the seeming fit between Converse and Lipset and Rokkan.
2   A search on scholar.google.ca reveals decade by decade citation rates ranging from 67 in the 1970s to 305 in the 2010s, with an increased number each consecutive decade.
3   Converse's own thoughts about the impact of parents starts at p. 154.
4   This point is made with considerable emphasis in Bartels and Jackman (2014).
5   The Lipset-Rokkan analysis of mechanisms starts at p. 52 and includes notable failures as well as successes. The focus is on:

> ... organizational developments and the freezing of political alternatives.... To understand the current alignments of voters in our different countries it is not enough to analyze the contemporary issues and the contemporary sociocultural structure; it is even more important to go back to the initial formation of party alternatives and to analyze the interaction between the historically established foci of identification and the subsequent changes in the structural conditions of choice. (p. 54)

6   This is not to say that history or memory do not matter. Bartels and Jackman (2014) show that new information weighs more heavily at certain stages of the life cycle than at others and does so in a manner consistent with Mannheim's (1952) notion of political generations. But the weights do not decrease monotonically with age and, indeed, are stronger in citizens' 30s than in their 20s.
7   Or even genetic transmission (Settle et al. 2009).
8   Sears' (1975) review of the early socialization literature finds little support for the quality of affective bonds as a condition for parent-child homology, however.
9   More precisely, the number of parties for which there is a plausible estimate of I_j^s.
10 The shares can sum to one.
11 The "closest to" wording mimics the standard US follow-up question, and it is tempting to infer that this correspondence pulls up the US percentage in the Political Action data set. As it happens, the Political Action data set also includes the standard US battery and the slippage between the two versions is not small. "Strong" partisans in the conventional format exhibit essentially no slippage between items. But for other categories the slippage is considerable. About 5 per cent of "weak" partisans and 13 per cent of "independent leaners" claim to be closest to

no party. Of respondents who are pure independents with the conventional question 33 per cent claim a party preference in the Political Action version.

12 The Political Action dataset also includes a corresponding question about the respondent's mother. I focus on the impact of paternal partisanship as, on average, fathers are more likely than mothers to have partisanship imputed to them. This is consistent with Converse (1969):

> Our first simplification is to hinge the whole political socialization process on the father, for *daughters* as well as *sons*. This decision flies in the face of so many recent and entirely credible findings that it may seem downright perverse …. The point is not that anything is wrong with the current socialization findings, but rather that the additional variance to be explained by taking account of permutations in parental identifications and sex of children (while of significance in themselves) is dwarfed by the extreme complications that would be entailed in this model. The cost-benefit answer was simply negative (155).

13 Figure 4.1 does not capture intensity of partisanship, in contrast to the exhibits in Converse (1969). Converse's coding could not be reproduced in these data, as the Political Action team simply did not ask about intensity. As it happens, the Civic Culture dataset he used also did not ask for partisan intensity in so many words. Rather it asked first-round non-partisans a follow-up for partisan leaning. Converse assigns respondents who react positively to the follow-up to a middle category of intensity, with respondents who acknowledge a party at the first query assigned to the maximum intensity. arguably, what the Civic Culture really captured was partisan direction only. The gaping measurement discrepancy between Converse and all who attempted to reproduce his findings may account for the apparent reproduction failures. See Byrne (2019) for a close analysis of the Converse data and for attempts to replicate its logic with other data sets.

14 These observations are not reported in a table or figure.

15 The fact that Australia, with rates of postwar immigration that rival Canada's, has a low percentage of non-partisan fathers is an interesting puzzle. This may reflect the fact that as of 1967, Britain and New Zealand, with substantially identical party systems to that in Australia, were more important sources of migration to that country than to Canada.

16 The basis for the choice of two decades is the following. First, using multiple elections takes us closer to notions of party systems and political generations than would the potentially idiosyncratic variance in, say, the most recent election. Second, a 21-year span starts with the coming of age of the median respondent in these surveys, which was 43. Third, as a practical matter, the span takes most of the systems back almost to the end of the Second World War, which for a large fraction of older respondents was the de facto coming of age. For the US, the calculation is for House elections.

17 Finland is represented by its parliamentary arena only. Finnish parliamentary elections are more frequent than presidential ones, newly elected presidents do

not usually dismiss the government in place, and the resignation of a government generally reflects parliamentary factors, not the pleasure of the president (Samuels and Shugart 2010).

References

Abramson, Paul R. 1976. Generational Change and the Decline of Party Identification in America: 1952–74. *American Political Science Review* 70: 469–78.
–   1992. Of Time and Partisan Instability in Britain. *British Journal of Political Science* 22: 381–95.
Achen, Christopher H. 1992. Social Psychology, Demographic Variables, and Linear Regression: Breaking the Iron Triangle in Voting Research. *Political Behavior* 14: 195–211
–   2002. Parental Socialization and Rational Party Identification. *Political Behavior* 24: 151–70.
Bartels, Larry M., and Simon Jackman. 2014. A Generational Model of Political Learning. *Electoral Studies* 33:7–18.
Berelson, Bernard R., Paul F. Lazarsfeld, and William N. McPhee. 1954. *Voting: A Study of Opinion Formation in a Presidential Campaign.* University of Chicago Press.
Butler, David E., and Donald E. Stokes. 1969. *Political Change in Britain.* Macmillan.
Byrne, Matthew. 2019. *The Social Learning Model: A Time to Review "Of Time and Partisan Stability."* The University of British Columbia, unpublished dissertation.
Converse, Philip E. 1969. Of Time and Partisan Stability. *Comparative Political Studies* 2: 139–71.
–   1976. *The Dynamics of Party Support: Cohort-Analyzing Party Identification.* Sage.
Converse, Philip E., and Georges Dupeux. 1962. Politicization of the Electorate in France and the United States. *Public Opinion Quarterly* 26: 1–23.
Durkheim, Emile. 1938. *The Rules of Sociological Method.* University of Chicago Press.
Green, Donald, Bradley Palmquist, and Eric Stickler. 2002. *Partisan Hearts and Minds: Political Parties and the Social Identities of Voters.* Yale University Press.
Inglehart, Ronald, and Avram Hochstein. 1972. Alignment and Dealignment of the Electorate in France and the United States. *Comparative Political Studies* 5: 343–72.
Jennings, M. Kent, Laura Stoker, and Jake Bowers. 2009. Politics across Generations: Family Transmission Re-examined. *Journal of Politics* 71: 782–99.
Johnston, Richard. 1985. The Reproduction of the Religious Cleavage in Canadian Elections. *Canadian Journal of Political Science* 18: 99–113.
Lijphart, Arend. 1977. *Democracy in Plural Societies: A Comparative Exploration.* Yale University Press.
Lipset, Seymour Martin, and Stein Rokkan. 1967. Cleavage Structures, Party Systems and Voter Alignments: An Introduction. In *Party Systems and Voter Alignments,* edited by Lipset and Rokkan, 1–64. Free Press.

Mannheim, Karl. 1952. The Problem of Generations. In *Essays on the Sociology of Knowledge*, edited by Paul Kecskemeti, 276–320. Routledge and Kegan Paul.

McPhee, William N., and Jack Ferguson. 1962. Political Immunization. In *Public Opinion and Congressional Elections*, edited by William N. McPhee and William A. Glaser, 155–79. Free Press.

Niemi, Richard G., G. Bingham Powell Jr, Harold W. Stanley, and C. Lawrence Evans. 1985. Testing the Converse Partisanship Model with New Electorates. *Comparative Political Studies* 18: 300–22.

Norpoth, Helmut. 1984. The Making of a More Partisan Electorate in West Germany. *British Journal of Political Science* 14: 53–71.

Pederson, Mogens. 1979. The Dynamics of European Party Systems: Changing Patterns of Electoral Volatility. *European Journal of Political Research* 7: 1–26.

Samuels, David J., and Matthew S. Shugart. 2010. *Presidents, Parties, and Prime Ministers: How the Separation of Powers Affects Party Organization and Behavior.* Cambridge University Press.

Sears, David O. 1975. "Political Socialization." In *Handbook of Political Science.* (Vol. 2.), edited by Fred I. Greenstein and Nelson W. Polsby, 93–136. Addison Wesley.

Settle, Jaime E., Christopher T. Dawes, and James H. Fowler. 2009. "The Heritability of Partisan Attachment." *Political Research Quarterly* 62: 601–13.

Shafer, Byron E., and Richard Johnston. 2006. *The End of Southern Exceptionalism: Class, Race, and Partisan Change in the Postwar South.* Harvard University Press.

5 Gods and Votes: A Granular Look at the Relationship between Religion and Voting Behaviour in Canada

ALEXIS BIBEAU, MARC ANDRÉ BODET, AND YANNICK DUFRESNE

Introduction

The interaction of religion and politics can be tense (Putnam and Campbell, 2010; Norris and Inglehart, 2011; Layman, 2001). While most mature parliamentary democracies have solved their old religious conflicts prior to the Second World War, some are still working hard to avoid the rise of religious cleavages in their politics. In the Canadian context, recent research suggests that traditional religious cleavages that gave birth to the Catholic-Liberal connection have simply disappeared without much of a fight (Rayside et al., 2017). But that does not mean that religion is not important in Canadian politics (Johnston, 2017; Blais, 2005; Guth and Fraser, 2001). It might simply be that its capacity to organize party and electoral politics has faded away.

Yet, there are some paradoxical aspects to the religion-election nexus in Canada. First, the Canadian federation went through a tumultuous first 50 years that led to the reorganization of party politics in a way that ensured the peaceful management of religious tensions (see Godbout and Høyland, 2013). Moreover, Canada has more recently attracted hundreds of thousands of people from parts of the world where religion is not only a central aspect of public life but also of electoral politics. Finally, while religiosity is often connected to social conservatism, religious identity among Catholic communities was aligned for almost a century with a Liberal Party that had strong roots in anti-clerical rhetoric and classical liberalism.

In this chapter, we try to tackle these issues at the intersection of religion and politics by investigating Canadians' political attitudes and voting behaviour in detail. In doing so, we make use of two sources of data. First, the 2015 Canadian Election Study is mobilized on its own. We then add for comparison and further inquiry purpose a dataset of 659,197 participants collected during the 2015 federal general election through passive sampling technique (Vox Pop Labs, 2015). These participants had to – among numerous other questions related to political and social issues – self-declare their religious affiliation, their vote intention, and numerous other individual characteristics and attitudes. The important part is that the sheer size of this dataset allows a granular look at different religious denominations that have, in the past, been either lumped together in vague categories, or simply been discarded due to lack of sufficient sample size. We first propose a critical look on previous works based primarily on the limits of pooling heterogeneous populations and its consequences. We then present our research design and provide a detailed description of the data at hand. Data analysis is presented in an exploratory fashion, followed by a general discussion on the future of research in the study of religion and politics in Canada.

This chapter focuses on political attitudes and electoral behaviour. We thus look at the effect of religion on civic duty, party identification, ideology, and vote choice. Though religion probably plays a role in many other contexts, we believe these four pillars play a fundamental role in Canadian politics. They also have been parts of the dominant research agenda in Canadian political behaviour since at least the 1960s.

Related to that, religion as a political factor has been one of Richard Johnston's constant preoccupations during his academic career. He has studied the topic thoroughly in the context of party politics, with a strong emphasis on Catholics. And because the Canadian ethno-religious landscape is changing at a rapid pace, it only makes sense to continue the work on the topic, to revisit what we think we know, and to refocus our efforts on new religious cleavages that have replaced the old *Catholic and Others* dynamics (Johnston, 2017).

The Role of Religion in Canadian Electoral Behaviour

Research on the predictors of voting behaviour in Canada has generally revolved around a series of determining predictors such as partisanship (Blais et al., 2002; Johnston, 2006), leader and party evaluation (Clarke et al., 1984), ideology (Cochrane, 2015; Blais et al., 2002), geography, and sociodemographic attributes (Anderson and Stephenson, 2010). As such, research on Canada most notably echoes findings on voting behaviour in the United States (Campbell et al., 1960) and the United Kingdom (Clarke et al., 2004).

The puzzling lack of partisan stability in Canada has, however, led to numerous critiques of such an import (see about partisanship LeDuc et al., 1984; Clarke and Stewart, 1987). Multipartyism and the absence of affiliation between provincial- and federal-level parties is in fact often thought to prevent the formation of strong partisan attachment (Gidengil, 1992). As such, the general academic consensus nowadays states that partisanship plays a role in structuring the electorate even though its importance is mitigated by other factors and appears weak when compared to what we observe in the United States (Nevitte et al., 2000).

In Canadian politics, religion has played a structural, sociological role for a long time. This might perhaps even be an understatement. In fact, as Johnston observes, "the single best predictor of major party support in Canadian elections was religious denomination" during most of the twentieth century (2017, 101). The effect of religious cleavages on electoral politics is a characteristic of the Canadian context. However, it has been largely underplayed in the media and mainstream political talk (Mendelsohn and Nadeau, 1997). In the Canadian scholarly debate, however, this powerful explanatory factor has been the object of numerous studies (see, for instance, Meisel, 1956; Anderson, 1966; Lijphart, 1979; Blais, 2005; Wilkins-Laflamme, 2016). But the conclusions of that debate were rather elusive and contentious. A major scholar of the religious cleavage in Canada, William Irvine (1974) called it a "house guest that had overstayed his welcome." That was 50 years ago.

Yet, the religious cleavage is especially striking when it comes to the relationship between Liberals and Catholics. This alliance had a lasting impact on the Liberals' successes for almost a hundred years.[1] Even looking at most recent decades, Blais notes that "[t]hroughout all these elections [from 1975 to 2004], everything else being equal, the propensity to vote Liberal in Ontario and Atlantic Canada increases by 18 points when the person is Catholic." (2005, 823) This electoral relationship was considered one of the lasting puzzles of Canadian politics, mainly because "Catholics vote differently but they do not appear to differ on the issues" (Blais, 2005, 829).

What could be made of this? Johnston, most notably, argues that the interplay of religion and electoral behaviour must be understood through "processes outside citizens' families of origin" (Johnston, 1985, 108). Instead, he proposes to consider it through the lenses of geographic and social context (Johnston, 1985; 1991). Socialization at the local level must be understood has a major determinant of political affiliation – an analysis extended and confirmed by Bélanger and Eagles (2006). This fact, in Johnston's account, induces a form of distinctly Catholic *ethos* which had its roots in a "non-British conception" of Canada's identity (Johnston, 2017, 130). That was highly consequential because the non-British, autonomous conception of Canada was a Liberal trademark for most of the twentieth century. Johnston's thesis is furthermore strengthened by the fact that – as debate surrounding the political identity of Canada faltered in the early 2000s – the Catholic-Liberal relationship almost entirely disappeared.

Catholics are not the sole denomination with historic ties to a party. Protestants also play a part in the heightening of religious cleavages. Studies demonstrate that Protestants had and still have a deep-running connection with the Conservatives. This relationship is perhaps historically less acute than the one between the Catholics and the Liberals, but there is strong evidence of a profound alignment of Protestant denominations with the Conservatives (Gidengil et al., 2006). For example, Guth and Fraser (2001) show that Evangelical

Protestants tilted towards what was then the Reform Party, while Mainline Protestants were a core electorate of the late-Progressive Conservatives. Even though there were important political distinctions between the two parties,[2] and while they were at first competitors for quite distinct segments of the electorate, their fusion in 2003 merely created a larger Protestant coalition. This growing strength of the Protestant-Conservative alliance is corroborated by recent studies (Malloy, 2011; Gidengil et al., 2009; Rayside et al., 2017).

The growth in cohesion is interesting in the face of issues specifically salient to Evangelicals, an active segment of the Conservative voting base. In fact, Kay et al. (2009) notice a distinct pattern between Evangelicals and other Protestants regarding issues such as same-sex marriage and abortion. As they note, 78.9 per cent of Evangelical partisans tied to the Conservatives are against same-sex marriage, compared to 59.2 per cent of Mainline Protestants and 58.4 per cent of Catholics. This intra-Protestant variation is also striking for abortion, where over 85.8 per cent of Evangelicals – but only 50.9 per cent of Mainline Protestants – are opposed to it (Kay et al., 2009, 6-7). Still, Minkenberg (2010) and Kay et al. (2009) remind us that our understanding of religious cleavages among Christian voters needs to be refined. What about Canadian voters of other denominations? The lack of sufficient data on these populations in traditional surveys has made empirical inference almost impossible. We thus know very little about their electoral behaviour, and what we know often comes from studies about immigration and diversity.

Research Design

In this chapter, we study the intersection of religious denominations, political attitudes, and electoral behaviour in more details. We estimate linear probability models using a series of religious affiliations as an explanatory variable of duty to vote, left-right ideology, party identification, and vote intention. To do so, we use two surveys conducted during the 2015 Canadian federal election by two different research teams.

The first survey is the 2015 Canadian Election Studies (CES). We only make use of the phone component of the survey conducted during the campaign where 4,202 respondents were interviewed on different days. The second survey is part of the 2015 Vox Pop Labs' Vote Compass project (VPL), in which 1,297,361 participants filled that large-scale online survey, conducted through a passive sampling campaign in traditional and social media. In both cases, some questions were asked about specific issues, the electoral campaign, and other political attitudes, in addition to conventional socioeconomic questions such as religious denominations and localization.

We begin our analysis with a series of parametric estimations with data taken from the CES. Since we are trying to make an argument for the study of all religions in electoral behaviour, we feel it is appropriate to start with the flagship of electoral surveys. We go as far as possible with the CES dataset before moving to a much larger pool of observations, included in the VPL data.

Data Analysis

The CES, Civic Duty, and Partisanship

The CES asks respondents to identify their religious affiliation. Respondents could either give a denomination or answer "None," "Don't have one," or "Atheist." These last three answers are lumped together in the "No religion" category. The other respondents are found in the following categories: Catholics, Orthodox Christians, Anglicans, Baptists, Lutherans, Pentecostalists, Presbyterians, members of the United Church of Canada, Other Christians (Protestants, Christians, Christian Reformists, members of the Salvation Army, and Mennonites), Jews, Muslims, Hindus, Sikhs, and Buddhists. Denominations with very few respondents are dropped. It is interesting to note that, contrary to Christian denominations, Muslims are considered a single group in the CES despite profound cleavages between Sunnis and Shias. The reader would notice that we have regrouped a very heterogeneous group of denominations in the "Other Christian" category. We have done so for two reasons. First, we want to ease comparison between the CES and VPL dataset. That necessitates some rounding in operationalization. Second, we want to make sure we have enough respondents in each category.

We thus have 3,905 valid respondents as our working sample, with large proportions of Catholics (36% of the raw data) and atheists and non-religious persons (26%), followed by Other Christians (13%), members of the United Church of Canada (7%), and Anglicans (7%). The residuals are composed of respondents from other denominations (all below >3%). There are 12 Sikhs in the 2015 CES sample. They are all found in Ontario and British Columbia. There is a single Buddhist in Atlantic Canada, with only a few in other provinces for a raw total of 11 respondents. There are no respondents who have declared to be Jewish neither in Atlantic Canada, nor in Saskatchewan or Alberta.

First, we want to see if religious denominations are correlated with certain attitudes and behaviours. We look at civic duty and then partisan identification. To measure civic duty, respondents were asked the following question: "Is voting a duty or a choice?" We estimate a linear model in probability[3] that includes, as control variables, if the respondent was born in Canada, and the respondent's gender, language of interview, age and age squared, education, and province of residence. We then add a series of dichotomous variables for each religious denomination, keeping atheists and non-religious respondents as the reference category.[4] Many other explanatory variables discussed in the previous section could have been added but we want to restrain our model to be able to compare the estimates with the VPL dataset variables. Data is weighted and robust standard errors are computed. In our weighted sample 72 per cent of respondents consider that voting is a duty.

As shown in figure 5.1,[5] we find differences between certain religious denominations and atheists on civic duty, though the gain in terms of variance explained compared to the base model is less than two percentage points. Still, results suggest that some who identify to a religious denomination are more likely to consider voting a duty than those who do not. We indeed find strong and statistically significant effects for Sikhs (+35%), Pentecostalists (+20%), Anglicans (+13%), Catholics (+9%), and members of the United Church (+9%) compared to the reference category. These differences with the reference category are also substantial but not statistically significant for Jews, Lutherans, and Hindus. Only Buddhists, Muslims and Presbyterians tend to consider the act of voting more as a choice than a duty compared to those who do not have a religion, though these relationships are not statistically significant. We suspect that a bigger sample among these denominations would have helped estimates to reach statistical significance since the size of these effects are quite important.

We now look at party identification as a measure of how partisanship is correlated with religious denomination. We make use of the classic question about closeness to a political party, and we add the condition that to be considered a partisan, a respondent needs to "very" or "fairly strongly" identify to that party. We find that 41 per cent of respondents do not identify with one of the five main parties. The Liberals and the Conservatives are the two parties with the most partisans with 22 per cent and 20 per cent respectively, followed by the New Democrats at 12 per cent. Less than 3 per cent of respondents identify with either the Bloc Québécois or the Greens. We have recoded this variable into a dichotomous measure that differentiates those who are strong partisans and those who are not. Again, we estimate a linear model in probability that includes, as control variables, country of birth, gender, language of interview, age, age squared, education, and province of residence. We then add the series of dichotomous variables for each religious denomination, keeping those with no religion as the reference group. Campaign and party-related variables are again excluded from the model.

Figure 5.1 shows that certain denominations tend to be associated with more partisanship. Jewish respondents (+16%) and Muslims (+16%) are more partisan than atheists and non-religious individuals, as are certain Protestant denominations such as Lutherans (+19%) and Pentecostalists (+20%). We also find strong effect for Presbyterians and Baptists, but these two estimates do not reach the usual level of statistical significance. Interestingly, Hindus and Sikhs seem to be less prone to declare partisanship than those with no religion

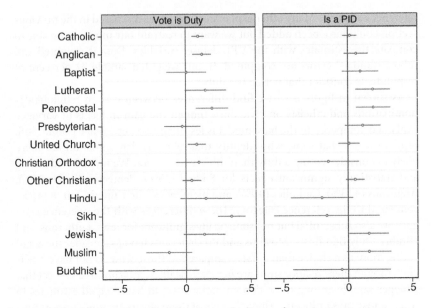

Figure 5.1. Civic duty, party identification, and religious denominations
Data: CES (2015).
Method: Multiple linear probability models.
Notes: n = 3,782. Points represent coefficient estimates from LPM models. Dependent variables are *Civic duty* and *Partisan identification*. The reference category is atheists and non-religious respondents. Models include covariates – born in Canada, gender, language of interview, age and age squared, education, and province of residence. See table 5.1 for details.

though the relationship is substantial but not significant. Raw cross-tabulations tend to suggest that these negative relationships might be caused by the absence of partisanship in these two communities outside the Liberal Party of Canada. The addition of religious denomination only improves the precision of the model at the margins.

VPL Survey and Ideology

The VPL data collected through Vote Compass is one of a kind. Despite making use of passive sampling techniques, this educative project has been able to reach hundreds of thousands of Canadians during federal and provincial general elections. Here, we focus on the 2015 Canadian federal election campaign version of this survey. These data offer a well-suited comparison with the CES data, at least on certain variables of interest.

There is no sample weight available for VPL data. The proportions of religious denominations are somewhat different than with the weighted CES, but the ranking of denominations remains roughly the same. There are fewer Catholics (29%) and more atheists and no religion (52%),[6] but the main difference is the number of respondents. This is especially spectacular for smaller denominations. For example, there are 3,783 Sikhs in the sample, 10,791 Jews, and 9,012 Buddhists. Some denominations are not very common in some provinces – especially in Atlantic Canada and the Territories – but this illustrates the heterogeneous religious landscape of Canada. And even in these cases, the quantities are sufficient. For example, there are 51 Hindus in the sample in Nova Scotia and 44 Muslims in Newfoundland and Labrador, quantities undoubtedly unheard of in traditional surveys.

We first look at the ideological positioning of participants on an 11-point scale, where lower values mean more to the left while higher values mean more to the right. Again, the reference category is those with no religion and atheists. Once list-wise deletion is performed, we are left with 653,281 observations. Statistical significance is thus less informative in this context, since standard error are extremely narrow with such a massive sample. What matters is the size of estimates.

Figure 5.2 show estimates where the reference category is atheists. Results clearly show that participants who declare having a religious denomination are more to the right, except for Buddhists. Pentecostalists (+1.7 on a 0 to 10 scale), Baptists (+1.6), and Orthodox Christians (+1.3) are on average the most on the right relative to the reference group. On the other hand, the least on the right are Buddhists (−.1), Jews (+.5), Muslims (+.5) members of the United Church of Canada (+.7), and Sikhs (+.8). There is a lot of variation among Protestant denominations, from Pentecostalists to Anglicans and members of the United Church of Canada. Finally, the sizes of these effects are much stronger than for sociodemographic variables and province of residence.

We also want to know if, among those with a religious affiliation, there are ideological differences. We thus exclude atheists and use Catholics as the reference category. Figure 5.3 shows the estimates. The darker dots are essentially a translation of what we had in figure 5.2 centred around Catholics. What is most interesting here is to compare lighter dots that represents the average ideological difference between very religious participants on each group and very religious Catholics. Also, if we compare for each group darker and lighter dots, we have the difference between the very religious participants and those with weaker religiosity.

There are no general patterns of variation between participants with very high religiosity of given religious denomination and the rest of their coreligionists. There are important exceptions, though. Among Christian denominations, very religious Anglicans are more to the left (−.48) than less religious ones, relative to their Catholic counterparts. The same thing is observed among Lutherans (−.26) and members of the United Church (−.91). There are also substantial

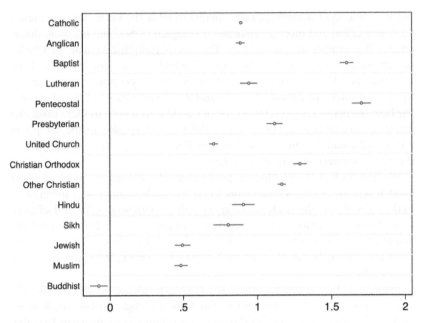

Figure 5.2 Left-right ideology and religion
Data: VPL (2015).
Method: Multiple linear probability models.
Notes: n = 653,281. Points represent coefficient estimates from LPM. The dependent variable is *Left-right ideology*. The reference category is atheists. Negative values show left-wing ideology and positive values show right-wing ideology. Models include covariates – born in Canada, gender, language of interview, age and age squared, education, and province of residence. See table 5.2 for details.

differences among Muslims (−.64) and Buddhists (−1.73). The most notable case in the opposite direction is among Jewish participants. We find that very religious members of this denomination are much more to the right than their less religious coreligionists, again relative to their Catholics counterparts.

Religions and Vote Intentions

Finally, we want to look at the flagship variable of electoral behaviour, that is, vote intention. The ideal scenario would be to estimate vote choice models (one in Quebec, one outside of it) that would include the usual sociodemographic (country of birth, gender, language, age, education, location) and campaign-related (feeling thermometers, strategic concerns, party identification) predictors and see if religious denomination plays a role in the process. Though the full model converges using a multinomial logit, we are left with serious concerns

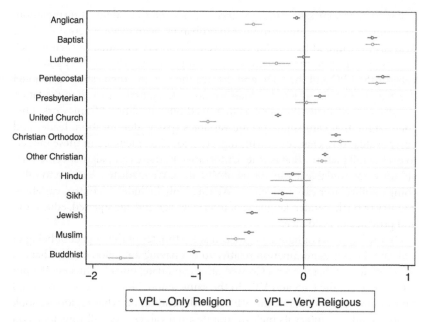

Figure 5.3 Left-right ideology and religious denominations only
Data: VPL (2015).
Method: Multiple linear probability models.
Notes: $n = 321,557$ for *Only Religion*; $n = 56,848$ for V*ery Religious*. Points represent coefficient estimates from LPM. The dependent variable is *Left-right ideology*. The reference category is Catholics. Negative values show left-wing ideology and positive values show right-wing ideology. Models include covariates – born in Canada, gender, language of interview, age and age squared, education, and province of residence. *Only Religion* includes all observations. *Very Religious* includes only those for whom religion is "very important." See table 5.2 for details.

regarding the quality of these estimates when we look at the number of cases in certain cells of the matrix. If we start by looking at the raw data for vote intention, location, and religious denominations, the pattern becomes even more concerning.

If we look at vote intentions for major parties and religious denominations, we find that among the 60 potential combinations outside Quebec (15 denominations and four parties), 32 (53%) have nine or more observations. In Quebec, the situation is even worst. Of the 75 potential combinations, only 8 (11%) have nine or more observations. We are making inference on very few cases, especially for New Democrats, Greens, and Bloc Québécois voters. VPL data does not suffer from such a shortcoming but is not representative of the voting population in the traditional sense. Therefore, it is better to compare estimates of the two datasets.

For comparison's sake with previous analysis and to facilitate interpretation, we estimate a series of linear models in probability with dyads where only those who say they intend to vote for two given parties are included in each model. In more practical terms, we choose for example, those who say they intend to vote for the LPC and the NDP and discard the rest. We then estimate a model that tries to explain why individuals would pick the first rather than the latter. Results are essentially the same as in a maximum-likelihood framework. One could argue that campaign-specific variables (party identification, leader and party evaluations, chances of winning, etc.) could be included in these models to get the full picture. That is true. Unfortunately, these campaign-specific variables are not available in our subset of VPL data. We made the decision to value comparability over exhaustiveness. We thus only include, as control variables, country of birth, gender, language of interview, age and age squared, education, and province of residence.

On the left panel of figure 5.4, we can see estimates of the impact of being of a given religious denomination relative to not having a religion on the chances of voting for a Liberal over a Conservative candidate, outside Quebec. We put estimates from the CES and VPL in the same graph. Since there are up to 200 times more respondents in the VPL data depending on what region we look at, its confidence intervals melt to infinitesimal values. We will thus focus on the magnitudes of point estimates. Again, one must keep in mind that these estimates represent differences between atheists and non-religious participants and religious ones.

The first conclusion is that, despite the difference in size and sampling techniques – plus the fact that the CES data is weighted while VPL data is not –, the differences in estimates for the Liberals/Conservatives dyad are quite small, apart from Sikh respondents. This is good news both for users of CES data who can still make use of very few cases in each religious denomination to estimate a multivariate model and users of passive samples such as VPL concerned with the lack of representativeness in the data. Only VPL estimates are discussed in detail here.

It is also interesting to note that most religious denominations lean more towards the Conservatives than the Liberals. There are exceptions, though. Muslims and the Sikhs are more likely to support the Liberals (+18% and +9%), while Hindus and Buddhists do not show a substantial tendency to vote one way or the other. There are strong effects in favour of the Conservatives also. Pentecostalists (44%), Baptists (38%), and Lutherans (20%) have the strongest effects among Protestants. Orthodox Christians (25%), Jews (21%), and members of the United Church of Canada (11%) are not far behind. Catholics (12%) and Anglicans (13%) are more likely to support the Conservatives than the Liberals relative to atheists and non-religious respondents. We find similar patterns in Quebec (see the right window) but with smaller magnitudes.

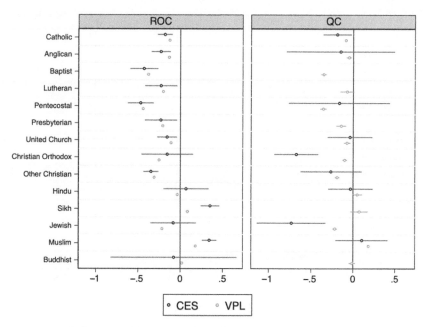

Figure 5.4. Difference in probability of voting for the LPC over the CPC
Data: CES and VPL, 2015.
Method: Multiple linear probability models.
Notes: $n = 1,621$ for CES and 318,075 for VPL in the ROC panel; $n = 228$ for CES and 106,696 for VPL in the QC panel. Points represent coefficient estimates from LPM. The dependent variable is the *probability of voting for the LPC over the CPC*. Positive values show the probability of support for LPC. Negative values show the probability of support for the CPC. Models include covariates – born in Canada, gender, language of interview, age and age squared, education, and province of residence. See table 5.3 for details.

Figure 5.5 shows estimates for the LPC/NDP dyad, both in Quebec and in the rest of Canada (ROC). While some Christian denominations such as Catholics (+12%), Anglicans (+10%), Presbyterians (+9%), and Orthodox Christians (+10%) tend to support the LPC more than the NDP, the margins are quite small. As with the LPC/CPC dyad, the Liberal Party benefits from a solid advantage among Sikh (+19%) but also Hindu (+17%) voters over the NDP compared to atheists and non-religious voters. The story in Quebec is one of amplification as the Liberal advantage among religious denominations is stronger in almost every case, except Catholics. For instance, differences in support for the LPC is up by 9 per cent among Anglicans, 14 per cent among Orthodox Christians, and 11 per cent among Muslims in Quebec compared to those same

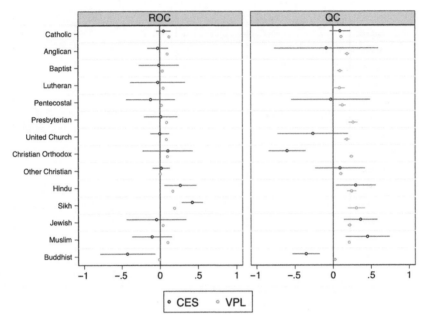

Figure 5.5. Difference in probability of voting for the LPC over the NDP
Data: CES and VPL, 2015.
Method: Multiple linear probability models.
Notes: $n = 1,324$ for CES and 363,505 for VPL in the ROC panel; $n = 327$ for CES and 206,725 for VPL in the QC panel. Points represent coefficient estimates from LPM. The dependent variable is the *probability of voting for the LPC over the NDP*. Positive values show the probability of support for LPC. Negative values show the probability of support for the NDP. Models include covariates – born in Canada, gender, language of interview, age and age squared, education, and province of residence. See table 5.4 for details.

denominations in the ROC. Catholics in Quebec are slightly more supportive of the LPC (+12%) than their coreligionists in other provinces (+11%).

The final estimations are from a CPC/NDP dyad. Figure 5.6 shows a clear advantage for the Conservatives among most religious denominations relative to the NDP, with the exceptions of Muslim, Buddhist, and Sikh voters. The strongest effects are for Pentecostalists (+44%), Baptists (+39%), Presbyterians (+29%), and Orthodox Christians (+33%), though the advantage for the Conservatives is apparent for every Christian denomination. In fact, levels of support for the CPC compared to the NDP are stronger for religious individuals compared to non-religious ones. Yet, unlike the LPC/CPC dyad, the story in Quebec is less straightforward. While patterns of support for the CPC are similar in both Quebec and the ROC, there is some variation in magnitude. For

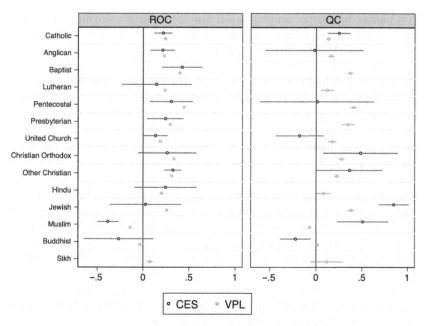

Figure 5.6. Difference in probability of voting for the CPC over the NDP
Data: CES and VPL, 2015.
Method: Multiple linear probability models.
Notes: *n* = 1,305 for CES and 270,670 for VPL in the ROC panel; *n* = 295 for CES and 175,607 for VPL in the QC panel. Points represent coefficient estimates from LPM. The dependent variable is the *probability of voting for the CPC over the NDP*. Positive values show the probability of support for CPC. Negative values show the probability of support for the NDP. Models include covariates – born in Canada, gender, language of interview, age and age squared, education, and province of residence. See table 5.5 for details.

instance, Catholics' probability of support for the CPC over the NDP is, again, more pronounced in the ROC (+24%) than in Quebec (+13%). These results – combined with the ones from the LPC/CPC and LPC/NDP models – attest to the heterogenous effect of religious denominations on voting behaviour.

Discussion

In this chapter, we have looked at four expressions of electoral behaviour, using two sources of data. Our main conclusions are threefold. First, it is necessary to go beyond the CES survey to study smaller religious groups and religiosity more thoroughly. The number of observations found in the CES is often sufficient for bivariate analyses but might raise concerns in a multivariate framework. Our conclusions suggest that sample size is an issue particularly when inferential analysis is at play. Adding more cases improves efficiency and allows for the confirmation of statistical relationships that otherwise would suffer from a lack of power.

Second, religious denomination matters beyond Catholicism. We do not claim to be original here. We show in the introduction that this topic has received good attention in recent work. But the more traditional stream of research on voting behaviour has still not incorporated this dimension in canonical models. For instance, we show that the effect certain religious denominations have on ideology is substantial. The sizes of some estimates are quite spectacular. As such, a larger dataset gives us the means to uncover previously hidden voting patterns. Among these patterns, findings related to the relationship between the Conservatives and certain branches of Protestantism matter because they provide a more granular look at the heterogeneous political implications of religion in Canada (Rayside et al. 2017; Malloy 2011). In fact, support towards the Conservatives appears to be correlated with specific Protestant denominations like Pentecostalism and Baptism. These findings have implications for research in Canadian politics because, in a country where religious and linguistic diversity is increasingly important, we need to adjust the canonical model and to move beyond simply adding a dichotomous variable for Catholics and maybe a measure of religiosity.

Third, the historical alliance between the Liberals and Catholics has disappeared by 2015. At least, we can say that Catholics do not vote differently anymore when they are compared to a mix bag of all other religious voters. As such, our findings corroborate Johnston's conclusions (2017), although they do not address the paradox raised by Blais (2005).

What are the consequences of emerging religious dynamics on the Canadian party system? Traditionally, Canadians voters from ethnocultural minority groups have opted en masse to support the Liberal Party even though their social and economic preferences would logically lead them to support the Conservative Party. The Liberal branding was simply too strong. Under Stephen Harper's leadership, the attempt to attract this religious electorate has somewhat been successful (Flanagan 2009). Our results highlight the high potential for right-of-centre parties among religious voters if these parties can reconcile the conflicting relationship between diversity and their ideology.

It would thus be a mistake to conclude that we can simply drop an important aspect of social identity like religion because the great paradox of Canadian electoral politics has dissolved. The fact remains that religion plays a crucial role in Canadian politics – a role that nowadays goes beyond simple denominational opposition between Catholics and Protestants (Minkenberg, 2010; Kay et al., 2009). As a matter of fact, in his recent book, Johnston (2017) titled his chapter on religion *Catholics and Others*. It is time to disentangle the *Others* into something much more sophisticated.

Appendix

Table 5.1. Civic duty, partisanship, and ideology

Dependent variables	Civic duty (CES)	Partisan identification (CES)
Catholic	.09* (.02)	.02 (.03)
Anglican	.12* (.04)	.06 (.05)
Baptist	.01 (.08)	.10 (.07)
Lutheran	.15 (.08)	.19* (.07)
Pentecostal	.20 (.06)	.20* (.07)
Presbyterian	−.02 (.07)	.12* (.07)
United Church	.09* (.04)	.01 (.04)
Christian Orthodox	.10 (.09)	−.15 (.12)
Other Christian	.05 (.04)	.06 (.04)
Hindu	.16 (.10)	−.20 (.12)
Sikh	.35* (.05)	−.17 (.21)
Jewish	.14 (.08)	.16* (.08)
Muslim	−.13 (.09)	.16 (.09)
Buddhist	−.25 (.18)	−.05 (.19)
Born in Canada	.02 (.03)	.02 (.04)
Female	.02 (.02)	.00 (.02)
French	.05 (.05)	−.21* (.05)
Age	.01* (.01)	−.00 (.00)
Age Squared	−.00 (.00)	.00 (.00)
More than HS	.08 (.04)	.07 (.04)
U. degree	.19* (.04)	.11* (.04)
(Provinces FE)	Yes	Yes
Intercept	.23* (.10)	.54* (.11)
N	3,782	3,782
R-Squared	.06	.04
Root MSE	.44	.49

Data: CES (2015).
Method: Multiple linear probability models.
Note: The reference category is atheists and non-religious respondents.
* $p < .05$; robust standard error.

Table 5.2. Left-right ideology and religion

Dependent variables	Ideology vs. Atheists (VPL)	Ideology vs. Catholics (VPL)	Ideology vs. Catholics – Very Religious (VPL)
Catholic	.89* (.01)		
Anglican	.88* (.02)	−.76* (.02)	−.48* (.04)
Baptist	1.60* (.02)	.65* (.02)	.65* (.04)
Lutheran	.94* (.03)	−.01* (.03)	−.27* (.07)
Pentecostal	1.70* (.03)	.75* (.03)	.69* (.04)

(Continued)

Table 5.2. Continued

Dependent variables	Ideology vs. Atheists (VPL)	Ideology vs. Catholics (VPL)	Ideology vs. Catholics – Very Religious (VPL)
Presbyterian	1.11* (.03)	.15* (.02)	.02 (.05)
United Church	.71* (.01)	−.25* (.02)	−.91* (.4)
Christian Orthodox	1.29* (.02)	.31* (.02)	.35* (.05)
Other Christian	1.16* (.01)	.20* (.02)	.17* (.03)
Hindu	.90* (.04)	−.11* (.04)	−.13 (.10)
Sikh	.80* (.05)	−.20* (.05)	−.22 (.12)
Jewish	.49* (.03)	−.49* (.03)	−.087 (.08)
Muslim	.48* (.02)	−.52* (.02)	−.64* (.04)
Buddhist	−.08* (.03)	−1.04* (.03)	−1.73* (.06)
Born in Canada	.01 (.01)	.05* (.01)	−.09* (.02)
Female	−.49* (.00)	−.51* (.01)	−.47* (.02)
French	.09* (.01)	−.01* (.01)	−.14* (.04)
Age	.02* (.00)	.01* (.00)	.00 (.00)
Age Squared	−.00* (.00)	−.00 (.00)	−.00 (.00)
More than HS	−.08* (.01)	−.06* (.01)	−.16* (.04)
U. degree	−.34* (.01)	−.28* (.01)	−.54* (.03)
(Provinces FE)	Yes	Yes	Yes
Intercept	3.90* (.02)	5.03* (.03)	5.86* (.10)
N	653,281	321,557	56,848
R-Squared	0.08	0.04	0.07
Root MSE	1.98	1.93	2.15

Data: VPL (2015).
Method: Multiple linear probability models.
Note: Refences categories are atheists (column 1) and Catholics (column 2 and 3).
* $p < .05$; robust standard errors.

Table 5.3. Probability of voting for the LPC over the CPC

Dependent variables	LPC/CPC (CES, ROC)	LPC/CPC (CES, QC)	LPC/CPC (VPL, ROC)	LPC/CPC (VPL, QC)
Catholic	−.18* (.04)	−.18* (.09)	−.13* (.00)	−.09* (.00)
Anglican	−.23* (.06)	−.15 (.33)	−.13* (.00)	−.05* (.02)
Baptist	−.42* (.09)	−.16 (.31)	−.38* (.00)	−.34* (.02)
Lutheran	−.22* (.10)		−.20* (.01)	−.07 (.04)
Pentecostal	−.47* (.08)		−.44* (.01)	−.35* (.02)
Presbyterian	−.23* (.10)		−.21* (.01)	−.14* (.03)
United Church	−.16* (.06)	−.04 (.13)	−.11 (.00)	−.07* (.02)
Christian Orthodox	−.16 (.16)	−.67* (.13)	−.25* (.01)	−.10* (.01)
Other Christian	−.34* (.05)	−.26 (.18)	−.31* (.00)	−.19* (.01)
Hindu	.07 (.14)	−.03 (.13)	−.04* (.01)	.05 (.02)
Sikh	.35* (.06)		.08* (.01)	.07 (.05)
Jewish	−.07 (.14)	−.73* (.21)	−.21* (.01)	−.22* (.01)
Muslim	.34* (.04)	.10 (.16)	.17* (.00)	.18* (.01)
Buddhist	−.08 (.38)		.02* (.01)	−.01 (.02)

(Continued)

Table 5.3. Continued

Dependent variables	LPC/CPC (CES, ROC)	LPC/CPC (CES, QC)	LPC/CPC (VPL, ROC)	LPC/CPC (VPL, QC)
Born in Canada	.04 (.04)	.02 (.11)	−.00 (.00)	−.00 (.01)
Female	.06* (,03)	.17* (.07)	.09* (.00)	.12* (.00)
French	.50* (.07)	−.27* (.08)	.09* (.00)	−.09* (.00)
Age	.00 (.01)	−.01 (.01)	−.01* (.00)	−.01* (.00)
Age Squared	−.00 (.00)	.00 (.00)	.00 (.00)	.00 (.00)
More than HS	.03 (.07)	−.19 (.13)	.03* (.00)	.04* (.01)
U. degree	.03 (.06)	−.09 (.13)	.11* (.00)	.12* (.01)
(Provinces FE)	Yes	No	Yes	No
Intercept	.50* (.15)	1.17* (.32)	.76* (.01)	.93* (.01)
N	1,621	228	318,075	106,696
R-Squared	0.15	0.17	0.11	0.06
Root MSE	0.47	0.47	0.45	0.46

Data: CES and VPL (2015).
Method: Multiple linear probability models.
* *p* < .05; robust standard errors.

Table 5.4. Probability of voting for the LPC over the NDP

Dependent variables	LPC/NDP (CES, ROC)	LPC/NDP (CES, QC)	LPC/NDP (VPL, ROC)	LPC/NDP (VPL, QC)
Catholic	.04 (.05)	.09 (.07)	.12* (.00)	.11* (.00)
Anglican	−.03 (.07)	−.09 (.35)	.10* (.00)	.19* (.02)
Baptist	−.01 (.13)		.03 (.01)	.09* (.02)
Lutheran	−.03 (.18)		.04* (.01)	.08* (.04)
Pentecostal	−.12 (.16)	−.03 (.26)	.02* (.01)	.12* (.02)
Presbyterian	.01 (.11)		.09* (.01)	.26* (.03)
United Church	−.00 (.06)	−.27 (.23)	.08* (.00)	.18* (.01)
Christian Orthodox	.10 (.17)	−.60* (.12)	.10* (.01)	.24* (.01)
Other Christian	.01 (.06)	.09 (.17)	.00 (.00)	.10* (.01)
Hindu	.27* (.11)	.30* (.13)	.17* (.01)	.24* (.03)
Sikh	.42* (.07)	.36* (.11)	.19* (.01)	.31* (.06)
Jewish	−.04 (.20)		.04* (.01)	.21 (.01)
Muslim	−.11 (.13)	.45* (.15)	.10* (.01)	.21* (.01)
Buddhist	−.42* (.19)	−.36* (.09)	−.01 (.01)	.02 (.01)
Born in Canada	.01 (.06)	−.12 (.11)	.02* (.00)	−.01 (.00)
Female	.01 (.04)	−.01 (.06)	−.02* (.00)	−.04* (.00)
French	−.25 (.15)	−.34* (.08)	−.05* (.00)	−.14* (.00)
Age	.01 (.01)	−.01 (.01)	.00* (.00)	−.01* (.00)
Age Squared	−.00 (.00)	.00 (.00)	.00* (.00)	−.01 (.00)
More than HS	.07 (.08)	−.21 (.11)	.01* (.00)	−.05* (.00)
U. degree	.15* (.07)	−.22* (.11)	−.00 (.00)	−.07* (.00)
(Provinces FE)	Yes	No	Yes	No

(Continued)

Table 5.4. Continued

Dependent variables	LPC/NDP (CES, ROC)	LPC/NDP (CES, QC)	LPC/NDP (VPL, ROC)	LPC/NDP (VPL, QC)
Intercept	.31* (.18)	1.25* (.28)	.49* (.01)	.65* (.01)
N	1,324	327	363,505	206,725
R-Squared	0.06	0.13	0.03	0.04
Root MSE	0.48	0.47	0.49	0.46

Data: CES and VPL (2015).
Method: Multiple linear probability models.
* *p* < .05; robust standard errors.

Table 5.5. Probability of voting for the CPC over the NDP

Dependent variables	CPC/NDP (CES, ROC)	CPC/NDP (CES, QC)	CPC/NDP (VPL, ROC)	CPC/NDP (VPL, QC)
Catholic	.22* (.05)	.25* (.06)	.24* (.00)	.13* (.00)
Anglican	.21* (.07)	−.18 (.27)	.23* (.00)	.16* (.02)
Baptist	.42* (.11)	.13 (.32)	.39* (.01)	.37* (.02)
Lutheran	.14 (.19)		.23* (.01)	.12* (.04)
Pentecostal	.30* (.11)		.44* (.01)	.41* (.02)
Presbyterian	.24* (.10)		.29* (.01)	.35* (.04)
United Church	.13* (.06)	−.18 (.13)	.18* (.00)	.17* (.02)
Christian Orthodox	.25 (.16)	.48* (.20)	.34* (.01)	.27* (.02)
Other Christian	.32* (.05)	.36* (.18)	.31* (.00)	.22* (.01)
Hindu	.24 (.17)	.85* (.08)	.20* (.01)	.08* (.04)
Sikh	.27 (.19)		.08* (.01)	.11 (.10)
Jewish			.25* (.00)	.37* (.02)
Muslim	−.38* (.06)	.50* (.14)	−.14* (.01)	−.07* (.01)
Buddhist	−.26 (.19)	−.22* (.08)	.03* (.01)	−.01 (.01)
Born in Canada	−.00 (.04)	−.15 (.11)	.14* (.00)	−.00 (.00)
Female	−.45* (.03)	−.21* (.05)	−.10* (.00)	−.10* (.00)
French	−.61* (.07)	−.06 (.12)	−.12* (.00)	−.03* (.00)
Age	.00 (.01)	−.01 (.01)	.01* (.00)	.00* (.00)
Age Squared	−.00 (.00)	.00 (.00)	−.00* (.00)	.00* (.00)
More than HS	−.00 (.06)	−.02 (.13)	−.02* (.00)	.01* (.00)
U. degree	.09 (.06)	−.12 (.13)	−.10* (.00)	−.14* (.00)
(Provinces FE)	Yes	No	Yes	No
Intercept	.27* (.16)	.80* (.32)	.21* (.01)	.24* (.01)
N	1,305	295	270,670	175,607
R-Squared	0.16	0.16	0.16	0.07
Root MSE	0.44	0.45	0.45	0.40

Data: CES and VPL (2015).
Method: Multiple linear probability models.
* *p* < .05; robust standard errors.

NOTES

1 See Johnston's figures on the emergence and decline of Catholic-Liberal alignment (2017, 111 and 121).
2 See Lustztig and Wilson (2005) on the moral dimension of the Protestant political cleavage.
3 Though logit and probit models are the most common parametric tools when the explained variable is a dichotomous response, we opt for a linear model in probability to facilitate interpretation and comparison between models. Results remain the same if maximum likelihood estimations are conducted instead.
4 It has been suggested to use Catholics as the reference category since the political science literature is mostly focused on that denomination. However, exploratory analyses have shown a clear difference between non-religious and religious persons. Having atheists as the reference category allows us to illustrate this difference.
5 Regression tables are found in the appendix.
6 VPL and CES data are also distinct in the distribution of respondents, since VPL are self-selected into the survey. We attend to this issue by controlling for socio-demographic factors on which we expect the sample to diverge from the general population, including age, gender, and education.

References

Anderson, C.D., and L.B. Stephenson. 2010. *Voting Behaviour in Canada*. UBC Press.
Anderson, G.M. 1966. "Voting Behaviour and the Ethnic-Religious Variable: A Study of a Federal Election in Hamilton, Ontario." *Canadian Journal of Economics and Political Science/Revue canadienne d'Économiques et Science Politique* 32 (1): 27–37. https://doi.org/10.2307/139946
Bélanger, P., and M. Eagles. 2006. "The Geography of Class and Religion in Canadian Elections Revisited." *Canadian Journal of Political Science/Revue canadienne de science politique* 39 (3): 591–609. https://doi.org/10.1017/S0008423906060227
Blais, A. 2005. "Accounting for the Electoral Success of the Liberal Party in Canada: Presidential Address to the Canadian Political Science Association London, Ontario, June 3, 2005." *Canadian Journal of Political Science/Revue canadienne de science politique* 38 (4): 821–40. https://doi.org/10.1017/S0008423905050304
Blais, A., E. Gidengil, R. Nadeau, and N. Nevitte. 2002. *Anatomy of a Liberal Victory: Making Sense of the Vote in the 2000 Canadian Election*. Broadview Press.
Campbell, A., P. Converse, W. Miller, and D.E. Stokes. 1960. *The American Voter*. University of Chicago Press.
Clarke, H.D., J. Jenson, L. LeDuc, and J.H. Pammett. 1984. *Absent Mandate: The Politics of Discontent in Canada*. Gage.
Clarke, H.D., D. Sanders, M.C. Stewart, and P. Whiteley. 2004. *Political Choice in Britain*. Oxford University Press.

Clarke, H.D. and M.C. Stewart. 1987. "Partisan Inconsistency and Partisan Change in Federal States: The Case of Canada." *American Journal of Political Science* 31 (2): 383–407. https://doi.org/10.2307/2111081

Cochrane, C. 2015. *Left and Right: The Small World of Political Ideas.* McGill-Queen's University Press.

Flanagan, Tom. 2009. *Harper's Team. Behind the Scenes in the Conservative Rise to Power.* McGill-Queen's University Press.

Gidengil, E. 1992. "Canada Votes: A Quarter Century of Canadian National Election Studies." *Canadian Journal of Political Science/Revue canadienne de science politique* 25 (2): 219–48. https://doi.org/10.1017/S0008423900003966

Gidengil, E., A. Blais, J. Everitt, P. Fournier, and N. Nevitte. 2006. "Back to the Future? Making Sense of the 2004 Canadian Election Outside Quebec." *Canadian Journal of Political Science/Revue canadienne de science politique* 39 (1): 1–25. https://doi.org /10.1017/S0008423906060069

Gidengil, E., P. Fournier, J. Everitt, N. Nevitte, N., A. Blais. 2009. "The Anatomy of a Liberal Defeat." In *Annual Meeting of the Canadian Political Science Association (May 2009).* Carleton University.

Godbout, J.-F. and B. Høyland. 2013. "The Emergence of Parties in the Canadian House of Commons (1867–1908)." *Canadian Journal of Political Science/Revue canadienne de science politique* 46 (4): 773–97. https://doi.org/10.1017/S0008423913000632

Guth, J.L., and C.R. Fraser. 2001. "Religion and Partisanship in Canada." *Journal for the Scientific Study of Religion* 40 (1): 51–64. https://doi.org/10.1111/0021-8294.00037

Irvine, W.P. 1974. "Explaining the Religious Basis of the Canadian Partisan Identity: Success on the Third Try." *Canadian Journal of Political Science/Revue canadienne de science politique* 7 (3): 560–63. https://doi.org/10.1017/S0008423900040786

Johnston, R. 1985. "The Reproduction of the Religious Cleavage in Canadian Elections." *Canadian Journal of Political Science/Revue canadienne de science politique* 18 (1): 99–113. https://doi.org/10.1017/S000842390002922X

– 1991. *The Geography of Class and Religion in Canadian Elections.* In *The Ballot and its Message: Voting in Canada,* edited by Joseph Wearing, 108–35. Copp Clark Pitman.

– 2006. "Party Identification: Unmoved Mover or Sum of Preferences?" *Annual Review Political Science* 9: 329–51. https://doi.org/10.1146/annurev.polisci .9.062404.170523

– 2017. *The Canadian Party System: An Analytic History.* UBC Press.

Kay, B.J., A.M. Perrella, and S.D. Brown. 2009. "The Religion Enigma: Theoretical Riddle Or Classificational Artifact?" *Laurier Institute for the Study of Public Opinion and Policy.*

Layman, G. 2001. *The Great Divide: Religious and Cultural Conflict in American Party Politics.* Columbia University Press.

LeDuc, L., H.D. Clarke, J. Jenson, and J.H. Pammett. 1984. "Partisan Instability in Canada: Evidence from a New Panel Study." *American Political Science Review* 78 (2): 470–84. https://doi.org/10.2307/1963376

Lijphart, A. 1979. "Religious vs. Linguistic vs. Class Voting: The 'Crucial Experiment' of Comparing Belgium, Canada, South Africa, and Switzerland." *American Political Science Review* 73 (2): 442–58. https://doi.org/10.2307/1954890

Lusztig, M., and J.M. Wilson. 2005. "A New Right? Moral Issues and Partisan Change in Canada." *Social Science Quarterly* 86 (1): 109–28. https://doi.org/10.1111 /j.0038-4941.2005.00293.x

Malloy, J. 2011. "Between America and Europe: Religion, Politics and Evangelicals in Canada." *Politics, Religion & Ideology* 12 (3): 317–33. https://doi.org/10.1080/215676 89.2011.596416

Meisel, J. 1956. "Religious Affiliation and Electoral Behaviour: A Case Study." *Canadian Journal of Economics and Political Science/Revue canadienne d'Économiques et Science Politique* 22 (4): 481–96. https://doi.org/10.2307/138709

Mendelsohn, M., and R. Nadeau. 1997. "The Religious Cleavage and the Media in Canada." *Canadian Journal of Political Science/Revue canadienne de science politique* 30 (1): 129–46. https://doi.org/10.1017/S0008423900014967

Minkenberg, M. 2010. "Party Politics, Religion and Elections in Western Democracies." *Comparative European Politics* 8 (4): 385–414. https://doi.org/10.1057/cep.2009.5

Nevitte, N., A. Blais, E. Gidengil, and R. Nadeau. 2000. *Unsteady State: The 1997 Canadian Federal Election*. Oxford University Press.

Norris, P., and R. Inglehart. 2011. *Sacred and Secular: Religion and Politics Worldwide*. Cambridge University Press.

Putnam, R.D., and D.E. Campbell. 2010. *American Grace: How Religion Divides and Unites Us*. Simon and Schuster.

Rayside, D., Sabin, J., and P.E. Thomas. 2017. *Religion and Canadian Party Politics*. UBC Press.

Vox Pop Labs. 2015. *Vote Compass, 2015 Canadian Federal Election*. Vox Pop Labs.

Wilkins-Laflamme, S. 2016. "The Changing Religious Cleavage in Canadians' Voting Behaviour." *Canadian Journal of Political Science/Revue canadienne de science politique* 49 (3): 499–518. https://doi.org/10.1017/S0008423916000834

6 Is Quebec's Distinctiveness an Artefact?

PATRICK FOURNIER AND ANDRÉ BLAIS

Quebeckers like to think that they are a distinct society. Indeed, the surveys regularly published about Canadian public opinion usually portray Quebeckers as holding views that differ substantially from those in the rest of Canada (ROC).[1] But are these differences real? We need to keep in mind that in all the surveys conducted in Canada there are in fact two questionnaires, one in English and one in French. There is always the possibility that the differences in answers that we observe reflect the fact that the questions are different rather than Quebec society's distinctiveness.

This is a real concern. Achieving linguistic equivalence is a formidable challenge, and so we should always ask ourselves, when we compare Quebeckers' and non-Quebeckers' views, whether the differences in opinion stem from differences in question wording. A good example of this can be found in Blais and Gidengil (1993). They observe that only 51 per cent of francophone Quebeckers responded in a 1990 survey that things would be worse if we stopped having elections, compared to 76 per cent in the rest of Canada. They go on to show that the difference vanishes when they control for the language of interview and suggest that the difference reflects subtle discrepancies in question wording.

This is an issue to which Richard Johnston has paid close attention. Johnston insisted on the necessity of including francophone scholars in the Canadian Election Study team. Furthermore, he was keenly aware of the challenges of achieving linguistic equivalence in the construction of the CES questionnaires, so much so that the 1988 team decided to simultaneously elaborate the French and the English questionnaires. That is, the team would first discuss the English version, then the French version, and then reconsider the English version, and so on until they were satisfied that the two versions were equally satisfactory and equivalent. This required a lot of time and effort, but there was no doubt in Johnston's mind that it was absolutely necessary. This was part of Johnston's broader preoccupation with measurement issues, especially with how small differences in question wording can have huge consequences. We have in mind

Johnston's (1992) masterful study about how the distribution of party identification depends immensely on how the party identification question is asked, a study that we discuss below.

One area in which Quebeckers have been found to hold distinct opinions has constituted a central portion of Richard Johnston's research program: views towards diversity (Johnston and Soroka, 2001; Soroka, Johnston, and Banting, 2004, 2006a, 2006b, 2007; Banting et al., 2006; Kay and Johnston, 2006; Stolle, Soroka, and Johnston, 2008; Johnston et al., 2010, 2017; Citrin, Johnston, and Wright, 2012; Soroka et al., 2016, 2017; Wright et al., 2017). Johnston's own work has shown that Quebec is less supportive of multicultural policies, Muslim religious garb, and religious accommodation than both the rest of Canada and the United States (Wright, Johnston, Citrin, and Soroka, 2017). Other studies have provided evidence along the same lines (Berry, Kalin, and Taylor, 1977; Lambert and Curtis, 1983; Bolduc and Fortin, 1990; Berry and Kalin, 1995; Bilodeau et al., 2012; Harell et al., 2012; Dufresne et al., 2019). For instance, using thermometer ratings, Bilodeau, Turgeon, and Karakoç (2012) document that Quebeckers express less positive feelings towards racial minorities than residents of any other province between 1988 and 2008. More recently, in the 2015 Canadian Election Study (CES), there is a 5-point gap between Quebec and the rest of Canada in average ratings of racial minorities (75 vs 80 points, on a 0–100 scale).

There are debates in the literature about whether these differences in views are produced by cultural insecurity, economic threat, group identity, secularism, support for independence, racism, or other factors (e.g., Harell et al., 2012; Turgeon and Bilodeau, 2014; Dufresne et al., 2019). We concentrate on a different question: Does the lower level of support for ethnic diversity in Quebec stem from a genuine difference in tolerance, or could it be attributable to differences in question wording? We examine this question by relying on a question-wording experiment regarding thermometer ratings that was included into the post-election wave of the web component of the 2015 Canadian Election Study.

The Relevance of Questionnaire Design

Why should public opinion be affected by question wording? The malleability of citizens' opinions is at odds with a traditional view of attitudes as preexisting crystallized evaluations of an object (Allport, 1935; Sherif and Cantril, 1947; Fazio, 1989). According to this perspective, people either have a position on, say, abortion or they don't. Public opinion surveys simply ask them to reveal the existence and nature of that position. Such an approach, sometimes dubbed the "file-drawer model" (Wilson and Hodges, 1992), has trouble accounting for the instability of responses over time (Converse, 1964), their susceptibility to context effects (Schuman and Presser, 1981), and the willingness of respondents to provide opinions on obscure and even fictitious issues (Bishop et al., 1986). These findings sometimes lead to the conclusion that many citizens hold "non-attitudes" (Converse, 1970).

More contemporary perspectives consider attitudes as "temporary constructions" (Strack and Martin, 1987; Tourangeau and Rasinski, 1988; Wilson and Hodges, 1992, 40; Sudman et al., 1996; Tourangeau et al., 2000). Survey answers emerge from a series of processes: "understanding the question, retrieving material about the issue, deriving an answer from what has been retrieved, and reporting the answer" (Tourangeau, 1992, 36). More specifically, judgments are formed by averaging across the sample of considerations currently accessible in memory (Zaller, 1992; Zaller and Feldman, 1992; Tourangeau et al., 2000). These are considerations that have been recently activated, whether by personal experiences, a discussion with a friend, or a news report. If, as Sudman and colleagues suggest, "human judgment is always context-dependent" (1996: 124), then opinions ought to fluctuate when context varies.

In fact, a substantial body of research has documented the impressive effects that questionnaire construction can have on survey responses (e.g., Schuman and Presser, 1981; Schwarz and Sudman, 1992; Tourangeau et al., 2000; Soroka et al., 2016). The way questions and response options are worded, formatted, and ordered influences the attitudes that are expressed. Thus, surveys do not simply capture pre-existing attitudes; they also, to some extent, mould and shape opinions. The most rigorous method to identify the effects of questionnaire design is a survey experiment. If respondents of a given survey are randomly assigned to two different design choices, then any difference in opinion between the two groups must be produced by the questionnaire.

A classic illustration of this work is the survey experiment conducted by Donald Rugg (1941) and later replicated by Schuman and Presser (1981). Respondents were asked: "Do you think the United States should [allow / forbid] public speeches against democracy?" People were much less willing to forbid such speeches than to not allow them (1941: 46% vs 62%; 1981: 21% vs 48%). Apparently, forbidding is perceived as tougher than not allowing; it is more difficult to agree to forbid, even though formally the meanings of the two terms are identical.

Richard Johnston transformed our understanding of political behaviour in Canada with a question-wording experiment. Prior research had concluded that party identification was basically meaningless in Canada, because it was too volatile and unstable, essentially following vote choice (Meisel, 1975; LeDuc et al., 1984). Johnston (1992) demonstrated that this reading was erroneous, due to a party identification question that failed to offer a response option capturing non-partisans. Individuals without a real attachment to a political party felt compelled to name the party for which they were voting. When appropriately measured, party identification is in fact a meaningful and powerful driver of Canadians' political behaviour (Nevitte et al., 2000; Blais et al., 2002; Gidengil et al., 2006, 2012; Fournier et al., 2013).

The Question-Wording Experiment

In this chapter, we focus on a common question battery that is found in many surveys, including the Canadian Election Study: feeling thermometers. Respondents are asked to indicate how they feel towards a variety of targets: political parties, party leaders, geographic entities, and social groups. Here are examples in both English and French of the formulations used in the Canadian Election Study since 1997.[2]

> And now some questions about countries and groups. How do you feel about CANADA? Use any number from zero to one hundred. Zero means you really DISLIKE Canada, and one hundred means you really LIKE Canada.
>
> Et maintenant quelques questions sur des pays et des groupes. Que pensez-vous du CANADA? Utilisez n'importe quel nombre entre zéro et cent. Zéro veut dire que vous n'aimez vraiment pas du tout le Canada, et cent veut dire que vous aimez vraiment beaucoup le Canada.

Several differences are evident, particularly with regards to the labelling of the endpoints of the scale. First, *aimer* may mean either "like" or "love," and thus the French question may have stronger emotional connotations. Second, in French, "not at all" is added to the low end of the scale, and "a lot" to the high end. Bottom line, "really dislike" is not the same as "really do not like/love at all," and "really like" is not the same as "really like/love a lot." Because the French endpoints are labelled in a more extreme fashion, it may be more difficult for francophones to give very high and very low ratings. Therefore, all else equal, the French questions could elicit ratings that are closer to the midpoint and that exhibit less variance than English questions. This could potentially produce artificially lower evaluations of minority groups among francophone respondents.

A survey experiment can shed some light on this. All thermometer questions in the post-election wave of the online component of the 2015 Canadian Election Study were the subject of a question-wording experiment. Half the respondents encountered the wording that has been used in the CES since 1997 (version 1 below), the other half received a formulation comparable to the wording employed during the Johnston era, i.e., the 1988 and 1993 CES (version 2 below). The second wording is more consistent across languages.[3] Both the English and the French versions label the endpoints of the scale as "very negative" and "very positive."

Version 1

How do you feel about the following countries and groups? Slide the slider to any number from 0 to 100. Zero means you really DISLIKE the country or group, and 100 means you really LIKE the country or group.

Que pensez-vous des pays et des groupes suivants? Glissez le curseur sur n'importe quel nombre entre 0 et 100. 0 veut dire que vous N'AIMEZ VRAIMENT PAS DU TOUT le pays ou le groupe, et 100 veut dire que vous AIMEZ VRAIMENT BEAUCOUP le pays ou le groupe.

Version 2

How do you feel about the following countries and groups? Slide the slider to any number from 0 to 100. Zero means a very NEGATIVE score, and 100 means a very POSITIVE score.

Que pensez-vous des pays et des groupes suivants? Glissez le curseur sur n'importe quel nombre entre 0 et 100. 0 veut dire un score très NÉGATIF, et 100 veut dire un score très POSITIF.

Assignment to question wording version was randomized. And randomization was conducted faithfully, since question version is unrelated to various demographic factors: notably, age, gender, education, income, geographic region, and language of interview.

If differences in public opinion disappear when we move from version 1 (with important differences across languages) to version 2 (which is more consistent across languages), then question wording creates artefactual discrepancies. If the differences in thermometer evaluations persist regardless of question wording, then this suggests that Quebec francophones are really distinct.

To make sure the comparison is clear, the analysis will be limited to two groups: (1) Quebeckers whose mother tongue is French and who completed the questionnaire in French, and (2) non-Quebeckers whose mother tongue is English and who completed the questionnaire in English. We deliberately avoid the complications linked to groups with "conflicting" characteristics (and small numbers in a typical survey) such as English Quebeckers and French non-Quebeckers.

Findings

To begin, let's focus on the impact of the survey experiment on the groups' mean thermometer ratings. We start with the measure from the introduction: evaluations of racial minorities. Quebec has significantly lower ratings than

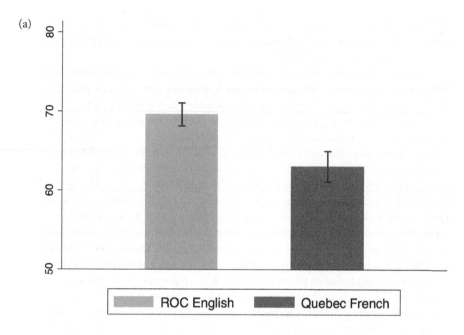

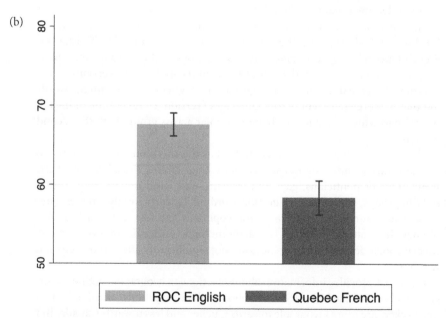

Figure 6.1. Mean evaluations of racial minorities: (a) Version 1 (like/dislike); (b) Version 2 (positive/negative)

ROC in both version 1 (figure 6.1a) and version 2 (figure 6.1b). Under both versions, francophone Quebeckers emerge as less supportive of racial minorities than anglophones from ROC.[4]

To simplify the presentation of results for other measures, we only report the differences between the two groups for each question wording. For instance, the first graph of figure 6.2 presents data already shown in figures 6.1a and 6.1b. The darker dot displays the difference in evaluations of racial minorities between French Quebec and English ROC under version 1 (as seen by the gap in figure 6.1a). Since the scores are lower in Quebec than in ROC, the difference is negative. The 95 per cent confidence interval around the dot indicates the difference between the two groups is statistically significant ($p < .05$). The lighter dot reveals the difference in thermometer ratings of racial minorities between Quebec and ROC under version 2 (as seen in figure 6.1b). As we noted previously, this difference is also significant, since the confidence interval does not span 0. The first graph in figure 6.2 also suggests that the Quebec/ROC difference in ratings of racial minorities is larger with version 2 than with version 1. However, this gap between the two Quebec/ROC differences is not statistically significant.[5] Throughout the analyses, we focus on whether there are significant differences between French Quebeckers and English non-Quebeckers under the two wording versions, and whether the size of the difference is significantly larger under one version or the other.

The other measures reported in figure 6.2 concern evaluations of immigrants, Muslims, and Aboriginals. The patterns are always the same. In all instances, French Quebeckers give significantly lower ratings of these groups than their English counterparts from the rest of the country under both versions of the question. And the difference is not significantly higher or lower with the wording that is more consistent across languages (version 2), except for ratings of Aboriginals which are statistically more similar across groups with the second version.

The results in figure 6.3 demonstrate that the thermometer questions do not necessarily lead to significantly lower ratings among French Quebeckers. Evaluations of politicians, gays and lesbians, and feminists are very similar in both groups, whatever the question wording. Unsurprisingly, French Quebeckers are more positive towards francophones and less so towards anglophones. The pattern, however, is exactly the same under the two versions, so we can conclude that the differences are not significantly affected by question wording.

Figure 6.4 provides information about reactions to geographic entities: Canada, Quebec, and the United States. Nobody will be surprised to see that French Quebeckers are more favourable towards Quebec and less towards Canada. But the differences are very small with respect to the United States, just borderline significant with version 2. More importantly, the differences between French

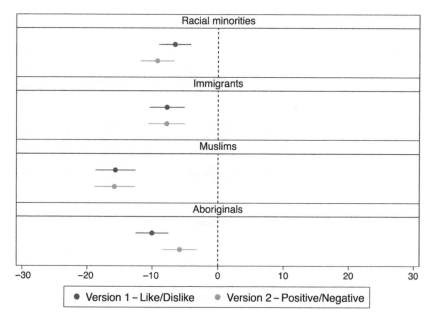

Figure 6.2. Differences in the evaluations of ethnic and religious groups between French Quebeckers and English Non-Quebeckers
Note: Estimates are OLS coefficients from separate bivariate models where the thermometer score (on a scale from 0–100) is regressed on a dichotomous variable that distinguishes French Quebeckers (score = 1) from English non-Quebeckers (score = 0). 95% confidence intervals are shown.

Quebeckers and English Canadians from other provinces are not statistically different across the two versions, except for ratings of Quebec, where the distance is smaller under version 2.

Finally, we consider the impact of the survey experiment on the variance in opinion distributions. We anticipate that the more extreme end labels of French wording 1 would reduce the amount of variance since respondents might be more likely to avoid the extremities. The first two columns of table 6.1 present the gap in standard deviations between versions 1 and 2. A positive difference means that variance is larger with version 1, while a negative difference means that variance is smaller with version 1. In ROC, question wording does not matter: the average difference is almost nil (.1). In Quebec, eight of the twelve differences are negative, and three are significant. Consistent with expectations, variance is more pronounced under French version 2, but only slightly so; the average difference (−.9) represents less than 4 per cent of the mean standard deviation.

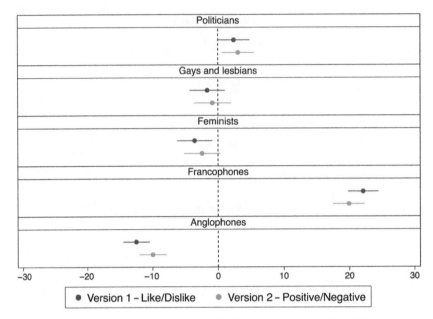

Figure 6.3. Differences in the evaluations of other groups between French Quebeckers and English Non-Quebeckers

Note: Estimates are OLS coefficients from separate bivariate models where the thermometer score (on a scale from 0–100) is regressed on a dichotomous variable that distinguishes French Quebeckers (score = 1) from English non-Quebeckers (score = 0). 95% confidence intervals are shown.

The last four columns of table 6.1 show the gap between versions in the proportion of ratings with values of exactly 0 and 100. Among both groups, very low scores were equally widespread across both question formulations. However, very high ratings exhibit a different pattern. Respondents were much less prone to give scores of 100 with the wording anchored by "very positive." This finding is unexpected, but it is present among both English non-Quebeckers and French Quebeckers to the same extent, so it is not responsible for differences in public opinion between the two groups. It seems that people are more willing to say that they really like something than they are very positive.

Conclusion

The starting point of this chapter is at the intersection of two of Richard Johnston's longstanding concerns during his career: the importance of survey question wording and of views regarding diversity. We investigated whether the way

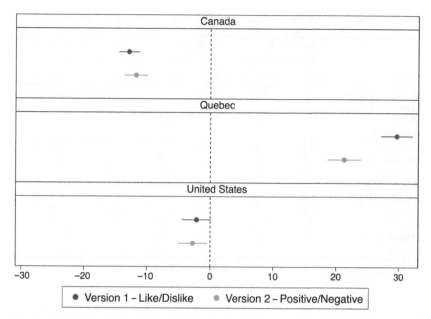

Figure 6.4. Differences in the evaluations of geographic entities between French Quebeckers and English Non-Quebeckers

Note: Estimates are OLS coefficients from separate bivariate models where the thermometer score (on a scale from 0–100) is regressed on a dichotomous variable that distinguishes French Quebeckers (score = 1) from English non-Quebeckers (score = 0). 95% confidence intervals are shown.

thermometer questions are formulated affects regional differences in evaluations of social groups in Canada. The study relied on a survey experiment conducted in the 2015 Canadian Election Study, where half the respondents received the regular wording that differs considerably between the English and French versions, while the other respondents received an older wording that is more consistent across languages.

It turns out that the patterns of public opinion observed in thermometer ratings among francophone Quebeckers and anglophone non-Quebeckers do not hinge on such question wording. No matter how the questions are asked, compared to the Rest of Canada, Quebeckers have significantly less positive evaluations of ethnic and religious minorities, English speakers, and Canada, significantly more positive evaluations of French speakers and Quebec, and similar evaluations of gays and lesbians, feminists, politicians, and the United States. Therefore, Quebec's distinctiveness does not appear to be a methodological artefact.

Table 6.1. Impact of question wording on opinion variance (version 1 *minus* version 2)

Categories	Difference in Standard Deviation		Difference in % of Very Low Scores (0)		Difference in % of Very High Scores (100)	
	ROC	Quebec	ROC	Quebec	ROC	Quebec
Racial minorities	.3	−1.6	−.1	−.5	4.3*	3.2*
Immigrants	−.2	.2	−.4	−.5	4.6*	3.1*
Muslims	.4	.7	−1.3	−1.5	4.6*	2.4*
Aboriginals	−.8	−.2	−.1	.1	5.2*	3.8*
Politicians	1.1	−.6	.2	−.5	.7	.3
Gays and Lesbians	−.9	−1.9*	−.8	.3	3.7*	1.5
Feminists	.4	−.6	−.5	−.7	4.2*	1.0
Francophones	.8	−1.7*	.1	.0	4.7*	12.7*
Anglophones	.0	.9	−.1	.5	6.7*	3.5
Canada	−2.7*	−.5	.0	−.6	23.3*	12.3*
Quebec	1.5*	−5.0*	−.7	−1.1*	3.0*	22.8*
United States	.8	.1	−.6	−.4	3.6*	3.5*
Average	.1	−.9	−.4	−.4	5.7	5.8

* significant at $p < .05$.

This does not mean that we should not pay attention to question wording and linguistic equivalence. There are instances where question wording does not make a big difference, and thermometer ratings appear to be such an instance, at least when comparing ROC and Quebec. But there are also cases where question wording matters a lot. Social scientists need to be preoccupied about measurement issues. Richard Johnston had many concerns in his quest for a deep understanding of Canadian society: concerns for geography, history, and religion most especially. But Canadian political science also gained tremendously because he took language, and the presence of a French community, most seriously.

NOTES

1 Some would argue that the Quebec/ROC comparison is not appropriate since it obfuscates regional differences within ROC. We cannot deal in detail with this issue here, but suffice it to say that the differences that we observe between Quebec and ROC hold when we can compare Quebec with only Ontario or only Western Canada.

2 These examples are drawn from the post-election wave of the RDD component of the 2015 CES.

3 Note that in both instances, the French introduction refers to *penser* ("think") rather than *sentir* ("feel"), the latter being less often used in French than the English "feel."

4   Also, the difference in support between versions 1 and 2 is significant in both ROC
and Quebec. Evaluations are less favourable, in both languages, when the question is
framed in terms of negative/positive than in terms of like/dislike.

5   More specifically, we performed OLS regressions with version 2 and French Quebec as
dichotomous independent variables along with the interaction term (version 2 x French
Quebec), and the interaction term is not significant. We have proceeded similarly for all
12 thermometer measures, and the few significant interaction effects are noted in the text.

References

Allport, Gordon W. 1935. "Attitudes." In *Handbook of Social Psychology*, edited by
C. Murchison, 798–844. Clark University Press.

Banting, Keith, Will Kymlicka, Richard Johnston, and Stuart Soroka. 2006. "Do
Multiculturalism Policies Erode the Welfare State? An Empirical Analysis."
In *Multiculturalism and the Welfare State: Recognition and Redistribution in
Contemporary Democracies*, edited by Keith Banting and Will Kymlicka, 49–91.
Oxford University Press.

Berry, John W., and Rudolf Kalin. 1995. "Multicultural and Ethnic Attitudes in Canada:
An Overview of the 1991 National Survey." *Canadian Journal of Behavioural Science*
27: 301–20. https://doi.org/10.1037/0008-400X.27.3.301

Berry, John W., Rudolf Kalin, and Donald M. Taylor. 1977. *Multiculturalism and Ethnic
Attitudes in Canada*. Supply and Services Canada.

Bilodeau, Antoine, Luc Turgeon, and Ekrem Karakoç. 2012. "Small Worlds of Diversity:
Views toward Immigration and Racial Minorities in Canadian Provinces." *Canadian
Journal of Political Science*, 45: 579–605. https://doi.org/10.1017/S0008423912000728

Bishop, George, Robert Oldendick, and Alfred Tuchfarber. 1986. "Opinions on Fictious
Issues: The Pressure to Answer Survey Questions." *Public Opinion Quarterly* 50:
240–50. https://doi.org/10.1086/268978

Blais, André, and Elisabeth Gidengil. 1993. "Things Are Not Always What They
Seem: French-English Differences and the Problem of Measurement Equivalence."
CanadianJournal of Political Science 26: 541–56. https://doi.org/10.1017
/S0008423900003449

Blais, André, Elisabeth Gidengil, Richard Nadeau, and Neil Nevitte. 2002. *Anatomy of
a Liberal Victory: Making Sense of the Vote in the 2000 Canadian Election*. Broadview
Press.

Bolduc, Denis, and Pierre Fortin. 1990. "Les francophones sont-ils plus 'xénophobes'
que les anglophones au Québec? Une analyse quantitative exploratoire." *Canadian
Ethnic Studies Journal* 22: 54–77.

Citrin, Jack, Richard Johnston, and Matthew Wright. 2012. "Do Patriotism and
Multiculturalism Collide? Competing Perspectives from Canada and the United
States." *Canadian Journal of Political Science* 45: 531–52. https://doi.org/10.1017
/S0008423912000704

Converse, Phillip E. 1964. "The Nature of Belief Systems in Mass Publics." In *Ideology and Discontent*, edited by D.E. Apter, 206–61. Free Press.

– 1970. "Attitudes and Non-Attitudes: Continuation of a Dialogue." In *The Quantitive Analysis of Social Problems*, edited by E.R. Tufte, 75–169. Addison-Wesley.

Dufresne, Yannick, Anja Kilibarda, André Blais, and Alexis Bibeau. 2019. "Religiosity or Racism? The Bases of Opposition to Religious Accommodation in Quebec." *Nations and Nationalism* 25: 673–96. https://doi.org/10.1111/nana.12429

Fazio, Russell H. 1989. "On the Functionality of Attitudes: The Role of Attitude Accessibility." In *Attitude Structure and Function*, edited by A.R. Pratkanis, S.J. Breckler and A.G. Greenwald, 153–79. Erlbaum.

Fournier, Patrick, Fred Cutler, Stuart Soroka, Dietlind Stolle, and Éric Bélanger. 2013. "Riding the Orange Wave: Leadership, Values, Issues, and the 2011 Canadian Election." *Canadian Journal of Political Science* 46: 863–97. https://doi.org/10.1017/S0008423913000875

Gidengil, Elisabeth, André Blais, Joanna Everitt, Patrick Fournier, and Neil Nevitte. 2006. "Back to the Future? Making Sense of the 2004 Canadian Election Outside Quebec." *Canadian Journal of Political Science* 39: 1–25. https://doi.org/10.1017/S0008423906060069

Gidengil, Elisabeth, Neil Neville, André Blais, Joanna Everitt, and Patrick Fournier. 2012. *Dominance and Decline: Making Sense of Recent Canadian Elections*. University of Toronto Press.

Harell, Allison, Stuart Soroka, Shanto Iyengar, and Nicholas Valentino. 2012. "The Impact of Economic and Cultural Cues on Support for Immigration in Canada and the United States." *Canadian Journal of Political Science* 45: 499–530. https://doi.org/10.1017/S0008423912000698

Johnston, Richard. 1992. "Party Identification Measures in Anglo-American Democracies: A National Survey Experiment." *American Journal of Political Science* 36: 542–59. https://doi.org/10.2307/2111490

Johnston, Richard, Keith Banting, Will Kymlicka, and Stuart Soroka. 2010. "National Identity and Support for the Welfare State." *Canadian Journal of Political Science* 43: 349–77. https://doi.org/10.1017/S0008423910000089

Johnston, Richard, and Stuart Soroka. 2001. "Social Capital in a Multicultural Society: The Case of Canada." In *Social Capital and Participation in Everyday Life*, edited by Paul Dekker and Eric M. Uslaner. Routledge.

Johnston, Richard, Matthew Wright, Stuart Soroka, and Jack Citrin. 2017. "Diversity and Solidarity: New Evidence from Canada and the US." In *The Strains of Commitment: The Political Sources of Solidarity in Diverse Societies*, edited by Keith G. Banting and Will Kymlicka, 152–76. Oxford University Press.

Kay, Fiona, and Richard Johnston. 2006. *Social Capital, Diversity, and the Welfare State*, UBC Press.

Lambert, Ronald, and James Curtis. 1983. "Opposition to Multiculturalism among Québécois and English-Canadians." *Canadian Review of Sociology* 20: 193–207. https://doi.org/10.1111/j.1755-618X.1983.tb00896.x

LeDuc, Lawrence, Harold Clarke, Jane Jenson, and John Pammett. 1984. "Partisan Instability in Canada: Evidence from a New Panel Study." *American Political Science Review* 78: 470–84. https://doi.org/10.2307/1963376

Meisel, John. 1975. "Party Images in Canada." *Working Papers on Canadian Politics.* McGill-Queen's University Press.

Nevitte, Neil, Blais, Elisabeth Gidengil, and Richard Nadeau. 2000. *Unsteady State: The 1997 Canadian Federal Election*, Oxford University Press.

Rugg, Donald. 1941. "Experiments in Wording Questions: II." *Public Opinion Quarterly* 5: 91–2. https://doi.org/10.1086/265467

Schuman, Howard, and Stanley Presser. 1981. *Questions and Answers in Attitude Surveys: Experiments on Question Form, Wording and Content.* Academic Press.

Schwarz, Norbert, and Seymour Sudman. 1992. *Context Effects in Social and Psychological Research.* Springer-Verlag.

Sherif, Muzafer, and Hadley Cantril. 1947. *The Psychology of Ego-Involvements: Social Attitudes and Identification.* Wiley.

Soroka, Stuart, Peter Loewen, Patrick Fournier, and Daniel Rubenson. 2016. "The Impact of News Photos on Support for Military Action." *Political Communication* 33: 563–82. https://doi.org/10.1080/10584609.2015.1133745

Soroka, Stuart, Richard Johnston, and Keith Banting. 2004. "Ethnicity, Trust, and the Welfare State." In *Cultural Diversity versus Economic Solidarity*, edited by Philippe van Parijs, 33–57. DeBoeck.

– 2006a. "Ethnicity, Trust, and the Welfare State." In *Social Capital, Diversity and the Welfare State*, edited by Fiona Kay and Richard Johnston. University of British Columbia Press.

– 2006b. "Immigration and Redistribution in a Global Era." In *Globalization and Egalitarian Redistribution*, edited by Pranab Bardhan, Sam Bowles, and Michael Wallerstein, 261–88. Princeton University Press and Russell Sage Foundation.

– 2007. "Ties That Bind? Social Cohesion and Diversity in Canada." In *Belonging? Diversity, Recognition and Shared Citizenship in Canada*, edited by Keith Banting, Thomas J. Courchene, and F. Leslie Seidle, 561–600. IRPP.

Soroka, Stuart, Richard Johnston, Anthony Kevins, Keith Banting, and Will Kymlicka. 2016. "Migration and Welfare State Spending." *European Political Science Review* 8: 173–94. https://doi.org/10.1017/S1755773915000041

Soroka, Stuart, Matthew Wright, Richard Johnston, Jack Citrin, Keith Banting, and Will Kymlicka. 2017. "Ethnoreligious Identity, Immigration and Redistribution." *Journal of Experimental Political Science* 4: 173–82. https://doi.org/10.1017/XPS.2017.13

Stolle, Dietlind, Stuart Soroka, and Richard Johnston. 2008. "When Does Diversity Erode Trust? Neighborhood Diversity, Interpersonal Trust and the Mediating Effect of Social Interactions." *Political Studies* 56: 57–75. https://doi.org/10.1111/j.1467-9248.2007.00717.x

Strack, Fritz, and Leonard L. Martin. 1987. "Thinking, Judging, and Communicating: A Process Account of Context Effects in Attitude Surveys." In *Social Information*

Processing and Survey Methodology, edited by H.-J. Hippler, N. Schwarz, and S. Sudman, 123–48. Springer-Verlag.

Sudman, Seymour, Norman M. Bradburn, and Norbert Schwarz, 1996. *Thinking About Answers: The Application of Cognitive Processes to Survey Methodology.* Jossey-Bass Publishers.

Tourangeau, Roger. 1992. "Context Effects on Responses to Attitude Questions: Attitudes as Memory Structures." In *Context Effects in Social and Psychological Research*, edited by N. Schwarz and S. Sudman, 35–48. Springer-Verlag.

Tourangeau, Roger, and Kenneth Rasinski. 1988. "Cognitive Processes Underlying Context Effects in Attitude Measurement." *Psychological Bulletin* 103: 299–314. https://doi.org/10.1037/0033-2909.103.3.299

Tourangeau, Roger, Lance J. Rips, and Kenneth Rasinski. 2000. *The Psychology of Survey Response.* Cambridge University Press.

Turgeon, Luc, and Antoine Bilodeau. 2014. "Minority Nations and Attitudes towards Immigration: The Case of Quebec." *Nations and Nationalism* 20: 317–36. https://doi .org/10.1111/nana.12068

Wilson, Timothy D., and Sara D. Hodges. 1992. "Attitudes as Temporary Constructions." In *The Construction of Social Judgments*, edited by L.L. Martin and A. Tesser, 37–66. Erlbaum.

Wright, Matthew, Richard Johnston, Jack Citrin, and Stuart Soroka. 2017. "Multiculturalism and Muslim Accommodation: Policy and Predisposition across Three Political Contexts." *Comparative Political Studies* 50: 102–32. https://doi .org/10.1177/0010414015626448

Zaller, John R. 1992. *The Nature and Origins of Mass Opinion.* Cambridge University Press.

Zaller, John R., and Stanley Feldman. 1992. "A Simple Theory of the Survey Response: Answering Questions Versus Revealing Preferences." *American Journal of Political Science* 36: 579–616. https://doi.org/10.2307/2111583

7 Concepts and Methods: How Definitions and Techniques Matter for Women's Political Participation

BRENDA O'NEILL

Introduction

Understanding how, when, and why different groups participate politically is a central question in democracies given that inequalities in political participation are very real. A well-functioning democracy requires minimum levels of engagement from all of its citizens, especially the most marginalized. Elections offer an opportunity for transmitting political preferences and selecting political representatives. Interest groups offer an indirect opportunity for influencing political decision-making. Social movements go further in shaping both the political agenda and in altering issue salience among the wider public. Protest activity offers an important alternative outlet for influencing the political agenda, often adopted when all and any alternatives are ineffective. Being heard and helping to influence political decision-making is central to the democratic experiment. Why individuals choose to become involved in these various forms of participation and engagement has received a great deal of attention from the political science community. One of the dominant theoretical frameworks highlights the importance of motivation, resources, and opportunity for helping to explain the range of factors that motivate participatory decisions and actions (Verba et al., 1995). People engage because they have the necessary combination of motivation, capacity, and opportunity – the latter often requiring little more than an explicit invitation – to participate.

Yet the study of citizen participation makes clear that we still have much to learn. For one, the conceptualization of political participation has direct implications for our conclusions regarding who participates. We know that the indicators that we employ to measure political interest (Ferrin et al., 2020) and political knowledge (Stolle and Gidengil, 2010), for example, have direct implications for our conclusions regarding women's supposed lower levels of political engagement. Other scholars are advancing our understanding of political participation by studying forms that have been largely overlooked, such as political deliberation (Beauvais, 2020). There are, of course, important theoretical reasons for interrogating what acts are considered to meet the criteria for political participation, including the most basic that researchers should be talking about the same behaviours when employing the same concept. But another, often overlooked reason is that our definition of political participation has direct implications for our understanding of who participates and why they participate in politics. If our definition excludes activity chosen by certain groups, then our conclusions regarding their levels of engagement will be skewed.

Additionally, as pointed out by Goss (2003), the "civic voluntarism model" developed by Verba, Schlozman, and Brady (1995), while providing a solid basis for understanding citizen participation, accounts for less than half of the total variance in these decisions. This understanding works best for our ability to model how many individuals, but not all, come to decide whether to participate in the political sphere. Scholars continue to work on identifying how various forces such as education and political interest influence participation, how these vary across groups in society, and which factors of importance are not fully captured by the model. The latter includes factors that are difficult to capture quantitatively and, as such, require that researchers move beyond experimental and survey methods towards more qualitative methods, ones not always wholly embraced within political science. Additionally, we have come to increasingly understand that context – infinitely variable – can affect how these explanatory variables work alone and in combination with each other.

One area of inquiry into political participation that has helped shed light on participation and the calculus that lies behind it focuses on women given that those scholars adopting this particular focus are more likely to question our understandings of what counts as political participation and why people get involved in politics. The most recent generation of feminists, for example, has embraced actions tied to cultural reclamation and individual resistance, including the #MeToo movement, needle work (Cadloff, 2018) and baking (Evans, 2015), in an attempt to bring about social and cultural change. Traditional measures of political participation do not always adequately capture these contemporary forms of activism. Scholars are also beginning the important work of interrogating longstanding concepts such as sex and their corresponding limitations (Bittner and Goodyear-Grant, 2017).

In this chapter I outline how our conceptual strategies and methodological approaches limit our understanding of political participation. I do so through two simple yet powerful strategies. The first is to demonstrate how our conceptualization of political participation renders the political activities of some groups invisible. The second is to underscore why an examination of the intersection of factors is minimally required for moving beyond a simple understanding of when, why, and how women choose to participate politically. As such, I argue that how we conceptualize and, importantly, operationalize the concept of political participation requires careful consideration that ought not be governed by the limits of quantitative analysis. And, further, that the methodological choices that we make in analyses of political participation are of consequence for our conclusions regarding the levels of political activity of certain groups.

This chapter links to Richard Johnston's research in at least three ways. First, the importance of questioning concepts, even those most basic to our political understandings, permeates his work. His work on political campaigns, for example, begins by asking what we mean when we use the concept of the political campaign. An important and yet too often overlooked step is to interrogate the meaning of basic concepts. Second, the importance of both our methodological choices and of modelling is a thread weaving through much of his research, highlighted perhaps by the development of the rolling cross-section design. As his work reveals, the strength of our conclusions rests in part on the quality and appropriateness of the data at hand. Continually challenging ourselves to improve how we investigate is imperative for advancing knowledge. And finally, much of his work investigates the importance of context for our theoretical conclusions, recognizing that generalizations can only get us so far. Exceptions and deviant cases – such as the Canadian party system in Anglo-American democracies – cannot and should not be ignored because their investigation reveals much.

Defining Women Out of Political Participation

The discipline of political science has long paid attention to political participation as a key element of the democratic enterprise. How the concept has been defined, however, has changed over time, with more recent definitions expanding to consider newer forms of participation. Scholars have had to modify their research definitions to address changes in political activity on the ground. Recent conceptualizations, and in particular the recent conceptualization offered by van Deth (2014), highlight the breadth and complexity of contemporary political activity.

The conceptual definition of political participation has direct implications for our conclusions regarding political activity, especially true for activity that is definitionally excluded from research. Fox (2014) provides a comprehensive summary of the evolution of the definition of political participation. As he notes, existing and multiple definitions of the concept reflect the research context and particular impact that the researcher understands for political participation, whether it to change or influence government outcomes, to establish societal goals, to allocate social values, to change the allocation of social goods, or to engage in a process of managing co-existence with other individuals (p. 497). There is no single commonly accepted definition of what counts as political participation.

Very briefly, Fox (2014) notes that the definition of political participation has expanded from its earliest version of legal or illegal active engagement either alone or as part of a group with the intent of influencing government (Almond and Verba, 1963). Revisions have added that behaviour must be voluntary (Brady, 1999; Pattie et al., 2004); be directed at the state and the services that it provides (Ibid, 2004); have an instrumental (i.e., produce a specific outcome) or symbolic intent (i.e., to express an opinion) (Whiteley, 2012); be undertaken by ordinary citizens rather than political elites or civil servants (Brady, 1999); and must include an attempt to influence the actions and decisions of political elites (Brady, 1999). There is tension among definitions, however, as some include civil participation in the definition of political participation (referred to as latent political participation), including political interest, donating to charities, reading newspapers, and volunteering (Ekman and Amnå, 2012).

As noted by Fox (2014), two recent changes have had a significant impact on how citizens engage politically: globalization and changes in information and communication technologies (ICTs). Globalization has decreased the state's role relative to other actors, with the results that it is less often a target of political activism, and that individualized forms of participation have increased (Hooghe, 2014). According to some, the growth in ICTs has allowed increased access to participatory arenas and expanded the participatory repertoire into a new form of participation (Theocharis and van Deth, 2018).

Jan van Deth's (2014) recently introduced a reconceptualization of political participation, one designed to capture new, complex activities and to address existing conceptual slippage. As noted by van Deth (2014), the concept lacks a common understanding, leading to conclusions that are not directly comparable. Rather than provide a definition of political participation, van Deth (2014) develops a conceptual map that lays out a set of decisions rules for identifying four distinct forms of political participation. The map begins with basic premise that to be considered participation, it must be an activity, it must be voluntary, and it must be performed by individuals in their role as citizens (and not in any professional capacity). One type of activity, *the minimalist definition of political participation* (political participation I), is performed within the sphere of government and politics, which is defined as "the sector directed by government under the jurisdiction of state power" (van Deth, 2014, 356). Activities in this category include voting, volunteering for political parties, and writing letters to political representatives. *Targeted political participation* is activity directed at government and politics. This form of participation is often referred to a "contentious politics" and includes protests and marches. A third type, a variant of targeted political participation, includes activity focused on problem solving and helping others, in recognition of the fact that non-political activity can have a political intent, that is to target a shared collective problem. As examples, he includes citizen initiatives and neighbourhood committees. The final category is the *motivational form of political participation*, which includes "voluntary, non-political activities by citizens used to express their political aims and intentions" (2014, 359). This type includes "individualized," "expressive," and "personalized" forms of participation, including political consumerism (Micheletti, 2003) and DYI politics (Bennett, 2012).

This new conceptualization has come under scrutiny. Both Hooghe (2014) and Hosch-Dayican (2014) take issue with the motivational form of political participation, noting in part the difficulty in trying to operationalize and measure intent quantitatively. Where they differ, however, is the importance ascribed to intent for activity to be considered political participation. Hosch-Dayican (2014) sees the motivational aspect of participation as essential to the concept's reconceptualization, whereas Hooghe (2014) sees intent as irrelevant to the impact of political participation and, thus, non-essential to its definition.

The fact that what constitutes political participation is debated has implications beyond the theoretical. The activities that are "counted" as political exclude some activities and thus some activists. The relatively recent inclusion of both political consumerism and online activism as forms of political participation are good examples of how the conceptual definition of the term has expanded to incorporate new forms of activity. One concern with expanding the definition of political participation is conceptual stretching, which renders it highly problematic if its definition varies across researchers (Ekman and Amnå, 2012). But of equal concern is conceptual shrinking if it renders some activity invisible. The definition ought to be broad enough to be able to capture the wide range of activities that hope to have a political impact. Instead, too often definitions reflect the experiences of the privileged and "obscure the experiences of those who are already marginalized" (Harnois, 2013, 131).

Insight into how the definition renders certain activities invisible can be gained by focusing on feminist activism, dominated by women actors. A simple, yet encompassing, definition suggests that what defines feminism is the "aim to make the empowerment of women a priority" and that organizations are feminist if they have as an explicit focus "women's status or gender oppression more generally" (Weldon, 2004, 3). As such, feminist activism has as its objective ending women's oppression. The feminist movement can be understood "as a socially constructed collective identity that emerges out of the interactions and accomplishments of participants in women's networks and organizations engaged in struggles for change in women's status and opportunities" (Staggenborg and Taylor, 2005, 44). There exists tremendous variation and complexity in the activities undertaken by contemporary feminist activists. For one, the repertoire of activities is expansive, having grown in recent years with the increasing use of the internet. Add to this that feminist activism rarely has a single strategic goal but rather is more often tied to several objectives at once. And the number of venues in which this activism occurs is wide. Feminist activity often occurs within groups, but the recent rise of neoliberalism has increased its individualization (Evans, 2015).

Concerns with new conceptualization as it relates to feminist activism can be identified. The first concerns the definition of politics. For van Deth (2014), participation is political if it takes place within the sphere of or is directed at government and politics, or, for non-political activity, has a political motivation. Politics, in this conceptualization, involves government, the political system, and the policy process. Norris has argued that focusing exclusively on politics as involving government and the state is unnecessarily narrow. As she notes, "the older definition of political participation, based on citizenship activities designed to influence government and the policy process within the nation-state, seems unduly limited today, excluding too much that is commonly understood as broadly 'political'" (Norris, 2002, 193). This is especially the case if we consider that feminists have been arguing for a broader definition of politics, one that includes "all activity aimed at changing, maintaining, or restoring power relationships in a society, its communities, or its institutions" (Vickers, 1997, 16).

Given that much of feminist activism is aimed at social relationships and institutions, it is clear that much of this activity is overlooked by definitions of political participation that adopt a limited understanding of politics. In her investigation of the processes and experiences of becoming a feminist, for example, Hercus's (2005, 155) interviews with feminists identified four strategies for bringing about feminist change, including employing feminist knowledge for personal empowerment and to empower other women, directly challenging taken-for-granted understandings or actions, whenever possible, and valuing and providing emotional and social support for other women. These strategies are not captured by conceptualizations of political participation that focus narrowly on the government and the state.

A further concern relates to the requirement that the activity be undertaken by citizens, which for van Deth (2014) excludes the

> activities of politicians, civil servants, office-bearers, public officers, journalists, and professional delegates, advisors, appointees, lobbyists, and the like. Essential as the accomplishments of these functionaries and officials might be for the political system, using the concept political participation in these instances would stretch the range of relevant behaviour to cover conceptually and functionally very different phenomena. (354–6)

Feminists engage in political activity in their capacity as citizens but also – and often – in their roles as employees. This includes feminist activism in the workplace that occurs outside of one's job description, but also feminist activity that occurs as part of one's occupational responsibilities. Indeed, feminists see themselves as citizens in the workplace. Femocrats and gender mainstreaming are two key strategies for influencing state action from inside governmental institutions of power (Chappell, 2002; True and Mintrom, 2001). Identifying as a feminist involves the adoption of an identity whose importance is not restricted to only certain roles in one's life. Indeed, the clear distinction between the *public* and the *private* is one that feminists challenge (Phillips, 1991). To the extent that our definitions of political participation exclude these activities, then this form of feminist activism is rendered invisible.

Van Deth's (2014) conceptual map includes actions that are not targeted to politics and government if they are "aimed at solving a collective or community problem" (p. 358), which he argues aligns with definitions of civic engagement that include activities aimed at the collective life of the polity. In short, he sees collective problems as political, and includes such activity as volunteering in this category. As he notes, "to deny the adjective 'political' to attempts to solve collective or community problems would imply a restriction to government- and state-centred definitions of political participation, and – what is more problematic – to an exclusion of activities by people who explicitly reject some borderline between 'politics' and 'society'" (2014, 357). This is most definitely a more expansive definition of the concept, one that would certainly capture more of feminist activity than many current definitions, but not one that has been embraced widely by researchers. The lack of objective criteria for what constitutes a collective and community *problem*, however, is problematic. For some acts, the answer is relatively straightforward; a group of parents organizing to erect a new community playground would seem to constitute an act of political participation designed to address a community problem. But for some others, such as a knitting groups (often called stitch 'n bitch groups) to reclaim a devalued and domestic craft (Kelly, 2014), the answer is less so.

The addition of the motivational form (voluntary, non-political activities by citizens used to express their political aims and intentions) in van Deth's conceptualization stems directly from the need to include more expressive forms of activity – such as boycotting and Tweeting – in the definition of political participation. In this expansion, non-political activities are considered political activity if the intention that lies behind the action is political. The activities are less about "politics" per se, that about being "political" in intent (van Deth, 2014, 359). This addition necessarily increases the possibility for including a greater number of feminist activities in our research. As noted above, however, concerns related to the ability to measure intent quantitatively have been raised and, as noted by van Deth, "qualitative explorations of expressions and public statements" are necessary "as they leave it to the citizens involved to define not only what is 'participation,' but especially what is considered to be 'politics' and 'political'" (2014, 363). The intent that lies behind non-political activity does not necessarily require more open-ended and qualitative explorations (see, for example, the question wording for boycotting and buycotting in the appendix). More problematic is that there are no criteria for identifying what constitutes a political aim and intention, related to the concern raised earlier. The lack of such criteria raises the potential for losing internal conceptual consistency and expanding the list of behaviours included in the definition so broadly that it becomes "a theory of everything" (Hosch-Dayican, 2014). If political aims and intentions are limited to ones designed to influence government and state activity, however, the concern is equally salient for it restricts much of feminist activity designed to bring about social and cultural reform.

Not All Women Participate in the Same Way nor for the Same Reasons

How we choose to define the concept of political participation has direct implications for which activities – and which individuals – we study. The choice is not neutral in highlighting certain activities and ignoring others. Beyond the definition of the concept, the methods that we adopt to study the concept also have implications for the conclusions that we reach and the groups that these conclusions ignore. The choices that we make in operationalizing the concept of political participation and the statistical techniques selected to model its determinants can also serve to render some groups invisible.

Our methodological choices can render the participation and the participation calculus of smaller and marginal groups invisible. As political behaviouralists, we are trained to seek out theoretical explanations for behavioural phenomena. Those theories should address important activities be predictively accurate, and, as much as possible, be simple (Shively, 2016, 16–18). The goal of theory is to help simplify a complicated world. Intersectional analysis, on the other hand, points out that striving for simplicity often means that we miss things.

Aggregation is one of the methodological practices that serves to create these invisibilities. Merging different political acts together in a single indicator of participation erases distinctions in participation across groups. Similarly, inserting a dummy variable for gender in a regression is a form of aggregation in that it renders different groups of women invisible, treats the dominant and largest group of women as the norm, and suggests that a simple comparison to men (also treated as a single group) is sufficient for "controlling" for gender (see also Harell, 2017). In doing so we lose the very context that could provide insight into expanding our explanatory power, albeit at a loss of some theoretical simplicity. But given that aggregation renders marginal groups largely invisible, these choices are not without cost. It marginalizes already powerless groups in that our theoretical explanations fail to capture their political realities.

Investigations into gender gaps in participation have revealed the limitations of existing models to account fully for participation decisions (see for instance

Coffé and Bolzendahl, 2010). In particular, research has shown that models fail to fully capture the manner in which the intersections of race, class, and gender influence the participatory decisions of many women (Brown, 2014; Harell, 2017). The inclusion of gender as a single variable into a model is insufficient for fully capturing the range of factors at play in these decisions, the various ways in which gender interacts with other variables in the model, and the range of factors that ought to be included in the analysis but which are difficult to capture quantitatively.[1] As noted by Brown (2014, 339), "Although scholars have indicated that minorities and women have fewer resources than whites and males, a scant few have articulated the effects of race-gender identity on political participation." Intersectional analyses in particular have underscored the importance of needing "to account for historical narratives, cultural representation, and legal discrimination to show how both race/ethnicity and gender operate in tandem to influence how minority women participate in American politics" (Brown, 2014, 315). Moreover, the limitations to focusing exclusively on the gender gap have been identified by both Burns (2005) and Gidengil (2007), ones that include the potential for ignoring differences across women themselves that can help further our understanding of factors central for assessing differences in political participation.

Adopting an intersectional lens adds to our understanding of political participation – not only women's – by moving away from explanations and theories that work largely for dominant groups and that are often devoid of context. Intersectionality argues that categories of difference including gender, race, class, and sexual orientation intersect in various ways that are relevant for how these different groups act and think (Hancock, 2007). An intersectional lens accepts that members of various groups do not experience the world in the same way and do not have equal access to political power (Holman, 2016; Brown, 2014). Part of this can stem from the relative lack of resources they enjoy, including access to education and income. Importantly, intersectionality argues that these differences, and how they play themselves out in terms of politics, will vary across groups depending on the intersections of these various categories. In short, not everyone participates in the same political activities nor at the same levels given their lived experiences. More specifically, Brown (2014) finds that while socio-economic status and education help to explain participation, they are insufficient for addressing the various structural barriers faced by traditionally marginalized women in the United States, including Black, Latina, and Asian women and their ability to overcome these barriers. Simply put, women of the same age or with similarly educational backgrounds will not participate in politics in similar ways given their varying experiences with the political system, their access to it, and the power that they wield within it.

Not surprisingly, racialized and Indigenous women in Canada display unique participation patterns in politics (Harell, 2017, Harell and Panagos, 2013,

Harell, Panagos, and Matthews, 2011). These differences arise due to an array of processes and circumstances that often restrict their opportunities, ability, and willingness to engage politically. A focus on explanations looking to socioeconomic resources such as occupation and education would necessarily suggest that both groups of women would have lower levels of participation because of the unique challenges they face on this front. Importantly, however, patterns for racialized women vary depending on the activity in question (Harell, 2017).

The motivations to participate in social movements are dynamic, changing over time, and dependent of the interaction between militant and personal environments and one's identity (Labelle, 2021). Key to this interaction is how the three "are interrelated through experienced marginalization at the intersection of sexuality, gender, and race" (Labelle, 2021, 819). Moreover, Indigenous women's struggle involves colonialism, which is often of greater consequence than gender for their participatory calculus (Harell and Panagos, 2013). This struggle can encourage Indigenous women to engage in certain types of political activity (Beauvais, 2020), often as a form of resistance such as the Idle No More and Sisters in Spirit movements. Their small numbers in the population mean, however, that any such differences in participation are lost when they are merged with other women into a single group in investigations, as is often the practice in gender gap research. The relative silence of political participation scholars on involvement with social movements – often left to other scholars – also means that these complex motivators are under-investigated.

Using survey data can help to highlight how marginalized women can be rendered invisible by our methodological practices. Not all political activities are similar, revealing differences in not only the degree to which individuals engage in them, but also how activity in them varies across groups of women. Modelling a range of factors often used to help explain rates of participation in various activities, but doing so separately for differently situated women highlights how standard explanations vary in their strength for different groups of women. In short, examinations of women as a single group fail to account for important distinctions between them.

Two surveys provide the data for this analysis: the 2007 Women's Political Participation Survey (WPPS) and the 2010 Quebec Women's Political Participation Survey (QWPPS).[2] The surveys asked women about a range of political activities (see question wording in the appendix). This included if they voted in the last federal election (2006 for the WPPS, and 2008 for the QWPPS); party and interest group membership; boycotting and buycotting; signed a petition or participated in a demonstration; and worked with others to bring about some kind of change in their neighbourhood or local school. These survey questions largely mirror commonly used questions designed to capture political participation, although political consumerism and grassroots engagement less so. As such, they fall victim to the complaint of failing to broaden our understanding of the concept and its operationalization. They nevertheless provide an opportunity for documenting the variation in participation across political activities by different women, in addition to providing a window into how the strength of our understanding of why women participate politically misses the mark for some groups of women.

The survey also asked respondents to identify up to four ethnic or cultural groups to which their ancestors belong (mirroring the strategy adopted in the Canadian Census). Racialized women were identified as those who indicated one non-European ancestral group (9.1 per cent).[3] Indigenous women were identified as those indicating Indigenous ancestry in one of these four groups (5.3 per cent). All other women were identified as white (85.5 per cent).

The first step is to highlight how participation practices vary across activities and across different women. Table 7.1 provides these results. The first column offers a breakdown on all women's participation rates, as a single group, in a range of political activities. The next three columns break down these data across different groups of women: white, racialized, and Indigenous. The first columns reiterate an important point made above: not all political activities are the same. Women engage in different activities at different rates. Women are most likely to vote, with just over two-thirds indicating that they had voted in the last federal election. Not surprisingly, very few are members of a political party or an interest group, and few have attended a demonstration in the past five years. Just over a quarter said they had boycotted a product and just under a third had signed a petition. And just over two in five women suggested that they had buycotted a product or been involved in some form of grassroots engagement. The variation in participation rates is significant. If political consumerism and grassroots engagement were not included in the list of activities, women's political engagement would appear to be much weaker than it is when they are included.

The next step is to compare the rates of participation across differently situated women (columns 2 through 4). The first point to draw from the breakdown of participation rates is the degree of variation across women, and not always in anticipated ways. The second is how closely the rates of participation for white women mirror those for the group that merges all women together. When one group far outnumbers other groups, aggregation means that the dominant group's characteristics prevail.

When we compare the political participation of racialized women to other women, a striking pattern emerges. Racialized women participate in some activities at rates close to white women (e.g., attended a demonstration, boycotted), but participate in rates far below them in a number of other political activities. They are much less likely to have voted in the last federal election (by 35 points), to have ever been a member of a political party or interest group (by roughly 10 points), to have signed a petition (8 points) and to have buycotted

Table 7.1. Women's participation in political activities by ethno-racial group

Categories	All Women (%)	White Women (%)	Racialized Women (%)	Indigenous Women (%)
Voted Federally***	79.1	83.0	48.0	64.9
Party Member***	14.9	16.2	6.3	8.3
Interest Group Member***	13.1	13.5	4.4	20.2
Signed a Petition in the Past Year***	32.2	31.9	24.1	50.0
Attended a Demonstration in the Last Five Years***	10.2	9.2	10.3	26.5
Boycotted	26.6	26.6	23.8	31.3
Buycotted**	43.1	43.6	34.7	50.4
Grassroots Engagement in the Last Five Years***	45.4	43.8	52.7	59.1
N (range, min–max)	2410–2497	2077–2141	202–224	130–132

Note: ** p < .010; *** p < .001.
Source: 2007 WPPS and 2010 QWPPS.

products (9 points). But not all of the gaps are negative: racialized women exhibit a higher level of participation (a 9-point difference) in a local or neighbourhood activity designed to bring about some kind of change than white women.

Indigenous women, on the other hand, exhibit a pattern of political activity that provides little evidence that they are less politically engaged than other women. In six of the eight activities recorded, Indigenous women have higher levels of participation than white women and they participate at higher levels than racialized women in all activities. They are less likely to have voted federally (by 18 points) and to be a member of a political party (by 8 points) than white women, reflecting in part the lack of legitimacy accorded to colonial electoral institutions (Ladner and McCrossan, 2007). They are, however, more likely to be a member of an interest group "working for change" (7 points), to have signed a petition (18 points), demonstrated (17 points), boycotted (5 points) and buycotted (7 points), and participated in a local or grassroots activity designed to bring about change (15 points). These findings suggest that while Indigenous women are less likely to participate in Canadian electoral democracy, they are nevertheless more likely to participate in processes and institutions designed to influence and pressure governments and other institutions to act, and to organize to get things done. Indigenous women are fully engaged in politics, although this point is only fully captured when they are examined separately from other women.

A final step is to examine the variation across a range of explanations often employed for modelling political participation. To do this, I run logistic

Table 7.2. Modelling women's voting by ethno-racial group

Categories	All Women	White Women	Racialized Women	Indigenous Women
Age	.06***	.05***	.09***	.08*
	(.02)	(.01)	(.02)	(.03)
High School Graduate or Less	−.42**	−.33†	−1.38*	−.47
	(.16)	(.18)	(.65)	(.64)
University Graduate	.51**	.82***	−.01	.92
	(.19)	(.24)	(.50)	(.95)
Professional Occupation	.13	.03	.56	−1.28
	(.20)	(.24)	(.53)	(.97)
Other Occupation	.17	.16	.31	−.59
	(.16)	(.18)	(.56)	(.66)
Immigrant	−1.25***	−.47†	−.87	
	(.17)	(.24)	(.64)	−
High Religious Attendance (at least once a month)	.27†	.37*	.25	−.28
	(.15)	(.17)	(.44)	(.67)
Young Child (preschool age) in Home	−.27	−.40†	−.46	−.15
	(.18)	(.21)	(.55)	(.75)
Efficacy	.01	.01	−.25	.14
	(.15)	(.18)	(.52)	(.64)
Political Interest	.98***	1.01***	1.12*	1.49†
	(.14)	(.16)	(.52)	(.58)
Traditional Gender Role	−.39**	−.23	−.67	−1.84**
	(.15)	(.17)	(.53)	(.66)
Constant	−1.83***	−1.33***	−3.85***	−2.36
	(.29)	(.34)	(1.14)	(1.24)
N	1932	1723	102	107
% Correctly Predicted	81.9	85.6	73.9	79.4
Nagelkerke R^2	0.286	0.218	0.382	0.422

Note: *** $p < .001$; ** $p < .01$; * $p < .05$; † $p < .10$.
Source: 2007 WPPS and 2010 QWPPS. Each column offers the results for a unique sample of women, with independent variables listed in the first column. Entries are binomial logistic regression coefficients (standard errors in parentheses). Reference categories are some college and/or university, no occupation, non-immigrant, no or school-age children in the home, low religious attendance, and non-traditional gender role beliefs.

regressions for three of the activities recorded in the survey: voting, participating in a demonstration, and grassroots engagement.[4] In order to run these, a number of controls were created. Age is coded in years. Education is measured by two dummy variables: completed high school or less (33.5 per cent) and completed an undergraduate degree or higher (28.1 per cent). The reference category is for those having completed some college and/or university or having earned a college diploma (38.4 per cent). Employment status is also measured by two dummy variables: professional occupation (21.0 per cent) and

Table 7.3. Modelling women's demonstration participation by ethno-racial group

Categories	All Women	White Women	Racialized Women	Indigenous Women
Age	−.02**	−.01†	−.02	−.016
	(.01)	(.01)	(.02)	(.02)
High School Graduate or Less	−.29	−.25	−1.11	.06
	(.23)	(.26)	(1.04)	(.70)
University Graduate	.42*	.35	.25	2.418*
	(.20)	(.23)	(.72)	(.99)
Professional Occupation	.54*	.70**	1.15	−1.51
	(.23)	(.27)	(1.01)	(1.05)
Other Occupation	.17	.16	.98	−.21
	(.22)	(.25)	(1.02)	(.67)
Immigrant	−.47†	−.33	−1.76*	–
	(.25)	(.35)	(.83)	
High Religious Attendance (at least once a month)	.17	.40*	.76	−3.11*
	(.17)	(.19)	(.63)	(1.39)
Young Child (Preschool) in Home	−.51†	−.28	−.79	−2.17†
	(.28)	(.32)	(.91)	(1.20)
Efficacy	−.08	−.12	1.27†	−1.36†
	(.18)	(.21)	(.71)	(.81)
Political Interest	.25	.27	2.00	−.59
	(.21)	(.24)	(1.39)	(.61)
Traditional Gender Role	−.32	−.64*	.02	.49
	(.22)	(.28)	(.97)	(.62)
Constant	−1.84***	−2.28***	−3.47†	.49
	(.39)	(.47)	(1.99)	(1.26)
N	1991	1758	125	108
% Correctly Predicted	91.3	92.4	88.4	83.4
Nagelkerke R^2	0.059	0.070	0.255	0.379

Note: *** $p < .001$; ** $p < .01$; * $p < .05$; † $p < .10$.
Source: 2007 WPPS and 2010 QWPPS. Each column offers the results for a unique sample of women, with independent variables listed in the first column. Entries are binomial logistic regression coefficients (standard errors in parentheses). Reference categories are some college and/or university, no occupation, non-immigrant, no or school-age children in the home, low religious attendance and non-traditional gender role beliefs.

non-professional occupation (41.1 per cent).[5] The reference category includes those women who are retired, unemployed, homemakers, students, and who reported their status as disabled (37.9 per cent). One dummy variable captures women's parental status, identifying women with preschool-age children living in the home (12 per cent) (see O'Neill and Gidengil, 2018). A control for religiosity was created – including women who attend religious services at least once a month (see O'Neill, 2006, 2009). An additional variable was created to

Table 7.4. Modelling women's grassroots engagement by ethno-racial group

Categories	All Women	White Women	Racialized Women	Indigenous Women
Age	−.04***	−.04***	−.04**	−.05*
	(.00)	(.00)	(.01)	(.02)
High School Graduate or Less	−.38**	−.32*	−.57	−.71
	(.12)	(.13)	(.53)	(.55)
University Graduate	−.01	.14	−1.16*	−.49
	(.13)	(.14)	(.52)	(.76)
Professional Occupation	.61***	.44**	1.71***	1.65†
	(.15)	(.16)	(.49)	(.87)
Other Occupation	.25*	.26*	−.43	.26
	(.12)	(.13)	(.50)	(.53)
Immigrant	−.35*	−.36*	−.30	−
	(.14)	(.18)	(.56)	
High Religious Attendance (at least once a month)	.53***	.52***	.61	.55
	(.11)	(.11)	(.40)	(.58)
Young Child (Preschool) in Home	−.03	−.12	.17	.02
	(.17)	(.19)	(.50)	(.78)
Efficacy	.01	.09	−1.28**	−.06
	(.11)	(.12)	(.46)	(.54)
Political Interest	.83***	.85***	1.28**	.41
	(.12)	(.13)	(.46)	(.51)
Traditional Gender Role	−.07	−.09	.10	−.78
	(.12)	(.13)	(.46)	(.56)
Constant	.71**	.62*	1.22	2.39*
	(.24)	(.27)	(.92)	(1.08)
N	1987	1756	123	108
% Correctly Predicted	65.7	63.3	72.1	69.6
Nagelkerke R^2	0.185	0.183	0.332	0.257

Note: *** $p < .001$; ** $p < .01$; * $p < .05$; † $p < .10$.
Source: 2007 WPPS and 2010 QWPPS. Each column offers the results for a unique sample of women, with independent variables listed in the first column. Entries are binomial logistic regression coefficients (standard errors in parentheses). Reference categories are some college and/or university, no occupation, non-immigrant, no or school-age children in the home, low religious attendance, and non-traditional gender role beliefs.

capture gender role socialization (see Lorenzini and Bassoli, 2015) by combining two surveys questions: the first asking whether society would be better off if parents stayed home with their children, and a second filter question asking those who agreed to the first whether they believed it should be the mother or the father who stayed home. All those who responded that it should be the mother were coded 1 on the traditional gender role socialization dummy variable (25.1 per cent of the sample). Finally, dummies were created to capture high levels of political efficacy and political interest. Respondents who indicated that they were strongly or somewhat interested in politics, and who strongly or somewhat disagreed that politics and government seemed complicated were coded as 1 on each.

Tables 7.2 through 7.4 provide the results of these analyses. Table 7.2 provides the regression results for voting federally. Focusing on the differences in causal mechanisms across groups rather than on the specific relationships between variables, three in particular stand out. The first is education. The results for all women show that those with lower education are less likely to turn out and those with higher education are more likely. These results hold for white women but not for racialized women (only those with a lower education are less likely to turn out) nor for Indigenous women (no difference across education levels). Religiosity is the second. Strong religiosity increases white women's likelihood of voting, but fails to present a statistically significant relationship in the racialized and Indigenous women's groups. Finally, women with a traditional understanding of women's gender role are less likely to vote, but this finding only applies for Indigenous women and at a much more substantive level. Examining women as a single group leads in some cases to slightly skewed understandings of what matters for women's decisions to vote.

Table 7.4 offers models for women's participation in demonstrations and here too the results indicate that not every explanation applies equally for different groups of women. Three factors that appear to be significant for all women only appear to matter for white women when it comes to demonstrating: age, a professional occupation, and a traditional gender role. Two appear significant for all women but are really only important for Indigenous women: education and motherhood. Being an immigrant appears to dampen women's willingness to demonstrate, but upon deeper investigation this is really only true of racialized women and at a much stronger level. A strong sense of political efficacy is insignificant across all women, and yet it appears to provide a boost for racialized women's participation in the event. By comparison, political efficacy dampens Indigenous women's willingness to participate. Similarly, strong religiosity does not appear to be a significant factor in explaining women's willingness to join a demonstration; when we break up the sample, however, we find that it boosts white women's likelihood but dampens Indigenous women's.

The modelling of women's grassroots engagement reveals similar variation. Noteworthy here are the effects of political efficacy and interest. Efficacy reveals little in the way of importance for encouraging women's participation in this political activity. Breaking the sample down, however, reveals that it has a strong dampening effect on racialized women's participation. Political interest, on the other hand, appears to play a strong positive role in encouraging women to participate in grassroots activities, a finding that holds for all groups except

Indigenous women. What helps to explain participation in grassroots engagement differs across women.

Moving Forward

The recent rise of the Black Lives Matter movement has brought to the forefront the degree to which seemingly innocuous practices and good intentions can nevertheless harm and deliver microaggressions to marginalized groups. As researchers, we are not immune to these tendencies in our research practices. Our conceptual and methodological practices can further marginalize the already marginalized.

Our conceptual definitions are important for ensuring that there is a common understanding of the phenomena in question. These definitions must, however, adapt to the changing nature of the concept as it is experienced and practised. The reconceptualization of political participation by van Deth (2014) stemmed in part from a need to ensure that newer forms of participation were captured by its definition and operationalization, actions not immediately recognized as political but with political motivations. Importantly, our concepts need to be measured not only against the degree to which they reflect contemporary phenomena as they are practised. They must also be measured against the degree to which they include the practices of the marginalized. Even with this more expansive conceptualization, the political activities of some groups are rendered invisible.

Our methodological practices – however well-intentioned from a methodological perspective – ought also to be challenged on the degree to which they create models and explanations that largely reflect dominant groups in society. This is neither simple to undertake nor without associated costs. It requires oversampling from marginalized groups – a practice rarely questioned for ensuring large enough samples from small geographic populations – to ensure that we can investigate how explanations that apply for majority groups might not extend to them. It means adopting more qualitative methods and practices when required to ensure that our seemingly valid and reliable indicators actually meet these tests upon deeper investigation. It means recognizing that striving for simple theories comes at a cost: the loss of context. And it means venturing beyond the disciplinary and field of study silos that inevitably become so comfortable. In short, we need to do better. We need to explore expanded understandings of political participation, using both qualitative and quantitative methods, to fully capture what is required for and the consequences of defining some activities as political and others not. We need to explore how our conceptualization of political participation shapes our conclusions regarding whether and how certain groups are democratically connected and motivated. And we need to recognize that our methodological choices have real, even if unintentional, consequences.

Appendix

Political Participation Questions:

- VOTE: Did you happen to vote in the last federal election in January 2006 [2008 for QWPPS survey]?
- PARTY MEMBER: Have you ever been a member of a political party?
- INTEREST GROUP MEMBER: Have you ever been a member of an interest group working for change on a particular social or political issue? [Interviewer, if necessary: We mean environmental groups, women's groups, and so on, but NOT political parties.]
- SIGNED PETITION: In the last 12 months, have you signed a petition?
- ATTENDED DEMONSTRATION: Have you EVER taken part in a demonstration? Was that in the last five years?
- BOYCOTTED PRODUCT: In the last 12 months, have you boycotted any products for political, ethical, or environmental reasons?
- BUYCOTTED PRODUCT: In the last 12 months, have you BOUGHT any products for political, ethical, or environmental reasons?
- GRASSROOTS ENGAGEMENT: Have you ever worked with others to bring about some kind of change in your neighbourhood or local school – for example, raising money to pay for playground equipment? Was that in the last five years?

NOTES

1 Indeed, part of the motivation for this paper was the claim made by a scholar at a talk I was giving that including gender as a dummy variable in a regression analysis was sufficient for claiming that a "gendered" analysis had been undertaken. I am fairly certain that I rolled my eyes – a bad habit of mine – at this suggestion.

2 The 1,264 WPPS telephone interviews took place between 18 July and 2 October with women 18 years of age and older in the nine largely English-speaking Canadian provinces; the overall response rate was 59 per cent. The 1,201 QWPPS interviews took place between 2 June and 3 July with women 18 years and older in the province of Quebec; the response rate was 34 per cent. The two samples were merged and weighted to reflect national population figures for a combined sample of 2,500 women. The sample includes a significant number of racialized, immigrant, and Indigenous women in the sample, while at the same time asking a range of questions on political participation.

3 This strategy likely errs most often in identifying majority women as part of the minority ethnic group; one result in that differences between minority and majority groups might be larger than those suggested by the data. The small percentage of

women in the minority ethnic group eliminates the possibility of examining ethnic background in any greater detail.

4 Note that the regressions are not meant to fully capture the range of possible factors explaining political activity. Instead, the goal is simply to illustrate how explanations vary across groups of differently situated women, an important argument behind intersectional analysis.

5 Income is left out of the models for two reasons. A significant percentage of respondents failed to provide a response to the household income and personal income questions (17.8 per cent). More importantly, perhaps, the inclusion of education and a measure for a professional or other occupation will adequately capture the importance of socio-economic status given the high correlation between these and income, without having to worry about the effects of high multi-collinearity between the variables.

References

Almond, Gabriel A., and Sidney Verba. 1963. *The Civic Culture: Political Attitudes and Democracy in Five Nations.* Princeton University Press.

Beauvais, Edana. 2020. "The Gender Gap in Political Discussion Group Attendance." *Politics & Gender* 16: 315–38. https://doi.org/10.1017/S1743923X18000892

Bennett, W.L. 2012. "The Personalization of Politics: Political Identity, Social Media and Changing Patterns of Participation." *The Annals of the American Academy of Political and Social Science* 644 (1): 20–39. https://doi.org/10.1177/0002716212451428

Bittner, Amanda, and Elizabeth Goodyear-Grant. 2017. "Sex Isn't Gender: Reforming Concepts and Measurements in the Study of Public Opinion." *Political Behavior* 39: 1019–41. https://doi.org/10.1007/s11109-017-9391-y

Brady, Henry. 1999. "Political Participation." In *Measures of Political Attitudes*, edited by J.P. Robinson, P.R. Shaver, and L.S. Wrightsman, 737–801. Academic Press.

Brown, Nadia. 2014. "Political Participation of Women of Colour: An Intersectional Analysis." *Journal of Women, Politics and Public Policy* 35 (4): 315–48. https://doi.org/10.1080/1554477X.2014.955406

Burns, Nancy. 2005. "Finding Gender." *Politics & Gender* 1: 137–41. https://doi.org/10.1017/S1743923X05221013

Cadloff, Emily Baron. 2018. "Not your grandma's needle work: Combining feminism and cross-stitch," *Globe & Mail* July 9. Online at https://www.theglobeandmail.com/arts/art-and-architecture/article-not-your-grandmas-needle-work-combining-feminism-and-cross-stitch/

Chappell, Louise. 2002. "The 'Femocrat' Strategy: Expanding the Repertoire of Feminist Activists." *Parliamentary Affairs* 55 (1): 85–98. https://doi.org/10.1093/parlij/55.1.85

Coffé, Hilde, and Catherine Bolzendahl. 2010. "Same Game, Different Rules? Gender Differences in Political Participation." *Sex Roles* 62 (5–6): 318–33.

Ekman, Joakim, and Erik Amnå. 2012. "Political Participation and Civic Engagement: Towards a New Typology." *Human Affairs* 22 (3): 283–300. https://doi.org/10.2478/s13374-012-0024-1

Evans, Elizabeth. 2015. *The Politics of Third Wave Feminisms: Neoliberalism, Intersectionality, and the State in Britain and the U.S.* Palgrave Macmillan.

Fox, Stuart. 2014. "Is It Time to Update the Definition of Political Participation?" *Parliamentary Affairs* 67 (2): 495–505. https://doi.org/10.1093/pa/gss094

Gidengil, Elisabeth. 2007. "Beyond the Gender Gap." *Canadian Journal of Political Science* 40 (4): 1–17. https://doi.org/10.1017/S0008423907071181

Goss, Kristin. 2003. "Rethinking the Political Participation Paradigm." *Women & Politics* 25 (4): 83–118. https://doi.org/10.1300/J014v25n04_04

Hancock, Ange-Marie. 2007. "Intersectionality as a Normative and Empirical Paradigm." *Politics & Gender* 3 (2): 248–54. https://doi.org/10.1017/S1743923X07000062

Harell, Allison, Dimitrios Panagos, and J. Scott Matthews. 2011. "Explaining Indigenous Turnout in Federal Elections: Evidence from Alberta, Saskatchewan and Manitoba." In *Indigenous Policy Research: Voting, Governance and Research Methodology*, edited by Jerry White and Julie Rachel Peters, 3–24. Thompson Education Publishing.

Harell, Allison. 2017. "Intersectionality and Gendered Political Behaviour in a Mulitcultural Canada." *Canadian Journal of Political Science* 50 (2): 495–514. https://doi.org/10.1017/S000842391700021X

Harell, Allison, and Dimitrios Panagos. 2013. "Locating the Indigenous Gender Gap: The Political Attitudes and Participation of Indigenous Women in Canada." *Politics & Gender* 9 (4): 414–38. https://doi.org/10.1017/S1743923X1300038X

Harnois, Catherine E. 2013. *Feminist Measures in Survey Research*. Los Angeles: Sage.

Hercus, Cheryl. 2005. *Stepping out of Line: Becoming and Being Feminist*. Routledge.

Holman, Mirya R. 2016. "The Differential Effect of Resources on Political Participation Across Gender and Racial Groups." In *Distinct Identities: Minority Women in U.S. Politics*, edited by Nadia E. Brown and Sarah Allen Gershon, 13–28. Taylor & Francis.

Hooghe, M. 2014. "Defining Political Participation: How to Pinpoint an Elusive Target?" *Acta Politica* 49 (3): 338–41. https://doi.org/10.1057/ap.2014.7

Hosch-Dayican, B. 2014. "Online Political Activities as Emerging Forms of Political Participation: How Do They Fit in the Conceptual Map?" *Acta Politica* 49 (3): 342–46. https://doi.org/10.1057/ap.2014.7

Kelly, Maura. 2014. "Knitting as a Feminist Project?" *Women's Studies International Forum* 44: 133–144. https://doi.org/10.1016/j.wsif.2013.10.011

Labelle, Alexie. 2021. "Why Participate? An Intersectional Analysis of LGBTQ People of Colour Activism." *Politics, Groups, and Identities,* 9 (4): 807–25. https://doi.org/10.1080/21565503.2019.1674671

Ladner, Kiera L., and Michael McCrossan. 2007. *The Electoral Participation of Aboriginal People.* Chief Electoral Officer.

Lorenzini, Jasmine, and Matteo Bassoli. 2015. "Gender Ideology: The Last Barrier to Women's Participation in Political Consumerism?" *International Journal of Comparative Sociology* 56 (6): 460–83. https://doi.org/10.1177/0020715215625726

Micheletti, M. 2003. *Political Virtue and Shopping: Individuals, Consumerism and Collective Action.* New York: Palgrave Macmillan.

Norris, Pippa. 2002. *Democratic Phoenix: Reinventing Political Activism.* Cambridge University Press.

O'Neill, Brenda. 2006. "Canadian Women's Religious Volunteerism: Compassion, Connections and Comparisons." In *Gender and Social Capital,* edited by Brenda O'Neill and Elisabeth Gidengil, 185–211. Routledge.

– 2009. "Religion, Political Participation and Civic Engagement: Women's Experiences." In *Faith in the Public Realm: Controversies, Policies and Practices,* edited by Adam Dinham, Robert Furbey, and Vivien Lowndes. Policy Press.

O'Neill, Brenda, and Elisabeth Gidengil. 2018. "Motherhood's Role in Shaping Political and Civic Behaviour." In *Mothers and Others: The Role of Parenthood in Politics,* edited by Melanee Thomas and Amanda Bittner, 268–87. UBC Press.

Pattie, C., P. Seyd, and Paul Whiteley. 2004. *Citizens and Politics: Democracy and Participation in Twenty-First Century Britain.* Cambridge University Press.

Phillips, Anne. 1991. *Engendering Democracy.* Polity Press.

Shively, W. Phillips. 2016. *The Craft of Political Research,* 9th edition. Taylor & Francis.

Staggenborg, Suzanne, and Verta Taylor. 2005. "Whatever Happened to the Women's Movement?" *Mobilization: An International Journal* 10 (1): 37–52. https://doi.org/10.17813/maiq.10.1.46245r7082613312

Stolle, Dietlind, and Elisabeth Gidengil. 2010. "What Do Women Really Know? A Gendered Analysis of Varieties of Political Knowledge." *Perspectives on Politics* 8 (1): 93–109. https://doi.org/10.1017/S1537592709992684

Theocharis, Yannis, and Jan W. van Deth. 2018. "The Continuous Expansion of Citizen Participation: A New Taxonomy." *European Political Science Review* 10 (1): 139–63. https://doi.org/10.1017/S1755773916000230

True, Jacqui, and Michael Mintrom. 2001. "Transnational Networks and Policy Diffusion: The Case of Gender Mainstreaming," *International Studies Quarterly* 45 (1): 27–57. https://doi.org/10.1111/0020-8833.00181

van Deth, Jan W. 2014. "A Conceptual Map of Political Participation." *Acta Politica* 49 (3): 349–67. https://doi.org/10.1057/ap.2014.6

Verba, Sidney, Kay Lehman Schlozman, and Henry E. Brady. 1995. *Voice and Equality.* Harvard University Press.

Vickers, Jill. 1997. *Reinventing Political Science: A Feminist Approach.* Fernwood Publishing.

Weldon, S. Laurel. 2004. "The Dimensions and Policy Impact of Feminist Civil Society: Democratic Policy Making on Violence Against Women in the Fifty U.S. States," *International Feminist Journal of Politics* 6 (1): 1–28. https://doi.org/10.1080/1461674032000165914

Whiteley, P. 2012. *Political Participation in Britain: The Decline and Revival of Civic Culture.* Palgrave Macmillan.

8 Multiculturalism Policy in the Vernacular: Public Opinion in Canada and the United States

MATTHEW WRIGHT

Introduction

Now more than ever, immigrant-receiving democracies confront a dilemma when it comes to fostering the preservation of immigrants' cultural traditions versus encouraging them to adopt the prevailing customs and norms of their new homes. Cultural "pluralists" support redefining host societies along more diversity-friendly lines, both symbolically and in policy, as a means of social inclusion. Cultural "monists," on the other hand, favour a common national culture, and worry about immigrants' unwillingness or inability to integrate to it. The debate, which began in earnest in the 1980s and 1990s, has taken on renewed urgency because of three broad developments: (1) a decades-long and widespread increase in mass migration and immigrant-driven diversity; (2) recent academic evidence demonstrating the threats demographic change poses to "social cohesion," and the spate of ensuing studies supporting, challenging, or contextualizing this finding; (3) the recrudescence of right-wing populism in Europe and the United States, and its roots in people's anxieties about immigration and other broad social trends.

In this chapter, I want to address a few mainly descriptive questions about the contours of public opinion on matters of immigrant diversity and, more to the point, policies designed to accommodate it. Specifically:

1 How supportive are people of policies designed to foster immigrants' cultural identity, and does this support vary depending on the policy in question?
2 How nuanced are people's assessments of these policies, or, put another way, do people tend to lump them together or differentiate sharply between them?
3 How strongly correlated is support for multicultural policies to that for other policies in the domain of immigration?
4 How closely tethered are attitudes about multicultural policies to more abstract sentiment about immigration and diversity?

I explore these questions using the IDSS survey, which canvassed a comprehensive set of attitudes on these topics from nationally representative samples of Americans and Canadians in 2014.

Background

Worries about immigrants either refusing or failing to "integrate" and how this might fray the broader social fabric are as old as the nations that receive them (e.g., Higham, 1955; Schrag, 2010). On the other hand, proponents of multiculturalism argue that immigrants have the right to maintain their traditional cultures, and that governments should facilitate this process both symbolically and practically (Taylor, 1994; Kymlicka, 1995). The debate between cultural monists and pluralists finds renewed urgency in light of (1) widespread increases in mass migration and immigrant-driven diversity (Castles, Haas, and Miller, 2013); (2) recent academic evidence on the negative relationship between ethnic diversity and indicia of social capital (e.g., Putnam, 2007), and a spate of ensuing studies supporting, challenging, or contextualizing this finding (Harell and Stolle, 2010; van der Meer and Tolsma, 2014); (3) the recent rise of so-called right-wing populism in Europe and the United States, a phenomenon that has roots in people's anxieties about immigration and other broad social trends (Gest, 2016; Mudde and Kaltwasser, 2017).

This impels us to understand both *what* citizens think about immigrants' cultural rights and obligations vis-à-vis their adoptive nations and *why*. Most recent literature explores this issue from the standpoint of national policy regimes (e.g., Goodman, 2014; Howard, 2009; Joppke, 2004; Soysal, 1994). Here, I turn the focus to public opinion, beginning with the broader literature on immigration in public attitudes. First, the "what" question. Surprisingly, the literature has yet to really grapple what people think about immigrant diversity in a rigorous way. The bulk of research on immigration attitudes contents itself with understanding abstract "anti-immigrant sentiment" (Hainmueller and Hopkins, 2012, although a few have examined immigration policy attitudes – mostly concerning flows of legal immigrants allowed to enter the country but also policy options on dealing with illegal immigration – in a more nuanced way (Muste, 2013; Schildkraut, 2013; Wright and Levy, 2019). A more recent line of work probes people's attitudes about whether immigrants should receive public benefits, and the bases upon which such decisions are made (e.g., Petersen, 2012; van Oorschot, 2006; Koostra, 2017; Banting et al., forthcoming; Levy and Wright, forthcoming).

With respect to attitudes about cultural pluralism and multiculturalism, however, we have less to go on. Researchers have, from time to time, asked questions about people's outlook on diversity in the abstract. The pioneering work on this topic is from Citrin and colleagues (Citrin et al., 2001), who begin by distinguishing multiculturalism as demographic "fact" from multicultural-ism as a political ideology, the latter being a normative understanding about diversity and a set of policies derived from this understanding. They go on to nuance ideological multiculturalism into so-called soft and hard varieties. "Soft" multiculturalism generally refers to symbolic (and often relatively cost-less) affirmations about the importance of diversity in society, or appreciation for the various ways in which immigrants and minority groups liven up the po-litical and social tapestry. "Hard" multiculturalism, on the other hand, favours concrete measures designed to reify and recognize cultural difference, and to de-emphasize the kind of "colour-blind," assimilationist liberalism that enforces white, middle-class, and Euro-American norms on ethnic minority groups.

We have a general sense from this work that native-born citizens in most immigrant-receiving democracies favour cultural monism to pluralism as a strategy for managing ethnic diversity and insist on linguistic assimilation and allegiance to the host country (Citrin et al., 2001; Citrin and Sears, 2014). We also have a handful of studies that look at whether policy context "matters" to these attitudes; some are focused comparisons of Canada and the United States on basic aspects of accommodation (Soroka et al., 2017; Wright et al., 2016), whereas others make comparisons on a wider scale (Weldon, 2006; Wright, 2011). However, these studies are short on nuance and policy specificity, and extremely limited in their ability to shed light on where these kinds of atti-tudes come from. At a minimum, we need better coverage of opinion on the range of issues that characterizes contemporary debates on multiculturalism policy (e.g., Banting and Kymlicka, 2017). Beyond this, we need to allow for the fact that (a) people's abstract preferences may not be that closely tied to their specific policy preferences; and (b) whatever cultural practices people think immigrants ought to either shed or retain is, at least potentially, disinct from whether or not they support government efforts to encourage or even enforce this preference. So, in a descriptive sense, the first task is to map out people's "belief system" about cultural pluralism in a nuanced and realistic way.

What should such a belief system look like? The aforementioned literature on immigration attitudes is short on nuance and generally doesn't worry much about answering this question. Instead, it typically works with only one or two measures or a handful boiled down to an underlying "anti-immigration" fac-tor and focuses on the correlates of that factor. The correlates of choice tend to be either "economic" or "cultural" motivations (e.g., Hainmueller and Hop-kins, 2012). The former understands immigration through the lens of narrow self-interest: people want to limit immigration when it threatens their job or wages, or when it seems likely to increase their tax burden. That said, *Homo economicus* has proved elusive, a figment of a "zombie theory," Hainmueller and Hopkins' recent review goes so far as to say (2012, 241). People simply do not reliably reject immigrants who would threaten their job and accept immigrants who would complement their skills and raise their marginal product of labour (Citrin et al., 1997). Links between opinions about immigration and personal exposure to higher tax burdens or reduced supplies of public benefits are also empirically tenuous. For example, there is at most a weak, contingent, complex, and indeterminate relationship between the size of immigrant populations in people's own states and localities and opposition to immigration (Citrin et al., 1997; Hopkins, 2010; Newman, 2013; though see McClain et al., 2013; Hood and Morris, 1998).

The prevailing storyline in and outside the academy is essentially ethnocultural rather than economic and premised on a *group-centric* understanding of mass political psychology. In the foreground we have an innate human tendency towards ethnic or national identification. This is set against (and set off by) structural forces – economic strain and perceived competition for resources, say, or more to the point here, political conflicts over inclusion/exclusion – that encourage such identifications, politicize them, and make their consequences real. This kind of argument has its roots in various social-psychological models of intergroup relations, among them Social Identity Theory (Tajfel and Turner, 1979), theories highlighting the role of group conflict over resources (Blumer, 1958, Bobo and Hutchings, 1996), and theories tied to relative group position (Sidanius and Pratto, 1999; Masuoka and Junn, 2013). What all share are the assumptions that groups and group identity are psychologically central in people's belief systems about immigration, that such questions are in general boiled down to questions of "us against them," and that this kind of thinking is set off when the ingroup is perceived as being "threatened" by outsiders (e.g., Abrajano and Hajnal, 2015; Kinder and Kam, 2009; Masuoka and Junn, 2011).

This approach to the psychology of immigration attitudes suggests that people ought to approach the issues in a largely undifferentiated way, and that their prime motive is threat to salient social group identities (either "ethnic" or "national"). Indeed, on the basis of these approaches, a sizable literature demonstrates that those who perceive cultural "threat" from immigrants tend to express anti-immigrant sentiment, whereas in the absence of such threat people tend to be more sanguine. It has also made a strong case that the cultural threat tends to overpower economic self-interest in most contexts and for most people (e.g., Ceobanu and Escandell, 2010; Hainmueller and Hopkins, 2012).

On the other hand, the idea that public opinion on these kinds of issues is less like an undifferentiated attitude and more like a nuanced belief system is something I have argued elsewhere with respect to immigration policy. More specifically, we have taken issue with the notion that anti-immigrant sentiment is an undifferentiated attitude and argued instead that people's abstract feelings about immigration are quite often only lightly tethered to what they think about specific immigration *policies*. Indeed, as pointed out earlier, people approach policy decisions in a far more ambivalent and nuanced way than simple recourse to "us against them" would suggest (Levy, Wright and Citrin, 2016; Wright, Levy and Citrin, 2016; Levy and Wright, forthcoming). They tend to see cleavages between issues to the degree that they become linked to alternative sets of values. For example, illegal immigration engages people's conceptions of legalism and egalitarianism in a way that legal immigration policy does not. Even within a given policy area, attitudes vary substantially based on whether people are encouraged to think about it in light of whatever underlying values are brought to the "top of the head" (Zaller, 1992).

While the focus to date has largely been on immigration policy (i.e., who should be allowed to immigrate and on what basis), the substantive leap to cultural pluralism and cultural rights is not especially large. Using Phillip Converse's path-breaking work on belief systems as a guide (1964; 2000), we can ask whether attitude cleavages exist between policy attitudes (within or across broader issues domains), something he referred to as "horizontal constraint." We can also explore "vertical constraint," or the degree to which attitudes on *specific* policies are tethered to more abstract attitudes about diversity immigration. It may be that they approach these issues in a largely undifferentiated way. If so, one this might reflect either non-attitudes or high levels of vertical and horizontal constraint. Assuming people have meaningful attitudes on these topics at all – a reasonable expectation given the subject but not one that should ever be taken for granted – the latter seems more likely of the two. It may also be, however, that the public *does* see nuance between domains of multicultural policy, and that these are in turn reflected in substantial breakdowns of vertical and horizontal constraint. Either way, the question is very much worth pursuing.

Data and Measures

As befitting a chapter offered in support of a volume on Richard Johnston's contribution to political science, the data I use here was developed in close cooperation with him and other collaborators – Keith Banting, Will Kymlicka, Jack Citrin, Stuart Soroka – all with a long-standing interest probing public support for multiculturalism and associated policies and predispositions. The survey, fielded online in late January 2014, includes three separate samples: 2,000 respondents in the United States, roughly 1,000 French-language respondents in Quebec, and 1,000 English-language respondents in the rest of Canada. The Canadian sample is divided between Quebec and the rest of the country because previous evidence suggest that *les québécois* respond differently than do other Canadians to immigration and the challenges of social integration (Banting and Soroka, 2012).

The items at the centre of this analysis were designed to capture, as closely as possible, support for the constituent policies of Banting and Kymlicka's cross-national "MCP" index (Banting and Kymlicka, 2020). We asked respondents whether they supported or opposed (using a scale running from "support strongly" to "oppose strongly" their national government in

a. Passing a law declaring that ethnic and cultural diversity is a fundamental characteristic of [American/Canadian] Identity
b. Ensuring that schools teach about the role of minorities and immigrants
c. Requiring that the mass media represent minorities fairly
d. Requiring employers to make a special effort to hire members of minority groups, including immigrants
e. Requiring employers to give special preference in hiring to members of minority groups, including immigrants
f. Allowing persons in the police or armed forces to wear religious headgear (for example, turban, head scarf, or skull cap) instead of the standard uniform while on duty
g. Allowing immigrants to [the U.S./Canada] to keep citizenship in the country they came from after they become [American/Canadian] citizens
h. Requiring that, where many immigrant children do not speak English, public schools offer classes in their native language

In order to head off fatigue, response set, and other problems associated with asking respondents sets of highly similar questions, they only received (at random) one of a, b, or c on this list. This leaves large enough subsets for meaningful descriptive analysis and, given the strong similarity between them, little is lost in subsequent indexing. Prior to analysis, all items were rescored in a pro-MCP direction, which is to say that 0 = "oppose strongly" and 1 = "support strongly" for all items. The means for all MCP items and a simple additive index (five items, four asked of all respondents, plus whichever "diversity" item they received, re-scaled from 0–1) are listed below in table 8.1. Note that henceforward all analyses are restricted native-born white respondents.

Three things are worth noting here. First, support for these policies tends to lean towards the negative end of the scale, as evidenced by index means (across all three subsamples) well below the nominal neutral point of .50. Second, as we have pointed out elsewhere, disaggregating by political context shows "Rest of Canada" and American respondents on the high side of policy support, and Quebeckers especially hostile (Citrin, Johnston and Wright, 2012; Wright et al., 2017). Third, support tends to vary along with specificity and, to use Citrin et al.'s terms, the "hardness" of the policy in question. That is, regardless of context policy support increases when items reflect abstract hat-tips to diversity in society, and decreases as the specific accommodations become more symbolically "costly" (for lack of a better term) to native-born citizens. Evidently, many who are fine in principle with their government endorsing cultural diversity in some general way draw the line at sustaining

Table 8.1. Mean support for multicultural policies by context

Categories	Quebec	Rest of Canada	United States
Diversity			
Fundamental	.49 (.02)	.49 (.02)	.52 (.01)
Taught in Schools	.58 (.02)	.66 (.02)	.65 (.01)
Media Requirements	.58 (.01)	.68 (.02)	.63 (.01)
Dual Citizenship	.40 (.01)	.40 (.01)	.38 (.01)
Affirmative Action	.38 (.01)	.34 (.01)	.32 (.01)
Accommodations			
Headgear	.12 (.01)	.32 (.01)	.26 (.01)
Immigrant Language	.15 (.01)	.24 (.01)	.26 (.01)
Scale	.32 (.01)	.38 (.01)	.36 (.01)

Note: Sample limited to white native-born respondents. Standard error in parentheses.

it with specific accommodations to religious headgear and multilingual language instruction in public schools.

One other noteworthy finding at the descriptive level is that, as is the case with immigration policy more generally (Wright and Levy, 2019), opinion may lean negative yet still reflect a great deal of ambivalence. For instance, recall that each respondent answered five questions on multiculturalism policy. The average white native-born respondent gave just over one positive answer (1.12), almost three negative answers (2.69), and just over one neutral answer (1.24). Indeed, most cluster around moderate responses, with very few respondents hitting the extremes: among white natives, 8.9 per cent answered negatively to all items put to them whereas, on the other side, only 2.9 per cent answered in Panglossian fashion. Finally, ambivalence does not appear to reflect pure indifference, as only 2.9 per cent of white native respondents answered neutrally to all questions.

Dimensionality

How strongly intercorrelated are peoples' assessments of these policies? Table 8.2, below, lists the policy items – the three "symbolic" diversity items asked of only a third of respondents each are combined into a composite measure – and explores bivariate correlations between them among each contextual subsample. What emerges is that, regardless of whether we are looking at Quebeckers, the Rest of Canada (ROC), or Americans, the items are positively correlated albeit not all that strongly. The correlation coefficients top out at around .50 and bottom out around .10, and, on average the pairwise correlation is .33 for ROC,

Table 8.2. Dimensionality of policy support items

Categories	Diversity (Composite)	Dual Citizenship	Aff. Act Preference	Accom. Headgear	Accom. Language
Diversity Composite	1.00	-	-	-	-
	1.00	-	-	-	-
	1.00	-	-	-	-
Dual Citizenship	.30	1.00	-	-	-
	.13	**1.00**	-	-	-
	.22	1.00	-	-	-
A.A. in Hiring	.37	.34	1.00	-	-
	.30	**.19**	**1.00**	-	-
	.41	.37	1.00	-	-
Accom. Headgear	.30	.38	.31	1.00	-
	.17	**.26**	**.31**	**1.00**	-
	.26	.43	.47	1.00	-
Accom. Language	.23	.31	.41	.36	1.00
	.17	**.27**	**.28**	**.52**	**1.00**
	.27	.42	.51	.49	1.00

Entries are Pearson correlation coefficients. ROC, **Quebec**, U.S. All entries are significant at the p = .05 level or better. Sample limited to white native-born respondents.

.26 for Quebec, and .39 for US respondents. Interestingly, it is with Americans where these attitudes are most closely tied. This may be surprising given that the United States is the least politically multicultural context of three; that said, the correlations are especially strong for issues that have achieved high degrees of salience there, namely affirmative action for minorities and language policy (see, e.g., Sears and Jessor, 1996, on the former and Schildkraut, 2005, on the latter).[1]

Another simple gauge of how well these items index together is Cronbach's Alpha, for which the items score a relatively high .71 in the full sample, and .71, .62, and .76 in the ROC, QC, and US subsamples respectively. Results from exploratory factor analysis were much the same: there is only a single factor worth mentioning, although the Eigenvalue associated with it is not overwhelmingly strong.[2] The upshot appears to be this: the measures appear somewhat "noisy," as evidenced by relatively weak pairwise correlations. Yet there is virtually no case to be made here for the idea that people are thinking about these items in a systematically distinct way in any of the three political contexts under investigation.

Vertical Constraint

For Converse, the notion of "vertical constraint" is the relationship between abstract opinions on a given topic and specific policy support item. In this case, the question is how closely support for multiculturalism policy (at least as

Table 8.3. Vertical constraint: MCP support and abstract attitudes about diversity and immigration

Categories	Immigration Consequences (4-Item)	Maintain or Adapt?	Society Better w/Shared Customs & Traditions	Society Better w/Variety of Religions	Society Better w/Common Language
Diversity					
Fundamental	.26	.29	.14	.26	.14
Taught in Schools	.42	.23	.23	.26	.12
Media Requirements	.26	.21	.15	.25	.09
Dual Citizenship	.29	.19	.13	.13	.18
Affirmative Action	.33	.16	.02	.21	.17
Accommodations					
Headgear	.28	.31	.15	.29	.22
Language	.21	.27	.06	.23	.24
MCP 5-Item Scale	.41	.34	.16	.33	.27

Notes: Entries are Pearson correlation coefficients. All items coded such that high scores indicate favourability towards immigration/diversity/MC. Sample is pooled across three political contexts but limited to white native-born respondents. Entries that are not statistically significant at the $p = .05$ threshold are italicized.

Banting and Kymlicka define it) is tied to broader conceptions of diversity in society. It isn't really a question of *whether* there is constraint in this domain, since it would be somewhat shocking if general opinions about diversity had nothing to do with one's support for policies designed to encourage it. Rather, it is a question of how much.

To find out, I pulled several items and scales out of the IDSS survey that were designed to tap general ideas about immigration and diversity. The first is an index based on four common "consequences of immigration" items.[3] The second is an item originally fielded in the 1992 American National Election Survey and designed to tap general sentiment on immigrant assimilation. It is worded as follows: "Some people say that it is better for a country if different racial and ethnic groups maintain their distinct customs and traditions. Others say that it is better if these groups adapt and blend into the larger society." Finally, we have a trio of items drawn from the European Social Survey designed to tease out whether "it is better for society if" (a) "almost everybody shares the same customs and traditions"; (b) "there are a variety of religions"; (c) "almost everyone is able to speak at least one common language." All of these items were rescored in a pro-MC direction. Table 8.3, below, shows how each item correlates with each of the MC policy support items and the MCP support index.

In general, the correlations here are positive across the board although generally rather modest. They are stronger for the immigration consequences index than for any other measure, although the "maintain or adapt" item also does well, perhaps unsurprisingly given the close kinship of that item's content and multiculturalism policy per se. Indexing the MCP items strongly boosts the correlations, which is to be expected as the process helps tamp down random measurement error. Overall, the takeaway here is as it was before: vertical constraint appears relatively high in this domain, in that there seems to be little case that people's policy judgments are departing strongly from their underlying feelings about immigration and immigrant diversity.

Horizontal Constraint

Horizontal constraint represents how well policy support on a given policy or set of policies predicts support for other, putatively related ones. In this case, I explore the extent to which people's support for multiculturalism policy is tied to pro- or anti-immigrant sentiment in other domains. Unfortunately, the IDSS cupboard of immigration policy support is somewhat bare. Even so, we did query respondents' desired level of immigration (the ubiquitous item eliciting whether immigration to the country ought to be "decreased," "increased," or "kept the same"), preference for family versus "skills-based" immigration, and a three-item index tapping whether immigrants should be eligible for various government benefits.[4] All items coded such that high scores indicate favourability towards immigration/diversity/MC. The "Family v. Skills" item, which has no obvious polarity in that regard, is coded "family" low and "skills" high.

As table 8.4 indicates, the MCP items are correlated in moderate-to-strong fashion with how much immigration people desire overall, a tendency that appears to ramp up as the accommodation shifts from "soft" to "hard" in character. The correlation between multiculturalism policy support and another immigration policy – a preference for skills versus family re-unification – is negative, meaning that "multiculturalists" seem to favour skills over family but only very weakly. Lastly, people's views on multiculturalism are somewhat positively correlated with their position on whether or not immigrants should have access to social benefits, but this correlation is also fairly weak.

Conclusions

My aim in this study was to paint a largely descriptive portrait of native-born Americans' and Canadians' attitudes about multiculturalism policy. The takeaways, at least as I see them, are as follows:

(1) Across countries, opinion on these policies leans negative overall (albeit with a substantial dose of ambivalence), and appears to do so more

Table 8.4. Horizontal constraint: MCP support and other immigration policy attitudes

Categories	Desired Immig. Level	Family v. Skills Preference	Immigrant Benefits Access (3-Item)
Diversity			
Fundamental	.25	−.16	.19
Taught in Schools	.31	*−.02*	.16
Media Requirements	.22	−.09	*.06*
Dual Citizenship	.30	−.13	.19
Affirmative Action	.38	−.10	.19
Accommodations			
Headgear	.35	*−.08*	.12
Immigrant Language	.34	−.15	.16
MCP 5-Item Scale	.47	−.16	.24

Notes: Entries are Pearson correlation coefficients. Sample is pooled across three political contexts but limited to white native-born respondents. Entries that are not statistically significant at the $p = .05$ threshold are italicized.

sharply as the policies themselves connote "harder-edged" forms of cultural accommodation. In short, the native-born seem largely content to acknowledge diversity in symbolic ways, much less so for policies that are either "costly" for them (affirmative action is one example) or manifestly geared against assimilation (uniform exceptions and native-language instruction in schools).

(2) Despite whatever ambivalence exists across the various policies, there is a substantial degree of correlation among them. This to say that, though the pairwise correlations across items are not overwhelmingly strong, when we consider all items together there is no evidence that more than one systematic "factor" underlies them.

(3) In terms of vertical constraint, attitudes on multiculturalism policy are quite closely tied with abstract sentiment about whether immigration is good or bad for the country, and whether immigrants should try to maintain their own cultures and traditions versus adapting to the host country. Connections between MCP support and broader sentiments about whether society is made better or worse by various forms of diversity are a little more weakly correlated, but the relationships are both consistent and in the expected direction.

(4) Finally, the picture was a little more uneven with respect to horizontal constraint: respondents' scores on the MCP index are strongly correlated to their overall preference for how many immigrants should be allowed to come to the country. On the other hand, they were much more weakly correlated with opinions about whether immigrants ought to be chosen with an emphasis on family reunification (versus skills), and whether they ought to have access to social benefits once they arrive.

I have said a lot about the "what" here without saying much about "why." In fact part of this depends on one's point of view, as many students of immigration attitudes model such attitudes as a function of the kinds of measures I explored under the heading "vertical constraint" (Ceobanu and Escandell, 2010; Hainmueller and Hopkins, 2012). So, on that interpretation scores on the MCP index are not merely *correlated* with one's underlying attitude about the economic and cultural consequences of immigration but caused by it. The difference between my largely descriptive story and the causal one is more than semantic, with the latter requiring assumptions about causal order that the data alone are generally unable to sustain. It may be the case that abstract sentiment causes people's specific policy attitudes, but we have no direct evidence of this from the data I have explored here. Regardless, deeper questions exist about whether attitudes over MCP are driven predominantly by group allegiances, on the one hand, or political values people associate with the social contract on the other.

Another issue to ponder is that what people thought in 2014, the year the IDSS was fielded, may bear little resemblance to the present day. What do they think now? On one hand, one sees in the rise of right-wing populist movements, the election of Donald Trump and the like, the possibility that these issues have become more even more politicized now than they were then.[5] It is difficult to say whether or how this might bear upon the findings presented here, as everything depends upon the nature of the change in rhetoric at the elite level and how this engages the preconceptions in the broader public and within key segments of it. It is conceivable that people have come to associate multiculturalism and associated issues even more closely with their national and ethnic identities than they did only a few short years ago, but it may also be the case that competing frames about the various policies has brought more nuance to the underlying belief system. The only way to find out is with more surveys, in more places.

Assuming we take the results of this study at face. What, then, should we make of the relative homogeneity of these policy attitudes, and their consistency with underlying sentiment about the nature of diversity in society? Of course, one could view this as little more than a measurement issue: survey research is messy, and while *researchers* tend to have no problem differentiating predisposition from policy, survey respondents either can't or won't. As a result, perhaps nothing much is gained by such a granular approach to policy support. Another possibility is that people lump these issues together because they have been encouraged to do so by the rhetoric they encounter from elites and the media, or even in the course of their day-to-day interactions. If the prevailing storyline on these issues encourages people to treat them together – whether that story line is predominantly pluralist or monist – then there is little reason to think that citizens encountering this storyline will bother to think about the issues in a nuanced way.

Yet we know that people *do* respond to cross-pressures when the "real world" makes them salient. In the United States, for example, we observed numerous cases where specific policy attitudes on immigration bore little resemblance to people's more abstract notions. Where do these cross-pressures come from? There is political culture in a big-picture sense, of course. More proximately, the same actors that might serve to tie these issues together might also, for one reason or another, pull them apart. The task moving forward, then, becomes twofold: (1) understanding the broader environment on these topics; and (2) understanding how this environment resonates with people's deeper conceptions of "us versus them" and the social contract that binds them to immigrants.

NOTES

1 This touches on broader conceptual questions about whether (and why) the policies reflected in the Banting & Kymlicka index should be called "multicultural policies" in domains where their implementation has not been tied to pro-MC arguments *as such*. For instance, affirmative action in the United States is generally framed not as a means to "boost" diversity but as a tool for redressing past injustice. Language policy is even more ambiguous, as "bilingual education" may reflect either "multicultural" or "integrationist" aims.

2 In the full sample, this value is 1.78. The second factor extracted has an associated Eigenvalue of a mere .05. The results are for all intents and purposes consistent across ROC, QC, and US subsamples.

3 Specifically, respondents were asked whether they agreed or disagreed that immigrants (a) "increase crime rates"; (b) "are generally good for [Canada's / the U.S.] economy"; (c) "take jobs away from people born in [Canada / the U.S.]"; (d) "improve [Canadian/ American] society by bringing in new ideas and cultures." The items index reasonably well (Cronbach's Alpha = .78 among native-born white respondents).

4 The immigration level item is worded: "Do you think the number of immigrants from foreign counties who are permitted to come to Canada to live should be …" and respondents are offered "increased a lot," "increased a little," "left the same," "decreased a little," and "decreased a lot." The family versus skills question is worded: "Every year, many more people apply to come to live in Canada permanently than current law allows. Some people think we should give preference to applicants who have family members already living in Canada, while others think we should prefer applicants with education and skills." Finally, the benefits access root question is: "Thinking of immigrants, after how many years living in Canada do you think they should obtain the same rights to government benefits and services as citizens already living here?" And respondents are queried with respect to "Publicly funded health insurance," "old-age pensions," and "cash welfare."

5 That said, however, one is struck by the relative lack of salience that immigration and multiculturalism brought to the recent Canadian federal election. Indeed, aside

from a brief flare-up caused by revelations about P.M. Justin Trudeau's exuberance for racially insensitive cosplay, and lingering concerns – proved meritless once returns were tallied – about Maxime Bernier's anti-immigrant and anti-multicultural People's Party.

References

Abrajano, M., and Hajnal, Z.L. 2015. *White Backlash: Immigration, Race, and American Politics*. Princeton University Press.

Banting, K., and W. Kymlicka. 2017. "Introduction: The Political Sources of Solidarity in Diverse Societies." In *The Strains of Commitment: The Political Sources of Solidarity in Diverse Societies*, edited by K. Banting and W. Kymlicka, 1–60. Oxford University Press.

– 2020. "Multiculturalism Policy Index." http://www.queensu.ca/mcp/

Banting, K., W. Kymlicka, H. Harrell, and R. Wallace, forthcoming. "Beyond National Identity: Liberal Nationalism, Shared Membership, and Solidarity," In *Liberal Nationalism and Its Critics*, edited by D. Miller and G. Gustavsson. Oxford University Press.

Banting, K., and S. Soroka. 2012. "Minority Nationalism and Immigrant Integration in Canada." *Nations and Nationalism* 18 (2): 156–76. https://doi.org/10.1111/j.1469-8129.2011.00535.x

Blumer, H. 1958. "Race Prejudice as a Sense of Group Position." *Pacific Sociological Review* 1: 3–7. https://doi.org/10.2307/1388607

Bobo, L., V. Hutchings. 1996. "Perceptions of Racial Group Competition: Extending Blumer's Theory of Group Position to a Multiracial Social Context." *American Sociological Review* 61: 951–72. https://doi.org/10.2307/2096302

Castles, S., H. de Haas, and M. Miller. 2013. *The Age of Migration*, (5th ed.) The Guilford Press.

Ceobanu, A.M. and X. Escandell. 2010. "Comparative Analyses of Public Attitudes toward Immigrants and Immigration Using Multinational Survey Data: A Review of Theories and Research," *Annual Review of Sociology* 36: 309–28. https://doi.org/10.1146/annurev.soc.012809.102651

Citrin, J., D.P. Green, C. Muste, and C. Wong. 1997. "Public Opinion toward Immigration Reform: The Role of Economic Motivations." *The Journal of Politics* 59: 858–81. https://doi.org/10.2307/2998640

Citrin, J., D.O. Sears, C. Muste, and C. Wong. 2001. "Multiculturalism in American Public Opinion," *British Journal of Political Science* vol. 31, no. 2: 247–75.

Citrin, J., R. Johnston, and M. Wright. 2012. "Do Patriotism and Multiculturalism Collide? Competing Perspectives from Canada and the United States." *Canadian Journal of Political Science* 45: 531–52. https://doi.org/10.1017/S0008423912000704

Citrin, J., and D.O. Sears. 2014. *American Identity and the Politics of Multiculturalism*. Cambridge University Press.

Gest, J. 2016. *The New Minority: White Working Class Politics in an Age of Immigration and Inequality*. Oxford University Press.

Goodman, S.W. 2014. *Immigration and Membership Politics in Western Europe*. Cambridge University Press.

Hainmueller, J., and D.J. Hopkins. 2012. "Public Attitudes Toward Immigration." *Annual Review of Political Science* 17: 225–49. https://doi.org/10.1146/annurev-polisci-102512-194818

Harell, A., and D. Stolle. 2010. "Diversity and Democratic Politics: An Introduction." *Canadian Journal of Political Science* 43 (2): 384–400. https://doi.org/10.1017/S000842391000003X

Higham, J. 2002 [1955]. *Strangers in the Land: Patterns of American Nativism, 1860–1925*. Rutgers University Press.

Hood, M.V. III, and I.L. Morris. 1998. "Give Us Your Tired, Your Poor, … But Make Sure They Have a Green Card: The Effects of Documented and Undocumented Migrant Context on Anglo Opinion Toward Immigration." *Political Behavior* (20): 1–15.

Hopkins, D.J. 2010. "Politicized Places: Explaining Where and When Immigrants Provoke Local Opposition." *American Political Science Review* 104: 40–60. https://doi.org/10.1017/S0003055409990360

Howard, M.M. 2009. *The Politics of Citizenship in Europe*. Cambridge University Press.

– 2004. "The Retreat of Multiculturalism in the Liberal State: Theory and Policy." *The British Journal of Sociology* 55 (2): 237–57. https://doi.org/10.1111/j.1468-4446.2004.00017.x. Medline: 15233632

Kinder, D.R., and C.D. Kam. 2009. *Us Against Them: Ethnocentric Foundations of American Opinion*. University of Chicago Press.

Koostra, A. 2017. "Us versus Them: Explaining the Perceived Deservingness of Minority Groups in the British Welfare State Using a Survey Experiment." In *The Social Legitimacy of Targeted Welfare: Attitudes towards Welfare Deservingness*, edited by W. van Oorschot, F. Roosma, B. Meuleman, and T. Reeskens, 263–80. Cheltenham: Edward Elgar.

Kymlica, W. 1995. *Multicultural Citizenship: Liberal Theory of Minority Rights*. Oxford University Press.

Levy, M., and J. Citrin, J. 2016. "Mass Opinion and Immigration Policy in the United States: Re-Assessing Clientelist and Elite Perspectives." *Perspectives on Politics* 14: 660–80. https://doi.org/10.1017/S1537592716001110

Levy, M., and M. Wright. forthcoming. *Immigration and the American Ethos*. Cambridge University Press.

Masuoka, N., and J. Junn. 2013. *The Politics of Belonging: Race, Public Opinion, and Immigration*. University of Chicago Press.

Mudde, C., and C. Kaltwasser. 2017. *Populism: A Very Short Introduction*. Oxford University Press.

Muste, C. 2013. "The Dynamics of Immigration Opinion in the United States, 1992-2010." *Public Opinion Quarterly* 77: 398–416. https://doi.org/10.1093/poq/nft001

Newman, B.J. 2013. "Acculturating Contexts and Anglo Opposition to Immigration in the United States." *American Journal of Political Science* 57: 374–90. https://doi.org/10.1111/j.1540-5907.2012.00632.x

Petersen, M. 2012. "Social welfare as small-scale help: Evolutionary psychology and the deservingness heuristic." *American Journal of Political Science* 56: 1–16. https://doi.org/10.1111/j.1540-5907.2011.00545.x. Medline: 22375300

Putnam, R.D. 2007. "*E Pluribus Unum*: Diversity and Community in the Twenty-First Century the 2006 Johan Skytte Prize Lecture." *Scandinavian Political Studies* 30 (2): 137–74. https://doi.org/10.1111/j.1467-9477.2007.00176.x

Schildkraut, D.J. 2005. *Press 'One' For English: Language Policy, Public Opinion, and American Identity*. Princeton: Princeton University Press.

– 2013. "Amnesty, Guest Workers, Fences! Oh My." *Public Opinion about "Comprehensive Immigration Reform."* In *Immigration and Public Opinion in Liberal Democracies*, edited by G.P. Freeman, R. Hansen, and D.L. Leal, 207–31. Routledge

Schrag, P. 2010. *Not Fit for Our Society: Immigration and Nativism in America*. University of California Press.

– 2007. "The Disconnect Between Public Attitudes and Public Policy on Immigration." In *Debating Immigration*, edited by C. Swain. Cambridge University Press.

Sears, D.O., and T. Jessor. 1996. "Whites' Racial Policy Attitudes: The Role of White Racism." *Social Science Quarterly* (77): 751–9. https://www.jstor.org/stable/42863528

Sidanius, J., and F. Pratto. 1999. *Social Dominance*. Cambridge University Press.

Sides, J., and J. Citrin. 2008. "Immigration and the Imagined Community in Europe and the United States." *Political Studies* 56: 33–56. https://doi.org/10.1111/j.1467-9248.2007.00716.x

Soroka, S., M. Wright, R. Johnston, J. Citrin, K. Banting, and W. Kymlicka. 2017. "Ethnoreligious Identity, Immigration, and Redistribution" *Journal of Experimental Political Science* 4: 173–82. https://doi.org/10.1017/XPS.2017.13

Soysal, Y. 1994. *Limits of Citizenship: Migrants and Postnational Membership in Europe*. Chicago University Press.

Tajfel, H., and J.C. Turner. 1979. "An Integrative Theory of Intergroup Conflict." In *The Social Psychology of Intergroup Relations*, edited by W.G. Austin, and S. Worchel, 33–7. Brooks/Cole.

Taylor, C. 1994. *Multiculturalism and the Politics of Recognition*. Princeton University Press.

van der Meer, T., and J. Tolsma. 2014. "Ethnic Diversity and Its Effects on Social Cohesion." *Annu. Rev. Sociol* 40 (1): 459–78. https://doi.org/10.1146/annurev-soc-071913-043309

van Oorschot, W. 2006. "Making the Difference in Social Europe." *Journal of European Social Policy* 16: 23–42. https://doi.org/10.1177/0958928706059829

Weldon, S. 2006. "The Institutional Context of Tolerance for EthnicMinorities: A Comparative, Multilevel Analysis of Western Europe." *American Journal of Political Science* 50: 331–49. https://doi.org/10.1111/j.1540-5907.2006.00187.x

Wright, M., 2011. "Diversity and the Imagined Community: Immigrant Diversity and Conceptions of National Identity." *Political Psychology* 32: 837–62. https://doi .org/10.1111/j.1467-9221.2011.00843.x

Wright, M., R. Johnston, J. Citrin, J., and S. Soroka. 2017. "Multiculturalism and Accommodation: Policy and Predisposition Across Three Political Contexts." *Comparative Political Studies* 50: 102–32. https://doi.org/10.1177/0010414015626448

Wright, M., and M. Levy. 2019. "American Public Opinion on Immigration: Nativist, Polarized, or Ambivalent?" *International Migration.* https://doi.org/10.1111 /imig.12660

Wright, M., M. Levy, and J. Citrin. 2016. "Public Attitudes Toward Immigration Policy Across the Legal/Illegal Divide: The Role of Categorical and Attribute-Based Decision-Making." *Political Behavior* 38: 229–53. https://doi.org/10.1007 /s11109-015-9311-y

Zaller, J. 1992. *The Nature and Origins of Mass Opinion.* Cambridge University Press.

9 Who Leads? The Delicate Dances of Party Elites and Partisans: Immigration Attitudes and Partisanship in Canada, 1980–2019

STUART SOROKA AND KEITH BANTING

In recent years, Canada has been seen as an exception to the major currents in contemporary democratic politics. Elsewhere, a powerful backlash against globalization and immigration has driven profound political shifts, including Brexit, the 2016 US presidential election, and the continued strength of radical anti-immigrant parties in Europe. To the outside world, Canada seems immune to these pressures, with continuing strong public support for a liberal immigration regime. Underneath the apparent stability, however, has been a growing polarization at two levels: a fraying of the historic multiparty consensus on immigration and diversity policy, and a striking polarization in the attitudes of the supporters of the major political parties in the country.

While there has been considerable commentary about the rupture in the multiparty consensus on immigration, there has been less attention to the growing divide in the attitudes of partisans of the major parties. More importantly, there has been little attempt to relate shifts at the level of parties to shifts at the level of partisan voters. Was polarization a top-down process in which growing conflict between party elites led to a sorting process in which voters moved to parties that articulated views close to their own? Or was polarization a bottom-up process, in which party leaders adopted divergent approaches to immigration to appeal to their partisan voters whose attitudes were shifting for other reasons?

This chapter explores these two processes. It does so by tracking polarization at the level of political parties and at the level of voters, comparing the trajectory at the two levels and the timing of shifts at each level. Undoubtedly, top-down and bottom-up processes were concurrent and reinforcing throughout the years of polarization. But as we shall see, comparing the trajectories and timing of change at the two levels generates interesting hints. Our discussion concentrates primarily on the Conservative Party and Conservative supporters. This is not to imply that polarization was driven solely by movement on the right. As we shall see, polarization among voters has reflected movement both by Conservative partisans, whose support for immigration has weakened, and by Liberal and NDP partisans whose support has strengthened (Besco, 2021). Nevertheless, the Conservatives, especially during the Harper government of 2006–15, provide a rich case study of the balance between top-down and bottom-up sources of change. To anticipate our conclusions, the timing of change in voter preferences and Conservative Party positions suggests that the story is, in part at least, more about following than leading opinion.

The chapter proceeds through three sections. The first section looks at relevant literatures that help inform our analysis. The second section traces the weakening of the multiparty consensus at the level of party elites, tracing their policy commitments during elections and decisions while in government. The third section analyses the growing divide in the attitudes of partisans of the major political parties during the same period. The final section compares the trajectory and timing of changes in policy positions of the Conservative Party on one hand and their supporters among the electorate on the other hand, and reflects on the implications.

Political Parties and Immigration Preferences

The first literature relevant to the analysis that follows highlights the relationship between the nature of party systems and the structure and nature of political debate in representative democracies. The literature has its origins in research linking European party systems to the structure of major "cleavages" in national politics (e.g., Lipset and Rokkan, 1967). That work made clear the connection between the structure of party systems and the nature and number of cleavages on which there will be electoral competition; it found that issue cleavages, electoral rules, and the number of political parties are intimately and reciprocally connected (e.g., Neto and Cox, 1997).

This is the case not just for the kind of stable issue dimensions which are the focus of the literature on cleavages, but also for new dimensions of political competition. Vote-seeking parties will adopt policy positions that may be advantageous electorally; and the institutionalization of that policy debate – in the form of party competition – can have an effect on issue salience as well as the degree to which the issue informs vote choice. This was a central lesson of Lijphart's (1979) seminal work on the varying impact of social cleavages on voting in Belgium, Canada, South Africa, and Switzerland, for instance; it is a feature of the literature on shifting cleavages and party systems (e.g., Kriesi, 1998) and the work on the impact of cultural change and postmodernism (e.g., Inglehart, 1990) as well.

The Canadian system has traditionally been characterized as a "brokerage" party system (Carty, 2010) in which parties have had to cobble together support from multiple constituencies, and consequently have tended to provide relatively few clear policy alternatives to voters. That said, both Reform and the Bloc Québécois are ideological parties (Carty et al., 2000); there is evidence of ideological differences across party members (Cross and Young, 2002); and evidence of differences in ideological and policy preferences across voters as well, both recently (Kevins and Soroka, 2018; Aytac et al. 2023) and in the 1980s (e.g., Perlin, 1988). In spite of a system that has been largely if not predominantly brokerage-style, then, Canadian parties have over the past 40 years regularly, visibly differed on salient policy issues.

Indeed, ideological and policy differences across parties and/or partisans have been central to Richard Johnston's account of Canadian electoral behaviour (Johnston et al., 1992; Johnston, et al., 2003), party systems (Johnston, 2013; 2017), and policy (Johnston, 1986). Parties have even staked out policy positions clearly outside the "middle" of public preferences, as suggested in Johnston, Fournier, and Jenkins's (2000) analysis of proximity versus directional voting in the 1993 and 1997 elections. They find that voters typically support the party with positions that are closest to their own, even if that position is on the opposite side of the policy debate, in line with the proximity model. That said, "the distribution of parties is not what a context-free proximity model would dictate" (1159). There are at times parties that perceive electoral or ideological advantages to espousing outlying positions in certain domains – notably including the Reform Party on the issue of aid to ethnic and racial minorities in 1993.

We take from these cross-national and Canadian literatures the understanding that (a) political parties (including Canadian ones) will stake out policy positions to increase vote share, and (b) when they do, citizens may either follow their party or switch to a party that better reflects their preferences on this new dimension of policy competition. This account is in one sense reciprocal, as both party positions and votes interact over time. That said, even as both parties and voters move, the direction of influence is primarily from the latter to the former: voters have preferences, and parties seek to represent the right combination (i.e., a plurality-winning combination) of those preferences. We view this as the standard account of Canadian party politics.

Which brings us to the second literature that has informed our analysis below, namely, the literature focused on the role of political parties in generating opposition to immigration and immigrants in democratic societies. This literature is especially extensive in the European context, where a potent backlash against migration has contributed to electoral volatility, voter realignment, and the rise of radical right parties. This backlash has placed immense pressure on mainstream parties, which have often responded by adopting increasingly restrictive approaches to immigration themselves (Arzheimer, 2009; Van de Brug et al., 2005). This literature sees the role of anti-immigrant parties not simply as a reflection of anti-immigrant sentiment among the public, but also as a causal force in immigration politics, legitimating public anxieties about immigrants, priming immigration as a salient issue in electoral choice, and mobilizing those anxieties in electoral politics (Koning, 2017).[1]

Just like the literature on the Canadian party system, then, the cross-national literature on the politics of immigration suggests bi-directional effects between parties and voters. But whereas the Canadian literature emphasizes the bottom-up influence of citizen preferences, the cross-national literature emphasizes the top-down influence of parties and party systems. Which account more accurately reflects the shifts in Canadian public attitudes and party policy on immigration over the past 40 years? How have the two levels interacted in the process of adjustment in Canada? These questions are the focus of the sections that follow.

The Trajectory of Party Support for Immigration

The 2000s witnessed the fraying of a longstanding multiparty consensus on immigration policy. The roots of polarization in party debates reached back to the disruption of the traditional party system in the early 1990s, with the dramatic fragmentation of conservative political forces, and their reunification in the early 2000s. The brokerage style of parties and politics, which dominated in much of the twentieth century was associated with a largely accommodative approach to immigration and diversity. Debates over immigration proceeded within "an unprecedented political and public consensus" on a generally liberal immigration policy, a pattern highlighted by the near-unanimous passage of the 1976 Immigration Act (Kelley and Trebilcock, 2010, 379). This consensus occasionally came under strain, usually in debates over refugee policy. But these fractious moments tended to obscure broad elements of continuing consensus. Notably, the Progressive Conservative government led by Brian Mulroney embedded multiculturalism in legislation in 1988 and steadily increased immigration levels during the economic turbulence of the early 1990s, breaking with the traditional pattern of cuts in admissions during recessions (ibid., 415-16).[2]

Where political parties are concerned, the shifting alignment between partisanship and immigration policy was principally about changes on the right. The multiparty consensus began to unravel in the aftermath of the 1993 election with the breakthrough of the populist Reform Party, which articulated a potent social conservatism and a highly individualist approach to diversity. The party opposed special status for Quebec, spending on Aboriginal peoples, gender equality, multiculturalism, and affirmative action, all of which they saw as catering to "special interests" (Harrison, 1995). Reformers also brought a distinctive voice to the immigration sector. Activists occasionally criticized the levels of non-white immigration that had emerged in the previous two decades, and in 1990 the party officially criticized immigration policy for changing the ethnic makeup of Canada (Laycock, 2012, 90). Following their breakthrough in the 1993 election, the 1994 Reform Party conference promised to lower the level of immigration and deny healthcare and social benefits to all immigrants before they became citizens (Flanagan, 1995, 197–8). Party leaders later sought to tone down anti-immigrant views in official party positions, but the party's 1997 election manifesto repeated its opposition to affirmative action and pledged to lead a campaign to repeal the multicultural section of the Charter (Reform Party, 1997).

Although the Reform Party proved a temporary feature of the party system, its views on immigration and diversity did not go away. The 1997 election demonstrated that Reform had reached the limits of its growth potential (Nevitte et al., 2000, ch. 8), and the party was absorbed in a restructured Conservative Party in the early 2000s. The social conservatism of Reform flowed into the newly united Conservative Party. As Farney has argued, "social conservatives are still allowed a seat at the conservative table" (Farney, 2012, 128). Their views are represented not only at the grassroots levels but also among the party's elected MPs, and social conservatives have represented an important block in successive party leadership contests (Thomas and Sabin, 2019; Wilkins-Laflamme and Reimer, 2019).

Leaders of the new Conservative Party faced twin imperatives common to political parties: to expand their electoral support and to retain the commitment and enthusiasm of their traditional base. This process proved complex, both ideologically and strategically. Ideologically, the party sought to combine a neoliberal approach to economic issues and a socially conservative approach to cultural issues, two imperatives that could sometimes be in tension. Strategically, the entire rationale for the unite-the-right movement was to win power federally. The new Conservatives therefore had to appeal to a broad spectrum of voters across the many cleavages that define the country, and to avoid the impression that they were intolerant of diversity and a haven for racists. Given the size of immigrant communities in Canada, especially in major urban conurbations such as Vancouver and Toronto, this meant that the party needed to appeal to immigrant voters. Yet the party also had to retain the support of social conservatives who constituted an important part of their base. This strategic necessity to appeal simultaneously to immigrants and social conservatives has been called the "populist's paradox" in Canada (Marwash et al., 2013; also Triadafilopoulos and Taylor, 2021. Crafting a response to these conflicting imperatives required a tricky balancing act, and the ways in the party responded proved critical to partisan debates over immigration.

While in opposition, the new Conservative Party studiously downplayed immigration issues. Its 2004 and 2006 election manifestos welcomed hardworking immigrants and promised to enhance recognition of their economic credentials, limiting negative tropes to a promise to speed up deportations of criminals and terrorists (Conservative Party, 2004, 2006). This pattern persisted into the first couple of years of minority government, with the government's most dramatic initiative being the prime minister's 2006 official apology for past wrongs to Chinese Canadians. Over time, however, the party's response emerged along three tracks, which were inevitably in tension with each other.

On the first track, reflecting the neoliberal strain in the party's ideology, the Harper government sought to define immigration generally in economic rather than cultural terms. They embraced the immigration levels established by their Liberal predecessors, and even raised the immigration target for 2007, the first full year for which they controlled the program (Citizenship and Immigration Canada 2006, Table 1). In addition, the Conservatives retained the high priority awarded to immigrants with high levels of education and skills, assuming they would become self-sustaining more quickly. Over time, this economic approach increasingly took on a pro-business form. Beginning in 2010, the government made an existing offer of employment an important consideration in admission decisions (Alboim and Cohl 2012). This trend reached its apogee in 2015 with the introduction of Express Entry, a revised program for economic migrants that gave more weight to offers of employment than their level of education and training. Responsiveness to business concerns was also reflected in dramatic growth in the Temporary Foreign Workers program, which allows employers to bring in temporary workers, with low-skilled temporary workers not having a path to permanent residency. In some years, Temporary Foreign Workers exceeded the total permanent admissions for the skilled, family, and refugee streams combined.

On the second track, the Conservatives worked hard to attract immigrant voters. The party assumed they could appeal to socially and fiscally conservative members of minority communities by emphasizing issues such as their opposition to same-sex marriage (Marwash et al., 2013; Triadafilopoulos and Taylor, 2021). But the Conservative government joined the mainstream appreciation of diversity in its early years. As noted earlier, in 2006, Prime Minister Harper offered a formal apology and financial restitution to Chinese Canadians for the punitive imposition of a head tax on Chinese immigrants in the late nineteenth and twentieth centuries. In 2008, the government launched the Community Historical Recognition Program, a five-year funding program for commemorative projects initiated by established ethnocultural communities that had been targets of discriminatory policies in the past, including for example the Jewish, Indian, and Chinese communities. This strategy gained momentum with the appointment of Jason Kenney as Minister for Immigration, Citizenship and Multiculturalism. Kenney's outreach campaign included ministerial participation in countless community events, strategic mailings, and the creation of large databases of minority voters. In addition, at a time when the government was squeezing public expenditures across the board, the Conservatives made a massive investment in enhanced integration programming, especially language training, which had the coincidental political benefit of generating more ministerial announcements of financial support at community events (Seidle, 2010, table 1). The neoliberal priority to economic migration did complicate efforts to appeal to immigrant voters, as it generated intense pressure on the family reunification program. The government struggled with its response. They narrowed the definition of the "family," challenged "marriage migration," criticized parents and grandparents as drains on health care, and stiffened the conditions immigrants had to meet if they wish to sponsor family members. In 2011, the government introduced a super-visa program, which would allow relatives to visit for up to 24 months, and which they hoped would ease the pressure for permanent immigration. However, the number of super visas available failed to meet the demand.

On the third track, the Harper government used cultural policies to provide symbolic reassurance to social conservatives through an often stealthy campaign of wedge politics (Abu-Laban, 2014; Abu Laban et al., 2023). Their cultural strategies were framed as an effort to protect Canadians and Canadian values from the alleged threat from newcomers and "others." Refugees were a favourite target. Conservative speeches repeatedly emphasized security, control, and fraud, promising to root out "cheaters," "queue-jumpers," and "terrorists," and in 2012 the government passed the Faster Removal of Foreign Criminals Act. Conservatives also frequently implied refugees were a drain on social programs, especially health care, and the government reduced federal health benefits provided to refugees in their first year. The cultural strategy also spread to the fields of diversity and citizenship. While the Harper government never explicitly attacked multiculturalism, they sought to redefine Canadian identity around conservative themes. Their 2009 revisions to the citizenship guide downplayed multiculturalism in favour of the history of Canada's military triumphs and its legacy of British institutions and traditions (Citizenship and Immigration Canada, 2009). They questioned the loyalty of dual citizens, and toughened standards in the citizenship test, driving down the success rate, especially among immigrants with low family income, low proficiency in official languages, and low educational levels (Hou and Picot, 2020). Perhaps most troubling, the Conservatives repeatedly targeted Muslims, the least popular minority in the country. They symbolically denounced "barbaric cultural practices" in the revised citizenship guide and countless ministerial speeches, and in 2011, Kenney announced that those wishing to become Canadian citizens would have to uncover their face during the citizenship oath. In 2015, the government legislated on a range of its complaints in the Zero Tolerance for Barbaric Cultural Practices Act.

Another indicator of the evolving balance among the different tracks in Conservative strategy in government can be seen in the party's election manifestos.[3] There is a striking contrast between the 2008 and 2011 manifestos on one hand, and the 2015 manifesto on the other. The 2008 document limited its discussion to a short section entitled "Ensuring an Immigration System that Responds to Economic Needs" (Conservative Party, 2008, 17). The 2011 manifesto did not devote a distinct section to immigration but sprinkled short references to assisting recognition of foreign credentials, deporting foreign criminals, and fighting terrorism in other sections of the document (Conservative Party, 2011). In contrast, the 2015 manifesto devoted expansive attention to immigration. A section on economic migration celebrated "our world leading immigration system" and promised refinements. However, the manifesto included a lengthy section on "Combating jihadi terrorism," which highlighted the government's 2015 Protection of Canada from Terrorism Act, promised to confront "the growing problem of terrorist radicalization and violent extremism among Canadian youth," and called for a more expansive definition of the crime of high treason. A later section on "Strengthening Canadian Citizenship" promised to battle against fraud, revoke the citizenship of dual citizens convicted of terrorism, and ban face coverings during citizenship ceremonies (Conservative Party, 2015, 32–4, 78–80, 151–2). Conservative political positioning had clearly shifted.

This complicated juggling act of appealing simultaneously to the mainstream, to immigrant voters and to social conservatives was widely seen as effective during the election of 2011, which produced a Conservative majority in Parliament (e.g., Bricker and Ibbitson, 2013).[4] However, the strategy fell apart during the election campaign of 2015. The pre-campaign period had been marked by the Syrian refugee crisis, and the Conservative government adopted a historically cautious policy of admitting only 10,000 refugees and only after a slow process of intense security screening. This position imploded politically early in the election campaign when pictures of the lifeless body of three-year-old Alan Kurdi, washed up on a Turkish beach, flashed around the world. The reaction in Canada was intensified by reports that the Kurdi family was hoping to reach Canada and by confusion over whether their application for asylum had been denied. Conservative spokesmen fumbled their responses, looking uncompassionate. With the collapse of the refugee strategy, the Conservatives turned to their anti-Muslim trope, campaigning hard on a promise to protect Canadian values against the alleged threat posed by Muslim women wearing a niqab. In the middle of the campaign, the courts struck down their ban on the niqab during citizenship ceremonies. Rather than conceding, the Conservatives doubled down in a series of moves, appealing the judicial decision, promising a "barbaric cultural practices" tipline on which Canadians were encouraged to inform on their neighbours, and suggesting a ban on the niqab not only during the oath of citizenship but also in the civil service (Kymlicka, 2021). These measures proved a step too far and generated a backlash. Support for the Conservatives dropped in the last weeks of the campaign, and the Liberals won the election and immediately raised the target intake of Syrian refugees. Later, the former Conservative immigration minister admitted that their emphasis on "barbaric cultural practices" made a lot of immigrants, including non-Muslims, nervous. "It's why we lost ... we allowed ourselves to be portrayed in the last election as unwelcoming. That was a huge mistake" (CTV News, 2016).

The Conservative strategy was built on separate economic and cultural logics. Do we find echoes when we examine the evolution of public attitudes, and especially the views of Conservative partisans in the same period?

The Trajectory of Partisans' Support for Immigration

We analyse Canadian experience by drawing on a data set that spans over three decades. Starting in the late 1970s, Environics Focus Canada surveys regularly fielded batteries of questions on Canadian public policy to representative samples of the Canadian public. Many questions were repeated, often entirely unchanged, over many years. The result is a wealth of data on Canadians attitudes, combined with a wide range of demographic and political variables. Environics Focus Canada surveys have played a starring role in past work on immigration attitudes in Canada (Wilkes and Corrigall-Brown, 2011; Lawlor, 2015; Lawlor and Tolley, 2017; Besco, 2021). They have been a core source of data for the Canadian Opinion Research Archive and, relatedly, were central to one of the first major projects on public preferences for policy in Canada: Richard Johnston's *Public Opinion and Public Policy in Canada: Questions of Confidence* (1986). Detailed information on survey data are provided in appendix table 9.1.

The top panel of figure 9.1 shows Environics Focus Canada data on Canadians' support for immigration levels over time. It is based on four-point agree–disagree responses to the statement "Overall, there is too much immigration to Canada." Here, we rescale the variable from zero to one, where increasing values indicate stronger support (for more immigration), and then we plot the average of that variable by year. Values below .5 indicate that a majority of respondents agreed with the claim that there is too much immigration; values above .5 indicate that a majority of respondents did not agree with that claim. Gray whiskers show 95 per cent confidence intervals at every point at which survey data are available.

Note that until the mid-1990s, just as in many other countries around the world, a majority of Canadians believed that there was too much immigration. The pattern changed dramatically in the late 1990s, however, at which point a new equilibrium emerged. By 2003, between 60 and 70 per cent of Canadians disagreed with the statement. Net support for immigration thus hovers between .55 and .62 for the last 16 years.

We have considered the role of macroeconomics and immigration flows on support for immigration elsewhere (Banting and Soroka, 2020). Our findings there suggest that these contextual factors may have been critical in the

(a)

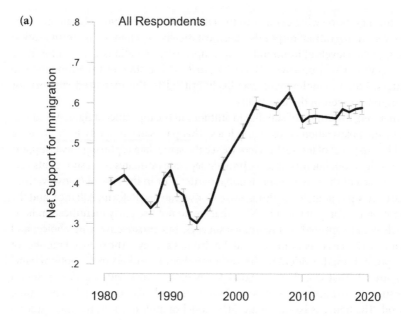

(b)

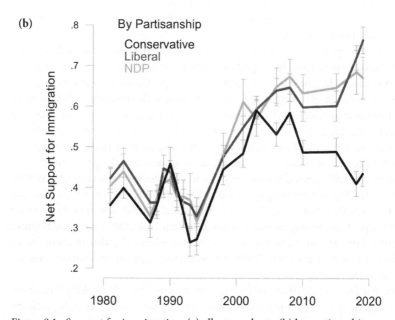

Figure 9.1. Support for immigration: (a) all respondents; (b) by partisanship

pro-immigration swing evident in the latter part of the 1990s. Canadians' support for immigration responds thermostatically to changes in immigration levels – when levels of immigration shift upwards, Canadians' support for more immigration shifts downwards, *ceteris paribus.* The state of the economy also matters. Low unemployment was likely critical to the increased support for immigration seen in the late 1990s.

That said, this image of stability in attitudes in the top panel of figure 9.1 masks a growing polarization across party lines. That partisan variability is the focus of the bottom panel of figure 9.1. Here we see the same data capturing mean support for immigration, but this time we provide separate estimates for respondents voting for each of the three major national parties – or in the case of Conservatives, a party group that includes Progressive Conservatives, Reform, Alliance, and the Conservative Party of Canada. Note that we do not use party identification here, which is not captured in Environics surveys, but prospective vote choice; and even vote choice is not available in all Environics surveys. The reduced number of data points is made evident by the lower number of whiskers in the bottom panel of figure 9.1. That said, there is a good deal of data to work with that *does* include a measure of prospective vote choice – 25,831 respondents, covering the entire time period. The figure is based on an OLS model of attitudes towards immigration levels, where immigration support is regressed on the following two interacted variables: (a) a factor variable for each year in the dataset, and (b) a factor variable with values for respondents who identify as Liberal, NDP, or Conservative (/Reform/Alliance/PC). Those who identify with other parties, or no party, are not included in this model.

The bottom panel of figure 9.1 suggests a fundamental shift in the relationship between vote choice and immigration attitudes in Canada. There are, first, few real differences in immigration support across partisans until the mid-2000s. There are some hints of what is to come, perhaps. In the early 1980s, in 1992 and 1993, and again in 2001 the mean for Conservative voters is lower than the mean for the Liberals or the NDP or both. It is notable that the largest differences are in 1992 and 1993, at the time when the Reform Party appeared as a national alternative to the Progressive Conservatives. But the gap between partisans in this early period is relatively low in comparison to what happens after 2004: a steadily increasing gap between Liberal and NDP voters on one side and Conservative voters on the other, where the former continue to increase their support for immigration, and the latter move in the opposite direction. By 2019, Liberal and NDP support for immigration is by this measure twice as high as it was in the early 1980s; Conservative support, in contrast, has returned to the same level as 1983.

The partisans of 2019 are of course not the same people as the partisans of 1980. Trends in the bottom panel of figure 9.1 may be less about stable partisans with steadily polarizing preferences so much as they are about voters sorting into parties. (The literature on polarization versus partisan sorting is helpful here; see, e.g., Mason, 2015; Kevins and Soroka, 2018.) Regardless, attitudes about immigration levels are more *aligned* with voting preferences now than in the pre-2004 period.

Past work has highlighted important cross-provincial differences, especially between Quebec and the rest of Canada (e.g., Banting and Soroka, 2012; Xhardez and Paquet, 2021). It is thus important to note that the overall trend observed in figure 9.1 is not different when we exclude Quebec, nor does it change substantially when we focus on Quebec alone. Appendix figure 9.1 replicates figure 9.1 results using only Quebec respondents and including Bloc Québécois supporters alongside the three major national parties.[5] From the mid-1990s to 2016 the primary distinction appears to be between pro-immigration NDP voters and all other partisans; but as of 2019, much like in the rest of Canada, Liberal voters are as supportive as NDP voters, with Conservative voters least supportive, and BQ voters somewhere in between. Similarly, as in the ROC, Quebec results suggest a shift from broad multiparty consensus in the mid-1990s to polarization afterwards. Large margins of error mean that few of these differences are statistically significant; and there are complexities to Québécois' immigration attitudes that are under-explored here, to be sure. But overall trends from 1980 to 2020 suggest that results in Quebec are not fundamentally different from the country as a whole.

To what extent is this shifting alignment evident in other measures of immigration support? Figures 9.2 and 9.3 examine trends in two other variables that have appeared regularly in Environics Focus Canada surveys. The first focuses on the economic benefits of immigration: "Immigration has a positive impact on the economy" (4-point response scale, agree strongly – disagree strongly). The second focuses on what the literature refers to as "cultural threat": "Too many immigrants are not adopting Canadian values" (4-point response scale, agree strongly – disagree strongly). Both variables are rescaled from 0 to 1 here; and values for the second variable are reversed so that for both measures increasing values indicate *pro*-immigration support. These questions were asked less frequently than the immigration levels question. For this reason, data in figures 9.2 and 9.3 begin only in 1992. Even so, there are over 25,000 respondents answering each question over a 27-year period.

Differences in mean values (and the range of y-axes) in figures 9.2 and 9.3 suggest that a majority of Canadians believes that there are economic benefits to immigration, but only a minority of Canadians is unconcerned about the cultural implications of that immigration. Our past work, reviewed above, suggests that this an accurate view of the nature of Canadian support for immigration. That said, part of the difference in the mean levels for these responses may have to do with question wording: note that agreement with the economic question indicates support, while agreement with the cultural question indicates a lack thereof. Acquiescence bias, the tendency for respondents to agree to survey questions (see Krosnick, 1999), may be part of what is going on here – from these data alone it is difficult to tell.

(a)

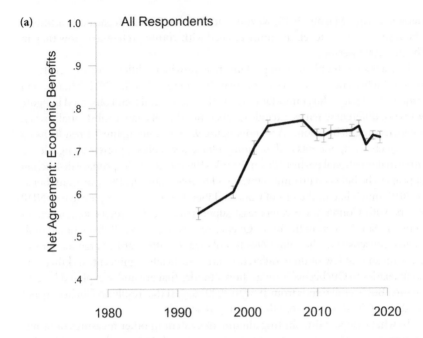

(b)

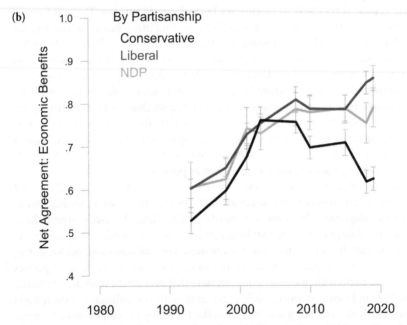

Figure 9.2. Agreement with economic benefits: (a) all respondents; (b) by partisanship

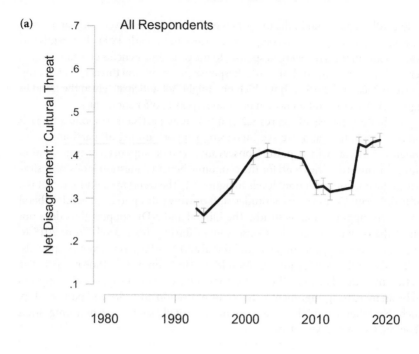

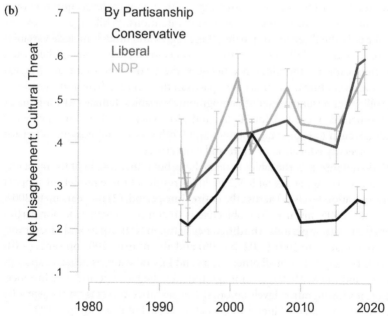

Figure 9.3. Disagreement with cultural threat: (a) all respondents; (b) by partisanship

Regardless, the trend in the top panels of the two figures is very similar. In each case, immigration support is comparatively weak in the early 1990s, but trends upward swiftly in the late 1990s. Responses to the economic benefits question remain relatively steady from 2001 onwards. Response to the cultural threat question drop between 2006 and 2016, a shift which one might not anticipate given the trend in figure 9.1. That said, differences in partisan responses offer some clues.

The bottom panels of figures 9.2 and 9.3 show partisans' responses to each survey question. Again, we see increasing support among all partisans up to roughly 2004, at which point Conservative voters' support for immigration shifts downwards. The trend for the economic benefits question looks very similar to the one for immigrant levels in figure 9.1. The trend for cultural threat is a little different: Conservative attitudes shift downwards up to 2010, while Liberal and NDP support remains steady. The Liberal and NDP support thus does not offset the downward shift by Conservatives during this period. From 2015 to 2019, however, support among both Liberal and NDP partisans moves upwards.

The dynamic seen for immigration levels (in figure 9.1) is thus not peculiar to that measure. For two other indicators of immigration support also appears to be an increasing alignment between immigration attitudes and partisanship, such that Liberal and NDP voters are more strongly supportive of immigration than are Conservative voters.

We can of course test this possibility more formally. Appendix table 9.2 shows results for OLS models regressing the immigration levels question on a factor variable capturing respondents' vote intentions. While figures show results for only the three major parties, these regression models include variables for Conservative, NDP, BQ and Other (mostly Green Party) voters, where each coefficient captures the difference between these voters and Liberals. Regression models capture a wider array of partisan differences, then; and they do so controlling for a standard set of demographic variables: female (=1 for females and 0 otherwise), age (=1 for 30–54, and 55+, where the baseline category is 18–29), French (=1 for Francophones and 0 otherwise) and education (=1 for some university education or more and 0 otherwise).

We do not interpret the tables in detail here, but rather highlight the most important results. Appendix table 9.2 includes results of three models of support for immigration levels (a) across the entire time period, (2) for years up to 2004, and (3) for 2005 onwards. The objective is to compare coefficients for parties across the two time periods. The difference between NDP voters and Liberal voters is marginal up to 2004 ($-.02$, $p < .05$) and absent from 2005 onwards ($-.01$, $p > .10$). The gap between all other voters and Liberal voters is negative and significant, and markedly larger in magnitude for the latter period. For instance: support for immigration levels amongst Conservative voters is on average $-.04$ ($p < .01$) lower than for Liberal voters before 2005; but it is $-.16$ ($p < .01$) lower than Liberals after 2005. To be clear: the gap between Conservative and Liberal partisans quadruples from one period to the next.

Appendix tables 9.3 and 9.4 include similar estimations for the economic benefits and cultural threat questions. Again, we see significant shifts across the two time periods. Support among Conservative voters is on average −.04 ($p < .01$) lower than among Liberal voters on the economic benefits measure before 2005, and −.13 ($p < .01$) lower after that. Conservatives are on average −.05 ($p < .01$) lower than Liberals on the cultural threat measure before 2005, and −.23 ($p < .01$) lower afterwards. There are small differences between NDP voters and Liberal voters over the two time periods. BQ voters are systematically less supportive of immigration than are Liberal voters, and more so after 2005.

Figures 9.1 through 9.3 and appendix tables 9.2 through 9.4 thus strongly support the contention that immigration attitudes became increasingly aligned with vote preferences after 2005; and that the major difference is the widening gap between Conservative voters versus Liberal and NDP voters.

Could it be that economic and culture concerns matter differently for partisan groups? There certainly is no hint that the difference in support for immigration levels is driven by concern primarily about economic or cultural factors. Both measures show roughly similar trends in figures 9.2 and 9.3; and both show roughly equivalent partisan differences in appendix tables 9.3 and 9.4. Insofar as there have been shifting attitudes among partisan groups, those shifts are equally evident for both the economic and cultural measures.

This does not necessarily preclude the possibility that the weight of economic and cultural factors matters differently for overall support of immigration across partisan groups, however. That is the focus of models in appendix table 9.5, which regress the immigration levels question on demographics and on responses to the economic benefits and cultural threat questions, across each partisan group, over the entire time period. Models rely on smaller numbers of cases, of course – we must now rely only on respondents for whom we have both partisanship and responses to all three immigration-related questions. Even so, results make clear that there is a robust ($p < .01$) relationship between the economic benefits and cultural threat questions and support for immigration levels, when all partisans are combined and when each is examined independently. Moreover, the coefficients for the two measures are similar in magnitude in every case. There is no partisan group for whom economic or cultural concerns seem to matter substantively more for immigration support.

This remains true in appendix table 9.6, in which the Liberal and Conservative models (for which we have a sufficient number of respondents) are broken down into the before 2005 and 2005 onwards periods. Here too, both economic benefits and cultural threat responses are significantly related to support for immigration levels, with roughly similar magnitudes. And there is little change in coefficients from one time period to the next.

In sum, the shifting alignment between partisanship and immigration attitudes does not appear to be linked primarily to economic or cultural concerns. There has been a marked change in partisans' support for immigration, however, beginning with Harper's leadership of the Conservative Party. From 2005 onwards, Conservative party voters have been less supportive of immigration levels, less inclined to see economic benefits to immigration, and more inclined to express concern about the impact that immigrants may have on Canadian culture. In contrast, Liberal and NDP voters have become more supportive. The result is Liberal and NDP electorates that are markedly more supportive immigration, and a base of Conservative support that is no more supportive of immigration than it was in the early 1980s.

Discussion: Who Leads? Policy Positions and Partisan Attitudes

Clearly, the image of Canada as a stable bastion of support for immigration and multiculturalism obscures change below the surface. The broad multiparty consensus of the late twentieth century has given way to more polarized party politics today. An important component of polarization has been the remarkable change in the attitudes towards immigration and cultural diversity among Conservative supporters. One obvious question at this stage concerns the nature of the relationship between the changes at the elite level and changes at the level of partisan supporters.

Did the Conservatives' policy responses lead or reflect changes in the attitudes of their partisans? Was the process top-down or bottom-up? The causal dynamics undoubtedly flowed in both directions, but comparing the trend and timing of government policy change with shifts in partisan opinion provides intriguing hints. First, it is difficult to attribute the erosion of Conservative voters' support for existing levels of immigration (figure 9.1) as well as their faith in the economic benefits of immigration (figure 9.2) to cues from "their" government. As we have seen, the Harper government steadfastly defined immigration as a positive economic benefit and maintained the existing immigration levels throughout their time in office. Over time, the pro-market and pro-business stance became stronger. Nonetheless, the same period saw a serious decline in support among Conservative partisans for existing immigration levels and the view that immigration was good for the economy. Admittedly, the erosion of faith in the economic benefits of immigration was somewhat slower while the Harper government was in power and sped up about the time they lost power in 2015. Nevertheless, in both cases, the turning point occurred during the Conservative government, and the process cannot be easily defined as a simple top-down process.

Timing of the growing anxiety about cultural values is even more intriguing. Here the decline among partisans was more dramatic. The relevant line in figure 9.3 turns in 2004, while the Conservatives were still in opposition, and plummets straight down and plateaus by 2010, staying there for the rest of the Harper government's tenure. Was this decline led by party cues? Once again, it is hard to see a simple top-down process. As we have seen, during its years in opposition, the leaders of the new Conservative party downplayed immigration issues; and their actions in their first couple of years as a minority government hugged the centre of the political spectrum. These years are typified by the 2006 Harper apology to Chinese Canadians, negotiations for which had begun under the previous Liberal government. The Conservatives more dramatic wedge politics emerged later, towards the end of the period of growth in their partisans' cultural anxiety, or more often after that anxiety had peaked. Kenney became minister of immigration in late 2008, and the government's more high-profile actions started the next year. The new citizenship guide and tighter standards in the citizenship test came in 2009. The ban on the niqab during the oath of citizenship and the first steps in tightening conditions for the sponsorship of parents and grandparents came in 2011. The reduction in health benefits for refugees and the automatic detention of "irregular" arrivals began in 2012; and legislation to allow the government to revoke the citizenship of terrorists came in 2013. The Zero Tolerance for Barbaric Cultural Practices Act was passed in 2015 and, as we have seen, the proposed tip line for Canadians to complain about their neighbours came later that year during the election. Once again, therefore, a simple top-down story is hard to sustain.

The same conclusion flows from a comparison of the party manifestos during the 2011 and 2015 elections. The 2011 manifesto gave little profile to cultural anxieties triggered by immigration, even though the support of Conservative partisans on this dimension of immigration and diversity had already bottomed out. In the 2015 manifesto, the party closed the gap between elite and partisan positions dramatically.

Obviously, it is difficult to discount more indirect processes. One possibility is that mere election of a Conservative government in 2006, even a minority one, meant that social conservatives no longer felt a need to repress anti-immigrant attitudes. Another is that the electorate responds only gradually to partisan differences set in motion years before, in this case perhaps by the brief prominence of the Reform Party. Perhaps what appears to be a leading electoral base in the mid-2000s is actually a following base, responding to partisan change set in motion in the early 1990s. Cochrane (2015) suggests that there was a lag of 10–20 years between ideological polarization at the party level and a similar dynamic among Canadian voters, for instance. In Carmines and Stimson's seminal account of issue evolution, "Following elite reorientations on contentious issues, comes a delayed, more inertial reaction in the mass electorate" (1986, 902). However, note that Carmines and Stimson's own evidence on attitudes towards racial desegregation in the United States suggests a delay of no more than a few years. Levendusky's (2009) work on partisan sorting in the United States portrays a dynamic more in line with the long-term change that Cochrane suggests – a gradual, increasing alignment of ideology and partisanship that was the product of polarizing cues from party elites. However, our account of conservative parties' positions over time does not portray decades of consistent, polarizing messaging on immigration from parties on the right in Canada. It is therefore difficult to avoid the conclusion that the more dramatic symbolic actions on culture during the majority Conservative government represented a reaction to a base which had was moving rapidly in response to a wider range of social cues.

The notion that parties respond to and then institutionalize change in public attitudes certainly fits with the causal story in the literature on social cleavages, party systems, and voting (e.g., Lijphart, 1979; Kriesi, 1998). It is also consistent with traditional interpretations of Canadian political parties. Given the historical record laid out here, it certainly seems possible that a shift in their voters' preferences led the Conservative Party to develop a dual immigration policy, simultaneously centrist on immigration levels and economic benefits but an outlier on cultural issues. This could be seen as an adaptation to a complex constituency consisting of mainstream voters, immigrant voters, and social conservatives among their traditional partisans. A complex constituency generates a complex policy strategy. It is striking (to us) that a dynamic at least resembling "brokerage" party politics is evident even when public attitudes are increasingly polarized. It would be more striking still if it was the practice of brokerage politics – that is, chasing either anti-immigration or pro-immigration voters – that contributed to party polarization on this issue.

This analysis calls out for further research. Most importantly, if Conservative party elites did not drive attitudinal change, what factors did lead to the weakening of support for immigration among Conservative voters? Analyses of the growth of anti-immigrant sentiment in other countries point to economic insecurity and cultural anxiety, both of which exist in Canada as well. Given the timing of the shift in support, we cannot discount the possibility that 9/11 and the securitization of immigration discourse also affected attitudes towards immigration, as has been suggested in the United States (e.g., Muste, 2013; on Canada, see McCoy, 2018). What is striking in the current context is that the Conservative base reacted to such external forces more quickly than did the party elite. Similar questions need to be asked about the other side of polarization. What has driven the increase in support for immigration among supporters of the Liberal and NDP parties?

Finally, the consequences of polarization are also critical. During the period under review here, aggregate opinion remained supportive of an ambitious immigration program. However, for decades, this stable support was based on a strong multiparty consensus. That consensus has given way to polarization, with what appears to be stable aggregate support reflecting declining support on the right and rising support on the centre-left. Is this a durable foundation for a stability in the politics of immigration in the years to come?

Appendix

Appendix table 9.1. Focus Canada surveys

	All Available Surveys		Including Immigration Question	
Year	No. of Surveys	No. of Respondents	No. of Surveys	No. of Respondents
1978	2	3,725	0	0
1979	5	9,751	0	0
1980	5	10,162	0	0
1981	5	9,951	0	0
1982	5	9,964	0	0
1983	5	10,091	1	2,018
1984	5	10,088	0	0
1985	5	10,233	0	0
1986	4	8,174	0	0
1987	4	8,069	1	2,019
1988	4	8,164	1	2,053
1989	4	8,019	1	2,005
1990	4	8,051	1	2,002
1991	4	8,256	1	2,021
1992	4	8,047	1	2,005
1993	4	8,047	1	2,002
1994	4	8,043	1	1,996
1995	4	8,067	0	0
1996	3	6,049	1	2,000
1997	4	8,045	0	0
1998	4	8,036	1	2,002
1999	4	8,177	0	0
2000	4	8,260	0	0
2001	4	8,115	1	1,493
2003	4	8,033	1	2,002
2004	4	8,082	0	0
2005	4	8,112	0	0
2006	4	8,273	1	2,045
2007	4	8,130	0	0
2008	4	8,095	1	2,026
2009	4	7,645	0	0
2010	1	2,020	1	2,020
2011	1	1,500	1	1,500
2012	1	1,500	1	1,500
2015	1	2,003	1	2,003
2016	1	2,000	1	2,000
2017	1	2,002	1	2,002
2018	2	4,000	2	4,000
2019	1	2,001	1	2,002

Appendix table 9.2. Modelling support for immigration levels

Categories	Dependent Variable: Immigration Levels		
	(1)	(2)	(3)
Female	−.011**	−.015***	−.036***
	(.004)	(.005)	(.008)
Age 30–54	−.018***	.014**	−.067***
	(.005)	(.006)	(.011)
Age 55+	.001	−.004	−.057***
	(.006)	(.007)	(.010)
French	−.013**	−.007	.008
	(.005)	(.006)	(.010)
Education	.219***	.225***	.164***
	(.005)	(.006)	(.008)
Vote: BQ	−.078***	−.059***	−.132***
	(.013)	(.014)	(.029)
Vote: Conservative	−.059***	−.037***	−.162***
	(.005)	(.006)	(.009)
Vote: NDP	−.012*	−.017**	−.010
	(.006)	(.007)	(.011)
Vote: Other	.013	−.017*	−.057***
	(.008)	(.010)	(.012)
Constant	.435***	.367***	.662***
	(.006)	(.007)	(.011)
Observations	27,090	18,642	8,448
R^2	0.083	0.084	0.093

Notes: Cells contain OLS regression coefficients with clustered standard errors. Model 1 includes all respondents; Model 2 uses respondents from before 2005; Model 3 uses respondents from 2005 onwards.
* $p < .10$; ** $p < .05$ *** $p < .01$.

Appendix table 9.3. Modelling agreement with economic benefits

Categories	Economic Benefits		
	(1)	(2)	(3)
Female	−.011**	−.017*	−.027***
	(.006)	(.009)	(.007)
Age 30–54	−.030***	.009	−.023**
	(.007)	(.011)	(.010)
Age 55+	−.001	.037***	−.020**
	(.007)	(.013)	(.009)
French	−.013*	.0002	−.021**
	(.008)	(.013)	(.010)
Education	.121***	.145***	.097***
	(.006)	(.010)	(.008)

(Continued)

Appendix table 9.3, continued.

Categories	Economic Benefits		
	(1)	(2)	(3)
Vote: BQ	−.119***	−.098***	−.132***
	(.017)	(.023)	(.025)
Vote: Conservative	−.075***	−.038***	−.134***
	(.007)	(.011)	(.009)
Vote: NDP	−.002	.003	−.040***
	(.009)	(.014)	(.011)
Vote: Other	−.041***	−.070***	−.075***
	(.010)	(.018)	(.011)
Constant	.720***	.625***	.814***
	(.007)	(.012)	(.009)
Observations	12,588	5,543	7,045
R^2	0.050	0.050	0.064

Notes: Cells contain OLS regression coefficients with clustered standard errors. Model 1 includes all respondents; Model 2 uses respondents from before 2005; Model 3 uses respondents from 2005 onwards.
* $p < .10$; ** $p < .05$ *** $p < .01$.

Appendix table 9.4. Modelling disagreement with cultural threat

Categories	Cultural Threat (reversed)		
	(1)	(2)	(3)
Female	.034***	.040***	.002
	(.006)	(.009)	(.009)
Age 30–54	−.106***	−.060***	−.132***
	(.008)	(.011)	(.012)
Age 55+	−.114***	−.109***	−.114***
	(.008)	(.012)	(.011)
French	−.027***	−.001	−.056***
	(.008)	(.012)	(.012)
Education	.181***	.202***	.155***
	(.006)	(.009)	(.009)
Vote: BQ	−.108***	−.089***	−.125***
	(.016)	(.018)	(.030)
Vote: Conservative	−.129***	−.052***	−.227***
	(.007)	(.010)	(.011)
Vote: NDP	.037***	.040***	−.003
	(.009)	(.014)	(.013)
Vote: Other	−.028***	−.030*	−.074***
	(.010)	(.017)	(.014)
Constant	.420***	.339***	.529***
	(.008)	(.011)	(.012)

(Continued)

Appendix table 9.4, continued.

Categories	Cultural Threat (reversed)		
	(1)	(2)	(3)
Observations	13,900	6,895	7,005
R^2	0.099	0.096	0.125

Notes: Cells contain OLS regression coefficients with clustered standard errors. Model 1 includes all respondents; Model 2 uses respondents from before 2005; Model 3 uses respondents from 2005 onwards.
* $p < .10$; ** $p < .05$ *** $p < .01$.

Appendix table 9.5. Modelling support for immigration levels across partisan groups

Categories	Immigration Levels				
	(1)	(2)	(3)	(4)	(5)
Female	−.009**	−.013	−.039***	−.004	.062**
	(.004)	(.009)	(.009)	(.013)	(.031)
Age 30–54	−.010*	−.028**	−.001	−.034*	−.074*
	(.005)	(.011)	(.012)	(.018)	(.038)
Age 55+	−.004	−.025**	.008	−.002	−.002
	(.005)	(.011)	(.012)	(.018)	(.040)
French	.030***	−.004	.090***	.073***	−.001
	(.004)	(.011)	(.015)	(.018)	(.080)
Education	.082***	.079***	.081***	.090***	.145***
	(.004)	(.009)	(.010)	(.015)	(.038)
Economic Benefits	.370***	.372***	.396***	.355***	.384***
	(.006)	(.015)	(.014)	(.023)	(.044)
Cultural Threat (rev)	.392***	.396***	.367***	.411***	.365***
	(.005)	(.012)	(.014)	(.019)	(.048)
Constant	.109***	.125***	.080***	.122***	.030
	(.006)	(.015)	(.014)	(.022)	(.090)
Observations	23,678	4,283	3,674	1,774	368
R^2	0.400	0.403	0.387	0.436	0.371

Notes: Cells contain OLS regression coefficients with clustered standard errors. Model 1 includes all respondents; Model 2 uses Liberal respondents; Model 3 uses Conservative respondents; Model 4 uses NDP respondents; Model 5 uses BQ respondents.
* $p < .10$; ** $p < .05$ *** $p < .01$.

Appendix table 9.6. Modelling support for immigration levels across Conservative and Liberal voters, over time

Categories	Immigration Levels			
	(1)	(2)	(3)	(4)
Female	−.036***	−.015	−.029*	−.049***
	(.012)	(.012)	(.015)	(.012)
Age 30–54	.001	−.013	−.007	.016
	(.015)	(.017)	(.019)	(.016)
Age 55+	−.006	−.023	−.002	.016
	(.017)	(.016)	(.022)	(.015)
French	.009	−.023	.065**	.092***
	(.015)	(.016)	(.028)	(.019)
Education	.108***	.045***	.091***	.070***
	(.013)	(.014)	(.016)	(.013)
Economic Benefits	.333***	.364***	.396***	.385***
	(.019)	(.026)	(.023)	(.018)
Cultural Threat (rev)	.399***	.369***	.405***	.353***
	(.017)	(.017)	(.022)	(.019)
Constant	.093***	.196***	.041*	.105***
	(.019)	(.025)	(.023)	(.017)
Observations	2,270	2,013	1,308	2,366
R^2	0.399	0.350	0.458	0.349

Notes: Cells contain OLS regression coefficients with clustered standard errors. Model 1 uses Liberal respondents before 2005; Model 2 uses Liberal respondents from 2005 onwards; Model 2 uses Conservative respondents before 2005; Model 2 uses Conservative respondents from 2005 onwards.
* $p < .10$; ** $p < .05$ *** $p < .01$.

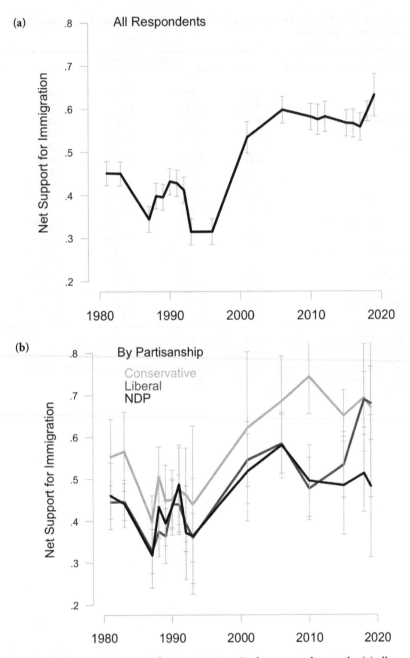

Appendix figure 9.1. Support for immigration, Quebec respondents only: (a) all respondents; (b) by partisanship

NOTES

1 Indeed, the reciprocal relationship between public attitudes and party policy/ competition proposed in work on social cleavages is readily evident in recent accounts of the politicization of immigration and integration in Europe (e.g., Grande et al., 2019; Green-Pedersen, 2012).

2 We have demonstrated elsewhere that rapid increases in immigration in these years weakened public support for the immigration program. See Banting and Soroka, 2020.

3 Unfortunately, the Manifestos Project does not currently provide data for immigration over this time period, and we are unable to conduct a quantitative analysis of the trajectory.

4 An analysis of the 2011 Canadian Election Study raises questions about whether the Conservatives actually did especially well with immigrant voters; they may simply have made small increases in support across the board.

5 We do not examine Quebec results in much detail in the text due to two factors: (1) low sample sizes, and (2) the absence of consistently coded BQ support in the vote variable. The former accounts for larger margins of error through the series. The latter accounts for the apparent absence of BQ voters from 2001 to 2015; though note that there are surveys in other years for which BQ votes are unidentifiable as well. For these reasons we do not look at Quebec-only results for the other time series examined below, for which even less data is available. Even so, we view appendix figure 9.1 as a useful diagnostic for comparing the available Quebec results with those in figure 9.1.

References

Abu-Laban, Yasmeen. 2014. "Reform by Stealth: The Harper Conservatives and Canadian Multi-Culturalism." In *The Multicultural Question: Debating Identity in 21st-Century Canada*, edited by Jack Jedwab. McGill-Queen's University Press.

Abu-Laban, Yasmeen, Ethel Tungohan, and Christina Gabriel 2023. Eds., *Containing Diversity: Canada and the Politics of Immigration in the 21st Century*. University of Toronto Press.

Alboim, Naomi, and Karen Cohl, 2012. *Shaping the Future: Canada's Rapidly Changing Immigration Policies*. Maytree Foundation.

Arzheimer, Aleandre. 2009. "Contextual Factors and the Rise of the Extreme Right Vote in Western Europe, 1980–2002" *American Journal of Political Science* 53 (2): 259–75. https://doi.org/10.1111/j.1540-5907.2009.00369.x

Aytac, Seyda Ece, Andrew Parkin, and Anna Triandafyllidou. 2023. "Why Are Public Attitudes towards Immigration in Canada Becoming Increasingly Positive? Exploring the Factors behind the Changes in Attitudes towards Immigration (1998–2021)." *Canadian Review of American Studies*: e2023012. doi:10.3138/cras-2023-012

Banting, Keith, and Stuart Soroka. 2012. "Minority Nationalism and Immigrant Integration in Canada." *Nations and Nationalism* 18 (1): 156–76.

– (2020). "A Distinctive Culture? The Sources of Public Support for Immigration in Canada, 1980–2019." *Canadian Journal of Political Science* 53 (4): 821–38. https://doi.org/10.1017/S0008423920000530

Besco, Randy. 2021. Forthcoming. "From Stability to Polarization: The Transformation of Canadian Public Opinion on Immigration, 1975–2019." *American Review of Canadian Studies* 51 (1): 143–65. doi:10.1080/02722011.2021.1902169.

Bricker, Darell, and John Ibbitson. 2013. *The Big Shift: The Seismic Change in Canadian Politics, Business, and Culture and What It Means for Our Future.* Harper Collins Publishers.

Carlaw, John. 2021. "Unity in Diversity? Neoconservative Multiculturalism and the Conservative Party of Canada." Working Papers Series produced jointly by the Ryerson Centre for Immigration and Settlement (RCIS) and the CERC in Migration and Integration at Ryerson University.

Carmines, Edward G., and James A. Stimson. 1986. "On the Structure and Sequence of Issue Evolution." *American Political Science Review* 80 (3): 901–20. https://doi.org/10.2307/1960544

Carty, R. Kenneth, and William Cross. 2010. "11 Political Parties and the Practice of Brokerage Politics." *The Oxford Handbook of Canadian Politics.* https://doi.org/10.1093/oxfordhb/9780195335354.003.0011

Carty, R. Kenneth, Lisa Young, and William Paul Cross. 2000. *Rebuilding Canadian Party Politics.* UBC Press.

Citizenship and Immigration Canada. 2006. *Annual Report to Parliament on Immigration.* Government of Canada.

– 2009. *Discover Canada: The Rights and Responsibilities of Citizenship.* Government of Canada.

Citrin, Jack, Richard Johnston, and Matthew Wright. 2012. "Do Patriotism and Multiculturalism Collide? Competing Perspectives from Canada and the United States." *Canadian Journal of Political Science* 45 (3): 579–605. https://doi.org/10.1017/S0008423912000704

Cochrane, Chris. 2015. *Left and Right: The Small World of Political Ideas.* McGill-Queen's University Press.

Conservative Party of Canada. 2004. *Demanding Better: Conservative Party of Canada, Platform 2004.* https://www.poltext.org/en/part-1-electronic-political-texts/electronic-manifestos-canada

– 2006. *Stand Up for Canada. Federal Election Platform 2006.* https://www.poltext.org/en/part-1-electronic-political-texts/electronic-manifestos-canada

– 2008. *The True North Strong and Free: Stephen Harpers' Plan for Canada.* https://www.poltext.org/en/part-1-electronic-political-texts/electronic-manifestos-canada

– 2011. *Here for Canada.* https://www.poltext.org/en/part-1-electronic-political-texts/electronic-manifestos-canada

– 2015. *Protect Our Economy. Our Conservative Plan to Protect the Economy.* https://
www.poltext.org/en/part-1-electronic-political-texts/electronic-manifestos-canada

Cross, William, and Lisa Young. 2002. "Policy Attitudes of Party Members in Canada:
Evidence of Ideological Politics." *Canadian Journal of Political Science/Revue canadienne
de science politique* 35 (4): 859–80. https://doi.org/10.1017/S0008423902778475

CTV News. 2016. "Chris Alexander on 'Barbaric Cultural Practices': It's Why We Lost."
October 9. https://www.ctvnews.ca/politics/chris-alexander-on-barbaric-cultural
-practices-it-s-why-we-lost-1.3106488

Farney, James. 2012. *Social Conservatives and Party Politics in Canada and the United
States.* University of Toronto Press.

Flanagan, Tom. 1995. *Waiting for the Wave: The Reform Party and Preston Manning.*
Stoddart.

Grande, Edgar, Tobias Schwarzbözl, and Matthias Fatke. 2019. "Politicizing
Immigration in Western Europe." *Journal of European Public Policy* 26 (10):
1444–63. https://doi.org/10.1080/13501763.2018.1531909

Green-Pedersen, Christoffer. 2012. "A Giant Fast Asleep? Party Incentives and the
Politicisation of European Integration." *Political Studies* 60 (1): 115–30. https://doi
.org/10.1111/j.1467-9248.2011.00895.x

Johnston, Richard, Keith Banting, Will Kymlicka, and Stuart Soroka. 2010. "National
Identity and Support for the Welfare State." *Canadian Journal of Political Science,* vol.
43 (2): 349–77. https://doi.org/10.1017/S0008423910000089

Harrison, Trevor. 1995. *Of Passionate Intensity: Right-Wing Populism and the Reform
Party of Canada.* University of Toronto Press.

Hou, Feng, and Garnet Pict. 2020. "The Decline in the Naturalization Rate among
Recent Immigrants in Canada: Policy Changes and Other Possible Explanations."
Migration Studies. doi:10.1093/migration/mnaa010.

Inglehart, Ronald. 1990. *Culture Shift in Advanced Industrial Society.* Princeton
University Press.

Johnston, Richard. 1986. *Public Opinion and Public Policy in Canada: Questions of
Confidence.* University of Toronto Press.

– 2013. "Alignment, Realignment, and Dealignment in Canada: The View from
Above." *Canadian Journal of Political Science / Revue canadienne de science politique*
46 (2): 245–71. https://doi.org/10.1017/S0008423913000474

– 2017. *The Canadian Party System: An Analytic History.* UBC Press.

Johnston, Richard, André Blais, Henry Brady, and Jean Crête. 1992. *Letting the
People Decide: The Dynamics of Canadian Elections.* (1st ed.) Stanford University
Press.

Johnston, Richard, Patrick Fournier, and Richard Jenkins. 2000. "Party Location and
Party Support: Unpacking Competing Models." *Journal of Politics* 62 (4): 1145–60.
https://doi.org/10.1111/0022-3816.00050

Kelley, Ninette, and John Trebilcock, eds. 2010. *The Making of the Mosaic: A History of
Canadian Immigration Policy.* (2nd ed.). University of Toronto Press.

Kevins, Anthony, and Stuart Soroka. 2018. "Growing Apart? Partisan Sorting in Canada, 1992–2015." *Canadian Journal of Political Science* 51 (1): 103–33. https://doi.org/10.1017/S0008423917000713

Koning, Edward. 2017. "Making Xenophobia Matter: The Consequences of the 2002 Elections for Immigration Politics in the Netherlands." In *The Strains of Commitment: The Political Sources of Solidarity in Diverse Societies*, edited by Keith Banting and Will Kymlicka, 268–99. Oxford University Press.

Kriesi, Hanspeter. 1998. "The Transformation of Cleavage Politics. The 1997 Stein Rokkan Lecture." *European Journal of Political Research* 33 (2): 165–85. https://doi.org/10.1111/1475-6765.00379

Krosnick, Jon A. 1999. "Survey Research." *Annual Review of Psychology* 50 (1): 537–67. https://doi.org/10.1146/annurev.psych.50.1.537. Medline: 15012463

Kymlicka, Will. 2021. "The Precarious Resilience of Multiculturalism in Canada." *American Review of Canadian Studies*, vol. 51 (1): 122–42.

Lawlor, Andrea. 2015. "Framing Immigration in the Canadian and British News Media." *Canadian Journal of Political Science* 48 (2): 329–55. https://doi.org/10.1017/S0008423915000499

Lawlor, Andrea, and Erin Tolley. 2017. "Deciding Who's Legitimate: News Media Framing of Immigrants and Refugees." *International Journal of Communication* 11: 967–91.

Laycock, David. 2012. *The New Right and Democracy in Canada: Understanding Reform and the Canadian Alliance*. Oxford University Press.

Levendusky, Matthew. 2009. *The Partisan Sort: How Liberals Became Democrats and Conservatives Became Republicans*. University of Chicago Press.

Lijphart, Arend. 1979. "Religious vs. Linguistic vs. Class Voting: The 'Crucial Experiment' of Comparing Belgium, Canada, South Africa, and Switzerland." *The American Political Science Review* 73 (2): 442–58. https://doi.org/10.2307/1954890

Lipset, Seymour Martin, and Stein Rokkan. 1967. *Party Systems and Voter Alignments: Cross-National Perspectives*. Free Press.

Marwash, Inder, Triadafilos Triadafilopoulos, and Stephen White. 2013. "Immigration, Citizenship and Canada's New Conservative Party." In *Conservatism in Canad*, edited by James Farney and David Rayside, 95–119. University of Toronto Press.

Mason, Lilliana. 2015. "'I Disrespectfully Agree': The Differential Effects of Partisan Sorting on Social and Issue Polarization." *American Journal of Political Science* 59 (1): 128–45. https://doi.org/10.1111/ajps.12089

McCoy, John. 2018. *Protecting Multiculturalism: Muslims, Security, and Integration in Canada*. McGill-Queen's University Press.

Muste, Christopher P. 2013. "The Dynamics of Immigration Opinion in the United States, 1992–2012." *Public Opinion Quarterly* 77 (1): 398–416. https://doi.org/10.1093/poq/nft001

Neto, Octavio Amorim, and Gary W. Cox. 1997. "Electoral Institutions, Cleavage Structures, and the Number of Parties." *American Journal of Political Science* 41 (1): 149–74. https://doi.org/10.2307/2111712

Nevitte, Neil, André Blais, Elizabeth Gidengil and Richard Nadeau. 2000. *Unsteady State: The 1997 Canadian Federal Election.* Oxford University Press.

Perlin, George, ed. 1988. *Party Democracy in Canada: The Politics of National Party Conventions.* Prentice Hall.

Reform Party of Canada. 1997. "A Fresh Start for Canadians: A 6-Point Plan to Build a Brighter Future Together." https://www.poltext.org/en/part-1-electronic-political -texts/electronic-manifestos-canada

Seidle, Leslie. 2010. *The Canada-Ontario Immigration Agreement: Assessment and Options for Renewal.* Mowat Centre for Policy Innovation, University of Toronto.

Stevenson, Randolph. 2001. "The Economy and Policy Mood: A Fundamental Dynamic of Democratic Politics?" *American Journal of Political Science* 45 (3): 620–33. https://doi.org/10.2307/2669242

Thomas, Paul, and Jerald Sabin. 2019. "Candidate Messaging on Issues in the 2016–17 Conservative Party of Canada Leadership Race." *Canadian Journal of Political Science,* vol. 52 (4): 801–23. https://doi.org/10.1017/S0008423919000246

Triadafilopoulos, Triadafilos, and Zack Taylor. 2021. "The Political Foundations of Canadian Exceptionalism in Immigration Policy." In *International Affairs and Canadian Migration Policy,* edited by Samy Yiagadeosen and Howard Duncan, 13–40. Palgrave Macmillan.

Van de Brug, Wouter, Meidert Fennema and Jean Tille. 2005. "Why Some Anti-Immigrant Parties Fail and Others Succeed: A Two-Step Model of Aggregate Electoral Support." *Comparative Political Studies* 38 (5): 537–73. https://doi.org /10.1177/0010414004273928

Veugeler, John. 2000. "State-Society Relations in the Making of Canadian Immigration Policy during the Mulroney Era." *Canadian Review of Sociology,* Vol. 37 (1): 95–110. https://doi.org/10.1111/j.1755-618X.2000.tb00588.x

Wilkes R., N. Guppy, and L. Farris. 2008. ""No Thanks, We're Full': Individual Characteristics, National Context and Changing Attitudes toward Immigration." *International Migration Review,* no. 42: 302–29. https://doi.org/10.1111 /j.1747-7379.2008.00126.x

Wilkins-Laflamme, Sarah, and Sam Reimer. 2019. "Religion and Grass Roots Social Conservatism in Canada." *Canadian Journal of Political Science,* vol. 52 (4): 865–81. https://doi.org/10.1017/S0008423919000544

Xhardez, Catherine, and Mireille Paquet. 2021. "Beyond the Usual Suspects and Towards Politicization: Immigration in Quebec's Party Manifestos, 1991–2018." *Journal of International Migration and Integration,* no. 22: 673–90. https://doi .org/10.1007/s12134-020-00764-3. Medline: 32837335

PART THREE

CAMPAIGNS AND PERSUASION

10 Do Election Campaigns Tighten the Margin of Victory? A Cross-National Analysis

JULIA PARTHEYMÜLLER

Introduction

It has often been mentioned – though sometimes rather as a side note – that the gap in the polls between the two main contenders tends to narrow over the course of US presidential election campaigns. For instance, Campbell (2008, 41) states that "the race routinely tightens up over the course of the presidential campaign." Erikson and Wlezien (2012, 34) point out that "starting with the conventions, election margins tighten as the campaign progresses" with large early leads being unsustainable. Despite being common knowledge in the US literature, however, the implications of the narrowing effect of election campaigns so far have received rather little attention. We also know hardly anything about whether narrowing can be observed in the context of other political systems.

This is somewhat surprising, given that narrowing has immediate implications for the predictability of election outcomes. Narrowing is considered to be the result of intense competition (Campbell, 2008, 41–8), and the winner of a close and highly competitive contest is by the very nature of the matter hardest to predict. Consider, for instance, the final match in the Champions League between two football teams of equal strength. Much is as stake: a prestigious victory and huge financial rewards. Both teams will optimize their strategies and fight intensely against each other. Much of the effort spent, however, will be offset by the other team, and who wins and who loses will remain highly uncertain until the end. The margin of victory for the eventual winner will most likely be small. In some cases, to arrive at a decision might even require the proverbial toss of a coin, with both teams possessing the same probability of winning.

Much is at stake at national elections, too, more than at any other level of government (Reif and Schmitt, 1980). The outcome of national elections should, therefore, be expected to be hard to predict. Surprisingly, though, previous research has instead emphasized the role of election campaigns for producing predictable outcomes (Gelman and King, 1993). Most notably, the "Theory of the Predictable Campaign" (Campbell, 2008) unifies the notions that election results are predictable by leading indicators and that election campaigns do influence voting decisions by arguing that election campaigns steer the public towards the predicted outcome by activating voters' latent political leanings (Lazarsfeld, Berelson, and Gaudet, 1948) and informing them about the true economic and political conditions (Gelman and King, 1993). This process has also become known as the "activation of fundamentals" (Johnston, 2017a).

Previous research has confirmed the presence of activating dynamics in the context of various institutional settings (Andersen, Tilley, and Heath, 2005; Arceneaux, 2007; Finkel and Schrott, 1995; Holbrook, 1996; Johnston, Partheymüller, and Schmitt-Beck, 2014). Recent comparative research on campaign dynamics has further examined two specific implications of theory of the predictable campaign (Johnston and Lachance, 2022): (1) whether frontrunners tend to lose ground and (2) whether election campaigns bring the election result closer to the predicted outcome. Broadly, the results confirm that both of these expectations are met, although with some exceptions and qualifications. But can we thus, based on the results from previous research, conclude that election campaigns are mainly predictable and conducive to enlightenment?

There is some reason to believe that systematic forces may not be the whole story. What has been emphasized less, so far, is that at the national level, where elections tend to be highly competitive, the predicted equilibrium will often be relatively close to a tossup, resulting in alternating governments over time. A corollary that follows from this proposition is that, ironically, some of the most important decisions in politics – national elections – are often decided by marginal strategic advantages and sheer luck. In fact, the small margin of victory in such highly salient elections makes the election outcome rather susceptible to "late shocks" and small shifts in public opinion, of which previous research has indeed demonstrated their presence in election campaigns (Johnston et al., 1992; Johnston, Hagen, and Jamieson, 2004). In this sense, national election campaigns can be said to make alternative futures imaginable and tangible, leading to a greater contingency of political outcomes that may seem unexpected, accidental, or unforeseen.

Against this background, this chapter investigates whether national election campaigns systematically narrow the margin of victory. The chapter assesses, in particular, whether narrowing can be found elsewhere outside the US context – in the absence of somewhat unique conditions that sometimes have been considered critical to the predictability of campaigns such as two sides, equally well equipped with enormous resources of money, and the importance of economic conditions (Johnston, 2017a; Johnston, Partheymüller, and Schmitt-Beck, 2014). The paper is structured as follows: First, previous research on the narrowing effect of election campaigns is reviewed. As a source of data, the chapter relies on the "Dataset on Polls and the Timeline of Elections" (Jennings and Wlezien, 2018), with a focus on a set of advanced democracies for which a sufficient number of polls are available to track the time path within campaigns across multiple elections. The dependent variable, the margin of victory, is calculated following the suggestions by Kayser and Lindstädt (2015) to measure competitiveness in cross-national studies. The analyses provide a comparison of the dynamics of vote margins under different types of political and electoral institutions as well as across individual countries. The results show that narrowing is present in other settings, yet some deviant cases display vote margins that show no systematic trends or even growth over time. The chapter concludes with a discussion of the implications of the results for collective decision-making.

Previous Research and Expectations

The US Case: Why Presidential Election Campaigns Narrow the Margin of Victory

Studying US presidential elections, Campbell (2008, 41–5) outlines five reasons why election campaigns may narrow the margin of victory: First, election campaigns are said to activate political predispositions and bring disenchanted partisans back into the fold (Berelson, Lazarsfeld, and McPhee, 1954; Finkel, 1993; Kaplan, Park, and Gelman, 2012; Lazarsfeld, Berelson, and Gaudet, 1948). In the United States, the general election campaign is preceded by primary elections with multiple candidates of the same party competing for the nomination. In this context, campaigning may make a bigger difference for the candidate nominated by a divided political party. These candidates are usually the ones who are behind at the outset of the campaign, but when partisans rally increasingly behind their nominee over the course of the campaign, the divided party may gain traction in the polls. Apart from that, some research suggests that parties attempt to mute discussion of divisive issues out of the electoral arena to strengthen party unity at election times (Aylott, 2002).

A second reason why vote margins narrow is the competitive, two-sided information flow (Chong and Druckman, 2007a, 2007b, 2007c; Zaller, 1992) that campaigns provide. Highly competitive campaigns tend to serve as an equalizer as both main competitors usually spend lots of resources to mobilize and persuade voters. News media cover the national elections intensively, trying to balance reporting between the competitors. Voters during elections, therefore, form their opinions in the context of competing bits of information.

A third reason for tightening vote margins can be that the frontrunner becomes the target of increased scrutiny by voters and the media during the campaign. Voters may increasingly ask themselves whether the candidate with the best chances to win represents their preferences well. In addition, the increased scrutiny might also be driven by the media's tendency to focus on the horse race (Banducci and Hanretty, 2014), negativity bias, and the media's general desire to create drama (Farnsworth and Lichter, 2007). Previous research suggests that the election coverage may indeed work towards the advantage of the trailing party by creating an underdog effect (Faas, Mackenrodt, and Schmitt-Beck, 2008; Fleitas, 1971; Schmitt-Beck, 2016; Simon, 1954).

Fourth, another argument about narrowing focuses on the electoral strategy of the competitors. The frontrunner, being in a good position to win the election, may opt for a risk-averse strategy, playing things safe. In contrast, the trailing candidate may pursue a more risky and more aggressive approach. As a result, many elections manifest themselves as a competition between a risk-averse and a risk-seeking party (Rose-Ackerman, 1991).

Finally, as a consequence of the balanced information environment, voters deciding during the campaign period tend to split about evenly between the main competitors. Although it is well known that many voters are already decided before the campaign has even begun, considerable numbers of voters remain who decide late in the process (Dalton and Wattenberg, 2002; Schmitt-Beck and Partheymüller, 2012). Due to the two-sided information, undecided voters are often divided in about equal proportions between the main competitors, to the effect that the gap in the polls between the competitors should shrink.

As a last point, Campbell (2008, 41–5) emphasizes that narrowing should not be confused with momentum effects as they have been found in presidential primaries (Bartels, 1988). Campbell argues that narrowing might sometimes look similar to momentum but the two are different. For example, in the presence of a bandwagon effect (Schmitt-Beck, 2016) – to the extent that it is driven by the desire of voters wanting to vote for the winner – the vote margin should rather widen between the frontrunner and the trailing candidate as the frontrunner attracts additional voters. Under narrowing, in contrast, the frontrunner is expected to lose support.

Narrowing in Other National Elections

Narrowing in US presidential elections, as described, thus, is the product of voter psychology, media logic, and party strategies. But can we expect to see similar dynamics to play out in the same way in other settings than the US presidential elections? Regarding voter psychology, previous research has demonstrated that election campaigns activate political predispositions in other settings. Activation effects have been found, for example, in British general elections (Andersen, Tilley, and Heath, 2005) as well as German federal elections (Finkel and Schrott, 1995; Johnston, Partheymüller, and Schmitt-Beck, 2014). Like in the United States, the party with the greatest internal divisions is likely, initially, not to do well in the polls but to gain the most from overcoming division in the campaign period, which potentially could lead to some narrowing.

Concerning media logic and party strategies, however, some questions arise whether the same playbook applies in other settings. National elections are likely to be competitive and intensely covered by the media. But, unlike in the United States, elections in most other advanced democracies involve multiparty competition. Multiparty competition can be similarly bipolar when parties aligned in two distinct blocs compete with each other (Kam, Bertelli, and Held, 2020), and in line with that, recent cross-national research by Johnston and Lachance (2022) has confirmed that frontrunners, who for the most part are the incumbents, tend to lose ground in election campaigns. Yet, in some cases, multiparty competition might instead be truly multipolar, when no competing proto-coalitions are in place. This can add another layer of complexity to the political dynamics, and some of the arguments about the narrowing effect in the United States, such as the framing of elections as horse race between a frontrunner and a trailing underdog, might not apply equally well in such a context.

Under multiparty competition, however, also additional reasons for possible narrowing effects emerge, both in majoritarian as well as under proportional systems. For instance, in majoritarian electoral systems, according to Duverger's Law (1954), voters should abandon non-viable third parties and opt for their second-best more viable alternative to avoid wasting their votes. In particular, supporters of trailing parties face an incentive to coordinate on the more viable option. As a consequence of such a desertion from non-viable parties, the margin of victory between the two main competitors may narrow.

The logic of Duvergerian voting to some extent also applies to proportional systems (Cox and Shugart, 1996). There are at least three different possibilities for strategic coordination in that context: First, when the voting system has an electoral threshold, supporters of minor parties with rather minimal support might be worried about wasting their votes and vote instead for a larger, more viable contender. Second, although not impossible, it is politically typically very difficult to form a government against the plurality party, even under a proportional system (Kayser and Lindstädt, 2015). Supporters of a trailing party, recognizing this logic, might opt for their second-best alternative to decide about who will become the formateur and likely prime minister ("strategic sequencing," see Cox, 1997). Finally, Bargsted and Kedar (2009) have outlined a similar logic of Duvergerian coalition-targeted voting where supporters of a trailing party, expecting that their preferred coalition might not receive enough votes to form, might opt for the more centrist party that they expect to be part of the coalition government. Thus, there are various additional mechanisms that might produce narrowing in other national elections.

One caveat applies, however: Strategic coordination may fail for various reason (Cox, 1997, ch. 12–14). For example, a dominant party of the centre can often prevent electoral alliances from being formed against it (Carty, 2006; Johnston, 2017b). Or opportunistic election timing followed by rather short campaigns may not allow for enough time for the opposition to coordinate, thereby granting the incumbent an advantage in the election (Schleiter and Tavits, 2016). And, also voter psychology limits strategic voting, as previous research has shown that most voters vote rather sincerely than strategically (Alvarez and Nagler, 2012). Hence, although there are several reasons to expect narrowing under multiparty competition, the extent to which narrowing can be observed might be limited by the multipolar nature of party competition and coordination failures.

Data and Methods

Data Set, Selection of Countries, and Time Frame

To assess narrowing in national elections, this chapter makes use of the "Dataset on Polls and the Timeline of Elections" (Jennings and Wlezien, 2018). The dataset includes poll aggregates (poll-of-polls), covering national elections from 45 countries, from 1942 to 2017. For the purpose of this analysis, a subset of countries and elections was selected to ensure a sufficient number of polls and elections per country and a certain level of homogeneity of cases for the comparison. The focus here is on advanced democracies. Apart from the United States, the remaining sample includes 11 parliamentary democracies with a single-member district electoral system such as in Australia, Canada, New Zealand (until 1993), and the United Kingdom as well as countries with a proportional electoral system such as in Denmark, Germany, Ireland, Netherlands, New Zealand (from 1996), Norway, Portugal, and Spain. Excluded were less advanced democracies (e.g., Latin American countries), countries with a two-round system (i.e., France), and countries with too few elections and too few polls for a meaningful country-based analysis (i.e., Austria, Belgium, Bulgaria, Croatia, Finland, Greece, Hungary, Iceland, Japan, Malta, Poland, Romania, Serbia, Slovakia, Sweden, Switzerland, Turkey). Overall, the used subset of the dataset covers 177 elections (table 10.1).

Regarding the time frame, all polls available during the last 365 days before election day enter the analysis. This period by convention has also been called the "long campaign" (Miller et al., 1990). Although some campaigns are rather short (Stevenson and Vavreck, 2000), studying the dynamics over the course of the entire year before the election does allow for observing the dynamics over the short campaign (i.e., the last few months before election day) at the same

Table 10.1. Countries and elections included in the analysis

Country	Political / Electoral System	Range of Years	No. of Elections
United States	Presidential (US)	1952–2016	17
Australia	Parliamentary (SMD)	1958–2013	21
Canada	Parliamentary (SMD)	1945–2015	22
New Zealand	Parliamentary (SMD)	1975–1993	7
United Kingdom	Parliamentary (SMD)	1945–2017	20
Denmark	Parliamentary (PR)	1960–2015	15
Germany	Parliamentary (PR)	1961–2013	15
Ireland	Parliamentary (PR)	1977–2016	12
Netherlands	Parliamentary (PR)	1967–2012	11
New Zealand	Parliamentary (PR)	1996–2011	6
Norway	Parliamentary (PR)	1965–2013	13
Portugal	Parliamentary (PR)	1987–2011	8
Spain	Parliamentary (PR)	1982–2016	10

Note: $n = 12$ (countries); $n = 177$ (elections).

time. The results will show whether narrowing occurs over the period of the long or the short campaign.

The Dependent Variable: Measuring Vote Margins in Comparative Research

Previous research has discussed various ways of how to best measure competitiveness in elections in comparative research (Cox, Fiva, and Smith, 2020). Some measures have been applied at the aggregate level (Kayser and Lindstädt, 2015), whereas others have tried to measure competitiveness at the district level (Blais and Lago, 2009; Grofman and Selb, 2011). Although in US presidential elections in particular, as well as under single-member district systems, the election outcome strictly depends on the localized competition, polls at the subnational level are rare and most of the public discussion focuses on the popular vote at the national level. As most arguments about narrowing focus on the aggregate, the focus here will be on the aggregate level.

At the aggregate level, Kayser and Lindstädt (2015) have proposed a measure of competitiveness for comparative research. They propose a measure focusing on the status of being the plurality party. They justify their measure in light of the fact that the *formateur* and prime minister will most likely be from the plurality party (according to their sample in 82% of the cases). This measure, hence, is in line with arguments about "strategic sequencing" (Cox, 1997, 194) as outlined above, as one possible rationale for narrowing dynamics.

Following this line of reasoning, the margin of victory, which will serve as the dependent variable in all analyses, will be defined here as the absolute difference in the poll share between the largest and second largest party, with the

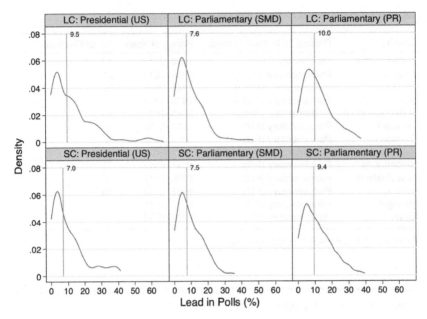

Figure 10.1. Distribution of the dependent variable

Note: Univariate kernel density estimation (kernel function: epanechnikov). Long campaign (LC): last 365 days before election day; short campaign (SC): last 60 days before election day. The vertical line shows the median of the distribution.

rank of the party being determined based on the final actual vote share in a given election. Figure 10.1 shows the univariate distribution of the poll-based measure for the long and the short campaign under three different types of institutional settings.

It can be seen that the vote margins tend to be tight in all national elections. All distributions are strongly right-skewed and the modal value of the poll-based vote margins in national elections typically hovers around 5 per cent. The median value for US presidential campaigns decreases from 9.5 to 7.0 per cent when moving from the long to the short campaign, suggesting some narrowing. Interestingly, the median lead in polls for elections under the single-member district plurality (SMDP) rule is always fairly tight, with 7.5 to 7.6 per cent, with little change from the long to the short campaign. In proportional systems (PR), the margins tend to be wider, with a median lead in polls of 10.0 per cent during the long campaign and 9.4 per cent during the short campaign. Considering that the 95 per cent posterior credible intervals for predicted vote shares taking into account various sources of uncertainty in election predictions have been reported to be as wide as +/- 10 percentage points (Lauderdale and Linzer,

2015), it becomes clear that the outcome of national elections will, on a regular basis, be fairly uncertain.

Strategy of the Analysis: Fitting a Smooth Time Path

The main independent variable to test for narrowing are the days left to election day. The analyses proceed in two steps. In the first step, the focus is on the dynamics in the US presidential elections, parliamentary elections under SMDP, and parliamentary PR elections, whereas in the second step a country-by-country analysis in conducted to assess heterogeneity within these groups of institutional design. This is particularly important as patterns of party competition might diverge despite a similar institutional framework.

In both steps of the analyses, a smooth time path is fitted to the data using a semiparametric multilevel model (SPMM) (Fahrmeir and Kneib, 2011; Lin and Zhang, 1999; Ruppert, Wand, and Carroll, 2003), alongside a random intercept to account for varying levels of competitiveness across elections. To allow for potentially diverging levels of competitiveness and trends across the type of the political and electoral system, a factor-smooth interaction (Hastie and Tibshirani, 1990) is included in the model between the time trend and the type of the political system, or country, respectively. In all models, dummy variables for different political periods (1945–2017) will be included as parametric terms to control for whether vote margins have changed over time. All models are estimated using the R package *mgcv* (Wood, 2016). An advantage of the approach is that we can observe when the margins start to tighten by allowing for potential non-linearities in the time path. At the same time, we do not run the risk that countervailing dynamics over the long and short campaign will offset each other.

Results

The Institutional Setting and the Dynamics of Vote Margins

Table 10.1 shows the results of the estimation of the SPMM model. The dependent variable is the poll-based margin of victory. Among the parametric terms, the model includes the main effect of the type of political and electoral system and the dummies for different political periods as a control variable. The results for the parametric terms show no significant differences in levels of competitiveness across time and institutional settings. In line with the univariate distributions in figure 10.1, we see, however, that the coefficient for the SMD systems is sizeable and negative, suggesting that the lead in the polls tends to be about 2.6 percentage points smaller on average than in US presidential elections. Likewise, the coefficient for the post-2000 era is, though insignificant,

Table 10.2. Dynamics of vote margins in three different types of elections

	DV: Lead in Polls
Parametric terms	
Intercept	13.69 (2.66)***
Political / electoral system (ref. presidential (US)):	
- Parliamentary (SMD)	−2.60 (1.99)
- Parliamentary (PR)	−.28 (1.96)
Period (ref. 1945–1959):	
- 1960–1979	−.67 (2.38)
- 1980–1999	−.83 (2.36)
- 2000–2017	−4.09 (2.42)
Non-parametric terms	
Days to election × Presidential (US)	3.80 (4.00)***
Days to election × Parliamentary (SMD)	.04 (4.00)
Days to election × Parliamentary (PR)	2.64 (4.00)*
Random effect (Election ID)	167.52 (171.00)***
R^2	.68
N(Polls)	7518

Notes: ***$p < .001$; **$p < .01$; *$p < .05$. For parametric terms, entries are unstandardized regression coefficients from a linear SPMM with standard errors in parentheses. For non-parametric terms, entries are the effective degrees of freedom (EDF) with the reference degrees of freedom in parentheses.

sizeable, suggesting that poll margins were about 4 percentage points tighter after 2000 than in the post-war era.

Regarding the narrowing hypothesis, the non-parametric factor-smooth interactions are, more importantly, capturing the dynamics of vote margins within elections in the three different types of systems. The smooth terms for US presidential and parliamentary PR elections are significant, indicating that vote margins change significantly over time in these types of elections. Interestingly, no significant trend is found in the case of parliamentary SMD elections. The effective degree of freedom (EDF) indicates how much variation there is, but it cannot tell us anything about the direction of the trend.

To investigate whether election campaigns narrow or widen the margin of victory, figure 10.2 displays the estimated smooth functions based on the estimates in table 10.2. The US presidential elections show the most pronounced changes in the poll margins over the course of the campaign. It can be seen that narrowing happens in two steps: First, during the early stage of the campaign (ca. 300 to 200 days before election) the vote margin seems to tighten. Then, after seemingly widening slightly, the lead in the polls continues to shrink further, starting from about 100 days before election day until the election. This two-stage process is probably driven by the distinct rhythm of US presidential

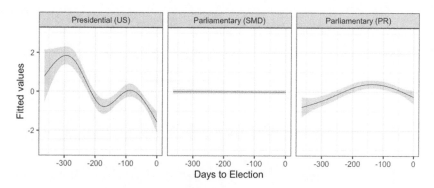

Figure 10.2. The dynamics of vote margins by institutional context
Note: Fitted values for smooth terms based on model in table 10.1 (centred). Shaded area shows 95% confidence interval.

campaigns where primary elections precede the general election campaign. Overall, the margins seem to shrink by about 3 percentage points.

The contrast with SMD systems, where we do not find any systematic dynamics, is striking. Partially, this lack of narrowing might be driven by the fact that margins, as shown, tend to be somewhat tighter in SMD systems in general. In an already very tight election, the campaign might not be able to tighten the margins even further. Also, coordination failure might play a role as some campaigns tend to be shorter due to opportunistic election timing in some of these elections. Another possibility is that the heterogeneity within the category of SMD systems somewhat masks the dynamics in some countries in this category, which will be investigated in the next section.

Finally, in parliamentary PR elections, the dynamics are overall more modest, but we do see some narrowing over the course of the short campaign at least. Similar to the US presidential elections, the tightening over the short campaign is preceded by a phase of widening margins. However, there this no first stage of narrowing. Instead, it seems that margins over the election year mostly widen and only come closer in the last few months. Overall, the amount of narrowing does not seem to be much greater than .5 percentage points. However, also in the case of PR systems, it seems possible that some of the narrowing gets masked by heterogeneity across countries.

Country-by-Country Analysis

Table 10.2 reports the results from the country-by-country analysis. The parametric estimates for the main effects of the countries show a few significant differences with regard to vote margins. Most notably, the gap in polls tends

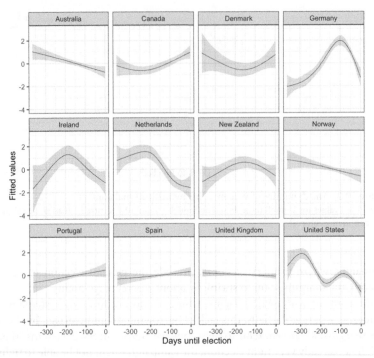

Figure 10.3. Dynamics of vote margins by country
Note: Fitted values for smooth terms based on model in Table 10.2 (centred). Shaded area shows 95% confidence interval.

to be larger in Canada, Denmark, Ireland, Norway, and the United States than elsewhere, with the remaining countries being statistically indistinguishable from the reference category (Australia). As before, we do not see any significant effects for the dummy variables controlling for different historical time periods.

Significant dynamics of vote margins are found in Australia, Canada, Germany, Ireland, the Netherlands, Norway, and the United States. For the remaining countries, changes in vote margins remain insignificant. To evaluate the direction of the changes in vote margins figure 10.3 shows again the fitted values for estimated smooth terms.

Apart from the familiar pattern for the United States, we find significant narrowing in Australia, Germany, the Netherlands, and Norway. However, in Canada, poll margins seem to widen significantly instead. For the remaining cases the evidence is rather inconclusive. Denmark, Spain, and Portugal seem to show a tendency towards widening, but it is not significant. New Zealand and the UK show a tiny tendency for narrowing but the confidence intervals overlap and, as shown in table 10.3, there is no significant variation for these

Table 10.3. Dynamics of vote margins by country

	DV: Lead in Polls
Parametric terms	
Intercept	8.01 (2.58)**
Country (ref. Australia):	
- Canada	5.99 (2.17)**
- Denmark	5.22 (2.38)*
- Germany	.31 (2.35)
- Ireland	10.37 (2.55)***
- Netherlands	−1.23 (2.59)
- New Zealand	4.57 (2.47)
- Norway	7.65 (2.46)**
- Portugal	1.95 (2.92)
- Spain	4.88 (2.73)
- United Kingdom	1.21 (2.22)
- United States	4.92 (2.27)*
Period (ref. 1940–1959)	
- Period: 1960–1979	.42 (2.32)
- Period: 1980–1999	.01 (2.32)
- Period: 2000–2017	−3.41 (2.34)
Non-parametric terms	
Days to election × Australia	1.13 (4.00)***
Days to election × Canada	1.90 (4.00)**
Days to election × Denmark	1.78 (4.00)
Days to election × Germany	3.65 (4.00)***
Days to election × Ireland	2.41 (4.00)*
Days to election × Netherlands	2.90 (4.00)***
Days to election × New Zealand	1.95 (4.00)
Days to election × Norway	.99 (4.00)*
Days to election × Portugal	.71 (4.00)
Days to election × Spain	.72 (4.00)
Days to election × United Kingdom	.60 (4.00)
Days to election × United States	3.81 (4.00)***
Random effect (Election ID)	158.37 (162.00)***
R^2	.69
N(Polls)	7518

Notes: ***$p < .001$, **$p < .01$, *$p < .05$. For parametric terms, entries are unstandardized regression coefficients from a linear SPMM with standard errors in parentheses. For non-parametric terms, entries are the effective degrees of freedom (EDF) with the reference degrees of freedom in parentheses.

countries. Hence, both the group of SMD and PR systems show some noticeable heterogeneity that was masked in the previous analysis by lumping the countries together.

The amount of narrowing in those countries where we do see significant dynamics is only slightly smaller than in the US case, but the rhythm of the campaigns differs. For Australia, we see a rather continuously narrowing trend over the long campaign, with vote margins shrinking by about 2 percentage points. In Germany, and also Ireland, we find a strongly non-linear pattern where narrowing follows after an initial period of widening gaps: During the last 100 days, vote margins in Germany tighten by about 2.5 percentage points; in Ireland vote margins decrease by about 2 percentage points over the last 200 days. In the Netherlands, the lead in polls shrinks by about 3 percentage points over the last 200 days, without a preceding period of widening margins. In the deviant case of Canada, poll margins widen by about 1.5 percentage points over the last 200 days.

All in all, the analyses demonstrate that election campaigns may narrow the margin of victory, both in the US and elsewhere, across a wide range of political institutions. Although the trend is not entirely universal, in various countries vote margins were found to decrease by about 2 to 4 percentage points. Yet, some qualifications need to be mentioned. First, the campaigns seem to follow different rhythms in different countries. For instance, in the US case, the campaign seems to be divided in two stages: Vote margins narrow at first early on and then again over the course of the short campaign. In other countries, such as Ireland and Germany, margins first widen before narrowing towards the end. Then, again, other countries show a more continuous trend towards narrowing, but differ with regard to the start when narrowing begins.

Second, for a number of countries there is no evidence of systematic narrowing (e.g., United Kingdom, New Zealand, Denmark, Spain, Portugal). This might suggest that margins sometimes narrow and sometimes widen in cases, with no predictable pattern. We have also found one deviant case, Canada, where vote margins predominantly widen. Possibly, the origins of this deviation are rooted in the complex structure and high volatility of party competition (Johnston, 2017b). A further in-depth analysis, however, is beyond the scope of this chapter. In general, further research into narrowing effects would be necessary to understand under what conditions we should expect vote margins to narrow or to widen.

Discussion and Conclusion

This chapter has investigated whether election campaigns narrow the margin of victory, taking a comparative perspective. Previous research has investigated other aspects of the "Theory of the Predictable Campaign" such as activation dynamics, or has focused, in particular, on narrowing in the US case. The review of the literature regarding the reasons underlying the narrowing effect has shown, however, that some of the same logics might indeed apply elsewhere. Yet, potential limits to narrowing dynamics have been identified also, such as the potentially multipolar nature of multiparty competition and coordination failures.

The results confirm that narrowing can be found outside the US context, with some qualifications. Most notably, the time path within campaigns seems to vary across countries. In particular, the United States shows a very distinct two-stage process over the long campaign where narrowing takes place in two distinct steps. This pattern appears to be quite unique and was not found in other cases. In most other countries, narrowing was confined to the short campaign, either manifesting itself as a rather continuous trend or being preceded by an initial widening of the gap. In general, in the group of SMD and PR systems significant heterogeneity was uncovered, with some countries not showing any systematic trends and one deviant case displaying a widening trend.

An implication of narrowing is that election campaigns make it harder to predict the winner of an election. It has been shown that the margin of victory in the polls will usually be too small to confidently predict the winner, considering the typical margin of error of vote share predictions. In that sense, the outcome of national elections will be typically uncertain – and election campaigns make the outcome even more uncertain. Election campaigns in this sense lead to a lower, not greater, predictability of election outcomes.

It is important to note, though, that this result does not contradict previous research indicating that election campaigns show predictable trends and steer public opinion towards the long-term equilibrium. However, what has not been emphasized enough is that at the national level the long-term equilibrium is often close to an even split between the main competitors. The election campaign may thus steer the vote towards the equilibrium and lead to greater contingency at the same time.

On the one hand, this might be beneficial as it makes alternative futures imaginable and tangible. Close elections facilitate the alternation of governments as one side or the other will win depending on rather minor advantages. In a world of perfect Downsian competition where the major competitors converge on centrist policies (Downs, 1957), it would hardly matter, if the decision was made one way or the other. On the other hand, though, the idea may seem unsettling, as we do know that parties in the real world do often not converge in terms of policy (Merrill and Grofman, 1999; Schofield, 2003). Minor short-term swings and random events can, as a result, turn out to be very consequential. Due to narrowing, elections, like highly competitive football matches, may in the end be decided by short-term deviations from the equilibrium, randomness, and sheer luck. Overall, the presence of narrowing might thus require us to accept the surrounding political world as more complex, unreasonable, and unpredictable than we would feel comfortable with. It is, however, also a call for short-term shocks to public opinion during election campaigns to be closely monitored.

References

Alvarez, R. Michael, and Jonathan Nagler. 2012. "A New Approach for Modelling Strategic Voting in Multiparty Elections A New Approach for Modelling Strategic Voting in Multiparty Elections." *British Journal of Political Science* 30 (1): 57–75. https://doi.org/10.1017/S000712340000003X

Andersen, Robert, James Tilley, and Antohony F. Heath. 2005. "Political Knowledge and Enlightened Preferences: Party Choice Through the Electoral Cycle." *British Journal of Political Science* 35 (2): 285–302. https://doi.org/10.1017/S0007123405000153

Arceneaux, Kevin. 2007. "I'm Asking for Your Support: The Effects of Personally Delivered Campaign Messages on Voting Decisions and Opinion Formation." *Quarterly Journal of Political Science* 2: 43–65. https://doi.org/10.1561/100.00006003

Aylott, Nicholas. 2002. "Let's Discuss This Later: Party Responses to Euro-Division in Scandinavia." *Party Politics* 8 (4): 441–61. https://doi.org/10.1177/1354068802008004005

Banducci, Susan, and Chris Hanretty. 2014. "Comparative Determinants of Horse-Race Coverage." *European Political Science Review* 6 (4): 621–40. https://doi.org/10.1017/S1755773913000271

Bargsted, Matias A., and Orit Kedar. 2009. "Coalition-Targeted Duvergerian Voting: How Expectations Affect Voter Choice under Proportional Representation." *American Journal of Political Science* 53 (2): 307–23. https://doi.org/10.1111/j.1540-5907.2009.00372.x

Bartels, Larry M. 1988. *Presidential Primaries and the Dynamics of Public Choice.* Princeton University Press.

Berelson, Bernard R., Paul F. Lazarsfeld, and William N. McPhee. 1954. *Voting: A Study of Opinion Formation in a Presidential Campaign.* University of Chicago Press.

Blais, Andre, and Ignacio Lago. 2009. "A General Measure of District Competitiveness." *Electoral Studies* 28 (1): 94–100. https://doi.org/10.1016/j.electstud.2008.07.007

Campbell, James E. 2008. *The American Campaign: U.S. Presidential Campaigns and the National Vote.* Texas A&M University Press.

Carty, R. Kenneth. 2006. "Political Turbulence in a Dominant Party System." *PS: Political Science & Politics*: 39 (4): 825–7. https://doi.org/10.1017/S1049096506061026

Chong, Dennis, and James N. Druckman. 2007a. "A Theory of Framing and Opinion Formation in Competitive Elite Environments." *Journal of Communication* 57 (1): 99–118. https://doi.org/10.1111/j.1460-2466.2006.00331.x

– 2007b. "Framing Public Opinion in Competitive Democracies." *American Political Science Review* 101 (4): 637–55. https://doi.org/10.1017/S0003055407070554

– 2007c. "Framing Theory." *Annual Review of Political Science* 10 (1): 103–26. https://doi.org/10.1146/annurev.polisci.10.072805.103054

Cox, Gary W. 1997. *Making Votes Count: Strategic Coordination in the World's Electoral Systems.* Cambridge University Press.

Cox, Gary W., and Matthew S. Shugart. 1996. "Strategic Voting Under Proportional Representation." *Journal of Law, Economics, and Organization* 12 (2): 299–324. https://doi.org/10.1093/oxfordjournals.jleo.a023365

Cox, Gary W., Jon H. Fiva, and Daniel M. Smith. 2020. "Measuring the Competitiveness of Elections." *Political Analysis* 28 (2): 168–85. https://doi.org/10.1017/pan.2019.28

Dalton, Russell J., and Martin P. Wattenberg. 2002. *Parties Without Partisans: Political Change in Advanced Industrial Democracies*. Oxford University Press.

Downs, Anthony. 1957. *An Economic Theory of Democracy*. Harper.

Duverger, Maurice. 1954. *Political Parties: Their Organization and Activity in the Modern State*. Methuen.

Erikson, Robert S., and Christopher Wlezien. 2012. *The Timeline of Presidential Elections: How Campaigns Do (And Do Not) Matter*. University of Chicago Press.

Faas, Thorsten, Christian Mackenrodt, and Rüdiger Schmitt-Beck. 2008. "Polls That Mattered: Effects of Media Polls on Voters Coalition Expectations and Party Preferences in the 2005 German Parliamentary Election." *International Journal of Public Opinion Research* 20 (3): 299–325. https://doi.org/10.1093/ijpor/edn034

Fahrmeir, Ludwig, and Thomas Kneib. 2011. *Bayesian Smoothing and Regression for Longitudinal, Spatial and Event History Data*. Oxford University Press.

Farnsworth, Stephen J., and S. Robert Lichter. 2007. *The Nightly News Nightmare: Television's Coverage of US Presidential Elections, 1988–2004*. Rowman & Littlefield.

Finkel, Steven E. 1993. "Reexamining the 'Minimal Effects' Model in Recent Presidential Campaigns." *Journal of Politics* 55 (1): https://doi.org/10.2307/2132225

Finkel, Steven E., and Peter R. Schrott. 1995. "Campaign Effects on Voter Choice in the German Election of 1990." *British Journal of Political Science* 25 (3): 349–77. https://doi.org/10.1017/S0007123400007249

Fleitas, Daniel W. 1971. "Bandwagon and Underdog Effects in Minimal-Information Elections." *American Political Science Review* 65 (2): 434–8. https://doi.org/10.2307/1954459

Gelman, Andrew, and Gary King. 1993. "Why Are American Presidential-Election Campaign Polls So Variable When Votes Are So Predictable?" *British Journal of Political Science* 23 (4): 409–51. https://doi.org/10.1017/S0007123400006682

Grofman, Bernard, and Peter Selb. 2011. "Turnout and the (Effective) Number of Parties at the National and District Levels: A Puzzle-Solving Approach." *Party Politics* 17 (1): 93–117. https://doi.org/10.1177/1354068810365506

Hastie, Trevor J., and Robert J. Tibshirani. 1990. *Generalized Additive Models*. Chapman & Hall.

Holbrook, Thomas M. 1996. *Do Campaigns Matter?* Sage Publications.

Jennings, Will, and Christopher Wlezien. 2018. "Dataset on Polls and the Timeline of Elections." https://liberalarts.utexas.edu/government/faculty/cw26629#datasets -on-polls-and-the-timeline-of-elections.

Johnston, Richard. 2017a. "Campaign Effects." In *The SAGE Handbook of Electoral Behaviour*, edited by Kai Arzheimer, Jocelyn Evans, and Michael Lewis-Beck, 709–32. Sage.

– 2017b. *The Canadian Party System: An Analytic History*. UBC Press.

Johnston, Richard, André Blais, Henry E. Brady, and Jean Crête. 1992. *Letting the People Decide: Dynamics of a Canadian Election*. Stanford University Press.

Johnston, Richard, Michael G. Hagen, and Kathleen Hall Jamieson. 2004. *The 2000 Presidential Election and the Foundations of Party Politics*. Cambridge University Press.

Johnston, Richard, and Sarah Lachance. 2022. "The Predictable Campaign: Theory and Evidence." *Electoral Studies* vol. 75: 102432. https://doi.org/10.1016/j.electstud.2021.102432

Johnston, Richard, Julia Partheymüller, and Rüdiger Schmitt-Beck. 2014. "Activation of Fundamentals in German Campaigns." In *Voters on the Move or on the Run?*, edited by Bernhard Weßels, Hans Rattinger, Sigrid Roßteutscher, and Rüdiger Schmitt-Beck 217–37. Oxford University Press.

Kam, Christopher, Anthony M. Bertelli, and Alexander Held. (2020). "The Electoral System, the Party System and Accountability in Parliamentary Government." *American Political Science Review*, 114 (3): 744–760. https://doi.org/10.1017/S0003055420000143

Kaplan, Noah, David K. Park, and Andrew Gelman. 2012. "Understanding Persuasion and Activation in Presidential Campaigns: The Random Walk and Mean Reversion Models." *Presidential Studies Quarterly* 42 (4): 843–66. https://doi.org/10.1111/j.1741-5705.2012.04021.x

Kayser, Mark Andreas, and René Lindstädt. 2015. "A Cross-National Measure of Electoral Competitiveness." *Political Analysis* 23 (2): 242–53. https://doi.org/10.1093/pan/mpv001

Lauderdale, Benjamin E., and Drew Linzer. 2015. "Under-Performing, Over-Performing, or Just Performing? The Limitations of Fundamentals-Based Presidential Election Forecasting." *International Journal of Forecasting* 31 (3): 965–79. https://doi.org/10.1016/j.ijforecast.2015.03.002

Lazarsfeld, Paul F., Bernard R. Berelson, and Hazel Gaudet. 1948. *The People's Choice: How the Voter Makes Up His Mind in a Presidential Campaign*. Columbia University Press.

Lin, Xihong, and Daowen Zhang. 1999. "Inference in Generalized Additive Mixed Models by Using Smoothing Splines." *Journal of the Royal Statistical Society: Series B (Statistical Methodology)* 61 (2): 381–400. https://doi.org/10.1111/1467-9868.00183

Merrill, Samuel III, and Bernard Grofman. 1999. *A Unified Theory of Voting: Directional and Proximity Spatial Models*. Cambridge University Press.

Miller, William L. et al. 1990. *How Voters Change: The 1987 British Election Campaign in Perspective*. Oxford University Press.

Reif, Karlheinz, and Hermann Schmitt. 1980. "Nine Second-Order National Elections: A Conceptual Framework for the Analysis of European Election Results." *European Journal of Political Research* 8 (1): 3–44. https://doi.org/10.1111/j.1475-6765.1980.tb00737.x

Rose-Ackerman, Susan. 1991. "Risktaking and Electoral Competition." *European Journal of Political Economy* 7 (4): 527–45. https://doi.org/10.1016/0176 -2680(91)90035-2

Ruppert, David, Matt P. Wand, and Raymond J. Carroll. 2003. *Semiparametric Regression.* Cambridge University Press.

Schleiter, Petra, and Margit Tavits. 2016. "The Electoral Benefits of Opportunistic Election Timing." *Journal of Politics* 78 (3): 836–50. https://doi.org/10.1086/685447

Schmitt-Beck, Rüdiger. 2016. "Underdog Effect." In *The International Encyclopedia of Political Communication,* edited by Gianpietro Mazzoleni, 1627–31. Wiley Blackwell.

Schmitt-Beck, Rüdiger, and Julia Partheymüller. 2012. "Why Voters Decide Late: A Simultaneous Test of Old and New Hypotheses at the 2005 and 2009 German Federal Elections." *German Politics* 21 (3): 299–316. https://doi.org/10.1080/096440 08.2012.716042

Schmitt-Beck, Rüdiger. 2016. "Bandwagon Effect." In *The International Encyclopedia of Political Communication,* edited by Gianpietro Mazzoleni, 57–61. Wiley Blackwell.

Schofield, Norman. 2003. "Valence Competition in the Spatial Stochastic Model." *Journal of Theoretical Politics* 15 (4): 371–83. https://doi.org/10.1177/0951692803154001

Simon, Herbert A. 1954. "Bandwagon and Underdog Effects and the Possibility of Election Predictions." *Public Opinion Quarterly* 18 (3): 245–53. https://doi.org /10.1086/266513

Stevenson, Randolph T., and Lynn Vavreck. 2000. "Does Campaign Length Matter? Testing for Cross-National Effects." *British Journal of Political Science* 30 (2): 217–35. https://doi.org/10.1017/S0007123400000107

Wood, Simon. 2016. "Package 'Mgcv.'" *R package version:* 1–7.

Zaller, John R. 1992. *The Nature and Origins of Mass Opinion.* Cambridge University Press.

11 Voters, Media Biases, and Rolling Cross-Sections: Persuasive Effects of TV News on Party Evaluations in the 2005 to 2017 German Federal Elections

RÜDIGER SCHMITT-BECK AND ALEXANDER STAUDT

Introduction

Media persuasion at elections is a phenomenon with a somewhat peculiar dual character. It is taken for granted by political actors like parties and politicians (van Aelst et al., 2008) as well as many citizens (Perloff, 1999). But over decades is has appeared stubbornly elusive to research. Just a few years ago Dobrzynska et al. characterized this unsatisfactory state of affairs in strong terms: "Do the media have a direct effect on the vote? Fifty years of research on electoral behaviour have left this question basically unanswered." (Dobrzynska et al., 2003, 27) Yet, from today's perspective this diagnosis appears too bleak. Taking advantage of improved theories, research methods, and data (Kinder, 1998), a small body of research has lately emerged which shows that media bias, that is, news content with a favourable or unfavourable valence towards certain parties or candidates, may indeed be consequential for voters' attitudes and behaviour at elections (e.g., Dalton et al., 1998; Druckman and Parkin, 2005; Brandenburg and van Egmond, 2011; Geers and Bos, 2017; Johann et al., 2018; Eberl et al., 2017).

Methodologically, these studies demonstrate the utility of merged data from dynamic voter surveys and media content analyses as a key resource for observational research aiming to detect media effects at elections (de Vreese et al., 2017). Many studies in this line of research have relied on panel data. But an impressive body of research also attests to the value of rolling cross-section (RCS) surveys where fieldwork is spread on a day-by-day basis over entire election campaigns and the dates of individual interviews are treated as random events (Johnston and Brady, 2002; Brady and Johnston, 2006; Schmitt-Beck et al., 2006; Kenski et al., 2013). Drawing on a unique set of merged RCS surveys and media content analyses, our study examines the persuasive influence of TV news on voters' evaluations of the major parties during the 2005 to 2017 German Federal Election campaigns. Specifically, we are interested in the effects of two kinds of media bias on electoral preferences: statement bias, that is, the evaluative tone of reporting on the parties, and coverage bias, that is, the amount of reporting that is devoted to them (D'Alessio and Allen, 2000).

A Revived Topic of Political Science

Whether and how mass media are capable of influencing their audiences' political attitudes and behaviour at elections was one of the first questions asked about this social institution after its emergence in the late nineteenth and early twentieth century. It was first raised by the "hypodermic" or "magic bullet" perspective that dominated thinking about the mass media's political role in the early decades of the past century. Media were believed to be capable of exerting a strong, immediate, and uniform persuasive impact on their audience (Brandenburg and van Egmond, 2011, 442). Simply put, they were ascribed the power to tell those attending to them "what to think" (Cohen, 1963, 13) about the competing actors at elections. Quite naturally, therefore, Lazarsfeld and his colleagues expected to see this huge power of the media first-hand in operation when they set out in 1940 to conduct the first large-scale survey of public opinion at a presidential election campaign (Lazarsfeld et al., 1944). However, despite its ingenious design this study failed to demonstrate persuasive media effects of any relevance. Voter "conversion," it concluded, was quite negligible as a possible outcome of campaign communication (Lazarsfeld et al., 1944, 94–100).

These findings led to the demise of the conception of powerful media and its swift replacement by what came to be known as the "minimal effects" model. After this model's canonization by authors like Klapper (1960), scholarly concern about persuasive media effects almost completely vanished. Communication scientists concluded that voters' preferences were simply the "wrong" dependent variable for research into media effects at elections and directed their attention instead at cognitive phenomena like agenda-setting, whereas political scientists did no longer much care at all about the role of mass media at elections.

This began to change only in the 1990s, when major advances in social science theory and methods spurred a renaissance of research on media persuasion at elections (Kinder, 1998). The most significant theoretical achievement was, arguably, Zaller's (1992) Receive-Accept-Sample model. Methodological progress not only supplied new statistical approaches to modelling media effects (Bartels, 1993), but also innovative techniques of data generation, such as the RCS design as a new approach to collecting time-sensitive survey data (Johnston and Brady, 2002; Brady and Johnston, 2006; Romer et al., 2006). As a result, over a period of half a century "research into the effects of mass communication has come full circle" (Iyengar, 1997, 215).

How Can Media Persuade Voters?

A proper understanding of media effects requires a precise determination of the attributes of media content that are assumed to be responsible for the hypothesized outcomes (Schmitt-Beck, 2012). Central for research on *persuasive* media effects at elections is reporting on parties or candidates that is characterized by some sort of "news bias" that is inherently favourable or unfavourable for these objects.

Most studies of media persuasion at elections focused on the tonality of news reports on parties or candidates, that is, the *statement bias* inherent in the media's coverage (D'Alessio and Allen, 2000). It concerns openly positive or negative evaluative content of media reports on certain electoral competitors. Voters are assumed to learn from such messages whether these parties or candidates are to be evaluated rather positively or negatively (Zaller, 1996). Ultimately, they are expected to take the direction of the media's tone as "an important cue as to whether one should vote for a party or not" (Hopmann et al., 2010, 391).

Several American studies have provided micro-level evidence that voters are indeed sensitive to statement bias in the news. At presidential elections, for instance, such effects were registered for newspapers (Dalton et al., 1998) as well as for TV news (Johnston et al., 2004). Studies of presidential primaries (Barker and Lawrence, 2006) and Senate elections (Druckman and Parkin, 2005) arrived at similar results. Effects of the tone of TV news on voters' orientations towards parties were observed by studies of Canadian parliamentary elections (Johnston et al., 1992: 187–91; Dobrzynska et al., 2003; Fournier et al., 2004). Similar findings were also reported by election studies from several European countries. Brandenburg and van Egmond (2011), for instance, found substantial tone effects for British newspapers at the 2005 parliamentary election. Effects of statement bias in newspapers on readers' party preferences were also reported for Austrian voters (Eberl et al., 2017; Johann et al., 2018). Studies of Dutch (Geers and Bos, 2017) and German elections (Boomgaarden and Semetko, 2012; Geiss and Schäfer, 2017) observed effects of news tone on voter preferences for both the press and TV.

Coverage bias is another manifestation of news bias that was also examined by several studies, either on its own or simultaneously with statement bias. It refers to the amount of attention that media devote to the various parties or candidates, and the concomitantly varying visibility of these competitors to voters (D'Alessio and Allen, 2000). The guiding assumption behind this research is that visibility translates into likability, so that a large amount of media coverage on a party or candidate leads to positive evaluations of this electoral competitor on the part of audience members. Voters can use the amount of coverage a competitor receives as a cue to infer its political importance, quality, and viability (Eberl et al., 2017, 1128). The familiarity created by a party's or candidate's visibility in the news can thus be expected to give rise to positive evaluations (Geiß and Schäfer, 2017, 445–6).

Several European studies accordingly recorded positive relationships between the amount of news coverage devoted to parties and audience members' electoral preferences. For instance, better evaluations in response to more coverage of the parties themselves were registered by research on the 2007 parliamentary election in Denmark (Hopmann et al., 2010). A study of the 2012 Dutch election observed a substantial visibility effect for parties with reference to both TV news and newspapers (Geers and Bos, 2017). Positive associations between measures of party visibility in the press and on TV and audience views were also recorded at the 2009 German and 2013 Austrian parliamentary elections (Boomgaarden and Semetko, 2012; Johann et al., 2018).

Against this backdrop our study aims to examine the *role of statement and coverage bias in the political reporting of the most important German primetime TV newscasts on their audiences' party preferences during the 2005 to 2017 federal election campaigns.* We test the expectation that both forms of news bias, that is, the tonality of reporting on the parties as well as the amount of visibility granted by the news media to these competitors, influenced audience members' party evaluations. More precisely put, we expect parties to be evaluated more (or less) favourably by viewers of TV news, when these newscasts' preceding coverage of these same parties was more positive (negative) or more (less) voluminous.

Data, Measures, and Strategy of Analysis

Our study relies on a unique set of survey and media content data that were collected during the campaigns of four subsequent German federal elections. The survey data include all *RCS surveys* ever conducted at German federal elections. They range from the 2005 pioneer application of the RCS design in Germany (Schmitt-Beck and Faas, 2009) to the three RCS surveys that were conducted under the auspices of the German Longitudinal Election Study (GLES) at the 2009, 2013, and 2017 federal elections (Rattinger et al., 2011, 2014; Roßteutscher et al., 2019).[1] All surveys were fielded by telephone as first waves of two-wave pre-post election panel studies with about 85 interviews on average per day in 2005, 100 interviews per day in 2009 and 2013, and 120 in 2017.[2]

The *content analyses of TV news* paralleled the RCS surveys in terms of substance and periods of observation (Schmitt-Beck et al., 2010; Rattinger et al., 2015a, 2015b; Roßteutscher et al., 2018). They included all primetime newscasts of the two public broadcasters ARD and ZDF and the two commercial broadcasters with the highest ratings, RTL and SAT.1. News stories were the coding units, coding was conducted by trained human coders. All news reports of the complete broadcasts were included in the content analyses. The periods of observation covered the last three (2005: two) months before the respective election.[3]

As *dependent variables* we refer to 11-point like–dislike scales (-5 to +5). The analysis includes the CDU/CSU,[4] SPD, FDP, Greens, The Left, and – only in 2017 – AfD. As *independent variables* two classes of instruments are of principal relevance for observational studies of the role of media at elections: measures of media exposure and of media content. Each of the common analytical strategies prioritizes one of these two factors (Jerit and Barabas, 2011). The "attentiveness approach" (Dobrzynska et al., 2003) focuses on media usage as independent variable and interprets its covariation with a dependent variable of interest as evidence for media effects (e.g., Bartels, 1993). Measures of media usage are thus interpreted as proxies for the reception of media content which is assumed to be responsible for the observed association. The evidence generated by such "mere exposure studies" (de Vreese et al., 2017, 222) typically involves a considerable amount of ambiguity, depending on how much external background knowledge exists about the content to which the studied media audience has been exposed.

Often such studies examine cases of what might be called "blatant media partisanship," that is, media whose coverage is unmistakably slanted, such as the British daily press (e.g., Ladd and Lenz, 2009) or American news providers like FOX (e.g., DellaVigna and Kaplan, 2007). Other studies rely on editorial endorsements to proxy media biases (e.g., Chiang and Knight, 2011). While such studies may offer important insights, they nonetheless lack the necessary indicators for examining the potentially quite subtle implications of fine-grained phenomena like coverage and statement bias. Moreover, in many media systems, including Germany's (Hallin and Mancini, 2004), neither blatant media partisanship nor endorsements are common.

Under such circumstances, assessing the electoral relevance of news media is impossible without direct measures of those aspects of media content that are assumed to be responsible for the media's impact. This renders the "linkage approach" (Dobrzynska et al., 2003), where "the central concept of interest – information from the mass media – is incorporated in the empirical analysis" (Jerit and Barabas, 2011, 144), a priori more adequate. Often such studies approach their object at the aggregate level, seeking to determine whether media content and public opinion covary across media or within media over time. This implies that the mechanisms of influence cannot be modelled. In particular it is not possible to distinguish between direct "message exposure" effects and indirect effects that come about through interpersonal secondary diffusion of media messages (Lazarsfeld et al., 1944). Hence, the ideal strategy for studying electoral effects of mass media is a fusion of both approaches that combines all three components – measures of electoral attitudes, media exposure, and media content – in the same model (Brandenburg and van Egmond, 2012, 442–5). Merging measures of media content with survey data by means of survey-generated indicators of exposure to the respective media is the strategy that optimally realizes the potential of such data (de Vreese et al., 2017). It allows modelling of direct media effects at the micro-level of individual media consumers where they occur. Since this approach is methodologically quite demanding, it has thus far rarely been used – overall (Scharkow and Bachl, 2017, 325; de Vreese et al., 2017, 223–4), but in particular also in research on persuasive effects of mass media at elections.

We pursue this research strategy by linking data from surveys and content analyses collected during four election campaigns. In doing so we take advantage from the fact that within RCS surveys every day of interviewing constitutes an independent random draw from the same population (Johnston and Brady, 2002). Combining interview dates and survey-generated information on respondents' personal exposure to TV news, we can construct precise measures of the specific news content received by individual viewers.

To determine the tonality of TV news coverage on parties, coders were asked to provide overall ratings on a bipolar scale.[5] For 2009, 2013, and 2017, a five-point scale was used whose extreme points (-2, +2) indicated that the respective party was overall judged in an unambiguously negative or positive way. More moderate scores of -1 and +1 signalled that the party was assessed overall rather negatively or positively, but not in an unanimously one-sided way. A score of 0 was assigned if a news report was neutral or ambivalent, that is, if it did not entail any discernible tonality or if it contained a roughly balanced amount of negative and positive statements. For 2005 a similar scale was used, but no distinction was made between unambiguously or only moderately negative tone values; we therefore assigned all negative reports a score of -1.5 to render them comparable to the GLES data. To obtain a base measure of the parties' visibility, the content analyses registered for each of the major parties (whether the party itself, any of its organizational sections, or any of its leading politicians) appeared among the first eight actors (in 2005: all actors) mentioned in a news report.[6] By dividing the number of mentions pertaining to a party by the total number of all actor appearances within the same report we constructed a measure that precisely indicates the extent to which a news report concentrated on this particular party.

Fusing these indicators to the survey data to obtain the "message exposure measures" (Scharkow and Bachl, 2017, 326) that we need to test our expectations required a number of further steps. The first consisted in aggregating them to the level of publication days and news outlets by means of averaging.[7] For the subsequent steps we adopted an approach proposed by Brandenburg and van Egmont (2011, 451–2). We split each of the content measures up into a party- and campaign-specific grand mean, indicating the overall leanings of the respective news program towards the various parties across each of the four campaigns, and daily deviations from these overall averages, which represented the various news programs' short-term fluctuations around the central tendencies of their coverage of each party. This allows for a more rigorous test of media effects, as the temporal heterogeneity of the RCS data (Kenski et al., 2013, 42–3) opens up "reception gaps" (Zaller, 1996, 23–6) that allow to attribute audience opinions unequivocally to the temporally preceding media content. Whereas associations between electoral attitudes and news programs' overall tendencies might reflect audience selectivity, this possibility can be ruled out for co-variations between the day-to-day changes of media content and subsequently measured audience attitudes. In the final step, we used the resulting variables to construct indicators of the content to which individual voters were exposed. We assigned each respondent aggregated measures of coverage and statement bias (separately for campaign- and party-specific grand means and deviations from these central tendencies) for the week before his or her interview, averaged across those news programs that he or she claimed to have watched, and weighted by the number of days the respective programs were followed by that person during that week. For the sake of comparability all four resulting measures of media message exposure were normalized to range 0 to 1.

Our models *control* for partisanship as a generic political predisposition. It has a strong impact on electoral attitudes and may be a powerful driver of selective exposure to news media (dummy variables indicating whether a respondent identified with respective party and whether or not he or she was an independent; implicit reference category: identification with other parties). In addition, we control for respondents' exposure to a range of alternative sources of electoral information (dummy variables for daily newspapers [0 = no newspapers read, 1 = at least one newspaper read during previous week], online news sites [0 = not used, 1 = used] and parties' campaign contacting [0 = no contact to campaign of respective party, 1 = contacted by respective party]). Our models also include education as a generic indicator of cognitive capacity (1 = secondary education completed, 0 = lower level of education) as well as age (rescaled to range 0 – 1), and gender (1 = female, 0 = male). Furthermore, the models contain a set of structural control variables. To neutralize differences in average levels of party evaluations we control for parties (reference category: CDU/CSU) and whether a party was a member of the incumbent government coalition at the time of the election campaign (dummy variable). Lastly, in order to model the effects of all independent variables simultaneously it is necessary to deal with structural missing values caused by features of media usage and content. The models therefore additionally control for two dummy variables (coded 1 for respondents that did not watch TV news, and for respondents exposed to newscasts that during the week assigned to their interview did not publish any reports with discernible tonality).

To achieve a comprehensive understanding of media effects we *model* the effects of all four measures of bias in TV news – grand means and deviations for both coverage and statement bias – in one simultaneous estimation. To model these predictors' impact on party evaluations we stack our data by parties within respondents, comparable to other recent studies of media effects at elections in multi-party systems (Hopmann et al., 2010; Geers and Bos, 2017; Eberl et al., 2017; Johann et al., 2018). This allows us to model "generic" party orientations, transcending parties' "proper names." Thus, for the 2005 to 2013 elections respondents appear five times in the models (for CDU/CSU, SPD, FDP, Greens, and the Left), and for 2017 six times (adding the AfD). Nesting parties within respondents means that party-specific predictors such as in particular our independent variables, but also partisanship and campaign exposure need to be turned into generic variables with different characteristics for each party. Since our dependent variable is continuous we use hierarchical linear models with varying intercepts (with party-respondent combinations as level 1, respondents as level 2 and elections as level 3). Given the low number of groups at the highest level, we rely on Bayesian instead of conventional maximum likelihood estimation techniques (Stegmüller, 2013).[8]

From a methodological point of view our approach to examining persuasive media effects is in several respects extremely conservative. The deck is thus stacked against detecting statistically meaningful media effects, minimizing the likelihood of false positives. For one, by including partisanship we opt for a control variable that erects high hurdles for any additional predictors of party evaluations. In Germany partisanship is so closely associated with electoral preferences that at times it has been debated whether it is actually a distinct phenomenon or rather endogeneous to orientations of the kind we refer to as dependent variables (Falter et al., 2000). Unlike many comparable studies we also include in our models a variety of alternative and potentially competing sources of electoral information as additional controls. Moreover, recent methodological research suggests that self-reports on media exposure like those used in our surveys as well as indicators of media content are often affected by issues of measurement imprecision. These problems are not tractable with current methodological approaches and tend to depress the effects sizes in linkage studies like ours (Scharkow and Bachl, 2017).

Findings

The results of our model are displayed in table 11.1 (unstandardized linear regression coefficients). Despite the high hurdles that our approach erected to the detection of media effects, three of our four measures of media bias show substantial effects in the expected direction. The overall means of TV newscasts with regard to both coverage and statement bias display effects that differ

Table 11.1. TV news message exposure and party evaluations

Visibility (mean across campaign)	.21 (.06)***
Visibility (centred on mean)	−.05 (.10)
Tone (mean across campaign)	.32 (.04)***
Tone (centred on mean)	.38 (.11)***
Party ID	3.03 (.92)***
No party ID	.32 (.02)***
Exposure to newspaper	.05 (.02)*
Exposure to online news	−.13 (.02)***
Campaign contact	.65 (.06)***
Higher education	−.04 (.02)*
Age	−.35 (.05)***
Female	.22 (.02)***
SPD	−.16 (.02)***
FDP	−.72 (.03)***
Greens	−.32 (.03)***
Left	−2.17 (.03)***
AfD	−4.46 (.04)***
Party in government	−.39 (.02)***
No TV news	−.22 (.03)***
No tone in TV news	−.05 (.02)**
Constant	6.13 (.26)***
Num. Obs.	121295
Num. Respondents	23050
Num. Election Studies	4
Var. (Residual)	5.29
Var. (Respondents)	.70
Var. (Election Studies)	.01

Notes: *$p < .05$, **$p < .01$, ***$p < .001$. Entries are unstandardized coefficients from a Bayesian hierarchical linear model (posterior standard deviations in parentheses).

significantly from zero. Viewers of news programs that overall covered parties more often tended to like these parties better than viewers of programs whose coverage concentrated less strongly on these parties. The same applies to the tone of party coverage. Viewers of news that reported overall more positively on parties tended to evaluative these parties better than viewers of news that presented them on average less favourably. Variation between news programs with regard to parties' visibility as well as the tonality of parties' coverage thus mattered for how strongly viewers liked or disliked these parties. In addition, TV viewers were also sensitive to deviations of the tonality of news programs from their long-term means. This suggests that short-term changes in how positively or negatively parties were covered by TV news led to accordingly oscillating evaluations of these parties on the part of the news audience, over and beyond the same news programs' baseline impact. The same does not pertain to coverage bias, however. The dynamic ups and downs of media attention during the campaigns were not reflected in voters' attitudes.

To put these effects into perspective, we can compare them to the effects of partisanship and exposure to alternative information sources. Since all independent and control variables have the same range (0–1), effect sizes can be directly compared. Unsurprisingly, partisanship exerted a very powerful influence on how voters assessed the electoral competitors. However, exposure to alternative media sources such as newspapers and online media also displayed statistically significant effects, although much weaker ones (and negative for online news). Voters exposed to a party's electioneering also tended to evaluate this party significantly more favourably. The effect sizes of the three measures of bias in TV news amounted to about half the impact of campaign contact. However, they were considerably stronger than the mere exposure effects of the daily press and online news. However, it would be premature to conclude from this that when it comes to media persuasion at elections TV is a stronger force than the press, whether conventional or online. Since they entail no information on the content conveyed to readers, mere exposure effects of the kind displayed in the table are by necessity weaker than effects of direct exposure to persuasive news content.

Conclusion

During the second half of the twentieth century, research on media effects at elections went "full circle" (Iyengar, 1997, 215). Whereas the canonization of the "minimal effects" model during the 1950s (Klapper, 1960) had led to the almost complete demise of the idea that mass media might have the capacity to exert persuasive influences on voters' attitudes, new theories, new methods, and new data stimulated a renaissance of this notion in the 1990s (Kinder, 1998), albeit to date a rather modest one. Relying on sophisticated research designs that linked media content data with dynamic survey data in order to model the consequences of respondents' exposure to specific media messages (De Vreese et al., 2017), a small number of studies about elections in the United States, Canada, the United Kingdom as well as several West European countries were meanwhile able to demonstrate persuasive effects of statement and coverage bias, that is the tonality and the amount of coverage devoted to parties or candidates (D'Alessio and Allen, 2000), on electoral preferences (e.g., Johnston et al., 2004; Johnston et al., 1992, 187-91; Dobrzynska et al., 2003; Fournier et al., 2004; Hopmann et al., 2010; Brandenburg and van Egmond, 2011; Geers and Bos, 2017; Johann et al., 2018; Eberl et al., 2017; Boomgaarden and Semetko, 2012; Geiss and Schäfer, 2017). Against this backdrop our analysis examined the role of bias in the political reporting of the most important TV news programs for voters' party evaluations at the 2005 to 2017 German

Federal Elections, using merged data from RCS campaign surveys (Johnston and Brady, 2002; Brady and Johnston, 2006; Schmitt-Beck et al., 2006; Kenski et al., 2011) and content analyses.

The perhaps most crucial message of our study is as simple as it is important: From a methodological point of view our approach to examining persuasive media effects was in several respects extremely conservative; nonetheless our model detected evidence for direct media persuasion with regard to how voters evaluated the major parties at the four most recent federal elections. In view of how elusive such effects have proven to be over decades in research, this appears quite remarkable in itself. We found that voters tended to evaluate parties more positively if they followed news programs that covered these parties overall more prominently and with an overall more favourable tonality. Even more importantly, we also found voters' evaluations to follow the dynamic short-term fluctuations in the tonality of news reporting during campaigns. To be sure, despite the strong controls that we included in our model, it is possible that the static overall patterns to some extent reflect audience selectivity rather than media effects. But for the short-term effects of the day-to-day oscillations of statement bias this can be ruled out. We consider this outcome of our study strong evidence for the existence of media persuasion.

How TV news portray the parties thus appears to leave a trace in voter's political attitudes; during election campaigns they do tell them "what to think" (Cohen, 1963, 13) about the parties. Specifically, we found more positive TV coverage leading to more friendly judgments on the part of viewers. Higher visibility in the news also seems to go along with more favourable viewer attitudes, but this relationship is more ambiguous. Cautiously generalizing from our findings, we may conclude that at elections TV news are not as all-powerful as they are often seen by politicians and citizens (van Aelst et al., 2008; Perloff, 1999), but they are certainly also far from a *quantité négligeable*. However, our findings also invite speculation about what the news media's power at elections could amount to if its coverage were less plural. The news audience exposes itself routinely to information from different sources whose coverage is quite diverse. This leads to a substantial amount of mutual cancellation between messages of varying directional content (Zaller, 1996). A crucial implication of this is that the media's direct impact on voters' electoral preferences could be considerably larger if the current plurality of news outlets would be transformed into a more uniform system where most media speak with the same voice. Under such circumstances a massive "mainstreaming" of public opinion is the likely outcome (Zaller, 1992, 97–117). Small wonder, then, that seeking to control the news media is foremost on governments' minds in an increasing number of countries where elected rulers have begun to convert liberal democratic regimes into "illiberal" or "guided democracies" (cf. https://freedomhouse.org /report/freedom-media/freedom-media-2019).

NOTES

1 German electoral research is deeply indebted to Richard Johnston for generously sharing his expertise when these surveys were planned and conducted. A comprehensive analysis of these data is provided by Partheymüller (2018).

2 In 2005, 2009, and 2013 fieldwork was based on multi-stage random sampling based on the ADM-design for landline telephones, a variant of RDD sampling. Sampling was regionally stratified; target persons in households were selected using the last-birthday method. In 2017 sampling was based on a dual sampling frame that comprised also mobile phones. The surveys covered 41, 60, 62, and 76 days respectively, with each day's interviews constituting random samples from the population of German citizens aged 18 and above (8 August to 17 September, 2005: N = 3,583, AAPOR response rate 37.7; 29 July to 26 September, 2009, N = 6,008, AAPOR response rate 19.6 per cent; 7 July to 21 September, 2013, N = 7,882, AAPOR response rate 15.5 per cent; 24 July to 23 September, 2017, N = 7,650, AAPOR response rate 9.6 per cent). IPSOS GmbH was responsible for fieldwork. The datasets can be obtained from GESIS – Leibniz Institute of the Social Sciences (dataset numbers ZA4991, ZA5303, ZA5703, and ZA6803).

3 Coding of the 2005 content analysis was conducted by GöFaK Medienforschung Berlin, the 2009 to 2017 content analyses were conducted by the GLES team. The datasets can be obtained from GESIS – Leibniz Institute of the Social Sciences (dataset numbers ZA4997, ZA5306, ZA5705, ZA6808). Numbers of cases: 2005: 5,191; 2009: 6,212; 2013: 5,947; 2017: 5,144.

4 CSU for Bavarian respondents, CDU for all others (the CSU exists only in Bavaria where the CDU in turn has no state party organization; in the Federal Parliament the two parties collaborate in a unified group).

5 For 2005 coders were instructed to refer to both explicit and implicit evaluations contained in news stories, whereas for 2009 to 2017 they referred only to explicitly evaluative judgments. Average reliability (Krippendorff's α; cf. Krippendorff, 2004) of the resulting ratings: .86.

6 Average reliability of these base measures (Krippendorff's α): .89.

7 See Schmitt-Beck and Staudt (2022) for descriptive information on these content data.

8 We assign the coefficients weakly informative normal priors (mean 0, standard deviation 2.5), the intercept a normal prior with mean 0 and standard deviation 10, and the variance components a Gamma prior with shape 1 and rate 1.

References

Barker, David C., and Adam B. Lawrence. 2006. "Media Favoritism and Presidential Nominations: Reviving the Direct Effects Model." *Political Communication* 23: 41–59. https://doi.org/10.1080/10584600500477013

Bartels, Larry M. 1993. "Messages Received: The Political Impact of Media Exposure." *American Political Science Review* 87: 267–85. https://doi.org/10.2307/2939040

Boomgaarden, Hajo, and Holli A. Semetko. 2012. "Nachrichten-Bias: Medieninhalte, Bevölkerungswahrnehmungen und Wahlentscheidungen bei der Bundestagswahl 2009." In *Wählen in Deutschland (PVS Special Issue 45),* edited by Rüdiger Schmitt-Beck, 345–70. Nomos.

Brady, Henry E., and Richard Johnston. 2006. "The Rolling Cross-Section and Causal Attribution." In *Capturing Campaign Effects,* edited by Henry E. Brady and Richard Johnston 164–95. University of Michigan Press.

Brandenburg, Heinz, and Marcel van Egmond. 2011. "Pressed into Party Support? Media Influence on Partisan Attitudes during the 2005 UK General Election Campaign." *British Journal of Political Science* 42: 441–63. https://doi.org/10.1017/S0007123411000445

Chiang, Chun-Fang, and Brian Knight. 2011. "Media Bias and Influence: Evidence from Newspaper Endorsements." *The Review of Economic Studies* 78: 795–820. https://doi.org/10.1093/restud/rdq037

Cohen, Bernard C. (1963). *The Press and Foreign Policy.* Princeton University Press.

D'Alessio, Dave, and Mike Allen. 2000. "Media Bias in Presidential Elections: A Meta-Analysis." *Journal of Communication* 50: 133–56. https://doi.org/10.1111/j.1460-2466.2000.tb02866.x

Dalton, Russell J., Paul A. Beck, and Robert Huckfeldt. 1998. "Partisan Cues and the Media: Information Flows in the 1992 Presidential Election." *American Political Science Review* 92: 111–26. https://doi.org/10.2307/2585932

DellaVigna, Stefano, and Ethan Kaplan. 2007. "The Fox News Effect: Media Bias and Voting." *Quarterly Journal of Economics* 122: 1187–1234. doi:10.1162/qjec.122.3.1187

De Vreese, Claes H., Mark Boukes, Andreas Schuck, Rens Vliegenthart, Linda Bos, and Yph Lelkes. 2017. "Linking Survey and Media Content Data: Opportunities, Considerations, and Pitfalls." *Communication Methods and Measures* 11: 221–44. https://doi.org/10.1080/19312458.2017.1380175

Dobrzynska, Agnieska, André Blais, and Richard Nadeau. 2003. "Do the Media Have a Direct Impact on the Vote? The Case of the 1997 Canadian Election." *International Journal of Public Opinion Research* 15: 27–43. https://doi.org/10.1093/ijpor/15.1.27

Druckman, James N., and Michael Parkin. 2005. "The Impact of Media Bias: How Editorial Slant Affects Voters." *Journal of Politics* 67: 1030–49. https://doi.org/10.1111/j.1468-2508.2005.00349.x

Eberl, Jakob-Moritz, Hajo G. Boomgaarden, and Markus Wagner. 2017. "One Bias Fits All? Three Types of Media Bias and Their Effects on Party Preferences." *Communication Research* 44: 1125–48. https://doi.org/10.1177/0093650215614364

Falter, Jürgen W., Harald Schoen, and Claudio Caballero. 2000. "Dreißig Jahre danach: Zur Validierung des Konzepts ‚Parteiidentifikation' in der Bundesrepublik." In *50*

Jahre Empirische Wahlforschung in Deutschland, edited by Klein, Markus, Wolfgang Jagodzinski, Ekkehard Mochmann and Dieter Ohr, 235–71. Westdeutscher Verlag.

Fournier, Patrick, Richard Nadeau, André Blais, Elisabetz Gidengil, and Neil Nevitte. 2004. "Time-of-Voting Decision and Susceptibility to Campaign Effects." *Electoral Studies* 23: 661–81. https://doi.org/10.1016/j.electstud.2003.09.001

Geers, Sabine, and Linda Bos. 2017. "Priming Issues, Party Visibility, and Party Evaluations: The Impact on Vote Switching." *Political Communication* 34: 344–66. https://doi.org/10.1080/10584609.2016.1201179

Geiß, Stefan, and Svenja Schäfer. 2017. "Any Publicity or Good Publicity? A Competitive Test of Visibility- and Tonality-Based Media Effects on Voting Behavior." *Political Communication* 34: 444–67. https://doi.org/10.1080/10584609.2016.1271068

Hallin, David C., and Paolo Mancini. 2004. *Comparing Media Systems: Three Models of Media and Politics*. Cambridge University Press.

Hopmann, David N., Rens Vliegenthart, Claes De Vreese, and Erik Albæk. 2010. "Effects of Election News Coverage: How Visibility and Tone Influence Party Choice." *Political Communication* 27: 389–405. https://doi.org/10.1080/10584609.2010.516798

Iyengar, Shanto. 1997. "The Effects of News on the Audience. Minimal or Maximal Consequences? – Overview." In *Do the Media Govern? Politicians, Voters, and Reporters in America*, edited by Shanto Iyengar and Richard Reeves, 209–16. Sage.

Jerit, Jennifer, and Jason Barabas. 2011. "Exposure Measures and Content Analysis in Media Effects Studies." In *The Oxford Handbook of American Public Opinion and the Media*, edited by Robert Y. Shapiro and Lawrence R. Jacobs, 139–55. Oxford University Press.

Johann, David, Katharina Kleinen-Von Königslöw, Sylvia Kritzinger, and Kathrin Thomas. 2018. "Intra-Campaign Changes in Voting Preferences: The Impact of Media and Party Communication." *Political Communication* 35: 261–86. https://doi.org/10.1080/10584609.2017.1339222. Medline: 29695892

Johnston, Richard, André Blais, Henry E. Brady, and Jean Crete. 1992. *Letting the People Decide. Dynamics of a Canadian Election*. Stanford University Press.

Johnston, Richard, and Henry E. Brady. 2002. "The Rolling Cross-Section Design." *Electoral Studies* 21: 283–95. https://doi.org/10.1016/S0261-3794(01)00022-1

Johnston, Richard, Michael G. Hagen, and Kathleen Hall Jamieson. 2004. *The 2000 Presidential Election and the Foundations of Party Politics*. Cambridge University Press.

Kenski, Kate, Jeffrey A. Gottfried, and Kathleen Hall Jamieson. 2013. "The Rolling Cross-Section: Design and Utility for Political Research." In *Sourcebook for Political Communication Research: Methods, Measures, and Analytical Techniques*, edited by Erik P. Bucy and Lance Holbert, 34–54. Routledge.

Kinder, Donald R. 1998. "Communication and Opinion." *Annual Review of Political Science* 1: 167–97. https://doi.org/10.1146/annurev.polisci.1.1.167

Klapper, Joseph T. 1960. *The Effects of Mass Communication*. The Free Press.

Krippendorff, Klaus. 2004. "Reliability in Content Analysis. Some Common Misconceptions and Recommendations." *Human Communication Research* 30: 411–33. https://doi.org/10.1111/j.1468-2958.2004.tb00738.x

Ladd, Jonathan M., and Gabriel S. Lenz. 2009. "Exploiting a Rare Communication Shift to Document the Persuasive Power of the News Media." *American Journal of Political Science* 53: 394–410. https://doi.org/10.1111/j.1540-5907.2009.00377.x

Lazarsfeld, Paul F., Bernard Berelson, and Hazel Gaudet. 1944. *The People's Choice. How the Voter Makes Up His Mind in a Presidential Campaign*. Columbia University Press.

Partheymüller, Julia. 2018. *Campaign Dynamics in German Federal Elections, 2005–2013*, PhD thesis, University of Mannheim.

Perloff, Richard M. 1999. "The Third Person Effect: A Critical Review and Synthesis." *Media Psychology* 1 (4): 353–78. https://doi.org/10.1207/s1532785xmep0104_4

Rattinger, Hans, Sigrid Roßteutscher, Rüdiger Schmitt-Beck, and Bernhard Weßels. 2011. *"Rolling Cross-Section-Campaign Study with Post-Election Panel Wave (GLES 2009)."* GESIS Data Archive, Cologne: ZA5303 Data File Version 6.0.0, doi: 10.4232/1.11604.

Rattinger, Hans, Sigrid Roßteutscher, Rüdiger Schmitt-Beck, Bernhard Weßels, and Christof Wolf. 2014. *"Rolling Cross-Section-Campaign Study with Post-Election Panel Wave (GLES 2013)."* GESIS Data Archive, Cologne: ZA5703 Data File Version 2.0.0, doi: 10.4232/1.11892.

Rattinger, Hans, Sigrid Roßteutscher, Rüdiger Schmitt-Beck, Bernhard Weßels, and Mona Krewel. 2015a. *"Campaign Media Content Analysis, TV (GLES 2009)."* GESIS Data Archive, Cologne: ZA5306 Data file Version 1.2.0, doi:10.4232/1.12211.

Rattinger, Hans, Sigrid Roßteutscher, Rüdiger Schmitt-Beck, Bernhard Weßels, Christof Wolf, Anne Schäfer, and Sebastian Schmidt. 2015b. *"Campaign Media Content Analysis: TV (GLES 2013)."* GESIS Data Archive, Cologne: ZA5705 Data file Version 1.0.0, doi:10.4232/1.12173.

Romer, Daniel, Kenski, Kate, Winneg, Kenneth, Adasiewicz, Christopher, and Kathleen Hall Jamieson. 2006. *Capturing Campaign Dynamics 2000 & 2004: The National Annenberg Election Survey*. Philadelphia: University of Pennsylvania Press.

Roßteutscher, Sigrid, Rüdiger Schmitt-Beck, Harald Schoen, Bernhard Weßels, Christof Wolf, Lena Marie Schackmann, Mona Krewel, and Anne Schäfer 2018. *"Campaign Media Content Analysis, TV (GLES 2017)."* GESIS Data Archive, Cologne. ZA6808 Data file Version 1.0.0, doi:10.4232/1.13186.

Roßteutscher, Sigrid, Rüdiger Schmitt-Beck, Rüdiger, Harald Schoen, Bernhard Weßels, Christof Wolf, and Alexander Staudt. 2019. *"Rolling Cross-Section Campaign Survey with Post-election Panel Wave (GLES 2017)."* GESIS Data Archive, Cologne. ZA6803 Data file Version 4.0.1, doi:10.4232/1.13213.

Scharkow, Michael, and Marko Bachl. 2017. "How Measurement Error in Content Analysis and Self-Reported Media Use Leads to Minimal Media Effect Findings in

Linkage Analyses: A Simulation Study." *Political Communication* 34 (3): 323–43. https://doi.org/10.1080/10584609.2016.1235640

Schmitt-Beck, Rüdiger. 2012. "Comparing Effects of Political Communication." In *The Comparative Handbook of Communication Research*, edited by Frank Esser and Thomas Hanitzsch, 400–9, Routledge.

Schmitt-Beck, Rüdiger, and Thorsten Faas. 2009. *Bundestagswahl 2005 Kampagnendynamik - Vor- und Nachwahlstudie*. GESIS Data Archive, Cologne: ZA4991 Data file Version 1.0.0, doi:10.4232/1.4991.

Schmitt-Beck, Rüdiger, Thorsten Faas, and Christian Holst. 2006. "Der Rolling Cross-Section Survey – ein Instrument zur Analyse dynamischer Prozesse der Einstellungsentwicklung." *ZUMA-Nachrichten* 58:13–49. https://nbn-resolving.org /urn:nbn:de:0168-ssoar-211128

Schmitt-Beck, Rüdiger, Mona Krewel, and Ansgar Wolsing. 2010. *Bundestagswahl 2005 Kampagnendynamik - Fernsehnachrichtenanalyse*. GESIS Data Archive, Cologne. ZA4997 Data file Version 1.0.0, doi:10.4232/1.4997.

Schmitt-Beck, Rüdiger, and Alexander Staudt. 2022. "Media Biases and Voter Attitudes." In *The Changing German Voter*, edited by Rüdiger Schmitt-Beck, Sigrid Roßteutscher, Harald Schoen, Bernhard Weßels, and Christof Wolf, 257-81. Oxford University Press.

Stegmüller, Daniel. 2013. "How Many Countries for Multilevel Modeling? A Comparison of Frequentist and Bayesian Approaches." *American Journal of Political Science* 57 (3): 748–61. https://doi.org/10.1111/ajps.12001

Van Aelst, Peter et al. 2008. "The Fourth Estate as Superpower?" *Journalism Studies* 9 (4): 494–511. https://doi.org/10.1080/14616700802114134

Zaller, John R. 1992. *The Nature and Origins of Mass Opinion*. Cambridge University Press.

Zaller, John R. 1996. "The Myth of Massive Media Impact Revived: New Support for a Discredited Idea." In *Political Persuasion and Attitude Change*, edited by Diana C. Mutz, Paul M. Sniderman and Richard A. Brody, 17–78. University of Michigan Press.

12 Media Image and Voter Perception of Candidates in the 2015 Canadian Election

AMANDA BITTNER AND DAVID A.M. PETERSON

Introduction

Candidates and party leaders influence election outcomes. To a typical voter, someone who pays moderate attention to campaign coverage, this is an obvious statement. Certainly, partisanship, the economy, and other factors matter for elections, but the amount of attention the personalities of the party leaders receive in media coverage indicates how important these factors are in elections. These typical voters would likely be skeptical of a large cross section of the political science literature on elections. A common refrain among scholars is that elections are more or less predictable based on the fundamentals. Our ability to predict the outcome, months ahead of time, with little to no information about the specific party leaders implies that the leaders themselves are probably inconsequential to the outcomes. In the American context, the resurgence of partisanship means that it is the letter after the name (D or R) that really matters and that the names before the party letters are essentially interchangeable.

The ability to forecast elections is remarkable. The accuracy of the models without regard to the nature of the party leaders is suggestive of the limits of the importance of party leaders, but we remain unconvinced. Notably, the existing work tends not to show that leaders do not matter, instead emphasizing what can be done without attempting to account for party leaders. This choice is somewhat odd. In most social science, researchers try to directly test how something is related to something else. We conclude that a concept does not matter if the empirical evidence is not strong enough for us to conclude that there is a relationship. We do not simply say that this other concept does a good job of explaining the dependent variable, therefore some other concept must not matter. That is, however, where some of the current literature has left us on the role of party leaders in elections.

In this chapter we revisit the role of party leaders in elections outcomes, using the context of the 2016 Canadian federal elections. In particular, we look at the interactions between three important pieces to this research question: (1) the image of the party leader's personality as portrayed in the media; (2) the perceptions in the minds of the voters; and (3) election outcomes, captured as both the overall levels of support for a party and an individual voter's preference. The combination of these three concepts helps us elucidate the role of leaders in elections and test several hypotheses about how voters and the media interact to construct election outcomes. Our results suggest that the interplay between candidates, voters, and the media is complicated, with evidence that the media both leads and responds to the voters' preferences for party leaders.

Voters' Perceptions of Leaders' Traits

The role of candidates has been a central piece in the literature about voter decision making at least since *The American Voter* (Campbell et al., 1960 and Converse, 1964). Stokes (1966) went so far as to argue that the variation in election outcomes over time is largely the result of the differences in the leaders across the elections. That is, parties rise and fall between electoral cycles as the attractiveness of the candidates for office changes.

Not surprisingly, these initial works were followed by a tremendous amount of research in subsequent decades. The first major shift in how scholars approached the study of the perceptions of leader's personalities was the inclusion of the standard closed-ended battery of trait questions in the 1980 American National Election Study (Abelson et al., 1982), although Patterson had included similar questions in his panel surveys of 1976 (1980). Given the limits of data acquisition and survey collection of the era, the inclusion of these questions in the main common resource of survey-based research jump-started research into how voters think about party leaders.

The bulk of research that followed assessed the way in which voters perceive candidates and party leaders (and the impact of those perceptions) based on analyses of cross-sectional survey data from a single election in a single country, particularly the United States. Much of this work became bogged down in secondary debates about the role of leader personality in voter decision-making. Scholars explored the dimensionality of trait perceptions (Funk, 1996), which voters were more or less likely to rely on personality trait perceptions when voting (Bittner, 2011) and the interaction between voters' other preferences and their perceptions of the candidates (Peterson, 2005).

But these works were usually tied to cross-sectional surveys and faced the limitations that single cross-sectional surveys face when trying to disentangle complicated empirical relationships. Not surprisingly, several scholars revisited some of the basic work on the role of personality perceptions by voters, noting the key limitations of cross-sectional observation data and challenging the foundations of the field. Bartels (2002), for instance, demonstrates that much of the empirical relationship between perceptions of party leader traits and vote choice is largely endogenous. He concludes that the independent causal effect of these trait perceptions is negligible, and the seemingly strong relationship is quite spurious. If we account for the systematic biasing effects of party and issues and the projection of positive traits onto candidates a voter prefers, these measures have little explanatory power left. His conclusion is that these character impressions are not responsible for voters' choices, and we should largely ignore them when trying to explain campaigns.

But if observational cross-sectional data is limited and inconclusive for understanding how the personalities of leaders shape elections outcomes, the solution is better designs. This was the importance of Johnston, Blais, Brady, and Crete's *Letting the People Decide* (1992). Their in-depth study of the 1988 Canadian federal election provides clear evidence of how the content of the campaign changed voters' perceptions of the leaders and how those changes fundamentally reshaped the election. This was the clearest evidence yet, and some of the clearest evidence to date about the role of leaders in shaping election outcomes. Johnston et al. did things differently than the standard cross-sectional analysis of survey data. First, the survey design was much more ambitious and complex. Instead of one or two surveys during the campaign, as is standard for election studies, they used a rolling cross-section approach, with repeated random sampling throughout the campaign.[1] Additionally, they included extensive data about the campaign itself. They were fortunate that the election campaign was one of the more interesting in recent memory, with the Progressive Conservatives making the choice to focus on Liberal Party leader Turner's leadership mid-way through the campaign. In combination, Johnston et al. are among the first to clearly show a link between the campaign information about a party leader's personality and voters' decisions.

Conceptually, what Johnston et al. were able to do was make the distinction between the *image* of a party leader's personality and the *perception* a voter or voters have about that leader. The former is the public depiction of who the party leader is. It is likely tied to his or her real personality, but it is the more general depiction of him or her. The latter of these are how individual voters perceive the leaders. The perception of these personalities is likely shaped by the image of the leader in the information environment, but each person filters this information by his or her predispositions. Cross-sectional survey data can only examine these perceptions and their connections to votes. Given that perceptions are filtered by things like partisanship it is not surprising that they are correlated with vote choice and that these simple correlations may, as Bartels suggested, overstate their effects.

The more subtle piece of the problem, however, is that a cross-sectional survey has to ignore the image of the candidate. If the image is a construction of the campaign environment and all the survey respondents are essentially drawn from the same environment, the image does not vary meaningfully. There may be differences in what information respondents attend to, but if we cannot effectively measure these (and there is ample evidence that this is quite difficult (e.g., McCann, 1990, Nimmo and Savage, 1976), then the image of a candidate is, essentially, a constant. A more positive image may lead to more support for the candidate, but this is difficult to test if we only observe voters at a single moment in time when the image does not vary.

Johnston et al. may have been the first to do this, but they were not the last. In addition to incorporating some temporal variation in the image of the candidates, scholars have made use of experiments (see Rahn, 1993, Rosenberg et al., 1986, Lodge et al., 1989 for early examples), and others have assessed the topic cross-nationally (Bean and Mughan, 1989, Bittner, 2011). In both cases scholars leverage the ability of their designs to get variation in the images of the candidates to test fundamental questions of the nature of how voters perceive leaders. In doing so, they address the central criticisms of endogeneity raised by Bartels and others.

The field has matured to have a broader understanding of the ways in which voters form these impressions of leaders. Still, at least three substantial questions remain confusing (Bittner and Peterson, 2019). First, even when there is agreement that the perceptions of leaders' personalities are influential in elections outcomes, the framework that citizens use to construct these perceptions remains unclear. Second, the specific role of the information environment and content available to voters is mixed, with only limited success in tying specific measures of information to voters' assessments of the candidates. Third, while the experimental evidence about the role of perceptions of leaders is clear about internal validity of the relationships, real world campaigns are messy and complicated and work is still needed to connect the results of experiments to real world elections. In this chapter, we provide additional evidence on each of these questions.

Leaders' Traits: What Are They?

Existing scholarship notes that perceptions of leaders' personalities are divided up into dimensions. How many dimensions depends on the study, but generally speaking scholars agree on between two and four categories, which include *competence, leadership, integrity,* and *empathy* (see Bittner, 2011 for a more detailed discussion of content of the various dimensions and how they fit together). Importantly, these trait dimensions fit within cognitive psychology understandings of how people perceive the world more broadly, that is, through the use of schema and stereotypes. These schemata (which can be likened to filing cabinets) affect (a) how we remember information we already have stored as well as (b) how we integrate new information into our understanding of the world (Lodge et al., 1986), by providing categories and labels to allow us to fit new information in with what already exists in our minds.

These categories or schemata are not invented by the individuals processing information but reflect collective understandings of the world around us. As Kinder et al., (1980) suggest, voters agree on the types of traits, for example, that presidents *should* have, and then evaluate candidates on that basis. These social understandings of the world are underpinned in language systems and communication. Humphreys et al., (1999) and Vigliocco et al., (2007) note the important link between language and concepts, suggesting that the two cannot be disentangled. As Peterson argues, we adapt our language to describe an individual's personality, and choose adjectives according to our (sometimes changing) impressions: "word choices fundamentally shape the audience's perceptions" (2014, 8). As such, focusing on the language used to describe candidates should give us some insight into the types of information voters are integrating into their existing "filing cabinets" when evaluating party leaders.

With a few notable exceptions (e.g., Peterson, 2018, McGraw et al., 1996), the work of political science scholars studying the role of candidate traits has generally not been *explicitly* linked to the work of personality scholars in psychology. Having said this, political science scholarship in this area is implicitly reliant upon the foundational work of psychology scholars who years ago established the existence of the "Big Five" personality traits, including (a) extroversion; (b) agreeableness; (c) conscientiousness; (d) openness to experience (or intellect); and (e) emotional stability or neuroticism (Ashton et al., 2004), and election studies around the world (including both the NES and CES) essentially use a pared down version of the approach when they ask voters to assess candidates based on a short list of personality traits.

The Big Five dimensions were established early on, but have been studied extensively (and verified frequently) by scholars (Goldberg 1982, Ashton et al., 2004), by asking individuals to rate others (or themselves) on a list of adjectives, and then using statistical analyses (e.g., factor analysis, principal components analysis) to identify and map these adjectives onto dimensions. Political science scholars have relied upon the Big Five and linked those personality trait dimensions to a number of different political phenomena, including political information, political attitudes, and political participation (Mondak, 2010). Not only have the Big Five been found to be important in relation to multiple orientations to politics, but the dimensions also travel across space, suggesting that English is not the only language of relevance (Ashton et al. 2004).

The link between the Big Five personality traits and voters' perceptions of candidates is an important one, and one that has not been explored in as much detail as it could be. Indeed, most studies assessing the role of candidates and leaders in the minds of voters make no mention whatsoever of the Big Five. However, McGraw et al. (1996) argue that the Big Five dimensions map quite closely onto the dimensions that have been identified and studied in the candidates literature. Table 12.1 draws links between (a) the dimensions established in the candidates literature; (b) the Big Five dimensions of personality; and (c) the types of candidate traits that are associated with each of the dimensions.

Note that one of the Big Five dimensions (emotional stability or neuroticism) does not clearly map onto the traits established in the candidate's literature. Our best guess for this is that there is traditionally little variation in the emotional stability of candidates. The selection processes of modern democratic parties potentially weed out candidates who lack emotional stability. The nomination and election of Donald Trump, however, demonstrates that this is not always the case. A second possibility is simply that survey researchers have not thought to ask the appropriate questions. The 2004 National Annenberg Election Study of the American presidential election asked voters how well "reckless" described the candidates. To the best of our knowledge, that is the closest any survey has come to asking voters how emotionally stable or neurotic a candidate is.

While McGraw et al. (1996) establish the links between the Big Five and the dimensions observed in the candidates literature, Caprara and colleagues (1999, 2002, 2006, 2007) confirm that the dimensions map onto one another, but also take the work one step further, demonstrating that not all of the dimensions matter equally in the minds of voters. They find that voters focus most heavily on the "intellect" and "agreeableness" of candidates (or competence and empathy, to use the language of the candidates literature). Indeed, that voters do not concentrate on all traits equally is a finding that was confirmed also by Bittner (2011), who argues that voters tend to focus more heavily on "character" (traits linked to both integrity and empathy) when evaluating candidates.

Even after the advances from Johnston et al., the field has been slow to try to directly incorporate specific measures of the image of the candidates as portrayed in the media or advertising. Certainly, there is a voluminous literature on documenting how campaign messages influence voters generally (Johnston et al., 1992, Johnston et al., 2000, Hillygus, 2005), but effective measures of how the personalities of leaders are portrayed are elusive. One recent advance (Peterson, 2018) relies on the link between language and the Big Five personality research to develop a measurement scheme for capturing the image of a leader's personality. He uses loadings between words used to describe a person and the latent measures of the Big Five (Ashton et al., 2004) to conduct a content analysis of media coverage and advertising about the candidates for the 2008 American presidential election. He finds that there is a systematic link between how the candidates are covered in the media and the image portrayed in advertising and their standing in the polls. This is the first example of how this type of nuanced measurement of the leaders' images can be used to explain electoral outcomes.

Table 12.1. Mapping trait dimensions from the candidates literature onto the Big Five

Candidates Literature	Big Five	Candidate Traits
Competence	Intellect (Openness to Experience)	Intelligent, Knowledgeable.
Strength of Leadership	Extroversion	Outgoing, Shy, Timid
Integrity	Conscientiousness	Honest, Trustworthy
Empathy	Agreeableness	Kind, Sympathetic, Caring

The idea that media depictions of candidates matter for elections should not be surprising. Existing scholarship demonstrates that media content influences voters' perceptions more broadly. Iyengar et al. (2010) suggest that television news has an important impact on public opinion even outside of a campaign. Sides and Vavreck (2014), although pointing to the important role of non-campaign events (like economic performance one year prior to an election), suggest that media coverage of primary candidates affects candidate standing in the polls during the primary campaign. In relation to perceptions of candidates more specifically, Johnston et al. (2004) note the impact of media construction of Gore's (dis)honesty on public perceptions of his character, and by assessing the tone of media stories (positive or negative), argue that the media helped shape voters' impressions. Just et al. (1996) assess the impact of media *exposure* and suggest that voters' perceptions of leaders were crystallized as a result of media emphasis on leaders' personalities.

The question that remains, however, is why these patterns emerge: Why do voters focus on some traits over others? Is it because these are somehow more intrinsically important? Or because this is the information that they are presented with? It is possible that the media encourages voters to think in the way that election campaigns and political candidates are covered (Caprara, 2002), but actual evidence is needed to really establish this link. Peterson (2018) begins this process and demonstrates a clear link between the language employed in media messaging and voter perceptions of candidates, and we build on this work in the Canadian context. Given that the Big Five dimensions are said to travel, we believe that testing the link between image and perceptions outside of the United States is an important next step.

In particular, we take two approaches to test how the image of the leaders are tied to election results. The first is to take a macro approach similar to Peterson (2018). He ties his measures of the image of the candidate to an existing measure of the trial heat tracking polls from the 2008 election. We take a similar approach here, constructing a new measure of the standing of the candidates during the campaign. Second, we combine the aggregate image measures based on media coverage to individual level data about voters' perceptions. In doing so, we try to uncover the micro level mechanism undergirding the macro level relationship.

Data and Analysis

This chapter seeks to understand the sources of information influencing voters' perceptions of party leaders. In particular, we want to understand whether the language and content of media stories affects the types of impressions that voters have of party leaders. Peterson (2014) relied upon media data, party advertising data, and survey data in order to make these connections in the 2004 American presidential election. Unfortunately, this information is not as readily available in the Canadian context (there is no comparable "Campaign Mapping Project" or "WiscAds project" (Hart, 2009, Goldstein and Rivlin, 2007) in Canada).[2] Canada does have a rich tradition of election studies, however, and. beginning in the 1960s, has run a Canadian Election Study (similar to the NES in design) in every federal election. The 2015 election study builds on this rich tradition, including the tradition of a rolling cross-section design (first seen in the 1988 Canadian context, directed by Johnston and his colleagues), and thus provides us with daily information about voters' perceptions.

In this analysis, we marshal data from two main sources: first, we make use of the CES and its daily tracking of perceptions of leaders. Second, we performed a content analysis of articles printed daily in the country's two national newspapers, the *Globe and Mail* and *National Post*, over the course of the election campaign.

The content analysis replicates the method we used in our earlier (2015) paper. A research assistant reviewed all articles written in the two newspapers throughout the campaign, separating out all articles that refer to one of the party leaders. Most articles included content about more than one candidate; therefore, we created three data files per article: one containing all the language in the article about Thomas Mulcair, one for Stephen Harper, and one for Justin Trudeau. Once this was complete, we applied coding rules to this processed text, based on the psycho-lexical work of Ashton et al. (2004). These scholars identified 1,710 adjectives that fit into the Big Five dimensions of personality, and we programmed Python's dictionary with these adjectives, and then had the program open an article and scan it for those adjectives, counting each appearance in each article. We then converted these counts into something similar to factor scores for each candidate by applying the factor loadings estimated by Ashton et al. (2004).[3]

By counting the use of adjectives and multiplying those counts by the factor loadings from Ashton et al. (2004), we were able to construct measures of the Big Five dimensions for each article, organized by date, leader, and newspaper. Because articles vary in length, scores are then divided by the number of words about the candidate in each article and multiplied by 1000 to provide scores that are comparable as well as interpretable, allowing us to explore dynamics across candidates and over time. The measures we use in the models that follow are the average ratings of the candidates from all the coverage up until that point.

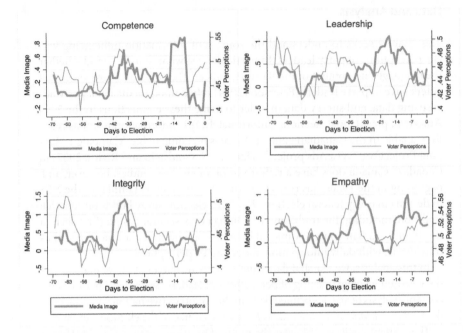

Figure 12.1. Media images and perceptions of Mulcair
Note: smoothed by loess (5-day moving avg).

Figures 12.1 through 12.3 present the constructed measures, against the backdrop of perceptions of leaders in Canada, as measured in the CES.[4] The first obvious aspect of the figures is that the variance of the *image* series declines over time. This is a function of how those variables were constructed. These measures are a five-day moving average of the image in the coverage. The moving average smoothes out the day-to-day variation and summarizes the underlying patterns in coverage and perceptions.

A few observations should be made. First, a broad observation that the patterns in image and perceptions are different across leaders. This suggests that the various measures are all measuring different things, which is what we want to see. Second, note the changes in the Y axes across graphs: for some leaders/traits, image and perceptions are more compressed, and for others, the distance between the trend lines is wider. The graphs do not all have the same aspect ratio, so interpreting them side by side can be difficult.

When we turn to the three sets of graphs, a few notable features emerge. For Mulcair, as depicted in figure 12.1, his leadership and competence receive slightly less positifve discussion and attention in national media than do his integrity

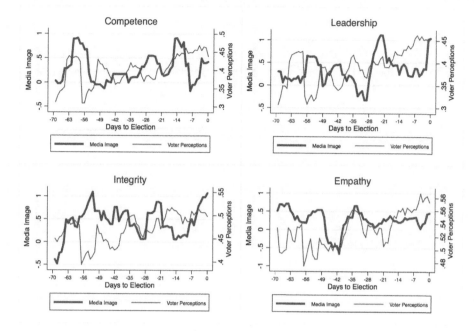

Figure 12.2. Media images and perceptions of Trudeau
Note: smoothed by loess (5-day moving avg).

and empathy (especially at the start of the campaign). Recall that the daily image scores reflect positive-negative mentions, and thus reflect a general tone in coverage. Towards the middle of the campaign, Mulcair received increasingly positive coverage of his traits, but then coverage of his integrity became more negative over time. Voters' perceptions of Mulcair loosely follow projections of his image in the media, but there are a number of instances – weeks, even – where perceptions of his leadership are much stronger than media portrayals might lead us to expect.

As depicted in figure 12.2, portrayals of Trudeau in the English-language national papers start out quite unfavourably at the beginning of the campaign (even starting with a negative tone in coverage of his "integrity"), and then fluctuates up and down over the course of the campaign, usually ending up more favourable at the end of the campaign than at the beginning. Voters' perceptions of Trudeau on these four traits fluctuates as well, but creeps upward over the course of the campaign.

For Harper, as depicted in figure 12.3, coverage of his traits faces many ups and downs, and in some cases ends up more positive at the end (integrity and empathy) and in other cases ends up more negative at the end (competence and leadership).

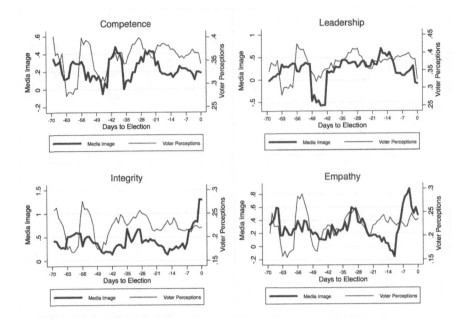

Figure 12.3. Media images and perceptions of Harper
Note: Smoothed by loess (5-day moving avg).

Voters' perceptions also move up and down, reflecting (for some weeks) coverage trends, and at other times not following media image at all. Perceptions of Harper's empathy go up over time (albeit only slightly) while perceptions of his other traits all become slightly more negative by the end of the campaign.

Taken together, figures 12.1 through 12.3 leave us with a mixed picture of the relationship between image and perceptions. Certainly, the impact of image on perception is not as obvious or as strong as seen in Peterson (2018).

The media measures are the key independent variables in the analyses. Our approach to understanding how they shape voter decision-making is to go through a series of models to best illustrate the effect of the media's image of the candidates. We do this at both the level of individual voters and the dynamics of the Canadian electorate.

Modelling Strategy

For each of the candidates, we go through three different models. The first treats each of the four main individual personality traits as a dependent variable and the specific media image connected to those traits as the independent variable (i.e., what is the effect of media coverage of the three leaders' intellect on perceptions of each leader's competence?). Note for this we include all three leaders' images on a given trait dimension as independent variables because of the likelihood that voters are considering all three leaders (or consuming media about all three leaders) simultaneously, and perhaps even comparing them.[5] The second approach uses the overall candidate evaluation from the feeling thermometer as the dependent variable and all five of the dimensions of the media image as the independent variables.[6] The correlations between these image dimensions are quite high in the media data. We did this twice: first, including only the media images for the leader in question (looking at the impact of Mulcair's media coverage on overall evaluations of him, for example); and second, we included the media images for ALL leaders as independent variables (looking at the impact of media coverage of all trait dimensions for all leaders on perceptions of Mulcair), again to address the possibility that voters think about leaders in comparison with one another rather than in isolation, and how they feel about one leader (e.g., Mulcair) is influenced by media portrayals of not only Mulcair, but also the other leaders. The final model pools the five images into a single measure of how positive the image of each candidate for each day is and uses this as an independent variable predicting the feeling thermometer. Again, we use these composite image measures collectively as independent variables, to determine the extent to which images of one candidate affect perceptions of both that candidate and the other candidates.

Our main independent variable is an aggregate measure that varies over time. There are several individual level controls that need to be included in the models predicting individual traits and candidate evaluations. We include sex, education, employment status, age, partisanship, and national economic perceptions. We also control for region, separating out all of the provinces (again, excluding Quebec) and including them separately in the model as dummy variables.[7]

The data has a multilevel structure to it. Individual voters are clustered within days and the main independent variables vary at this higher level. Usually, this particular data structure requires some type of hierarchical or multilevel model (Gelman and Hill, 2007). These models include a random error term at the upper level of aggregation. We have estimated all of the models in the chapter as multilevel, including a random effect for the day of interview. In every case, the diagnostics indicate that including this upper-level error term does not improve the fit of the model, and the variance estimate for these terms is always indistinguishable from zero. As a result, we estimate the models as regressions with robust standard errors, clustered by day.

Macro Level Models

The models focusing on the electorate-level patterns between candidate support and media coverage deal with the potential reciprocal nature of the two phenomena. Our approach will be to estimate the relationships as Vector Autoregressions (VAR) and test for the Granger causality of the various series. Our measure of the poll numbers is the percentage of the respondents who indicated that they intend to support Harper, Trudeau, or Mulcair in the election, aggregated up to the day. Our media measures are the same as those used in the individual level analyses.

Results

We begin with the macro time series models. The main goal of this test is to compare the relative effects of the media image on voters' preferences to the effect of voters' preferences on the media image of the candidates. Essentially, we are asking whether the media lead or lag the general success and failure of the campaign of each leader. Table 12.2 presents a summary of the Granger causality tests for each candidate. Because we are more interested in the interplay of the media and voters than the interconnections between the various media measures, we are only presenting the results that summarize the key relationships.

For all three candidates, several of the media measures predict poll numbers. For Mulcair, the media image of this leadership and emotional stability Granger cause his vote share. For Harper, the dimensions that Granger cause poll numbers are the image of his empathy, leadership, and integrity. Finally, the media image of Trudeau's integrity and emotional stability Granger cause his poll numbers. In short, there is ample evidence that the media images drive the poll numbers.

As we note, however, there is also reason to expect that the media coverage itself will respond to changes in the polls. For two of the candidates (Mulcair and Harper) there is no evidence of this effect. For Trudeau, however, it appears that the image of his competence responds to changes in his poll numbers. Given the pattern of the results, the higher his numbers went, the more positive the coverage of his competence.

These results are suggestive of the interplay between the media and the perceptions of the voters. The media's image of the candidates seems to influence the perceptions of the voters. At the same time, the members of the media are responding to the general status of the race. We are not implying that they are responding to precisely these measures of the state of the race, but our measure of the electorate's preferences should be thought of as a proxy for the state of the race. If reporters have a general shared sense of how each leader is faring, this could easily translate in to shifts in coverage. For Trudeau, it seems, reporters were likely to describe him more positively as he fared in the campaign. This essentially suggests that the media would sense a shift in public preferences and portray Trudeau more positively as a result.

Individual Level Models

We begin the results with models predicting the individual trait ratings for each candidate. The results in tables 12.3, 12.4, and 12.5 present the results

Table 12.2. Granger causality results (chi-square statistics from Wald test)

Variable	Mulcair	Harper	Trudeau
Media predicting poll numbers			
Empathy	.47	4.70*	.86
Leadership	8.81*	5.90*	2.18
Integrity	.85	8.02**	5.25*
Emotional Stability	6.51*	.19	4.66*
Competence	.07	1.60	.26
Poll numbers predicting media			
Empathy	.24	1.65	.47
Leadership	2.59	2.76	.98
Integrity	1.22	.83	.04
Emotional Stability	.23	1.82	2.92
Competence	.39	1.39	10.91***

Notes: $N = 68$.
$* = p < .05$, $** = p < .01$, $*** = p < .001$

predicting the trait ratings for Mulcair, Trudeau, and Harper, respectively. Each table presents the results of eight separate OLS models, in which trait perceptions of each of competence/leadership/integrity/empathy are regressed on media images of the three leaders on the affiliated Big Five trait dimensions. These analyses include control variables as described above.

The results of all models are surprising, based on Peterson's (2018) findings, but perhaps not surprising if we consider the patterns seen in figures 12.1 through 12.3 – and not surprising at all if we look back to the results we got in our 2015 paper, which explored similar dynamics for the 1988 Canadian election. Perceptions of Mulcair on the four trait dimensions, for example, reflect the corresponding media image of the leader's trait only sometimes and not always in the direction expected, and often are not statistically significant. Also confusing was the impact of media images of the other leaders: with increasingly positive coverage of Harper's integrity, for example, perceptions of *Mulcair's* integrity became more positive (similarly, with more positive images of Trudeau's empathy, Mulcair's empathy score went up among the electorate).

For Trudeau, results are similarly scattered. Media portrayal of Trudeau's image has no impact on perceptions, but positive portrayals of Mulcair and Harper's leadership leads to less positive perceptions of Trudeau. The impact of image on perceptions of Harper is also inconsistent and mixed. It is only images of leadership that had any effect on perceptions of Harper on that trait: positive media portrayal of Harper led to negative perceptions of him on that trait, while positive images of Trudeau led to positive impressions of Harper on that same trait. The results are not as we expected.

The influence of the media on these traits is only one step in assessing the relationship between media images and voters' perceptions. In table 12.6 we

Table 12.3. Trait perceptions of Mulcair

Variable	Competence	Leadership	Integrity	Empathy
Media image of Mulcair	.008*(.004)	.004 (.004)	−.005 (.005)	.008 (.006)
Media image of Harper	−.003 (.012)	.003 (.003)	−.000 (.005)	−.017***(.009)
Media image of Trudeau	−.006 (.005)	−.002 (.004)	.005 (.004)	.017**(.007)
Intercept	.483***(.015)	.485***(.016)	.460***(.015)	.477***(.017)

Notes: N = 4.260.
* = p < .05, ** = p < .01, *** = p < .001

Table 12.4. Trait perceptions of Trudeau

Variable	Competence	Leadership	Integrity	Empathy
Media image of Mulcair	.007 (.007)	−.002 (.016)	.003 (.006)	−.002 (.006)
Media image of Harper	.017 (.017)	.003 (.005)	−.003 (.006)	−.013 (.011)
Media image of Trudeau	.008 (.007)	.005 (.005)	.002 (.004)	.003 (.007)
Intercept	.467***(.018)	.485***(.016)	.460***(.016)	.517***(.018)

Notes: N = 4.262.
* = p < .05, ** = p < .01, *** = p < .001

document how these same trait measures influence the feeling thermometer ratings of the candidates, and similarly to the relationship between images and trait perceptions, results remain inconsistent.

Again, very few of the media images are statistically significant. There is very little evidence that evaluations of Mulcair are being driven by media images of his personality. Images of Trudeau's leadership and emotional stability have an influence on overall evaluations of him. Positive images of his leadership lead to positive feelings towards him, while positive images of his emotional stability lead to more negative feelings towards him.[8] Media portrayals of Harper's image have no impact on voters' feelings towards him. Again, these results are confusing, and do not point to a clear relationship between media image of personality traits and perceptions of leaders.

One potential problem with the results of all the multivariate models is that the media series tend to trend together over time. While it is clear from Figures 12.1 through 12.3 that they are independent series, the collinearity might be masking some of the patterns. To test for this, we average together the five media measures into a single composite measure of the personalities of the candidates. This approach loses some of the important nuance in the candidate images, but it might uncover some patterns in the results that the more specific image measures mask.

The results in table 12.7 show that this is an unfounded concern. Once combined into a single measure, media images of the leaders have no impact on general feelings towards leaders.[9] We are stumped.[10]

Table 12.5. Trait perceptions of Harper

Variable	Competence	Leadership	Integrity	Empathy
Media image of Mulcair	.000 (.005)	.002 (.004)	.003 (.005)	−.002 (.007)
Media image of Harper	.011 (.014)	−.008***(.003)	−.012 (.009)	−.007 (.010)
Media image of Trudeau	−.003 (.006)	.012**(.005)	.007 (.004)	−.003 (.008)
Intercept	.266***(.019)	.266***(.021)	.153***(.018)	.205***(.017)

Note: N = 4.259.
$^* = p < .05$, $^{**} = p < .01$, $^{***} = p < .001$

Table 12.6. Feeling thermometers for candidates, all media measures for a single leader

Variable	Mulcair	Trudeau	Harper
Media image of Empathy	.007 (.006)	−.004 (.006)	.004 (.010)
Media image of Leadership	.008 (.005)	.008**(.004)	−.002 (.003)
Media image of Integrity	.001 (.005)	−.002 (.005)	−.009 (.007)
Media image of Emotional Stability	.003 (.006)	−.02*(.011)	−.01 (.015)
Media image of Competence	−.004 (.004)	−.001 (.004)	−.012 (.011)
Intercept	.532***(.012)	.531***(.015)	.267***(.017)

Note: N = 3.389.
$^* = p < .05$, $^{**} = p < .01$, $^{***} = p < .001$

Table 12.7. Feeling thermometers for candidates, composite media measure for all leaders

Variable	Mulcair	Trudeau	Harper
Composite Media image of Mulcair	.014 (.009)	.01 (.01)	−.006(.011)
Composite Media image of Harper	.015 (.011)	.012 (.011)	−.017 (.014)
Composite Media image of Trudeau	−.012 (.010)	.006 (.011)	−.013 (.001)
Intercept	.534***(.017)	.527***(.016)	.27***(.017)

Note: N = 3.389.
$^* = p < .05$, $^{**} = p < .01$, $^{***} = p < .001$

Conclusions

In looking at these results, one might conclude that there is no "real" relationship between media coverage of leaders' personalities and voters' perceptions of either personality traits or overall evaluations of the leaders. Two things seem clear from these results: first, media image of leaders influences voters' perceptions, sometimes, and for some leaders. Second, voters include information about other leaders in their assessments of a given individual. That is, voters compare and contrast leaders and don't evaluate individuals in a vacuum. A clear, predictable, "logical" pattern, however, has not emerged here.

More research is necessary. Our approach is limited to English language media and, as a result, excluded Quebec from our analyses. Including additional local media sources may help us to better understand voter perceptions in that province. In the rest of Canada, the *Globe and Mail* and the *National Post* are widely read, but it is possible that other regional/local newspapers were providing voters with additional information that may have influenced their perceptions. Integrating additional media sources is, therefore, likely to help us better understand the relationship between media image and voters' perceptions of leaders.

An additional potential avenue would be to look for heterogeneity in how individual Canadians respond to the changes in media coverage. Our approach looks for a common effect across all voters. It is plausible that some Canadians are more sensitive to the narrative about leaders. Voters who get more information or have weaker connections to the parties may base their decisions more on how the media portrays the candidates. Another option is that voters look for candidates who are like them. Rather than preferring a candidate who is an exemplar of these personality traits, some voters may want someone who is more typical or more like them (Sullivan et al., 1990).

Finally, our analysis relies solely on newspaper articles. It is quite possible that voters base a lot of their understanding of party leaders on what they *see* rather than what they read. Indeed, visual cues are likely to be quite important, because they most closely mirror the way that we normally evaluate individuals who we encounter daily in our regular lives. We may not be able to fully understand how voters integrate media coverage of personality into their understanding of personality without including TV news coverage of party leaders into our analysis. This information is not readily accessible in the Canadian context, however, which makes obtaining these media images a difficult process.

NOTES

1 This design had been used by the ANES for the 1984 Campaign Monitoring survey, but the small samples in the 1984 survey made the over time design relatively under-powered.
2 We think these would be an excellent resource, however, and would love to see them established in the Canadian context.
3 Peterson obtained these loadings from Goldberg when performing this analysis for the 2004 election in his 2014 paper, and we re-apply them here.
4 Our analyses exclude Quebec. The measures we develop are based on English language newspapers and likely do not capture the ways in which the candidates are covered in French language media.
5 This follows from Bittner (2007, 2011), who suggests that voters think about leaders en masse, rather than in isolation.

6   There are five in these analyses (rather than four) because we have a measure of the image of the candidate's emotional stability. There is, however, no comparable measure of the individual survey respondent's impression of the candidate on these dimensions. This omission is standard in surveys about candidates (Peterson, 2014).

7   For ease of presentation and interpretation of the relationships of interest, none of these control variables appear in the tables presented but were included in all models.

8   The emotional stability results are odd, but it does tend to be a significant predictor in similar models of candidate evaluations (Peterson, 2014).

9   The same is true when we regress traits on the composite measures, and when we collapse the variables into two "dimensions" ("character" and "competence") for both image and perceptions. When we regress perceptions of each leaders' character (composed of integrity and empathy) and competence (composed of leadership and competence) there is no statistically significant effect.

10 We also considered the possibility that these models conceal individual-level heterogeneity and ran models in which we interacted media measures with both knowledge and interest in the campaign. While the impact of media measures on perceptions did move in predictable ways with both knowledge and interest, very few of the coefficients achieved traditional levels of statistical significance.

References

Abelson, R.P., D.R. Kinder, M.D. Peters, and S. Fiske. 1982. "Affective and Semantic Components in Political Person Perception." *Journal of Personality and Social Psychology* 42: 619–30. https://doi.org/10.1037/0022-3514.42.4.619

Ashton, M.C., K. Lee, and L.R. Goldberg. 2004. "A Hierarchical Analysis of 1,710 English Personality-Descriptive Adjectives." *Journal of Personality and Social Psychology* 87 (5): 707. https://doi.org/10.1037/0022-3514.87.5.707. Medline: 15535781

Bartels, L. 2002. Beyond the Running Tally: Partisan Bias in Politcal Perceptions." *Political Behavior* 24: 117–50. https://doi.org/10.1023/A:1021226224601

Bean, C., and A. Mughan. 1989. "Leadership Effects in Parliamentary Elections in Australia and Britain." *American Political Science Review* 83: 1165–79. https://doi.org/10.2307/1961663

Bittner, A. 2011. *Platform or Personality?: The Role of Party Leaders in Elections.* Oxford University Press.

Bittner, A., and D.A. Peterson. 2019. "Personality, Party Leaders, and Election Campaigns." *Electoral Studies* 54: 237–9. https://doi.org/10.1016/j.electstud.2018.04.005

Campbell, A., P.E. Converse, W.E. Miller, and D.E. Stokes. 1960. *The American Voter.* John Wiley & Sons.

Caprara, G.V., C. Barbaranelli, and P.G. Zimbardo. 1999. "Personality Profiles and Political Parties." *Political Psychology* 20 (1): 175–97. https://doi.org/10.1111/0162-895X.00141

– 2002. "When Parsimony Subdues Distinctiveness: Simplified Public Perceptions of Politicians' Personality." *Political Psychology* 23 (1): 77–95. https://doi.org/10.1111/0162-895X.00271

Caprara, G.V., S. Schwartz, C. Capanna, M. Vecchione, and C. Barbaranelli. 2006. "Personality and Politics: Values, Traits, and Political Choice." *Political Psychology* 27 (1): 1–28. https://doi.org/10.1111/j.1467-9221.2006.00447.x

Caprara, G.V., M. Vecchione, C. Barbaranelli, and R.C. Fraley. 2007. *Political Psychology* 28 (5): 609–32.

Converse, P.E. 196N. "The Nature of Belief Systems in Mass Publics." In *Ideology and discontent*, edited by D.E. Apter. Free Press.

Funk, C.L. 1996. "The Impact of Scandal of Candidate Evaluations: An Experimental Test of the Role of Candidate Traits." *Political Behavior* 18: 1–24. https://doi.org/10.1007/BF01498658

Gelman, A., and J. Hill. 2007. *Data Analysis Using Regression and Hierarchical/Multilevel Models*. Cambridge University Press.

Goldberg, L.R. 1982. "From Ace to Zombie: Some Explorations in the Language of Personality." *Advances in Personality Assessment* 1: 203–34.

Goldstein, K., and J. Rivlin. 2007. "Presidential Advertising, 2003–2004." *The University of Wisconsin Advertising Project*, the Department of Political Science at the University of Wisconsin, Madison.

Hart, R.P. 2009. *Campaign Talk: Why Elections Are Good for Us*. Princeton University Press.

Hillygus, D.S. 2005. "Campaign Effects and the Dynamics of Turnout Intention in Election 2000." *The Journal of Politics* 67 (1): 50–68.

Humphreys, G.W., C.J. Price, and M.J. Riddoch. 1999. "From Objects to Names: A Cognitive Neuroscience Approach," *Psychological Research Psychologische Forschung* 62: 118–30. https://doi.org/10.1007/s004260050046. Medline: 10472198

Iyengar, S., J. Curran, Q.B. Lund, I. Salovaara-Moring, K.S. Hahn, and S. Coen. 2010. "Cross-National versus Individual-Level Differences in Political Information: A Media Systems Perspective." *Journal of Elections, Public Opinion and Parties* 20 (3): 291–309.

Johnston, R., A. Blais, H.E. Brady, and J. Crête. 1992. *Letting the People Decide: Dynamics of a Canadian Election*. Stanford University Press.

Johnston, R., M.G. Hagen, and K.H. Jamieson. 2004. *The 2000 Presidential Election and the Foundation of Party Politics*. Cambridge University Press.

Just, M., A. Crigler, D.E. Alger, T.E. Cook, M. Kern, and D.M. West. 1996. *Citizens, Candidates, and the Media in a Presidential Election*. University of Chicago Press.

Kinder, D.R., M.D. Peters, R.P. Abelson, and S.T. Fiske. 1980. "Presidential Prototypes." *Political Behavior* 2: 315–37. https://doi.org/10.1007/BF00990172

Lodge, M., and R. Hamill. 1986. "A Partisan Schema for Political Information Processing." *American Political Science Review* 80: 505–20. https://doi.org/10.2307/1958271

Lodge, M., K.M. McGraw, and P. Stroh. 1989. "An Impression-Driven Model of Candidate Evaluation." *American Political Science Review* 83 (2): 399–419. https://doi.org/10.2307/1962397

McCann, J.A. 1990. "Changing Electoral Contexts and Changing Candidate Images during the 1984 Presidential Campaign." *American Politics Quarterly* 18 (2): 123–40.

McGraw, K.M., M. Fischle, K. Stenner, and M. Lodge, M. 1996. "What's in a Word?" *Political Behavior*, 18: 263–87. https://doi.org/10.1007/BF01498602

Mondak, J.J. 2010. *Personality and the Foundations of Political Behavior.* Cambridge University Press.

Nimmo, D.D., and R.L. Savage. 1976. *Candidates and Their Images: Concepts, Methods, and Findings.* Goodyear: Pacific Palisades.

Peterson, D.A. 2005. "Heterogeneity and Certainty in Candidate Evaluations." *Political Behavior*, 1–24.

Peterson, D.A. 2014. "The Social Construction of Candidate Image." *Atlantic Provinces Political Science Association.*

– "The Dynamic Construction of Candidate Image." *Electoral Studies* 54: 289–96. https://doi.org/10.1016/j.electstud.2018.04.012

Peterson, D.A., and A. Bittner. 2015. "Candidate Image and Voter Perception: Unpacking the Impact of Personality." *Biennial Meeting of the Association for Canadian Studies in the United States*, Las Vegas, Nevada, October 14–17, 2015.

Rahn, W.M. 1993. "The Role of Partisan Stereotypes in Information Processing about Political Candidates." *American Journal of Political Science*, 472–96. https://doi.org/10.2307/2111381

Rosenberg, S.W., L. Bohan, P. McCafferty, and K. Harris. 1986. "The Image and the Vote: The Effect of Candidate Presentation on Voter Preference." *American Journal of Political Science*, 108–24. https://doi.org/10.2307/2111296

Sides, J., and L. Vavreck. 2014. *The Gamble: Choice and Chance in the 2012 Presidential Election.* Princeton University Press.

Stokes, D.E. 1966. "Some Dynamic Elements of Contests for the Presidency." *American Political Science Review* 60: 19–28. https://doi.org/10.2307/1953803

Sullivan, J.L., J.H. Aldrich, E. Borgida, and W. Rahn. 1990. "Candidate Appraisal and Human Nature: Man and Superman in the 1984 Election." *Political Psychology*, 459–84. https://doi.org/10.2307/3791660.

Vigliocco, G., and D.P. Vinson. 2007. "Semantic Representation." *The Oxford Handbook of Psycholinguistics*, 195–215. https://doi.org/10.1093/oxfordhb/9780198568971.013.0012.

13 Cognitive Preconditions for Direct Poll Effects on Voters: Evidence on Attention, Retention, and Judgments of Applicability

FRED CUTLER, J. SCOTT MATTHEWS, AND MARK PICKUP

Introduction

Modern election campaigns are virtually inconceivable without polls (Patterson, 2005). Yet many observers worry that polls distort voters' choices through the infamous bandwagon effect, by supplying the wrong information relevant to strategic voting (Johnston et al., 1992), and many other direct and indirect mechanisms (see, for example, Simon, 1957; Bartels, 1988; Blais, Gidengil, and Nevitte, 2006; Kenney and Rice, 1994; Morwitz and Pluzinski, 1996; Mutz, 1998). Scholars have therefore been concerned with the relative balance of "horse race" versus other coverage of elections, including Richard Johnston in "What's the primary message: Horse race or issue journalism?" (Brady and Johnston, 1987). One of the prominent forms of strategic voting has also been central to Johnston's career-long interest in party system change, as he has assessed the possibility that in non-proportional systems the "viability" of parties can narrow the choices voters see as plausible (e.g., Johnston et al., 1992).

Poll effects are tantalizing for scholars, but they do not appear to be strong enough to generate any sort of consensus about their *direct* effect on voters during campaigns or in other political contexts (Sonck and Loosveldt, 2010). One explanation is that voters enjoy the entertainment and forecasting functions of polls but keep that information separate from their voting calculus. Another possibility is that poll reports are noticed, accurately retained, and found credible and relevant by too few voters for survey researchers to observe the direct influence of polls. Most of the existing literature, however, asks how polls might affect voters' choices *given that voters take in poll information*. This is especially so in experimental work examining poll effects, which by design holds informational conditions constant (e.g., Ansolabehere and Iyengar, 1994; Mutz, 1998). But it is also true of survey-based "campaign effects" research, including prominent work by Richard Johnston and his colleagues (Johnston et al., 1992; Johnston, Hagen, and Jamieson 2004). As we argue below, thinking through the various mechanisms of poll effects highlights the importance of voters' levels of *attention* to and *retention* of poll information, along with voters' judgments regarding the *applicability* of polls to electoral choice. It cannot be assumed that most, or even many, voters hear about and remember poll information, nor that they think it is relevant for their voting decisions.

Based on analysis of survey data collected during general elections in Canada and the United Kingdom, we supply answers to these questions: Are voters attentive to polls? Do they accept and retain poll information? Do they find poll information applicable to the voting decision? In this way, this paper shifts the focus backward in the chain of causation. Leaving *poll effects* proper to one side, that is, we consider the *preconditions for poll effects*. In *describing* voters' engagement with polls, we shed light on unresolved questions about polls' possible causal effects (cf., Gerring, 2012).

As we explain below, attention to and retention of poll information are important precursors of all the major mechanisms of direct poll influence examined in previous research, whereas voters' judgments of applicability are primarily relevant to those mechanisms that posit that voters "rationally" and consciously incorporate poll information. Further, the nature of the poll information required by the various poll effects mechanisms varies in important ways, with some processes imposing a heavier informational burden. We leverage this variation in cognitive demands to advance tentative conclusions about the prevalence of the several mechanisms of poll effects that have been theorized in the literature and observed in laboratory settings.

Though absent from our analysis, it should be emphasized that polls may affect the behaviour of the media or other political actors and thereby exert an *indirect* effect on voters (e.g., Matthews, Pickup, and Cutler, 2012). Equally, persuasive communications may exert direct effects on voters through less active or conscious processes, such as "mere exposure" (Zajonc, 1968). However, most of the literature on poll effects, including all the research canvassed below, assumes relatively active and conscious processing of poll information (see also Hardmeier, 2008). Further, as we note in our conclusion, understanding whether and how polls might *directly* influence voters is relevant to the normative evaluation of poll effects.

Theory

The psychology of persuasion. What we term "direct poll effects" consist of persuasion as a function of the reception of information about the standings of parties or candidates, where persuasion is defined as a change in an attitude or choice, even a small change in attitude strength or a slight weakening or reinforcement of a preference. A vast literature on persuasion in social and political psychology (e.g., McGuire 1969; Zaller, 1992; Petty and Wegener, 1998) suggests that three preconditions must be met. First, persuasion requires attention in order to receive, comprehend and, ultimately, to accept and be influenced by information. Second, persuasion requires retention of the information contained in persuasive communications – at least long enough for the information to be involved in attitude formation or change. Retention assumes reception of messages and, generally, comprehension and acceptance of (or "yielding to") those messages. Finally, persuasion often – but not always – requires that the information contained in a message is seen as applicable to attitudes, that is, the information is seen as having implications for relevant evaluations (cf., Chong and Druckman, 2007).

As we argue in the next section, attention and retention are generic preconditions for poll results to directly affect voter cognition: voters must attend to reports of poll results and they must retain (for at least a short period; see below) some cognitive representation of the information received from those reports. We also suggest that certain mechanisms of poll influence additionally require that voters find poll information relevant, or applicable, to political attitude formation or decision-making. Our key claim is that polls cannot *directly* influence the voter unless the relevant cognitive prerequisites are satisfied (even if they shape attitudes or behaviour through an indirect or less conscious process).

Note that these conditions are relevant even if voters process political information "online" (Lodge and Hamill, 1986), actively incorporating new information into their political evaluations as that information is encountered, but not (necessarily) retaining the information in long-term memory. Such "online-processors" must still attend to poll information, find it applicable to political judgments and, crucially, retain that information for at least a short period in order for it to influence their attitudes or behaviour. Our analysis of retention is sensitive to the fact that memory for poll information may fade relatively quickly.

Mechanisms of poll effects. We now canvass the most prominent direct poll effects and their theorized mechanisms. This will permit us to offer, in the penultimate section of the paper, tentative conclusions regarding the likely prevalence of each kind of poll effect, given our findings. We cannot, however, offer a firm pronouncement on the existence of poll effects; that is, the present paper contributes only indirectly to the poll effects literature that assesses the prevalence and power of these mechanisms themselves. In that literature, including the contributions of Richard Johnston, the tendency has been to "black box" the effects and offer multiple possible mechanisms for observed correlations between changes in poll standing and voters' choices. We consider our theoretical and empirical dissection of the possible mechanisms as a form of elaboration of some of Richard Johnston's contributions.

The first mechanism of poll influence is brute emotional contagion – the *bandwagon effect* (Simon, 1957; Marsh, 1985; Bartels, 1988). A voter may simply enjoy being on the winning, or gaining, side. The bandwagon requires voters to be informed of the identity of either the leading choice (party, candidate) or of that choice seen to be gaining support. While acquiring the former information should be relatively easy, acquiring the latter could take various forms entailing varying levels of informational complexity. A voter who "jumps on the band-wagon," of course, need not consciously believe that polls are a sensible basis for political judgment; such voters may, in other words, be influenced by polls even if they would not state that poll results are applicable to vote choice. The conditions of attention and retention, thus, are precursors to the bandwagon effect, while the condition of applicability is not.

The second way polls may impinge on voter choice is by informing strategies of *cue taking* (Ansolabehere and Iyengar, 1994). The basic idea is that voters can compensate for a lack of "encyclopedic" knowledge of parties and candidates by relying on their peers' collective judgment (Lupia, 1994; Cukierman, 1991; Sinclair and Plott, 2012). Large or increasing support for the leading choice is interpreted as a positive evaluation of the party's or candidate's qualities by the general public. Such cue-taking makes informational demands much like those of the bandwagon effect (Ansolabehere and Iyengar, 1994). What distinguishes cue taking from the bandwagon effect, and arguably positions it as a "rational" response to poll information, is a more or less conscious belief that the "wis-dom of the crowd" can compensate for a deficit of political knowledge. Cue takers, thus, not only attend to and retain poll information – they regard poll information as applicable to political judgment.

A third, less familiar mechanism for poll effects, brought into the literature by Mutz (1998), is *cognitive responding*. Here, voters are not directly moved to a leading or rising candidate, but instead take note of such facts and then seek to explain them. This is "self-persuasion," responding to thoughts that are brought to conscious processing in reaction to hearing the poll information. Depending on the strength of pre-existing attitudes, the direction of these thoughts will either reinforce (among those with strong, directionally complimentary atti-tudes) or offset (among those with weak, directionally opposite attitudes) the voter's *ex ante* vote intentions. An important case of cognitive-response-based poll effects, and the one on which we focus below, involves voters attempting to explain a surprising poll result (cf., Maheswaran and Chaiken, 1991). When a lead changes hands late in the campaign, swing voters who follow polls and engage in cognitive responding may well gravitate towards the new leader without taking a direct cue from their fellow citizens nor mindlessly jumping on a bandwagon (Mutz, 1998). The informational demands of such cognitive responding are relatively heavy: a current poll result and, for comparison, a sense of the relevant standing prior to the current result. We would not neces-sarily expect cognitive responders to consciously judge poll results as applica-ble to political judgments; rather, the poll results simply motivate reflection on reasons to support (or oppose) a given candidate (or candidates), and it is these reasons – not the poll results themselves – that exert an effect on voters' choices.

A final way poll reporting may affect voter choice is by facilitating the calculus of *strategic voting*, that is, the practice of "voting for a second-preferred party (candidate) rather than for the most preferred one, motivated by the perception that the former has a better chance of winning the election" (Blais and Nadeau, 1996, 40; Johnston et al., 1992).[1] Richard Johnston has emphasized the importance of this logic in Canadian politics. Voters' judgments of party viability may affect outcomes in one election and the party system over a longer term. Johnston has pointed out these viability dynamics in many contexts, be it US primaries, the 1988 Canadian election that re-volved around the Free Trade issue, bloc voting by the Quebec electorate to maximize collective representation, anti-labour voters in British Columbia needing to converge on one party to defeat the social democratic parties, and so on (Johnston, 2017).

The information required concerns the relative standings of the candidates and parties. In particular, any kind of strategic voting calculus requires three "bits" of poll information: the expected vote share or rank of one's most favoured candidate, the share or rank of one's least (or lesser) favoured candidate, and the share or rank of some third candidate that is preferable to the latter but dominated by the former (Blais and Nadeau, 1996, 39–40). Further, the voter engaged in strategic voting, inasmuch as that voter is engaged in a conscious evaluation – conditioned by poll results – of the expected utility of voting alternatives, necessarily finds poll information relevant to the vote decision. The strategic voter must attend to the information obtained from polls, retain it, and find it applicable to political judgment. One obvious complication in parliamentary systems, though, is that the locus of the information ought to be at the local level, while poll information is almost always at a higher level of aggregation (Johnston et al., 1992; Johnston and Cutler, 2009); In this chapter we simply assume that some voters may find national poll information relevant to their strategic choice in the local district.

The implication of this discussion is that as attention, retention, and judgments of applicability pertaining to polls vary, so does the probability that the necessary preconditions for different mechanisms of poll influence are met. The preconditions for a bandwagon effect are met with minimal poll information. Cue-taking from polls is no more informationally demanding than the bandwagon effect but requires a belief that poll results are relevant to political evaluations (specifically, as valuable cues that can compensate for knowledge deficits). Cognitive responding to expectation-divergent polls carries a heavier informational burden than either of the foregoing possibilities; like the bandwagon, however, cognitive responders need not consciously judge poll information as applicable to political choice. Strategic voting entails both a high informational demand and a belief that such information is a sound basis for political, and specifically electoral, choice.

Previous Research

Attention. Our expectations concerning levels of attentiveness to polls are mixed. On one hand, political knowledge and interest are notoriously found wanting in the mass public (Delli Carpini, and Keeter, 1997; Fournier, 2002). On the other hand, insofar as the "horse race" is central to political news (Patterson, 2005), polls are likely to be more widely disseminated than other kinds of political information. Furthermore, poll results, especially surprising ones, may be intrinsically interesting, even to otherwise "tuned-out" voters (Iyengar, Norpoth, and Hahn, 2004).

The handful of attempts to measure voter attention to polls suggest that poll attention differs little from political interest and attention generally (see Blais and Bodet, 2006). Few voters are poll "junkies," and few pay no attention at all to the polls. A representative study is by McAllister and Studlar (1991), who report British exit poll data showing that about 70 per cent of voters said they had "seen or heard the results of an opinion poll in the last few days." Likewise, the 1980 American National Election Study found that 77 per cent of respondents said they had heard the result of a presidential poll over the last month (West, 1991). Similar results have been obtained for more recent elections in the United States and Israel (Giammo, 2004; Tsfati, 2001). Even if we revise these numbers downward for sample selection and social desirability biases, it seems clear that more than half of voters *say* they notice the polls in at least a minimal fashion.

Retention. Having attended to poll information, will it be retained? And if so, is the retained information accurate? If one were to generalize from levels of knowledge in other areas relevant to politics, one would form low expectations. Voters who are low in political engagement may fail to encode the information deeply or accurately, while strong partisans may be motivated to distort perceptions of the polls, either at encoding or retrieval (Babad and Yacobos, 1993; Babad, 1997; Granberg and Brent, 1983; Johnston et al., 1992).

Empirical work is sparse on the retention of poll information. Those studies that do exist, moreover, tap retention very crudely, relying exclusively on questions querying respondents about "who is ahead in the polls." This question, of course, can be guessed at without any poll information. No previous research has attempted to measure retention of poll information on the natural, numerical scale of the polls themselves. Not surprisingly, then, past work suggests high levels of retention. For instance, McAllister and Studlar (1991) found that a majority of Britons queried in exit polls were able to identify the leading party correctly and nearly all could do so when that party held a commanding lead.

Likewise, in US presidential races with a clear leader, few voters are ignorant of the fact by election day (1991). Yet we caution that correct responses to the "who is ahead" question could easily come from information sources other than polls themselves. A further complication, with countervailing implications, is that measures of retention collected following an election campaign require, for validity, that voters retain poll information in long-term memory. As such, post-campaign measures may miss considerable short-term retention of poll information (Lodge and Hamill, 1986). In contrast, the present analysis is unique in observing retention of numerical poll information within the campaign itself, which enhances validity by both reducing susceptibility to guessing and permitting detection of retention over the short-term.

Applicability. As noted, studies of cue-taking and strategic voting take it as a theoretical given that at least some voters find poll information applicable or relevant to political judgments. The literature also contains direct empirical evidence pertaining to the applicability issue. Two dimensions relevant to applicability judgments have been measured: the credibility of poll results and perceptions of the influence of poll information in voters' own and fellow citizens' vote decisions.

The credibility dimension is relevant to applicability since voters should find poll information more applicable as it becomes more credible. We know that source credibility – including both the expertness and trustworthiness of sources – moderates the impact of persuasive communications (Petty and Wegener, 1998; Zaller, 1992). Evidence from a number of countries shows that credibility assessments of polls improved over the second half of the twentieth century. More recently, however, citizens have become more skeptical of the value of polls in the electoral process. For instance, in Dran and Hildreth's (1995) study of Illinois voters, a majority (54%) thought polls were right "only some of the time" or "hardly ever." These authors conclude that "a plurality (of the negative respondents) misunderstand the theory supporting survey research, but large percentages also attribute poll inaccuracy to characteristics of respondents and to worries about manipulation" (1995, 141). Along the same lines, three-quarters of Americans in 2000 believed pollsters themselves influence the results "so they come out a certain way" (Price and Stroud, 2006).

The second dimension of applicability, perceptions of the influence of poll information in vote decisions, has even more direct relevance. Beliefs regarding the importance of a given consideration to a particular judgmental task are commonplace in political psychology, particularly in work on framing effects (e.g., Slothuus, 2008). Unfortunately, this dimension has rarely been examined with respect to poll effects. Nonetheless, it is significant that, queried in 2000, just one in four Americans agreed that the polls affected their vote to some degree (Price and Stroud, 2006). Presumably, this estimate is a lower bound on applicability judgments: in deference to liberal democratic norms, individuals may be reluctant to cede their political independence to collective social forces. More indicative, perhaps, may be the finding, also from Price and Stroud (2006), that 90 per cent of respondents thought polls affected "most voters' choices."

New Evidence on Preconditions for Poll Effects

Data. The present study reports the results of the most comprehensive sounding of voters' awareness of and attitudes towards polls to date: the 2007 Ontario Election Study (OES). Among other things, the survey incorporated measures of attention to polls, reception of poll information, perceptions of poll accuracy, perceptions of momentum, and attitudes to the role of polls in the electoral process. We fielded the survey by telephone with a rolling cross-section design: ~45 interviews were conducted per day over the 30 day campaign (*N*=1352) from 10 September to 9 October 2007.

As regards the generalizability of the results from this study, it bears noting that provincial elections in Canada feature much the same level of attention, media coverage, and voter turnout as national elections in Canada and elsewhere (Cutler, 2008). Moreover, we have no reason to believe Canadians are atypical when it comes to hearing about and thinking about polls. The polling industry and its relationship to the media is remarkably similar in most mature democracies. No less than 22 separate polls were reported in the media in Ontario over the 30-day campaign – a level of poll density similar to that in national campaigns elsewhere. The polls showed a Liberal Party lead over the Progressive Conservatives (PC) that ranged from 2 to 15 points.

We supplement the data from Ontario with similar but more limited survey data gathered by the 2011 Canadian Election Study (CES) and the 2009–11 British Co-operative Campaign Analysis Project (BCCAP). The CES, like the OES, was fielded as a rolling cross-section survey over the length of the 2011 campaign, from 1 April to 1 May 2011, with an *N* of 4308. The BCCAP was a multi-wave panel study. We draw mainly on the election period wave, which was fielded during the last two weeks of the 2010 campaign (22 April–5 May 2010) and has an *N* of 975. Details of measurement and operationalization are introduced as the analysis unfolds.

Attention to poll information. Did voters attend to poll reports? A caveat: all assessments of voter attention are susceptible to the many challenges of generalizing from survey respondents to the population of voters. Nonetheless, we deploy two survey-based approaches to answering this question. The first is to query attention directly – that is, we can ask respondents if they "pay attention to" the polls (e.g., Price and Stroud, 2006). The second is indirect: we can infer attention from the accuracy of retention, on the assumption that attention is a necessary condition of accurate retention (Price and Zaller, 1993; Zaller, 1992).

We directly measure attention to polls in two steps. First, following existing research, we ask: "How much attention are you paying to the polls in this Ontario election campaign?" Surprisingly, in response to this item, nearly half our sample (46%) chose "no attention at all." The others pay at least some attention to the polls: 26 per cent pay "little attention," 22 per cent pay "some attention," and only 6 per cent pay "a great deal of attention." On their face, these numbers suggest a significantly lower level of poll attention in Ontario than elsewhere.

However, there is reason to suspect that the standard measure underestimates poll attention, owing to a possible ambiguity in the question from two different meanings of the phrase "pay attention to." Saying "I don't pay attention to" something can mean, in principle, that one does in fact take in the information, but consciously ignores it when it might be relevant to a decision. We asked, therefore, a follow-up question[2] for those who claimed to be paying "no attention at all" to polls: "Even though you're not paying attention to the polls, have you read or heard anything about the polls during this election?" Strikingly, among these respondents, fully one in three confirmed that they had, in fact, heard or read about polls in the campaign. If we adjust our estimate of poll attention accordingly, Ontario respondents fall into line with estimates of poll attention elsewhere: about 70 per cent claim to receive poll information.

We can compare these numbers with the BCCAP survey from the UK. Of the 932 respondents giving valid responses, only 10 per cent indicated they were paying "no attention at all." Nine per cent indicated they were paying "a great deal of attention" and the remaining 81 per cent were paying "some" (49%) or "little" (32%) attention. Of those indicating they were paying "no attention at all" to polls, 70 per cent indicated that they had still read or heard about a poll. Clearly, attention to polls during the final weeks of the 2010 UK general election was very high, though it must be acknowledged that the BCCAP panel has relatively more elevated education levels than the Ontario respondents. We take the difference in the follow-up question – Ontario, 33 per cent; UK, 70 per cent – to indicate that these online panelists are a more attentive set of citizens.

Of course, both the Ontario and UK estimates are taken from the whole campaign period, obscuring significant over-time change in poll attention, at least in Ontario. Focusing on dynamics in the corrected measure of poll attention (i.e., adjusting for those that read or heard polls but claimed not to be paying them any attention), we defined attention dichotomously ("little," "some," or "a great deal" versus "no attention at all") and estimated a logit regression of the measure on an indicator for campaign time.[3] The estimates reveal that the probability of at least minimal poll attention increases by a full percentage point ($.0098, p < .05$) with each passing day in the campaign. Whereas the probability of attending to the polls is .39 on the first day of the campaign, by election day, voters' probability of attending to polls is .77. These dynamics imply that the preconditions for poll effects are maximized as election day approaches.

We can also provide a dynamic breakdown of the data collected for the UK election. We replicated the estimation described above and found that the level of attention to polls did not change over the last two weeks of the campaign (logit estimates; not reported). In other analysis using the panelists' responses six months prior to the campaign, however, we found that attention to polls in the UK during the six months leading into the 2010 general election was consistently very high in this group – consistent with the assumption that the panel is comprised of a relatively politically attentive group. The absence of a within-campaign increase in attention, thus, may reflect a ceiling effect. In any case, our UK and Ontario data together indicate that perhaps three-quarters of survey respondents are typically at least minimally exposed to poll information in modern campaigns. The Ontario data suggest, furthermore, that this proportion grows over the campaign. Still, even on election day, a significant minority of voters would seem to be immunized against poll influence by a lack of attention.

Retention of poll information. The next link in the chain of poll influence is retention. Operationally, our definition of retention entails accuracy: retained information is poll information that can be accurately recalled, at least to an approximation. As noted above, poll effects can occur in the absence of accurate, long-run retention of poll results, assuming poll information is integrated into political evaluations and then forgotten (Lodge and Hamill, 1986). Accordingly, our indicators of poll information retention (described below) concern accurate recall over the very short term. For a given indicator of accuracy we compare respondents' reckonings with the most recent poll result reported or with a range of results that includes the most recent polls. We think it implausible that voters could forget their intake of poll information over a few days, even if they ultimately do so. So retention-based poll effects require retention over the interval between poll release and the interview. In the Ontario campaign, for example, the mean and median intervals between commercial poll releases were, respectively, only 1.88 and 1.5 days.

The Ontario survey fielded three separate indicators of the retention of poll information. The simplest indicator, in terms of informational demands, addresses perceptions of which party is "ahead" in the polls. On one hand, of those who said they had "read or heard about" a poll, 70 per cent correctly responded that the Liberal party, which led in all polls throughout the campaign, was in the lead. Roughly 10 per cent wrongly gave the Conservatives or the NDP as leading. Another 2 per cent thought the parties were tied, while fully 15 per cent indicated that they did not know which party was ahead in that poll.

On the other hand, reinforcing their validity, all these figures moved significantly over the campaign. Whereas at the start of the campaign just over half of those who read or heard about a poll put the Liberals in the lead, fully 80 per cent did so by election day.[4] Conversely, the proportion placing the

Conservatives in the lead dropped from 18 to 6 per cent over the campaign and the share of the sample answering "don't know" fell from 29 to just 8 per cent (all changes significant, $p < .05$). By this standard, retention of poll information is rather impressive among those who attended to polls, in keeping with earlier research (Lavrakas, Holley, and Miller, 1991; McAllister and Studlar, 1991). Further, the analysis adds to existing findings by showing that retention levels are greatly elevated with the approach of election day.[5] Even so, on election day only 60 per cent (.77 * 0.8) of the whole sample knew that the Liberals were ahead in the polls they had read or heard.

In the 2011 Canadian Election Study data we find that a combination of more polls and probably slightly greater attention seems to have created more poll awareness. Unfortunately, we could not fit into that survey an initial attention question, so the national-level Canadian numbers are not directly comparable with those from Ontario. Respondents were asked, "Which party is ahead in the national polls right now? If you are not sure, just let me know." Fifty-eight per cent correctly gave the Conservative Party, which never trailed and had leads ranging from 3 to 20 points in the 81 major polls released over the 35-day campaign.[6] This figure is very close to the Ontario figure of 60 per cent and, thus, reinforces our estimate about overall retention of poll information generally and bolsters our confidence in measurement validity.

In the BCCAP study in the UK, 66.4 per cent of those who indicated they had read or heard a poll correctly identified the Conservatives as the leading party. This equates to 52.6 per cent of respondents in total. Notably, just before the survey went into the field one widely reported poll suggested the Liberal Democrats were in the lead, while another suggested the Lib Dems were tied with the Conservatives. Therefore, despite the somewhat harder task of identifying the leading party, given the informational environment, this measure of retention produces results similar to those for the elections in Ontario and Canada.

We now consider a second, and more demanding, indicator of poll retention that taps reckonings of the poll numbers themselves. As noted earlier, in addition to measuring retention, we consider this indicator a more difficult, objective measure of attention (Price and Zaller, 1993). All three surveys asked for a respondent's "best estimate" of the current "poll numbers" in percentage terms. To minimize difficulty, we advised that respondents should not "worry too much if [the poll numbers] don't add up to 100%."[7] We define as accurate those numerical poll estimates that fall within one point of the range defined by the minimum and maximum standing for a given party over three days prior to the interview.[8] We define a range of accuracy because a consumer of polls who had seen more than one may reasonably provide an average of recent polls or simply remember only one of them.[9] This measure of accuracy speaks to respondents' sensitivity to the magnitude of a party's share of vote intention, rather than simply its rank, unlike previous research in this area.

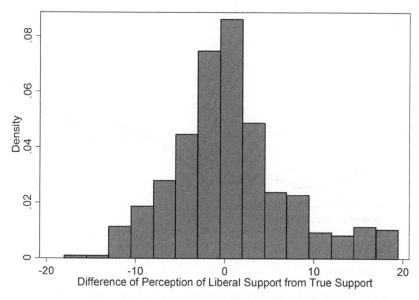

Figure 13.1. Accuracy of Perceptions of Leading Party Support, Ontario 2007

The overall accuracy of poll perceptions looks considerably less impressive given this more difficult standard. In the Ontario data, just 32, 35, and 29 per cent of those who said they paid attention to polls accurately gave the Liberal, Conservative, and NDP shares, respectively. Only 16 per cent of all respondents in the second half of the campaign were able to accurately provide the level of Liberal support.[10] Figure 13.1 presents a histogram of the accuracy of estimates of Liberal support. The figure shows plenty of respondents close to the true poll support of the governing Liberal party, but many a good distance away. More importantly, the distribution is very close to normal, so that in the aggregate, errors of accuracy will cancel each other.

The comparable follow-up question in the 2011 Canadian Election Study asked: "What per cent did the [fill leading party answer] get in the latest polls?" We use the same standard for accuracy but recognize that more polls means a wider range of estimates as a result of sampling error, making the test somewhat easier. Again, we see fewer than one in five respondents, 18 per cent, giving Conservative support within one point of the maximum and minimum poll readings from the previous three days. This figure doubled from 10 per cent to just over 20 per cent during the campaign but seems strikingly low for a national election where correct answers were defined on average within a *seven*-point range. Only 31 per cent of the sample gave a Conservative support

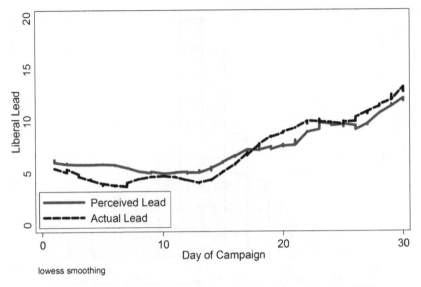

lowess smoothing

Figure 13.2. Liberal lead: Actual and perceived (less smoothing), Ontario 2007

figure within the range of the lowest and highest poll readings over the whole campaign. This makes it plain that a great many of the 60 per cent who are identifying the party leading in the polls are doing so without attending closely to the actual poll information.

Using the same retention measure we can also determine how responsive citizens are to the ebb and flow of the campaign – what we might call "aggregate dynamic accuracy." For respondents in Ontario, we regress the daily mean of respondents' numerical estimates on the two-day lag of the party's share as reported in the polls. The results indicate a significant ($p = .043$), positive, and substantively important relationship for only the leading Liberals. A unit increase in the Liberals' most recent poll result produces a corresponding gain in the party's perceived vote share of 1.28 points. The implication is that average awareness of Liberal fortunes was not only highly accurate, it was updated quickly – if somewhat over-enthusiastically. This pattern is clearly apparent in figure 13.2, which plots the relationship between the Liberal lead in the most recent published poll and the daily sample average of respondents' estimates of the party's lead over the PCs. Nevertheless, we infer that the systematic movement in aggregate perceptions of the lead are driven by a small minority of attentive respondents who retain accurate poll numbers in memory.

Our final indicator of retention tracks Ontario respondents' awareness of changes in poll standings. Apart from its value in assessing retention, the measure speaks directly to claims that perceptions of *momentum* based on poll standings are central to poll effects (e.g., Bartels, 1988). Specifically, we asked, "Did the last poll you heard about show the Liberals [Conservatives, NDP] going up, going down, or staying about the same?" We compare these perceptions of party momentum to "real" changes in party shares in the polls.[11] Note that, in defining objective momentum we confront the issue of how much change is necessary to reasonably consider a party to be on the rise or on the way down. Presumably, larger changes should produce greater awareness, so we classify a result as positive ("going up") or negative ("going down") if its difference from the previous reading exceeds various thresholds: greater than 0, 1, 2, and 3 points. Poll results not falling above these various thresholds are coded as neutral ("staying about the same"). Periods during which a party experienced no movement (according to the polls) were excluded from the analysis for each party.

The analysis reveals a level of awareness of party momentum as modest as the levels of awareness suggested by the other indicators of numerical poll information retention. Considering all changes (i.e., nonzero differences) in party standings, 32, 29, and 13 per cent of respondents (who said they had read or heard a poll result) were aware of changes in the Liberals', PCs', and NDP's standings, respectively. This effectively means that one in five voters accurately keeps track of changes in the polls. As regards the possibility that larger changes yield greater awareness, awareness of the Liberal trajectory (only) increases from 32 to 38 per cent as the change threshold increases from > 0 points to ≥ 3 points.[12]

Finally, knowledge of trajectories is modestly elevated over the campaign. The probability of correctly perceiving even small changes (i.e., all those > 0) in the Liberal trajectory increases by just under 1 point per day. Conversely, the comparable effect estimate for awareness of the PC trajectory is less than half as large and it is insignificant for the NDP. (Of course, absolute levels of knowledge of party trajectories did increase over the campaign because, although accuracy among those reading or hearing polls remained constant, the size of this group increased).

Applicability of poll information. The final precondition for poll influence is applicability. Consider, first, indicators of poll credibility in the Ontario survey. We queried agreement with the following statement: "The people who conduct election polls manipulate the questions to get the answers they want." In addition to paralleling previous work (Price and Stroud 2006), the item goes to the heart of common-sense concerns about polls: if the results are manipulated, I should ignore them, and so should my fellow citizens. Roughly half of

Ontarians find poll manipulation plausible: 49 per cent of respondents agreed. Interestingly, the level of confidence in pollsters is substantially higher than Price and Stroud (2006) found in the United States in 2000, where three-quarters of Americans suspected manipulation.

A second measure of perceptions of credibility is agreement with: "In general, the polls reported during election campaigns usually give a reliable indication of how the parties are doing." The concept of reliability is closely linked to the ideas of trustworthiness and expertness that are central to source credibility effects. Further, in comparison with the "manipulation" item, this "reliability" question sets a lower bar, as even those who are suspicious of pollsters' motivations may, nevertheless, think that polls "in general" are "usually" reliable. And indeed, fully 74 per cent of our Ontario respondents find polls reliable in this sense. Another 22 per cent disagreed, and 5 per cent did not give a response.

The results for Ontario compare well with the responses to a question in the election wave of the BCCAP survey asking those respondents that had claimed to have read or heard about a poll: "Do you think the recent polls you've seen have been reasonably accurate?" As in Ontario, about one quarter (24%) indicated that they did *not* think the recent polls were reasonably accurate. However, a further 38 per cent of respondents were uncertain about the accuracy of the polls (i.e., they responded "don't know"). Only 38 per cent of those that had read or heard a poll felt the results were reasonably accurate.

These results shrink further the pool of voters who might be influenced by poll information. At least one quarter, but possibly as much as one half, of voters have reason to dismiss poll information, given that they see polls as manipulated, unreliable or of uncertain reliability. Even among those who say they pay some or little attention to polls, 20 per cent think polls are unreliable. Importantly, perceptions of manipulation do not covary with attention (analysis not reported); thus, half of those that pay some attention to polls believe that pollsters manipulate the results.

Finally, we turn to voters' own conscious admission of influence by polls. Given the possibility, noted earlier, that conceding influence to polls may be constrained by democratic norms of independent judgment, it is important to formulate a measure that enables respondents to acknowledge influence from polls without obviously ceding much judgmental autonomy. Accordingly, we asked respondents if they agreed that "[p]olls reported during elections sometimes help me make my choice." We interpret response to this item as a plausible, if imperfect, proxy for perceptions of the applicability of poll information to political judgment. More specifically, we reason that both cue-takers and strategic voters ought to agree that polls "sometimes help" them to render voting decisions. As it happens, just 1 in 4 Ontarians reported that they found polls helpful in this fashion.

Discussion

We now return to the question that motivates the paper: Are the necessary conditions in place for polls to affect voters? Put differently, in light of our findings on attention, retention and applicability, what share of voters could, in principle, be directly influenced by poll results, and through what mechanisms could they be influenced? We organize our discussion in terms of the mechanisms of direct poll effects presented earlier, treating each mechanism in turn.

The classic metaphor of poll influence, and its most normatively troubling manifestation, is the bandwagon effect. We reason that the mechanism entails attention to and retention of poll information and find that both conditions are satisfied, at least to some degree, for a significant number of voters. From 70 per cent (Ontario) to 90 per cent (UK) of survey respondents pay at least some attention to polls, and from 28 per cent (Ont.) to 60 per cent (UK) pay a "great deal" of attention to them. If we assumed attention entailed meaningful retention of poll information, then these numbers set the upper bound on the share of voters susceptible to the bandwagon effect (or any other direct poll influence mechanism). Yet it is clear that not all those attending to polls retain poll information. To be sure, large shares of survey respondents can correctly identify the leading party in recent polls: from 53 per cent (UK) to 60 per cent (Ont., Canada [national estimate]) know "who's ahead" on a day-to-day basis. Many of these respondents, however, may have inferred this information from non-poll sources. If we apply a more difficult test of retention, then the proportion of voters seemingly susceptible to direct poll influence shrinks considerably: just 16 per cent (Ont.) to 18 per cent (Can.) of respondents accurately report the share of the leading party in recent polls, and a similar proportion (16 to 17%; Ont. only[13]) correctly register over-time changes in the shares of major parties. These stricter indicators of retention undoubtedly provide lower-bound estimates for the share of voters directly susceptible to abandwagon effect generated by poll information. Despite our efforts to simplify the task (see above), survey respondents commonly have difficulty reporting numerical estimates. Also, as we have noted, influence from polls can, assuming online processing (see above), co-exist with fairly short-term retention of poll information. While we have measured retention over much shorter intervals than previous research, we may still have failed to detect some meaningful, but very short-term, retention of poll information. Even so, we conclude that it is only a minority of voters, albeit potentially a sizable one, that are susceptible to a bandwagon effect resulting from direct reception of poll information.

The informational demands of cue-taking are similar to those of the bandwagon effect; at least as many voters, therefore, must meet the criteria of attention and retention applying to the former effect as do for the latter. In addition, however, we have argued that cue-taking entails a conscious belief that poll information is a sensible basis for political judgment. Given that not all those retaining poll information find it applicable to political choice, then, we know that it is a smaller minority of voters that could conceivably take rational cues from the polls. Notably, retention of poll information is generally uncorrelated with applicability judgments (Ont. only; analysis not reported). If we assume that a belief that polls are reliable also implies a belief they are applicable to vote choice, then as many as 74 per cent (Ont.) of those susceptible to bandwagon effects may be engaged in cue-taking. This is very likely an over-estimate, however, as many of those finding polls credible may not actually use them in political reasoning. A more conservative estimate relies on the fact that just 25 per cent (Ont.) consciously acknowledge the influence of polls. It seems likely that a much smaller group of voters is, in principle, engaged in cue-taking than the group susceptible to the bandwagon effect.

Compared with cue-taking, it is conceivable that the generation of cognitive responses is a more commonplace reaction to surprising poll results. To be sure, the demands of the mechanism are steeper, inasmuch as cognitive responding implies awareness of both current and prior poll standings. Unlike cue-taking, however, we do not require that cognitive responders will actively regard poll information as applicable to judgment. Further, on more stringent retention indicators, we find awareness of changes in poll standings very similar to awareness of parties' levels in the polls (see above). In the absence of a simpler test of awareness of change, we do not know for certain whether the upper-bound on susceptibility to bandwagon effects – roughly 60 per cent – applies to cognitive response effects. Nonetheless, it is plausible, in light of the evidence from the stringent indicators, that a sizable proportion of those who know "who's ahead" also know "who's pulling ahead" or "who's falling behind." A large proportion of the minority susceptible to the bandwagon, in other words, is likely also subject to cognitive response processes.

Strategic voting specifically informed by poll information is accessible to only a modest group of voters. The informational demands of this mechanism are the heaviest of the direct poll effects we have considered, requiring awareness of the absolute or relative vote shares of three parties (or candidates). In terms of awareness of relative vote shares, we find that as many as 25 per cent of respondents (Ont.) are able to correctly *rank* three parties. While this proportion falls dramatically when more stringent accuracy criteria are applied – just 4 per cent give accurate (absolute) numerical estimates for these parties' province-wide vote shares – the fact that 1-in-4 voters can correctly rank the parties suggests non-trivial scope for strategic voting. That scope is narrowed, however, by the fact that only a subset of voters – at least 25 per cent, but no more than 74 per cent (see above) – find poll information applicable to political judgment. If party standings in the polls are to inform strategic voting, our estimates suggest that only 6 per cent (i.e., the product of the percentage with

knowledge of relative shares and the percentage who find polls "help" with political choice) of voters are prepared by poll information to engage in strategic
voting.[14]

Conclusion

This chapter has examined the preconditions for direct poll effects – the cognitive precursors to the diverse mechanisms of poll influence (i.e., the bandwagon effect, cue-taking, cognitive responding and strategic voting) prominent
in the existing literature and touched on in much of the research of Richard
Johnston. While it suggests that polls sometimes influence voters' decisions,
and there may be normative consequences, the literature has not spoken to the
breadth of this effect across a typical electorate. We believe that the normative
evaluation of poll effects may be very different indeed if the effects are assumed
to affect all voters or if they are found, instead, to be potentially at play in the
calculus of only a small minority of voters.

Analysis of attention to and retention of poll information, and of voters' judgments of the applicability of polls to the vote decision, has yielded insight into
overall levels of cognitive engagement with polls and, more importantly, conclusions regarding the likely prevalence of various mechanisms of poll effects.
We conclude that a minority of voters – although potentially a sizable one –
may be directly subject to the bandwagon effect from poll information. It is
likely that a large subset of this minority meets the preconditions for cognitive
responding to polls, and a similar (if somewhat smaller) subset is likely to satisfy the prerequisites for cue-taking. Strategic voting would appear a plausible
response to polls for a much smaller group of voters, a finding that is quite
consistent with previous research (e.g., Johnston et al., 1992; Blais and Nadeau,
1996; Blais, Young, and Turcotte, 2005; Abramson et al., 2011).[15] Our findings
jibe perfectly with the account of Richard Johnston and his colleagues nearly
three decades ago, where it was suggested that sophisticated voters, a minority
of the electorate, may use the national polls to decide which parties are viable
options to defeat a least-liked party (Johnston et al., 1992).

As regards the broader significance of the findings, we observe, first, that
the relative prevalence of the various poll-effects mechanisms is normatively
important. In short, our results suggest that the least rational type of response
to polls – the bandwagon effect – is the mechanism for which the cognitive
preconditions are most prevalent. Given their differing cognitive demands, the
more rational uses of poll information (cue-taking and strategic voting) are almost certainly less common than "emotional contagion" as a response to polls,
as we would expect given what is known about political sophistication. Second,
at the most general level, the findings on retention are relevant to students of
political knowledge. Both the supply of and demand for information about the

"horserace" are, as compared to information in other political domains, exceptionally high (Brady and Johnston, 1987; Patterson, 2005; Matthews, Pickup, and Cutler, 2012; Iyengar, Norpoth, and Hahn, 2004). This seems reflected in the high levels of awareness of "who's ahead" that we find in our survey data. At the same time, large majorities fail stricter tests of poll knowledge (i.e., those involving numerical estimates or perception of change). One plausible interpretation, therefore, is that the voters' appetite for the horserace is a mile wide, but an inch deep. Critiques of modern campaigns often assume that the gap between substantive and horserace information is so large that horserace information will dominate voters' decisions. Our findings show that the two streams of information are on a more level playing field than many scholars have assumed.

NOTES

1 This is the dominant image of the effect of election polls among scholars in single-member first-past-the-post parliamentary systems (e.g., Blais, Gidengil, and Nevitte, 2006; Johnston et al., 1992; but see Blais, Young, and Turcotte, 2005).
2 The follow-up was asked of all respondents after the 16th day of fieldwork.
3 Similar conclusions are obtained with the 4-category dependent variable and using the root question only, controlling for the design change, and for time since the most recent poll.
4 Unless otherwise indicated, all statements of campaign dynamics reflect logit regression estimates of the quantity in question on an indicator of the day of the campaign, as described in the previous section.
5 The increase in retention may in part reflect the Liberals' increasing lead over the campaign.
6 In contrast with the Ontario study, accuracy on this measure was only marginally higher in the second half of the campaign.
7 More than 70 per cent of those who had "read or heard about" a poll offered numerical estimates for one of the parties; nearly all of these respondents did so for all three parties.
8 An analysis using a continuous accuracy variable produced results substantively similar to those reported in the text.
9 As random guesses are more likely to fall within larger ranges, when considering over-time dynamics (below), range size is included as a control variable in all regressions.
10 Recall that only in the second half of the campaign were respondents given the second chance to say they had noticed polls even though they said they did not pay them any attention. And in the second half of the campaign the Liberal lead had been identified by at least seven major published polls.

11 We take the average of poll results on days when more than one poll was released.
12 Regressions of momentum perceptions on raw party changes yields similar conclusions.
13 These proportions are the products of the accuracy percentages for the Liberal and PCs, reported above, and the share of respondents paying at least "a little" attention to polls (54%).
14 Notably, this figure is exactly the same as Blais and Nadeau's widely cited estimate of the share of strategic voters in the 1988 Canadian election (1996, 45).
15 One reason that relatively few voters satisfy the preconditions for strategic voting may be a form of rational ignorance: given that the available poll information – typically national- or provincial-level results – may not be diagnostic of conditions at the local level, voters may, quite sensibly, ignore it. We thank an anonymous reviewer for highlighting this possibility for us.

References

Abramson, Paul, J. A. Aldrich, M. Blais, A. Diamond, I. Diskin, D. Indridason, D. Lee, and R. Levine. 2011. "Comparing Strategic Voting under FPTP and PR." *Comparative Political Studies* 43: 61–90. https://doi.org/10.1177/0010414009341717

Ansolabehere, S., and S. Iyengar. 1994. "Of Horseshoes and Horse Races – Experimental Studies of the Impact of Poll Results on Electoral Behavior." *Political Communication* 11: 413–30. https://doi.org/10.1080/10584609.1994.9963048

Babad, E. 1997. "Wishful Thinking among Voters: Motivational and Cognitive Influences." *International Journal of Public Opinion Research* 9: 105–25. https://doi.org/10.1093/ijpor/9.2.105

Babad, E. and E. Yacobos. 1993. "Wish and Reality in Voters' Predictions of Election Outcomes." *Political Psychology*, 37–54. https://doi.org/10.2307/3791392

Bartels, L. 1988. *Presidential Primaries and the Dynamics of Public Choice.* Princeton, NJ: Princeton University Press.

Blais, A. and M. Bodet. 2006. "How Do Voters Form Expectations about the Parties' Chances of Winning the Election?" *Social Science Quarterly* 87: 477. https://doi.org/10.1111/j.1540-6237.2006.00392.x

Blais, A., E. Gidengil, and N. Nevitte. 2006. "Do Polls Influence the Vote?" In *Capturing Campaign Effects*, edited by H.E. Brady and R. Johnston, 263–79. University of Michigan Press.

Blais, A., and R. Nadeau. 1996. "Measuring Strategic Voting: A Two-Step Procedure." *Electoral Studies* 15: 39–52. https://doi.org/10.1016/0261-3794(94)00014-X

Blais, A., R. Young, and M. Turcotte. 2005. "Direct or Indirect? Assessing Two Approaches to the Measurement of Strategic Voting." *Electoral Studies* 24:163–76. https://doi.org/10.1016/j.electstud.2004.03.001

Brady, H.E., and R. Johnston. 1987. "What's the Primary Message: Horse Race or Issue Journalism?" In *Media and Momentum: The New Hampshire Primary and*

Nomination Politics, edited by Gary R. Orren and Nelson W. Polsby, 127–86. Chatham House.

Chong, D., and J. Druckman. 2007. "Framing Public Opinion in Competitive Democracies." *American Political Science Review* 101: 637–55. https://doi.org /10.1017/S0003055407070554

Cukierman, A. 1991. "Asymmetric Information and the Electoral Momentum of Public Opinion Polls." *Public Choice* 70: 181–213. https://doi.org/10.1007/BF00124482

Cutler, F. 2008. "One Voter, Two First-Order Elections?" *Electoral Studies* 27 (3): 492–504. https://doi.org/10.1016/j.electstud.2008.01.002

Delli Carpini, M., and S. Keeter. 1997. *What Americans Know about Politics and Why It Matters*. Yale University Press.

Dran, E., and A. Hildreth. 1995. "What the Public Thinks about How We Know That It Is Thinking." *International Journal of Public Opinion Research* 7 (2): 128–44. https:// doi.org/10.1093/ijpor/7.2.128

Fournier, P. 2002. "The Uninformed Canadian Voter." In *Citizen Politics: Research and Theory in Canadian Political Behaviour*, edited by J. Everitt and B. O'Neill. Oxford University Press.

Gerring, J. 2012. "Mere Description." *British Journal of Political Science* 42: 721–46. https://doi.org/10.1017/S0007123412000130

Giammo, J. 2004. Polls and Voting Behavior: The Impact of Polling Information on Candidate Preference, Turnout, and Strategic Voting.

Granberg, D., and E. Brent. 1983. "When Prophecy Bends: The Preference-Expectation Link in U.S. Presidential Elections." *Journal of Personality and Social Psychology,* 45: 477–91. https://doi.org/10.1037/0022-3514.45.3.477

Hardmeier, S. 2008. "The Effects of Published Polls on Citizens." In *The SAGE Handbook of Public Opinion Research*, edited by W. Donsbach and M. Traugott. Sage Publications Ltd.

Iyengar, S., H. Norpoth, and K. Hahn. 2004. "Consumer Demand for Election News: The Horserace Sells." *Journal of Politics* 66: 157–75. https://doi.org/10.1046 /j.1468-2508.2004.00146.x

Johnston, R. 2017. *The Canadian Party System: An Analytic History*. UBC Press.

Johnston, R., A. Blais, H. Brady, and J. Crête. 1992. *Letting the People Decide*. McGill-Queen's University Press.

Johnston, R., and F. Cutler. 2009. "Canada: The Puzzle of Local Three-Party Competition." In *Duverger's Law of Plurality Voting*, 83–96. Springer.

Johnston, R., M.G. Hagen, and K.H. Jamieson. 2004. *The 2000 Presidential Election and the Foundations of Party Politics*. Cambridge University Press.

Kenney, P., and T. Rice. 1994. "The Psychology of Political Momentum." *Political Research Quarterly* 47: 923–38. https://doi.org/10.1177/106591299404700409

Lavrakas, P., J. Holley, and P. Miller. 1991. "Public Reactions to Polling News during the 1988 Presidential Election Campaign." *Polling and Presidential Election Coverage*, 151–83.

Lodge, M., and R. Hamill. 1986. "A Partisan Schema for Political Information Processing." *The American Political Science Review* 80: 505–20. https://doi.org /10.2307/1958271

Lupia, A. 1994. "Shortcuts Versus Encyclopedias: Information and Voting Behavior in California Insurance Reform Elections." *American Political Science Review*, 63–76. https://doi.org/10.2307/2944882

Maheswaran, D., and S. Chaiken. 1991. "Promoting Systematic Processing in Low-Involvement Settings: Effect of Incongruent Information on Processing and Judgment." *Journal of personality and social psychology* 61: 13–25. https://doi.org /10.1037/0022-3514.61.1.13. Medline: 1890583

Marsh, C. 1985. "Back on the Bandwagon: The Effect of Opinion Polls on Public Opinion." *British Journal of Political Science* 15 (1): 51–74. https://doi.org/10.1017 /S0007123400004063.

Matthews, J., M. Pickup, and F. Cutler. 2012. "The Mediated Horserace: Campaign Polls and Poll Reporting." *Canadian Journal of Political Science* 45: 261–87. https:// doi.org/10.1017/S0008423912000327

McAllister, I., and D. Studlar. 1991. "Bandwagon, Underdog, or Projection? Opinion Polls and Electoral Choice in Britain, 1979–1987." *The Journal of Politics* 53: 720–41. https://doi.org/10.2307/2131577

McGuire, W. 1969. "The Nature of Attitudes and Attitude Change." In *Handbook of Social Psychology*, edited by G. Lindsay and E. Aronson. Addison-Wesley.

Morwitz, V., and C. Pluzinski. 1996. "Do Polls Reflect Opinions or Do Opinions Reflect Polls? The Impact of Political Polling on Voters' Expectations, Preferences, and Behavior." *The Journal of Consumer Research* 23: 53–67. https://doi.org/10.1086/209466

Mutz, D. 1998. *Impersonal Influence: How Perceptions of Mass Collectives Affect Political Attitudes.* Cambridge University Press.

Patterson, T. 2005. "Of Polls, Mountains – US Journalists and Their Use of Election Surveys." *Public Opinion Quarterly* 69: 716–24. https://doi.org/10.1093/poq/nfi065

Petty, R., and D. Wegener. 1998. "Attitude Change: Multiple Roles for Persuasion Variables." *The Handbook of Social Psychology* 1: 323–90.

Price, V., and N. Stroud. 2006. "Public Attitudes toward Polls: Evidence from the 2000 US Presidential Election." *International Journal of Public Opinion Research* 18 (4): 393–421. https://doi.org/10.1093/ijpor/edh119

Price, V., and J. Zaller. 1993. "Who Gets the News? Alternative Measures of News Reception and Their Implications for Research." *Public Opinion Quarterly* 57: 133. https://doi.org/10.1086/269363

Simon, H. 1957. "Bandwagon and Underdog Effects in Election Prediction." In *Models of Man: Social and Rational*, 79–97. Wiley.

Sinclair, B., and C.R. Plott. 2012. "From Uninformed to Informed Choices: Voters, Pre-Election Polls and Updating." *Electoral Studies* 31 (1): 83–95. https://doi.org /10.1016/j.electstud.2011.03.002.

Slothuus, R. 2008. "More Than Weighting Cognitive Importance: A Dual-Process Model of Issue Framing Effects." *Political Psychology* 29 (1): 1–28. https://doi.org/10.1111/j.1467-9221.2007.00610.x.

Sonck, N., and G. Loosveldt. 2010. "Impact of Poll Results on Personal Opinions and Perceptions of Collective Opinion." *International Journal of Public Opinion Research* 22: 230–55. https://doi.org/10.1093/ijpor/edp045

Tsfati, Y. 2001. "Why Do People Trust Media Pre-election Polls? Evidence from the Israeli 1996 Elections." *International Journal of Public Opinion Research* 13: 433–41. https://doi.org/10.1093/ijpor/13.4.433

West, D. 1991. "Polling Effects in Election Campaigns." *Political Behavior* 13: 151–63.

Zajonc, R.B. 1968. "Attitudinal Effects of Mere Exposure." *Journal of Personality and Social Psychology* 9 (2): 1–27. https://doi.org/10.1037/h0025848.

Zaller, J. 1992. *The Nature and Origins of Mass Opinion.* Cambridge University Press.

Contributors

Keith Banting is a Stauffer Dunning Fellow in the School of Policy Studies and a professor emeritus and Queen's Research Chair Emeritus in the Department of Political Studies at Queen's University at Kingston, Ontario.

Alexis Bibeau is a PhD student in the Department of Politics at the University of Virginia.

Amanda Bittner is a professor in the Department of Political Science at Memorial University of Newfoundland and Labrador.

André Blais is a professor emeritus in the Département de science politique at the Université de Montréal, where he was the University Research Chair in Electoral Studies.

Marc André Bodet is a professor in the Département de science politique at Université Laval.

R. Kenneth Carty is a professor emeritus of political science and a former Brenda & David McLean Chair in Canadian Studies at the University of British Columbia.

Fred Cutler is an associate professor in the Department of Political Science at the University of British Columbia and founder of Prograds – The Graduate Student Progress System.

Yannick Dufresne is an associate professor in the Département de science politique at Université Laval.

Patrick Fournier is a professor in the Département de science politique at the Université de Montréal.

Richard Johnston is a professor emeritus in the Department of Political Science at the University of British Columbia.

J. Scott Matthews is a professor in the Department of Political Science at Memorial University of Newfoundland and Labrador.

Brenda O'Neill is dean of the Faculty of Public and Global Affairs and Professor in the Department of Political Science at Carleton University.

Julia Partheymüller is Senior Scientist at the Department of Government and a member of the Vienna Center for Electoral Research (VieCER) at the University of Vienna.

David A.M. Peterson is the Lucken Professor in Political Science in the Department of Political Science at Iowa State University.

Mark Pickup is a professor in the Department of Political Science at Simon Fraser University.

Rüdiger Schmitt-Beck is a senior professor of political science at the University of Mannheim.

Byron E. Shafer is a professor emeritus in the Department of Political Science at the University of Wisconsin.

Stuart Soroka is a professor in the Departments of Communication and Political Science at the University of California, Los Angeles.

Matthew S. Shugart is a distinguished professor emeritus in the Department of Political Science at the University of California, Davis.

Alexander Staudt is a former research associate at the Mannheim Centre for European Social Research (MZES) of the University of Mannheim.

Cory L. Struthers is an assistant professor at the Evans School of Public Policy and Governance at the University of Washington.

Matthew Wright is an associate professor in the Department of Political Science at the University of British Columbia.

Printed and bound by CPI Group (UK) Ltd, Croydon, CR0 4YY

10/10/2024

14572325-0002